Trekking in Nepal, West Tibet, and Bhutan

THE SIERRA CLUB
ADVENTURE TRAVEL GUIDES

Adventuring Along the Gulf of Mexico, The Sierra Club Travel Guide to the Gulf Coast of the United States and Mexico from the Florida Keys to Yucatán, by Donald G. Schueler

Adventuring in Alaska, The Ultimate Travel Guide to the Great Land, Completely revised and updated, by Peggy Wayburn

Adventuring in the Alps, The Sierra Club Travel Guide to the Alpine Regions of France, Switzerland, Germany, Austria, Liechtenstein, Italy, and Yugoslavia, by William E. Reifsnyder and Marylou Reifsnyder

Adventuring in the Andes, The Sierra Club Travel Guide to Ecuador, Peru, Bolivia, the Amazon Basin, and the Galapagos Islands, by Charles Frazier with Donald Secreast

Adventuring in the California Desert, The Sierra Club Travel Guide to the Great Basin, Mojave, and Colorado Desert Regions of California, by Lynne Foster

Adventuring in the Pacific, The Sierra Club Travel Guide to the Islands of Polynesia, Melanesia, and Micronesia, by Susanna Margolis

Adventuring in the Rockies, The Sierra Club Travel Guide to the Rocky Mountain Regions of the United States and Canada, by Jeremy Schmidt

Adventuring in the San Francisco Bay Area, The Sierra Club Travel Guide to San Francisco, Marin, Sonoma, Napa, Solano, Contra Costa, Alameda, Santa Clara, San Mateo Counties and the Bay Islands, by Peggy Wayburn

Trekking in Nepal, West Tibet, and Bhutan, by Hugh Swift

Walking Europe from Top to Bottom, The Sierra Club Travel Guide to the Grande Randonnée Cinq (GR-5) through Holland, Belgium, Luxembourg, Switzerland, and France, by Susanna Margolis and Ginger Harmon

Trekking in Nepal, West Tibet, and Bhutan

by Hugh Swift

with additional material by
Charles Gay, Peter H. Hackett, M.D.,
Rodney Jackson, and Milan M. Melvin

Sierra Club Books   San Francisco

The Sierra Club, founded in 1892 by John Muir, has devoted itself to the study and protection of the earth's scenic and ecological resources—mountains, wetlands, woodlands, wild shores and rivers, deserts and plains. The publishing program of the Sierra Club offers books to the public as a nonprofit educational service in the hope that they may enlarge the public's understanding of the Club's basic concerns. The point of view expressed in each book, however, does not necessarily represent that of the Club. The Sierra Club has some sixty chapters coast to coast, in Canada, Hawaii, and Alaska. For information about how you may participate in its programs to preserve wilderness and the quality of life, please address inquiries to Sierra Club, 730 Polk Street, San Francisco, CA 94109.

Library of Congress Cataloging in Publication Data

Swift, Hugh.
  Trekking in Nepal, West Tibet, and Bhutan.

  Bibliography: p. 314
  Includes index.
  1. Hiking—Nepal.   2. Hiking—China—Tibet.
3. Hiking—Bhutan.   4. Nepal—Description and travel.
5. Tibet (China)—Description and travel.   6. Bhutan—
Description and travel.   I. Title.
GV199.44.N46S85   1989   915.49'6   88-23863

Photographs are by the author unless otherwise credited.

Production by Felicity Gorden

Cover design by Bonnie Smetts

Book design by Drake Jordan

Maps by Tom Dolan

Printed in the United States of America

10 9 8 7 6 5 4 3 2 1

Table of Contents

Foreword

By Galen Rowell

While trekking the streets of Washington, D.C., I almost tripped over a plump man lying in the street. He held a sign that read, "Help me! I'm starving!" Just a few feet away from him, a man in a three-piece suit stuffed bills from an autoteller window into his pocket. Fascinated, I stopped to see if other passersby noticed the incongruity of the "starving" fat man lying beside the "instant" rich man. No one gave them a second glance.

In Asia, we foreign tourists are fascinated by similar extremes when they are expressed through an exotic culture. As I walked on, I wondered if any of my friends would have spotted this display in America. Immediately I thought of Hugh Swift. Not only would Hugh chuckle quietly, but also he would write himself a note for future reference. Some of his friends refer to him as the "Archivist" because he records little details of his travels and files them away along with news clippings, maps, and notable quotes. I couldn't think of any use for what I had just seen, but just thinking of Hugh prompted me to write myself a note on a scrap of paper.

When I began this foreword, I found the note in my file, and realized that the vignette in Washington had a much deeper relation to Hugh's book than I had imagined. Spotting the juxtaposition of the two men and their social extremes was only one dimension. They represent the breadth in social class and buying power that Asians see in tourists from the Western world. In a very real sense, Hugh has written a guidebook both for the rich man who will effortlessly pay for his trip with plastic and for the poor man who may save for months or years to reach Kathmandu or Lhasa with little more than pocket change and a copy of this book.

Trekking in the Himalaya did not begin with the broad middle class. The original prerequisite was time rather than money. As the saying goes, at either end of the social scale there lies a leisure class, and from these extremes came a substantial portion of the first trekkers. Only after air flights, hotel reservations and trekking services became more certain did average citizens, who needed to plan their vacation time precisely, begin to visit the Himalaya in large numbers.

The natural world is a great equalizer. After a few weeks in the mountains, the panhandler and the man in the three-piece suit I saw in Washington are likely to have much more in common. Not only might they talk to each other on the trail, but they might also bear considerably more resemblance to each other than either would care to admit. Either one could carry this guidebook and think it was written for someone just like himself.

Hugh's words speak both to the low- and high-budget traveler in a voice so skillful that those who don't know him might think it contrived.

The voice is very much his own, due in great part to his own travel experiences with different styles of hiking. When guiding high-impact adventure-travel treks, he goes in the reasonably high style of his clients. When traveling alone, he spends almost nothing and leaves no sign of his passage except goodwill.

Recently I was a beneficiary of Hugh's goodwill. I was assigned by the *National Geographic* magazine to go into an area of western Tibet where one of their other journalists had been stopped by a local official and eventually sent back by a higher authority. His story was a failure. When I was briefed before the assignment, the editors were much more worried than I was about my success in that region. My ace in the hole was a note from Hugh introducing me to the local official as Hugh's good friend. The two of them had gone on a pilgrimage trek together. They now called each other "dharma brother" for life. Needless to say, my travels in that area were successful.

On that journey into western Tibet, I visited a place where the chasm between low- and high-budget travel is at its widest. I spent over thirty thousand dollars on logistical support to photograph for the *National Geographic,* while Hugh traveled longer than I did through the same region on just three hundred dollars. Yet when we go running together in the hills behind our Berkeley homes and talk about Tibet, none of this matters. We have shared a common journey, an experience that transcended the mode of travel.

Exceptions to this rule of the common experience are mostly due to bizarre situations that seem to occur with surprising regularity in isolated parts of the Himalaya. Hugh and I found little in common between his 1977 trek up the Kondus Glacier in the Karakoram and my 1986 flight up the same glacier in a Pakistan Army helicopter. Between the two trips, a border war had closed the area to foreigners. Pristine villages through which Hugh had walked now housed military camps and new roads had been carved through virgin valleys. Soldiers were shooting the last remaining wild sheep and goats for food and sport.

North of the Kondus lies the Siachen Glacier, which was administered by Pakistan in 1980 when I traveled it on skis without porters on the first leg of a 285-mile traverse of the Karakoram Range. I saw absolutely no sign of human presence and considered the Siachen to be the most remote place I had ever been. When I returned in 1986, the Siachen was held by Indian soldiers. Snowmobiles ran back and forth between fixed camps. Helicopters and transport planes dropped supplies to the camps. Expeditions were obtaining permission to travel there from India instead of Pakistan. An American group on their way to a peak at the head of the Siachen was forced to turn back after mortar shells landed near them; the shells had been fired from a Pakistan military camp at 20,500 feet.

The Siachen is but one of the regions where significant changes have occurred in the Himalaya in the brief years since the first edition of this guide was published in 1982. Major guidebook revisions are far more necessary in Asia than in America, where mountain regions do not have permanent native residents in the backcountry or international borders along the crest of the peaks. Himalayan regions are forever opening and closing at the whim of governments vying for power along the contested international borders that crisscross valleys and mountains.

Hugh and I are two among many mountaineers and trekkers who bide their time, waiting to be in the first wave allowed into a newly opened region. We each take notes and photographs to use later for publication in our own way. My own books emphasize adventure and beauty; I rarely take them trekking. Hugh's work emphasizes information; whenever I travel into a region covered by this guide, I keep it in the top flap of my pack along with my two other indispensables: a map and a journal. I hope you will find Hugh's book as useful, concise, and accurate as I have over the years.

Berkeley, California
August, 1988

Acknowledgments

This book could not have been written without the assistance of many knowledgeable and generous friends and collaborators. To all of them I am most grateful, and because of them the scope of the book is far greater than my experience alone would have allowed.

My parents, Charles and Mary Lou Swift, took me camping and hiking as a child, and from them I first came to feel at home in the mountains. Don Cohon, Ken Scott, and Bonnie Smetts have been most helpful with noneditorial assistance. Putting a keyboard on my lap has been a major change from the old portable typewriter. My appreciation to Richard Cleverly knows no bounds, for he has time and again patiently advised me on the intricacies of the Machine.

Several people have contributed important sections to this book. Peter H. Hackett, M.D., one of the world's foremost authorities on altitude sickness, provided the comprehensive, valuable chapter on medicine. Rodney Jackson, who has studied the snow leopard in the wild for years and knows more about this elusive and symbolic creature than anyone, developed his informative chapter on Himalayan natural history. Galen Rowell, a preeminent writer, climber, and photographer (and one strong runner), wrote an excellent foreword. Charles Gay's "Introduction to Spoken Nepali" is *ek dum* first class, and Milan M. Melvin's "Tibetan Glossary" will hopefully get more people out of than into trouble.

I am most appreciative to Debra Denker for her section, "Making the Most of Being a Woman Trekker," and to Pam Ross for "Trekking with Children." Gerry Spence kindly added an eloquent contribution to my favorite section, "Trekking as Metaphor."

Anne Frej described the way to the northeasternmost corner of Nepal; John V. Bellezza wrote about the track to the source of the Indus River; and Peter Overmire added his literate account of the tricky southern road to western Tibet. Daniel Miller assisted with the description of Langtang and also advised on the Bhutan chapter.

Others have also helped with suggestions and information: Dena Bartolome, Edwin Bernbaum, Stephen Bezruchka (whose elevations I have often shamelessly used, as have Nepal's map makers), Marie Brown, Kevin Bubriski, Hugh R. Downs, Bill Frej, K. Garnay, R. V. Giddy, Richard Kohn, John Mock, Pam Shandrick, Stan Stevens, Ted Worcester, and Chris Wriggins. Thanks also to Subhu Sengupta, without whom I might not have reached Toling and Tsaparang.

Tom Dolan drew the fine maps, and Benjamin Ailes made the excellent photo conversions from color to black and white. Mushkeel Baba relentlessly typed the entire manuscript. At Sierra Club Books, I am most appreciative to Jon Beckmann, Felicity Gorden, and David Spinner. My greatest huzzah is reserved for my copyeditor, Mary Anne Stewart, who worked extremely hard to unscramble the manuscript and make it readable for the uninitiated.

Finally, I wish to thank the many friends and those whom I may never see again in the hills of Nepal, Tibet, and Bhutan, who have walked with me, opening my eyes to the people, their ways, and their environment. Especially I am grateful to Karma Chumbey, Choying Dorje, and Pasang Khambache Sherpa. Also I thank Dambar Bahadur, Karma Chun Chun, Pasang Gyalgen, Nim Gyaltshen, Dawa Norbu Kharte, Dil Bahadur Rai, Nanden Singh, Prem Singh, Changba Tamang, Ram Bahadur Tamang, and Yeshe Wangchuck.

Acknowledgment is made for permission to reprint material from the following sources:

Nepal Himalaya, by H. W. Tilman. London: Cambridge University Press, 1952.

Mountain Monarchs, by George B. Schaller. Chicago: University of Chicago Press. Copyright © 1977 by George B. Schaller.

"Mr. Tambourine Man," by Bob Dylan. Los Angeles: Warner Bros. Music. Copyright © 1964 by Warner Bros., Inc. Used by permission; all rights reserved.

The Scottish Himalayan Expedition, by W. H. Murray. London: J. M. Dent and Sons Ltd. Copyright 1951 by W. H. Murray.

That Untravelled World, by Eric Shipton. Kent: Hodder and Stoughton Ltd. Copyright © 1969 by Eric Shipton.

Throne of the Gods, by Arnold Heim and August Gansser, translated by Eden and Cedar Paul. New York: Macmillan, Inc. Copyright 1938 by Arnold Heim and August Gansser.

Vagabonding in America, by Ed Buryn. New York: Random House, Inc. Copyright © 1975 by Ed Buryn.

The Waiting Land, by Dervla Murphy. London: John Murray Ltd. Copyright © 1967 by Dervla Murphy.

Preface

*A guide is someone who helps you build a raft
and gets you across to the far shore of the river.
Then he burns your raft.*

Ancient Tibetan Buddhist text

In 1967 I made the first of several overland trips across Asia. My interest in Asian cultures grew rapidly as I traveled from Vietnam (where I had taught school for two years) to Europe. During my next trip to the subcontinent my passion for South Asia quickly centered on trekking in the Himalaya. I always felt liberated from the thrall of time and Western materialism whenever I walked among the world's grandest mountains and met the people who live in these remarkable regions.

This book was written for wide-eyed Norman Neophyte, stumbling down the street in Kathmandu on his first day in Asia, as well as for Jungly Jaan who has been trekking for three years solid in the Himalaya. Since writing *The Trekker's Guide to the Himalaya and Karakoram* in 1980, I've spent over eighteen months hiking in these ranges. I've tried to incorporate what I've learned into this new volume for you, whether your walking style is funky, fancy, or somewhere in between.

When it came time to revise *Trekker's Guide,* Sierra Club Books publisher Jon Beckmann wisely suggested that the material be expanded and divided into two books: this one, covering Nepal, Bhutan, and western Tibet, and a companion volume, *Trekking in Pakistan and India.* Although some introductory material is essentially the same in each book, the majority of each volume is completely different and expanded from the original book. This volume covers everything from Tsaparang and Mt. Kailas to Annapurna, Mt. Everest, and Bumthang; from the Drokpas to the Limbus; from Khaptad Baba to the fine art of tungba preparation; from maps to medicine. You'll find new places, people, and tales to give you fresh ideas about where to walk on your first or fifth Himalayan sojourn.

Most of this book is about Nepal. Five full chapters, greatly expanded from the previous book, describe hiking routes from west to east through Nepal's 500-mile span. Two completely new chapters cover western Tibet and Bhutan. Western Tibet adjoins northwestern Nepal, is culturally linked with that region, and is often visited by Nepalis on pilgrimage. An exciting possibility is the derestriction of the main Humla Karnali Valley trail crossing the remote boundary between northwestern Nepal and southwestern Tibet. Bhutan lies adjacent to Nepal's eastern border. As you read about this small monarchy, you'll see what a unique kingdom it is and how it is carefully opening itself up to the outside world.

The excellent chapter on natural history kindly provided by Rodney

Jackson will introduce you to the flora and fauna of the Himalaya. Charles Gay's fine "Introduction to Spoken Nepali" and Milan M. Melvin's "Tibetan Glossary" will help you begin speaking with the locals. And Peter H. Hackett, M.D., has written an up-to-date and authoritative chapter on staying healthy in the Himalaya.

Keep in mind that the maps located in the descriptive chapters, while drawn to scale, are intended only for general orientation. You should purchase a more detailed map of your route before leaving for your walk. The map you buy may even be a blue ammonia dye print, the kind available at every trekking shop in Kathmandu (see Appendix A for all map information).

Once you arrive in Kathmandu, you can be resourceful enough to accomplish some of the preliminaries, such as finding a hotel on your own, without my making a list of recommended places. That is for another book to do (or just let your cab driver take you somewhere). My aim in the descriptive chapters is to give you enough information to plan a route and hike along it, but not so many facts as to remove the wonderful sense of discovery as you trek. Rather than precise itineraries, I have given approximate times in days or weeks for the walking routes mentioned. If you hike on your own, the precise number of trekking days shouldn't matter, and if you go with a group, you'll have no choice in the matter.

Before you commit the time and money for traveling to Asia, consider your decision carefully. Trekking involves hard physical exertion. Whether you hike by yourself or go under the wing of a good tour operator or trekking outfitter, there are bound to be times that will test your capacity for humor, your adaptability, and your desire to walk in mountainous regions. This is not to say that you must be in superior condition to consider Himalayan trekking. My experience with escorting trekking groups leads me to believe that the most important requirements for a person to be happy on the trail are that he or she be accustomed to hiking and have strong determination. The rest can come. The information in this book should help you appreciate an important principle: know where you are going and what it will require of you.

Your time in the Himalaya will be enriched immeasurably by learning even a little Nepali or Tibetan. Imagine how much a traveler in your country is handicapped if he or she speaks none of your language. Use the appropriate glossary and add words to your vocabulary list as you walk. Even if you speak just a few words that are out of order and mispronounced, people will listen and respond to your efforts, just as you would be sympathetic to a foreign traveler visiting your home town.

Harka Gurung, an extremely knowledgeable native son of Nepal, said, "To me, the very act of being on the road was as important as reaching the destination." What you see, whom you meet, and what happens to you in the Himalaya depend less on where you go than on who you are. I hope you can approach trekking as a passage, an experience of exploration. It is more important to enjoy the hike and see the country than to count the hours. You miss the point of traveling to the other side of the world if you don't pause occasionally to smell the flowers, to meet the locals, and to

see a bit of what's along the way. This book tries to emphasize the rich
cultural and human experience that these regions offer. Parts of the text
describe religious, cultural, and historic sites and introduce some of the
many clans that inhabit these regions.

People have said, "Please don't tell about the unspoiled, secret places."
And I'm aware of Oscar Wilde's line, "Yet each man kills the thing he
loves." So I'll mention the main trails, but not the hidden valleys where
tahr (wild goats) practically eat salt from your hand or the backdoor passes
that have barely felt the footsteps of foreigners. You'll have to find those
special places for yourself.

Hugh Swift
Berkeley, California

A steep couloir called the "Stairway to Heaven" bisects the south face of holy Mt. Kailas in west Tibet.

1
Trekking in the Himalaya

The soul of a journey is liberty, perfect liberty to think, feel, do just as one pleases.

William Hazlett

The art of Himalayan travel—and indeed of all adventure—is the art of being bold enough to enjoy life now.

W. H. Murray, 1951

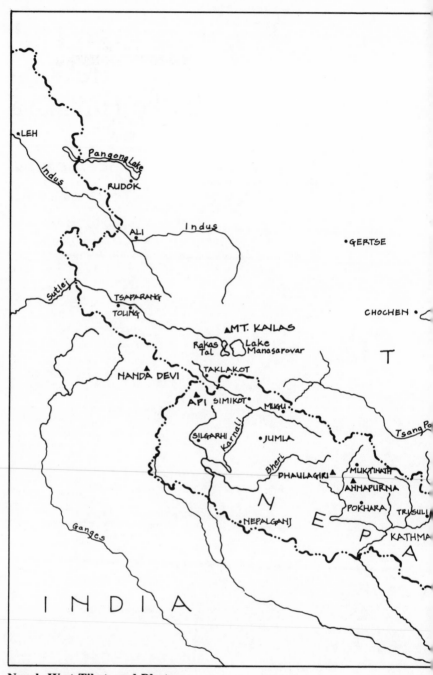

Nepal, West Tibet, and Bhutan

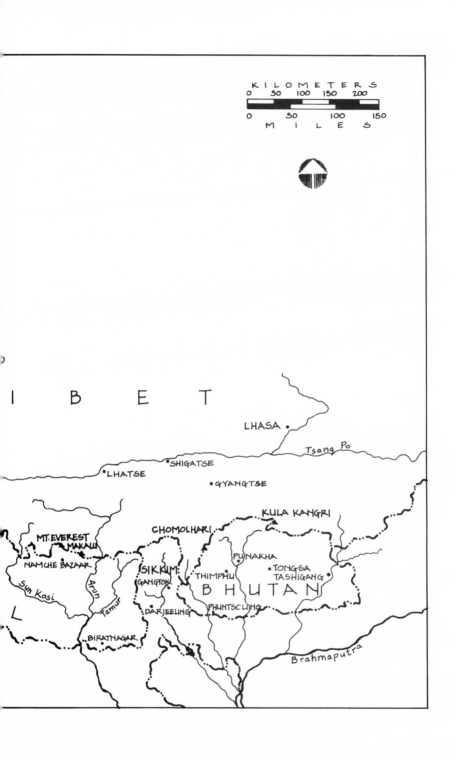

KILOMETERS
0   50   100 150   200

0   50   100   150
M I L E S

T I B E T

LHASA •

Tsang Po

• SHIGATSE
• LHATSE

• GYANGTSE

KULA KANGRI

CHOMOLHARI

MT. EVEREST
MAKALU

PUNAKHA

NAMCHE BAZAAR

SIKKIM
GANGTOK

THIMPHU

TONGSA
TASHIGANG

B H U T A N

Sun Kosi

Arun

Tamur

DARJEELING

PHUNTSCLING

BIRATHAGAR

Brahmaputra

L

A Thumbnail History of Himalayan Trekking

*No, not shooting; not rocks-collecting, not flowers keeping; not
heads measuring, not mountains measuring, not pictures taking.
This my Sahib and my Mem-Sahib traveling where their felt are
liked, camping always high place to look the country.*

Rasul Galwan, 1923

From the outset of travel by Westerners into the Himalaya, a trek or
a climb could be in either of two styles. Some people preferred to walk
with a small group that ate the local diet and replenished food supplies
along the way, eschewing large numbers of porters. Others traveled as
befitted a proper sahib, with porters, servants, cooks, guides, and if not
all the comforts of home, enough to take the edge off. Each method of
travel has had its enthusiastic participants, and trekking styles today have
evolved from the parties that went into the Himalaya a hundred years ago.

A perfect example of the grand, well-provisioned approach to
Himalayan trekking was carried off first class by Robert and Katherine
Barrett in 1923–24. Well read in both Tibetan lore and Francis Galton's
Art of Travel—the period's required reading prior to an Asian trip—this
unique American couple left Kashmir and trekked for a year in Ladakh
and Baltistan, calling themselves Gypsy Davy and Lady Ba. En route, they
reached the Baltoro Glacier, made a winter camp above Leh, and stayed
by Tibet's Pangong Lake before returning to British India. Their book, *The
Himalayan Letters of Gypsy Davy and Lady Ba,* is a little-known classic,
with an unexcelled map showing every night's camp and depicting the
glaciers as firewater-breathing dragons.

Toward the beginning, Lady Ba writes to a friend, "It is our pilgrimage
to Mecca, this Himalayan journey. We go about in a sort of rapture. It may
be years before we get back." Davy, in his fifties, went about in "neatly
patched Shetlands" and liked to meditate on high viewpoints. The Barretts
lived Tibetan style in handsome embroidered tents. They hired Rasul
Galwan from Leh, the best *sirdar* (caravan foreman) of the day, and allowed
him to outfit the caravan to his liking. Davy and Rasul had traveled together
twenty years earlier, and it was Rasul's knowledge that bestowed their
pilgrimage with an extra dimension. "Up to now," Lady Ba wrote, "the
mountains have been earth to us, beautiful, austere, impersonal. To Rasul
they are places, backgrounds for stories of people."

The opulent style of Gypsy Davy and Lady Ba's journey "to the high
quiet places" cannot be duplicated today, but it is quite possible to go with
a sizable crew, eat Western food, and maintain many amenities. However,
many Himalayan travelers today, given economics and recent innovations
in lightweight gear, are taking an unencumbered approach to trekking, and
this style too had its enthusiasts in the days when few valleys had yet been
breached by outsiders.

The first mountain explorer to advocate traveling lightly was Dr. Tom
Longstaff, a British explorer and climber who made discoveries and ascents
in the Gilgit valleys, Baltistan, Garhwal, and the Everest area at the begin-

ning of this century. Another exponent of the unencumbered approach was the legendary British mountaineer Eric Shipton, who in 1934 amazed even Longstaff by telling him that he (Shipton) and Bill (H. W.) Tilman planned to travel to India by cargo ship, hire two Sherpas, and travel in the Himalaya five months for a total of £300. Not only were Shipton and Tilman £14 under budget for that trip, they were the first Westerners to reach the meadows of the Nanda Devi Sanctuary, and they explored the three major sources of the sacred Ganges River. Shipton later wrote in his autobiography, "Bill and I used to boast that we could organise a Himalayan expedition in half an hour on the back of an envelope."

In 1949, several years before Nepal opened its doors to tourism, Bill Tilman, Maj. James O. M. ("Jimmy") Roberts, and two scientists were allowed into the upper Marsyangdi and Kali Gandaki valleys to look about and climb a few peaks. Like Tilman, Roberts knew the mountains, but the major lived higher off the land on his trip than had Tilman and Shipton with their wheat flour, *tsampa* (roasted barley flour), butter, and tea. Even the hardy Sherpas, while emphasizing that Shipton and Tilman were always fair, complained of the spartan diet they shared with these two *Angrezi* (Englishmen). Major Roberts was fluent in Nepali, having commanded a Gurkha Rifles regiment, and had gone many times into the hills on recruiting missions. From time to time he did some climbing and was leader of the only expedition ever sanctioned to attempt Machhapuchhare ("The Fishtail"), but his party was forced to stop a respectful distance below the summit of the sacred peak.

A Tamang joke. These girls are from Dhunche near the Langtang Valley. (Photograph by Daniel Miller.)

When Roberts retired, by then a colonel, he opened the first trekking agency, called Mountain Travel, Nepal, in the mid-1960s. Roberts's idea was that to trek comfortably in the exquisite and remote Nepal Himalaya, people would be willing to pay for porters, supplies, and Sherpas with know-how. It was a prescient decision, as events have proven.

After Nepal began issuing trekking permits (sometime around 1960), a world traveler named Jan Peiper became an early recipient. I met Jan in August 1967, and he told me about the incredible experience of trekking there, describing a particularly fine *bhatti,* or village inn, at a town called Tatopani, where hot springs were close at hand. At that time neither Jan nor I could have imagined the number of trekkers who would begin to pass through Tatopani and stay at that inn surrounded by tangerine trees.

Today's Styles of Trekking

A hundred years ago, you would have been foolish to travel in some parts of the Himalaya without being capable of repelling a raid by the locals. As time has passed, however, the people who live in and govern the Himalaya have changed their minds a great deal about foreigners. Economics have been a factor in many areas. With population pressures and deforestation, many people need income to purchase foods they can't grow, as well as other necessities they can no longer produce. Outsiders are now seen to be a source of revenue, not spies or representatives of a distant government. Consequently, many areas have opened to trekkers: far more than the three most popular areas in Nepal.

Today's trekker has a number of options as to trekking style. You can trek completely alone (recommended for very few except on the major routes) or with one or more friends; with just a porter, with or without friends (my preferred style); with a sirdar and crew; or with a group arranged by a tour operator. The descriptions below will help you decide which style is closest to your inclination and means.

Note that while styles of trekking differ in terms of convenience and the load you carry, the one doing the walking is always you. The first few days of a Himalayan trek can be daunting even though rationally you know that thousands of people (some of them quite out of shape) have preceded you and that for countless thousands of mountain dwellers in the Himalaya, walking mountain trails is an everyday fact of life. A good way to break in is to hike in the mountains near your home before setting off halfway around the world to trek. Be sure you like hiking before buying your ticket to South Asia if you're going there solely to trek. Most people who go trekking have previous hiking experience, but surprisingly, some do not.

If you are already in Asia and are considering a long hike, then you might try a short walk into the country to get a feel for the land and see whether you like trekking: there are easily accessible one-day walks you can take out of Kathmandu, Pokhara, and Lhasa. You can practice your trekking act and shove aside mountains of inhibitions by carrying a small pack to or beyond the day-hike viewpoint, then setting up camp and staying for the night. Two quick considerations if you do this: do not sleep in any religious temple or shrine and be certain that you are well above town and away from a road. As at home, the laws and denizens of the city can be very different from country ways and people.

Another way to warm up for a longer trek, or to help decide which style of trekking fits you, is to walk solo or with a porter for a couple of days or more to get the feel of things. The danger is that in a day or two you will indeed have a feel for the trail yet lack the gear or permission to continue. Returning to "Go" is frustrating, as I learned the irst time I went trekking when I had to return to Kathmandu from Pokhara to get a permit.

Here are the four basic styles of trekking.

Alone or with Friends

Yes, to dance beneath the diamond sky with one hand waving free. . . .

Bob Dylan, 1965

When we hike in the Sierra, Rockies, Appalachians, or the Alps, we plan for our food needs, take shelter, and head for the trail. This kind of trekking can be done in the Himalaya too, but several ifs and warnings are attached to going completely alone. The first-time trekker who will set off alone is rare, although many have done it. My decision to go trekking for the first time was arrived at one day in 1971 during a delightful morning walk west of Pokhara. In the course of that walk I easily came to the realization that, yes, the trail just kept going along, and all I had to do was follow it. Luckily, however, I met some Peace Corps volunteers (PCVs) who were about to leave also and we agreed to trek together. Now by nature I like to explore new places by myself, but I know that for the first two to three days of that trek I was very glad to be with the PCVs, learning the ropes and more vocabulary.

Solo trekking is most appropriate for the young and intrepid. Walking alone is easiest if you are hiking on a well-trekked route in the Annapurna, Langtang-Helambu, or Khumbu regions, where there are plenty of inns. Trekking alone can also be done by the strong Himalayan veteran who knows the ways of the land. Trekking solo, however, is not appropriate for women (see "Making the Most of Being a Woman Trekker," below); remember that the local women don't do it.

Trekking by yourself can be wonderful, but to do it you must be prepared to put more than walking along the trail into your day. If you plan to camp out and cook your own food, then you must have the stamina to do it. In many areas you may stay in inns or homes; in them you will need to know some basic vocabulary in your host's native language. Also, you must be prepared for the funky environment of most homes. This includes smoke from the family fire, the inevitable squalling child, and the possibility that family members will stay up much later than you and talk into the night.

Walking alone or with one or more friends over Himalayan periods of time (typically ten days out at the absolute minimum) takes a knack that comes as you proceed. If you are intrepid enough to trek alone off the main routes, you probably have good trail sense and should have a good map. A hundred-word vocabulary and a friendly disposition are two of the best assets for any foreign walker, but they are particularly helpful to the solo trekker. Just as families have traditionally given the traveler shelter and a meal, the traveler has traditionally reciprocated with local gossip, the word-of-mouth newspaper. Since you are not fluent in the language and don't know the issues and personalities of the valley, you can talk with people about other subjects, such as their livestock, the children, or a neighboring valley, or you can ask and comment about the trail in the vicinity. Practicing your food words with the cook may lead to eating a better meal. You will be surprised how many subjects can be handled with a few words and how quickly you will learn new words if you jot them down and actively use the language.

You need to be alive to what is going on about you. Recently I met an individual trekker who asked querulously, *"Mastey,* what means this *mastey?"* The fellow was four days up the trail and still didn't understand the meaning of *namaste,* the Nepali word of greeting. He thought the children saying "Namaste" to him were asking for something. More than other kinds of trekkers, individual trekkers can walk along, self-righteously burdened by their packs, and be out of touch with what is going on about them. This book aims to assist you toward communicating with the locals you meet and being in touch with the land you are passing through.

A solo trek can be the most rewarding walk possible. It can bring you almost mystically close to both the people and the land in a way impossible when traveling with a group. Carrying all your gear is the most tiring way to walk in the mountains, but you will be compensated by the freedom to come and go as you wish.

With a Porter

> *There came a time when I realized that he was teaching me more than I was teaching him.*
>
> Edward W. Cronin, Jr., 1979

For a great many people, trekking with a porter—who carries gear and (lacking inns on your route) cooks—or trekking with friends and several porters is the best way to walk in the Himalaya. Going with a local person will introduce you to much that might otherwise pass by unnoticed and spare you the labor of lugging all your belongings and food. If you show an interest in crops, forest plants, or people along the trail, your porter will be able to pass on much lore, because he knows the country. You will often be reminded that you may be the *sahib,* but he is the teacher.

Soon after you begin walking with a porter, a lingua franca will develop, probably a pidgin version of Nepali. Speaking even minimal Nepali will set you apart from most other trekkers. Using a modest amount of the language is extremely important in establishing good relations with your porter. If he knew English well, he would probably be working elsewhere. But if your porter wants to work for trekkers in the future, he may try to learn as much English as he can with you.

I had been on three treks without using a porter, but then one spring I found myself, along with friend Chris Wriggins, in dusty, windy Jumla, the wild west of Nepal. We would need porters for the long, rugged trip we planned. When we first saw the two thin, grinning Tibetan Drokpas (nomads) who were to cook and carry for us, we thought they might not be sturdy enough to carry a good load. That erroneous notion was erased quickly. The first night away from Jumla, I wondered, too, whether our preparations had been adequate. But we ate a fine dinner, and during the eight weeks we were on the trail together we needed to replenish only basic food items. By the time we reached Pokhara, the four of us had walked halfway across Nepal together. Another time, in central Nepal, a Sherpa who was accompanying two of us hired a Gurung fellow to porter on ten minutes' notice. Our new hiree did an excellent job of carrying for the next five months!

Longstaff, Shipton, Tilman, and Murray walked the mountain trails with a similarly minimal approach to trekking. Because they trekked for months at a time and departed from trailheads that were farther from the ranges than the trailheads used today, they needed more than one porter to a sahib. But everyone carried a load. If you are willing to carry at least a small load yourself, you and a friend can have a rewarding trek far into the Himalaya with one or at most two porters each. When I reached my mid-forties, I found I couldn't carry the loads I did in my twenties and still have any energy by the end of the day. That is part of the reason why I have learned to walk with a porter. Going with a local frees me to enjoy the walk, not just carry a load all day, and gives me the pleasure of having a good companion along as well.

Do not assume that you can get a first-class porter on snap notice. If you must count every day of your time in the Himalaya, you should weigh the merits of trekking with a sirdar and crew or with a group arranged by a tour operator. The important subject of whom to hire as porter and how is discussed in Chapter 3.

With a Sirdar and Crew

It was clear that we must field a light party and live on the country, after the manner set by the pioneer of Himalayan climbing, Dr. Longstaff—a manner that subsequently lapsed but which had again been demonstrated by Shipton and Tilman in the nineteen-thirties.

W. H. Murray, 1951

If you want to walk a chosen route through the mountains for a limited time with several friends, and if expense is not a prime concern, then hiring a sirdar (also known as a guide), cook, and porters is a good way for you to go trekking. By making arrangements with a tour operator at home or a trekking outfitter in Nepal, or by hiring a sirdar after you arrive (which can be tricky), you can go on a private trek with all of the comforts enjoyed by commercial trekking groups. A local trekking outfitter can do anything for you from merely arranging permits to completely outfitting a crew for your own group of friends.

If you have never been to Nepal before and want to have everything arranged for you when you arrive, you can write or call one or more of the established tour operators at home at least six months before you plan to leave. Tell the tour operator you choose where and for how long you or your group would like to walk, discuss terms, and you can have the company's local trekking outfitter completely outfit your trek before you arrive in Nepal. Then you will not waste time in-country, and although working with a tour operator is more expensive, you can be reasonably sure that your group will have an experienced sirdar, adequate supplies, and a dependable crew. It is not easy to make these arrangements on your own in Nepal. The tour operator you contact at home will make the arrangements for your trek through a trekking outfitter it works with in Kathmandu. The company at home and the trekking outfitter in Nepal have established working relationships (and probably telex facilities) that greatly facilitate matters. West Tibet and Bhutan each have their own special situations, which are elaborated on in Chapters 9 and 10.

Alternatively, you can write directly to a trekking outfitter in Nepal and ask it to plan things for you. (See Appendix B, "Trekking Outfitters in Nepal.") People usually use this method after they have already been to Nepal and set up some contacts there. With the exception of the few largest agencies, it can be difficult to make these arrangements directly with a company in Nepal if you don't know someone who will take a personal interest in your request. Sometimes outfitters in Nepal that you have contacted directly, yet do not know personally, will do nothing until you actually show up. Making arrangements directly with a company in Nepal will cost less than going through a tour operator at home, but negotiating through international mail will take longer than working with a tour operator at home.

If you wait to organize your crew until you arrive, you will need at least several days to a week to make plans. Again, once you are in Kathmandu, you can go to a trekking company and ask for assistance in putting together a sirdar and staff. Alternatively, look for the type of shop in the Thamel area of Kathmandu that sells used trekking gear and ask the manager to find a sirdar who can make arrangements for you. You might try telling your hotel manager that you are looking for a trekking crew, but he will probably just put you in contact with a friend of his who works at or runs a trekking outfitter. The outfitter may not be the best—it will just be his friend's. The busiest time of year is from the beginning of October until the latter part of November; you are unlikely to find the most experienced sirdars available then, but you might get lucky if there has been a cancellation.

If you sign with a trekking agency in Kathmandu, you will pay a fixed price for everything and that will be it. But if you deal directly with a sirdar, you will make a verbal arrangement, and then you must agree on everything. Any points left vague or open to interpretation may get hauled out later for renegotiation. If you go with an established company, it will provide equipment, but if you hire a sirdar, you may find yourself in the bazaar following him around as he purchases everything from pots to spices. Many people like to call themselves sirdars nowadays. You must always ask for a person's chits, his letters of reference from former employers. Read the letters carefully and form an intuitive sense of the man. Note particularly whether he has been along the specific route you want and whether he is recommended by someone you know or know of. Be certain, too, that the chits are his and not on loan from a friend.

With a Group Arranged by a Tour Operator

So-called adventure travel is going mainstream. People who have never been camping before now sign up to walk around Annapurna. Many folks now have the money for such foot-propelled vacations but want everything arranged for them when they arrive. For these people, there are numerous tour operators that offer treks in the Himalaya. The oldest of these companies have been organizing walking excursions for over twenty years, and the best do an excellent job. Mountain Travel was the first tour operator in the U.S.A. to send people to Nepal and elsewhere, but it has been joined by a host of competitors, each with its own flashy catalog. Organized trekking groups from Japan, England, Germany, France, Italy, Australia, and the United States fan out in many seasons, sometimes with itineraries leading to obscure places or with sophisticated specialities. Before long some enterprising company will offer a cross-cultural tour to observe the making of first-class *rakshi* (Nepalese grain liquor, known colloquially as "local wine") from rice, then corn, and finally from barley as the participants stagger up a valley.

If you go with an organized group, you can have confidence to trek that you might not have otherwise. But you need to be realistic about your abilities before deciding to go. Groups may have a physician along, and the leader can be helpful in calming beginners and advising on pace, but you must be physically fit and prepared to leave behind many comforts of home.

The first thing many people ask when they inquire about going with a particular tour operator is, Who will I be going with? Who is already signed up? Indeed, you will be walking with strangers on a group trek, but usually people get along quite well with each other, and you will always find some congenial souls to pass time with. One of the characteristics of people who join an organized group is that they are generally inclined to relate exclusively to others in the group and therefore often miss opportunities to meet locals or other trekkers along the way. Recently a man on a group I was escorting became ill and could not continue. He and his wife stayed behind with a Sherpa, and when he was ready to walk again, the three of them retraced their steps over the way we had come. When we met again in Kathmandu, they told me that the return by themselves had been the most rewarding part of the trek, for they had been able to walk utterly at their own pace and get closer to the locals than had been possible with the group. They didn't hesitate to seek out their own encounters and paint their own canvas. Yet many people prefer the friendship and sociability engendered in group trekking.

One question you should ask before deciding which group to sign up with is, Who is the group leader and what are his or her qualifications? How many times has the escort been over the route before? Does that person speak the language of the area? How well? Your escort can assist you to learn a lot about where you are going if he or she is familiar with the region. Sometimes group members trekking with a savvy leader become more knowledgeable about an area than individual trekkers who just put their heads down and start walking.

An important feature to keep in mind about group treks is that the participants agree to a set schedule. They all know, before leaving, where they will be on any day of the trek, and no one can follow an individual impulse to set off on an overnight side trip, to rest for a day, or to climb a tempting minor peak. The group must always camp together, although they don't by any means need to walk in a cluster. For many, the security and comradeship offered by group trekking is the ideal way to go. Group trekking has opened windows to remarkable areas and cultures that the participants would otherwise have never been able to experience.

Making the Most of Being a Woman Trekker   *by Debra Denker*

[Debra Denker has traveled in Tibet and trekked in India, Pakistan, and Nepal, sometimes with her mother, Maria Denker. She has kindly contributed the following thoughts for women who go trekking.]

Being a woman gives you wonderful, sometimes unique, opportunities to get to know local people while trekking. You will probably have very different experiences depending on whether you are trekking with a porter-guide, with a group, with another woman, or with a male companion. The composition of your group will affect how local people relate to you, but ultimately it's your own attitude that will make or break your relationships with people along the trail.

In some cultures where men and women are separate, being female gives you a special chance to relate to the female half of society. Even in Buddhist and Hindu cultures where men and women live and work closely together, women respond to other women with spontaneous sisterhood, and children respond to women as mother or aunt figures. You can enrich your trip immensely by learning about a hundred simple words and phrases of the local language. Learn to ask questions like, "How many children do you have?" and to answer other people's questions about you and your family. Bring pictures of your own family if they're not with you. Local people are just as curious about you as you are about them. It always helps to have a respectable profession, such as teaching, writing, or photography, that you can tell people about in the local language. When all else fails, use sign language. Be spontaneous! One of my fondest memories is of my mother, Maria Denker, and a *lama* (a Tibetan Buddhist priest) from Mustang making hand shadows of animals by firelight on the wall of a lodge near Muktinath.

Whether you are with a friend or with a group, pictures and small instruments, such as wooden flutes or harmonicas, make great conversation starters. Children also like to sing into tape recorders and are thrilled to hear the playback. In a lodge, you can sometimes enter the kitchen and watch women cook, make *chang* (beer), or churn butter tea. They'll be flattered by your interest, and you may be able to lend a hand in cleaning grain or even making bread. An exception, of course, is in Hindu households; non-Hindus are outside the caste system, and thus we would be viewed as polluting their food and kitchen.

Trekking completely by yourself isn't advisable. Remember that local women don't walk alone beyond their village. If you are alone, it is safest to hire a porter-guide from a reputable outfitter unless you have lived and traveled in the area for years. You might also consider hiring a Sherpa or Tamang woman as a guide if you speak enough Nepali to communicate with her. After being frustrated with male porters who sometimes didn't listen to what we were saying, Mother and I vowed to hire a Sherpa woman the next time we walk in the Khumbu region.

One of the difficulties of being female is that local men will sometimes be overly interested. The best way to handle this is to make clear at the beginning your lack of reciprocation. Generally, a sweetly uttered "But I think of you as my brother" is enough to make any male back off and, in fact, treat you with great respect. (Unfortunately, the introduction of video-cassette recorders and the X-rated films that may accompany them has sometimes given a wildly inaccurate impression of Western women to the locals.) Remember that you are far safer in Kathmandu or the hills, compared to traveling in Latin America or any city in the United States.

Dress is very important, perhaps more so for a woman than for a man.

These monks are at the monastery in Manang village; the second man from the right is a visiting lama from India.

If you want to be culturally sensitive and avoid misunderstandings, shorts and halter tops are definitely not recommended. Aside from being revealing, they are impractical, and you will end up scratched, bitten, and sunburned. Some women like to wear a *chuba,* the wraparound Tibetan-style robe, but usually Tibetan and Sherpa women walk better in them than we do over long distances. They are nice for lounging around a lodge, however, and people always appreciate foreigners who dress as they do. Learn from the local women and make sure your local dress actually goes together and is not a hodgepodge of styles or cultures that locals will look at oddly.

I have personally found the *shalwar kameez,* the long loose shirt and baggy trousers worn in Pakistan and northern India, to be comfortable, practical, and acceptable for trekking nearly anywhere. Loose cotton trousers for summer, loose wool trousers for winter, and especially long skirts, if you can walk in them, are also recommended. Remember that in remote areas a woman in pants may not be recognized as a woman. Nude bathing (unless you are with village women in a private place) or even wearing a bathing suit under an enticing waterfall is not recommended. If it's hot, it's nicer to bathe in your clothes and let them dry on you anyway.

If you have long hair, wear it in braids to keep it untangled and out of the way. Even better, let a village woman or girl braid it for you in the local fashion. I find a scarf or other head covering helps keep the dust out of my hair and the direct sun off my head.

A mundane but important consideration is what to do when you have your period. Bring plenty of tampons or sanitary napkins from home, because you won't necessarily find them in Kathmandu, or they won't be the right brand, or they will be very expensive. Disposal is another problem. One could burn the stuff, but lots of brands don't burn easily. Never burn sanitary or toilet materials, including facial tissues, in a kitchen fire or stove (considered sacred in Hindu and Buddhist locales), only in a private campfire out of sight of locals. Many well-traveled trails have lodges with marked toilets, and one can deposit used sanitary materials in these, unless you think the night soil will be used as fertilizer. The most ecologically conscious thing to do is to wrap tampons and sanitary napkins up in layers of plastic and take them back to a city for disposal. If you're absolutely sure they are biodegradable, it's okay to bury them, but like toilet paper, they should be buried deep enough. (Note that many women temporarily lose their period when they travel overseas and sometimes also for a month or two after they return. This is nothing to be concerned about.)

Personal cleanliness is sometimes hard to maintain, especially if you are trekking in a cold season and tend to wear your clothes for days at a time because it's too cold to undress. Panty liners are useful, and a babywipe at the end of the day does wonders for one's mood and feeling of cleanliness.

Many women have problems with cold hands and feet. I recommend a hot water bottle, to be filled last thing at night from the kettle. This can also provide lukewarm washing water in the morning. Be sure, too, that you take a warm-enough sleeping bag and perhaps down booties.

Whoever you are, however you trek, you can make the most of your experiences by being open to people around you and by going out of your way to be friendly, whether you've learned a little Nepali or Tibetan, or play the flute, or simply smile and use sign language.

Trekking with Children *by Pam Ross*

[Pam Ross has lived in Nepal and assisted her husband, Charles Gay, as escort on several group family treks. They have walked with their grade-school-age son Forrest on these and other hikes in various regions of Nepal. Pam has many words to the wise about hiking with children.]

Do you really want to take your kids with you to the Himalaya? For many first-time trekkers, the prospect of staying happy and healthy while walking in the mountains of Asia is daunting enough without the added responsibility of making sure that their offspring have a good time as well. Certainly you should already know that you enjoy traveling, camping, and hiking with your child before you contemplate a family trek in the Himalaya. In fact, having a child along can enrich the experience of trekking and encountering a new culture, and it definitely opens doors into that culture. Aside from parental anxiety, there is absolutely no reason why kids can't trek successfully.

How will taking kids along change the trek? As every parent knows, lack of energy is never the problem. Boredom or lack of perseverance is what causes a child to say, "I'm tired, I need to rest," and then to spend the entire rest time climbing the nearest steep rock and jumping off the top. Having other kids along makes both walking and playing more enjoyable for most kids. Go with friends or join a group set up for families; some tour operators offer family treks.

Plan on relatively short days: four or five hours of walking, with lots of fifteen- to twenty-minute stops to throw rocks in rivers, climb things, watch insects, etc. Plan on a two-hour stop in the middle of the day (most treks do this anyway so the staff can prepare a hot meal for everyone). While walking, be ready sometimes to tell stories or play word games with your children instead of drinking in the spectacular scenery in meditative silence.

Hire an extra person to carry each child under eight. The wives of Sherpas often do this job in Nepal. Even if your children end up walking most of the time, it's great for them (and you) to know that they can be carried if they need it, if they get sick, or if you have to get over a pass to reach a good campsite. Himalayan terrain is steep and often difficult, and even if your children's porters never carry them, it's reassuring to have someone who holds their hand in dicey places; carries their raingear, sun hat, and rock collection; and picks up their gloves when they leave them in a teashop. There are two options for child-carrying packs: your own child carrier, which can be simple or high-tech and has the advantage of being the one your child is accustomed to, or the local Nepali basket (*doko*), which can be cut down to make room for the legs and is easily padded with a sleeping bag. These woven baskets work beautifully, especially for older kids, and have the advantage of being good load carriers when the child is walking.

Can you keep your children healthy on a trek? This is the big question, the one that makes people think you're crazy for even considering taking a child trekking, but there's no reason, given adequate precautions and the cooperation of the child, why your kid shouldn't stay just as healthy as you. Read Chapter 12, "A Himalayan Medical Primer," and follow Peter Hackett's advice. The only extra risk with children is that they do tend to put their dirty hands (and other even less savory objects) in their mouths. I dealt with this problem quite successfully when my son Forrest was three years old by starting a big campaign of No Hands in Mouths as soon as we left the United States. To reinforce this idea, we *both* painted on bad-tasting stuff designed to stop nail biting. He loved reminding me not to bite my nails and soon got into the habit of washing his hands before eating anything. A thumb-sucker would be more of a challenge—perhaps regular cleaning with alcohol pads would do it.

Pediatric solutions of all the common medicines are available over the counter in India and Nepal. Carry child dosages of whatever you take in your medical kit. (Cough syrup is especially important for those night coughs that keep everyone awake.) *Travel note:* For long plane flights I highly recommend a kiddie sleeping medicine. The one my pediatrician prescribed was aptly called Noctec, but anything that induces sleep will do.

Altitude sickness in children has not yet been documented as any more likely to occur than it is with adults. Obviously it is important to acquaint yourself with the early symptoms of the disease and to make sure your child drinks plenty of fluids and reports any headaches or nausea. The key is alertness to both your own and your child's physical state, and willingness to rest for a day or to descend if it seems warranted. Be sure to keep in mind that dehydration from diarrhea can be particularly serious with children and that the younger the child, the more quickly he or she can become dehydrated. If you child develops diarrhea, be sure to give him or her lots of liquids.

Should special food or equipment be carried? Most children like the rice-and-lentil diet, and many enjoy the sweet milky tea served in most parts of the Himalaya. Some suggestions for extras: soy sauce to flavor rice; powdered drink mixes to mask the taste of iodine in water and to promote fluid consumption; and granola bars, dried fruit, or nuts for quick treats on the trail. These items are generally not available in Asia.

Your child's clothing and sleeping bag should be just as good as yours, with the additional reminder that children who are being carried are not generating heat of their own and should be warmly dressed. A warm hat is particularly important.

A few small, familiar toys are definitely worth taking: tiny stuffed animals, pens and notebooks, a small tape player with earphones, and kids' music and stories. Keeping a daily journal (for younger kids, pictures plus narrative dictated to you) is a wonderful occupation and the best possible souvenir. Having a teacher assign the task may make this more palatable to some kids.

Even if you plan to stay in lodges and houses most of the time, a tent provides welcome privacy for a child who may be overloaded with attention from local villagers. For all but the most gregarious child, the constant attention of strangers gets to be too much from time to time. A tent is an ideal retreat for some quiet time with familiar playthings.

Diapers and toileting are a problem in the mountains. Disposable diapers are not all that disposable where there is no garbage pickup. Probably the best solution is to bury used diapers *deeply* once a day. On organized treks the staff digs a latrine, and a separate hole for diapers could be dug nearby. Check to make sure the hole is covered properly before you leave any campsite, otherwise dogs will dig into it. Do not attempt to burn diapers: they don't burn easily, and such fires are offensive to the locals. Older kids may object to the lack of proper facilities. Have younger kids practice ahead of time outdoors if possible, and if in doubt, buy a small plastic potty (available in Kathmandu) or cut the seat out of one of the bamboo stools commonly carried on organized treks.

How can you foster interaction with local kids? For Himalayan villagers, the arrival of trekkers is a lot like having the circus pull into town. You are definitely a show, and even on the well-traveled routes, foreign kids are still a rarity. The traditional cultures along the trail are very family oriented and are usually thrilled to see that trekkers do indeed reproduce and travel as families, but to turn the existing fascination and goodwill into meaningful interchange requires some effort. Despite what we'd all like to believe, kids do not instantly overcome language and cultural differences and play together, especially if it's with a new set of kids each day.

An English-speaking staff person can help to get games started. In Nepal, many village children play a version of duck-duck-goose, which any kid can learn to play in two minutes. Tug-of-war is known everywhere, as are different forms of tag. Take a ball and a frisbee. But please do *not* take small gifts to hand out to kids: this practice just starts them begging.

If your child is of school age, try to visit a school. English is taught from the early grades, and participation in an English class would be enlightening for your child as well as the students. And the game of naming things in English and the local language can be fun anytime there is an opportunity for one-on-one play.

A valuable relationship to foster is that between your child and an English-speaking local staff person, who can expand your child's observation into learning. How the locals go about their daily lives (the details of food production, animal husbandry, and housekeeping) is generally more fascinating to kids than the elevations of peaks or the names of deities. Children specialize in minute observations of the natural world, and mountain people are of necessity excellent naturalists, with a vast knowledge of the plants and animals around them. Identification of animal droppings found along the trail is fun, and so is birdwatching, especially with a good picture guidebook.

Like many activities that people don't often do with kids, trekking in the Himalaya requires some extra effort and advance planning, but the rewards of sharing one of the great adventures of your life with your children are great indeed. Even if they don't remember the specifics of the trek in a few years, the experience of visiting a culture where people live in harmony with their mountain environment without roads, machinery, or modern entertainment is bound to make a lasting impression on your children.

These sisters from Mugu have distinctive round earrings; leather-covered amulets and musk deer tusks hang from their necks. (Photograph by Kevin Bubriski.)

2
Getting Ready to Go

As often as possible, do what the others are not doing: go off-season instead of on, go in bad weather instead of good, walk when others ride, laugh when others cry. . . .

Ed Buryn, 1971

In every journey, there are as many objectives missed as there are objectives gained.

Arnold Toynbee, 1960

General Preparation

Many of us tempt ourselves for years with the possibility of going to the Himalaya. Scenes from books come to mind, and we imagine ourselves being in those faraway places. We fantasize trekking north of the world's highest massifs into land indistinguishable from Tibet, or walking up a glaciated pass between two medieval valley kingdoms. When the decision is finally made, it is as if you had been walking up a rolling hill and imperceptibly crossed its ridgeline, finding yourself going down the far side. You *are* going. This chapter takes you from that decision to the airplane ride that will whisk you to Asia.

Eric Shipton could organize his excursions to the Himalaya "in half an hour on the back of an envelope," but you will require considerably more time and at least two full-size sheets of paper for making lists of inoculations to have, visas to obtain, and more. My second overland trip to Nepal was completely organized on two weeks' notice, from inspiration to departure. This can be done and we proved it, but if you take such a hasty approach, you'll likely be exhausted by the time you reach Asia. Two and a half months is a much better minimum time to consider planning such a sojourn. A Himalayan trek requires planning, and there are several projects to start at once.

Physical Conditioning

If you plan to trek in addition to sightseeing, you should initiate or continue a good conditioning program. Vigorous exercise that strengthens the cardiovascular system, lungs, and legs is the best way to prepare yourself for Himalayan walking. Running, swimming, bicycling, and cross-country skiing will help toughen you for walking in country so vertical that you may trek steadily uphill for days at a time. The best exercise, of course, is to hike uphill and down, carrying a day pack if you are going with a group, or more if you will be carrying a load in the Himalaya. Exercise continuously for sixty to ninety minutes every other day, or every day, if you have the time, and certainly work up to that much exercise before leaving. This will not fully condition you for a full day of walking day in and day out, but it will strengthen your system to the point that your body can accept the rigors of trekking. Backpacking in your favorite hilly location is the best approximation of what you will do in the Himalaya and will help remind you of your physical capabilities. One of the many joys of a Himalayan trek is that you get far beyond the achy-muscles-and-groggy-evenings stage of hiking by the end of the first week. To get in shape if you have done no physical preparation, however, will take far longer than a week on the trail. Many people who set off on a whim don't get far without wishing fervently that they were in shape. Spur-of-the-moment trekkers are sometimes forced to turn back by physical ailments that might well not have occurred if they had been adequately prepared.

Background Reading

This book describes many trekking possibilities in Nepal, western Tibet, and Bhutan, but you will enjoy your trip more if you do further background reading. After perusing this book, you may have a greater interest in two or three areas and might want to seek out additional reading about them. One likely source is the *National Geographic;* the stories are colorful, and most libraries have the magazine's back issues. The annotated bibliography at the back of this book will lead you a long way toward gathering all the information you will need or can absorb.

Of the introductions to walking Asian mountain trails, Eric Newby's *A Short Walk in the Hindu Kush* remains one of the classics. Newby, his friend, and their crew of three Afghans trekked in Nuristan, Afghanistan, in 1956. With minimal paraphernalia, they walked in the Panjshir and Ramgul valleys, then tried to reach the top of 19,880-foot Mir Samir, reading how-to-climb books on the ascent. After failing in three attempts, they had an eventful look at rarely seen Ramgul in Nuristan before returning to Kabul. Newby experienced and humorously detailed the range of predicaments and pitfalls facing the neophyte trekker. A more scholarly but nonetheless fascinating book is *Himalayan Pilgrimage*. In it, David Snellgrove describes his study trek to Dolpo and north-central Nepal's other Buddhist areas during a five-month period in 1956. He gives tribute to his guide and friend Pasang, without whose assistance "the whole venture would scarcely have been possible." Snellgrove describes his book as "a kind of scholar's travelbook." It is also an excellent evocation of village people and life in truly remote Himalayan places. You can also find many other volumes that tell about walking Himalayan trails specifically from the contemporary outsider's perspective.

Aside from reading for background, try to absorb some vocabulary from "Introduction to Spoken Nepali" if you are going to Nepal, or the Tibetan glossary if you are going to Tibet (see the end of this book). If you are going to Bhutan, keep in mind that you can often use Nepali there, because many Bhutanese understand Nepali. Every word learned is another opportunity to speak with the locals when you go trekking.

Maps

As you narrow down the areas you are interested in and plan your trek, you need to consider purchasing maps. When you are trekking, a map can mean a lot to you, especially if you are walking in more remote regions. You can find very inexpensive ammonia dye maps that cover most of the mountainous areas in Nepal, but these locally made maps can be purchased only in Kathmandu. These purple-colored maps are of only limited reliability, but they help give you some sense of where you are when trekking. For information about these and other more detailed maps of Nepal, Tibet, and Bhutan, consult Appendix A, "Map Information." The maps in this book, while drawn to scale, are meant only to give you an overview of the regions covered. Do read the appendix to learn the range of what is available, and consider purchasing more complete maps before you leave.

If maps are difficult for you to comprehend, you can familiarize yourself with them in several ways. When you fly in a plane and look down, what you see is very similar to a map. You can become accustomed to route finding by tracing on a map the paths described in this or other accounts as you read them. Once in the Himalaya, you can read towns off the map and talk with locals about them, even if you haven't figured out the exact relationship of one place to another. You will become more familiar with an area by referring to your map and looking at the lay of the land as you walk through the countryside. Use a map to figure out alternate routes, ask the locals about those paths, and try them if you want to see some different trails than other trekkers are taking. If at first a map appears to be a jumble of lines, you can become accustomed to the area represented by returning to the map and getting to know it in relation to what you see. Some people like to mark their maps with different-color felt-tip pens, using one shade for the main rivers and another for the ridgelines. Such lines following valley bottoms and ridges can particularly help you visualize the country shown on xeroxed or one-color maps. Don't hesitate to make notes right on a map or its border if your reading of the land disagrees with what the map shows.

Passport, Visas, and Immunizations

All U.S. citizens need a current U.S. passport for travel abroad. If your passport has expired or is due to expire, you will need a new one. Most post offices in the United States can give you passport application forms, or you can apply at one of the passport agencies operated by the State Department in major cities. For a first application you will need a certified copy of your birth certificate, a driver's license, two identical recent photographs with your head size 1 to 1½ inches tall, and a fee. For renewal you will need your old passport, the two identical recent photos, and a fee. You should also get about a dozen smaller photos for visas and trekking permits in Nepal.

Citizens of most countries except those that adjoin Nepal need visas to enter or transit Nepal. The Nepalese tourist visa is good for a one-month stay within three months from the date of issue. In Nepal, you can have a visa extended for a total stay of three months by paying the necessary fees. Alternatively, you can get a one-week visa at your arrival point by land or air in Nepal and arrange extensions once in-country (see "Trekking Regulations" in Chapter 3). No matter where you get your Nepalese visa, you will need to pay a fee (which has been $10 but may increase) and provide two photographs.

Likewise, citizens of most countries, including Commonwealth countries, need visas in order to enter or transit India. Please note this if you plan to stop overnight in India on your way to Nepal or Bhutan. The Indian visa can be validated for single, double, or multiple entries. The visa can be issued for up to a three-month stay, and the first entry must be within six months of the date of issue. A fee will be charged, probably depending on the number of entries requested. The visa is extendable for three more months once you are in-country. Extensions are granted at district police stations. Please check current regulations carefully when you apply for a visa, for these regulations can change.

To travel in Tibet you will need a Chinese visa. Up to now, the procedure for obtaining visas for individual travel to China has been complicated and lengthy, but it appears that this process is being eased and revised. Check with the Chinese embassy or nearest consulate for the present formalities. Visas for China can always be obtained overnight (during working days) by applying at the Chinese consulate or approved travel agencies in Hong Kong. If you are traveling to Tibet with a group, your travel agency or tour operator will assist you in getting your visa.

Travel in Bhutan is limited to groups, as noted in Chapter 10. To obtain information on travel to Bhutan, you will have to contact a tour operator used to arranging trips there, because all overseas offices of the Bhutan Travel Service have been closed. Alternatively, you can write to the Bhutan Tourism Corporation, P.O. Box 159, Thimphu, Bhutan.

To get a visa, you must first request an application from the appropriate embassy or consulate. After filling out the visa application, mail it back with payment, photos, a self-addressed stamped envelope (SASE), and your passport. To be absolutely safe when mailing your passport, send the letter by express or registered mail and include postage on the SASE sufficient for your stamped passport to be returned likewise by registered mail. Allow as much as three weeks for each visa to be processed. Many cities have visa services that, for a fee, can obtain visas for you far faster and far more easily than you can get one on your own.

In the United States, you can contact the officials for Nepal, India, and China at the following addresses:

Royal Nepalese Embassy, 2131 Leroy Place NW, Washington, DC 20008.

Royal Nepalese Consulate General, 820 Second Avenue, Suite 1200, New York, NY 10017.

Embassy of India, 2107 Massachusetts Avenue NW, Washington, DC 20008. (India also has consulates that can issue visas in the following cities: New York, Chicago, and San Francisco.)

Embassy of the People's Republic of China, 2300 Connecticut Avenue NW, Washington, DC 20008. (China also has consulates that can issue visas in the following cities: New York, Chicago, Houston, and San Francisco.)

At the time of this writing, no immunizations were required for entry to Nepal, China, or Bhutan, but this situation could change at any time. In any case, certain immunizations are recommended for your health and safety. For complete information, see Chapter 12, "A Himalayan Medical Primer," by Peter H. Hackett, M.D.

The Trekker's Complete List of What to Take

You will also be the final judge of what to take when you go trekking, and you should also have some hiking experience to build on before you travel halfway around the world to walk in the Himalaya. To assist you, I have compiled the following rather exhaustive list. It is divided into six categories so you can visualize what you will be adding to your pack if you wish to trek on your own carrying camping and cooking gear, or if you go into the high snows off the trail. Not everything is applicable to everyone's use; the equipment in category 5, for instance, is only for those intending to walk up high peaks or glaciers. Far more important to your enjoyment while walking than the latest synthetic piles, miracle fabrics, and fancy gear are prudence (in high places or changeable weather) and enthusiasm for the trekking experience.

Here are the six categories, then the complete list, item by item:

1. Clothing and personal gear
2. Camping equipment
3. Cooking equipment
4. Miscellaneous
5. Equipage for the snows and glacier walking
6. Optional accessories

Clothing and Personal Gear

If you are going to be walking in the Himalaya for any length of time, the chances are quite good that you will need the clothing listed here. You may also have to help equip a porter with clothing essentials acquired locally. As you choose what to pack, keep in mind that you will be hand-washing the most used items in cold stream water.

Underwear. Three pairs are enough. Wash and rewear.

Bras. For women, a couple. Bras are recommended for modesty in traditional societies.

Tampons or sanitary napkins. For women. These will be difficult or impossible to locate in the local bazaar. (See "Making the Most of Being a Woman Trekker" in Chapter 1.)

Socks. Take three pairs each of thin liner socks and heavier outer socks. Liner socks of nylon or cotton are good. Wool or a blend of mostly wool (not synthetics) should be your choice for outers. You must have, at minimum, two complete changes of socks plus an extra pair in case you need another layer. Keep washing your socks, and your feet will thank you by not blistering (given well-broken-in hiking boots or shoes).

Tights. For women, one pair for warmth.

T-shirts. Take several. T-shirts with snazzy designs on the front make great gifts for your porter or Sherpa.

Lightweight shirts. You should have one or two loose-fitting wash-and-wear shirts.

Medium- to heavyweight shirt. Two button-down pockets on your upper-altitude shirt will come in handy. Wool's still best.

Long, loose-fitting walking skirts. Long skirts are recommended for women. I am also advised that they can be very practical when you have to dodge off the trail. The baggy, locally made pants described below are also appropriate for women and offer wonderful freedom of movement.

Loose-fitting trekking pants. For men or women, a pair of pants in addition to those you wear on the plane. Loose pants are a must if you want freedom of movement on the trail. Baggy pants are often worn in the hills and, even if you are not used to them, will prove extremely comfortable as soon as you try them. In the West, the nearest we have to Himalayan-style pants are knickers. These give room for the knee to bend unconstricted, but many are tight in the crotch and pelvis unless you make or buy yours large on purpose. Jeans are much too tight for trekking, and if they get wet, they take forever to dry.

Better than knickers is the Nepalese *suruwal* or the Muslim *shalwar,* those wonderfully baggy pajama-style pants with a drawstring at the waist. When you arrive in Kathmandu, or even Lhasa, consider having a local tailor measure you for a pair to take on your trek. After measuring you, the tailor will know how much cloth is necessary. You can then purchase the material (dark colors hide stains), and the pants can be sewn within hours. I ask the tailor to make the ankle openings just wide enough to fit around my trekking boots. For me, walking in shalwar is the only way to go except on tricky, exposed places off the trail, where the voluminous material can snag. These pants breathe when the temperature is hot yet seem to retain heat during cold weather. Their primary asset is that they permit unrestricted leg movement in any direction without rubbing.

Thermal underwear. (The shirt is optional.) Polypropylene is the favorite material nowadays. In winter and in high camps, if you wear long johns under your pants and the rest of your body is kept warm, the wind will have to become quite intense before you become uncomfortable. For most treks, even with several high camps, these two garments will be enough cover on your legs. (If you carry rain chaps, you will have a third layer.)

Rain pants or chaps. Coated nylon or Gore-Tex rain pants are great for rain and wind, but I've always done fine with just rain chaps. If they are tied at one end, you can carry flour in them.

Down, pile, or fiberfill jacket or parka. You will want to have a good down or pile jacket or a down or fiberfill parka on most treks to ensure comfort. Don't take an expedition parka, however, unless you are going up a high peak or have extremely slow metabolism. Remember that you can always add layers. When you trek with a porter, he can use your down jacket to sleep under, with his blanket beneath him. A synthetic-fill jacket will be better if you trek in the monsoon, but remember that fiberfill jackets take up more room. You may want to add a woolen sweater if you are trekking in the winter.

Trekking boots. The medium- to lightweight trekking boots of your preference are the best to walk in. If you buy used boots, *they must be in good condition*. If you buy new boots, *they must be broken in*. Never take new boots to the Himalaya without being certain that the boots and your feet are well acquainted. Do be extremely careful where you put your boots when you are not wearing them. Trekking boots (and sleeping bags) can disappear faster than any other items in the mountains.

Some boot manufacturers now make hiking boots that cannot be re-soled. When their soles wear out, you must toss away the hiking boots. Consider this when you purchase your next pair. When you go to get your boots resoled, be sure the repairman knows his business. You might take along some Barge cement or Shoe Goo II if you have any qualms about how your soles will last.

Running shoes or tennis shoes. Running shoes are useful as backup footgear, around camp, when you are not carrying much, must ford a fast-moving stream, or have blisters. The light shoes are great for switching off with your regular footgear, but beware of taking them as your only shoes. If you sprain your ankle, you'll feel mighty funny hobbling out to a roadhead or airfield halfway around the world for lack of a pair of shoes that would adequately protect you. When you wear running shoes on the trail, walk carefully until you get the feel of them. Some kinds of treads are tricky; they tend to grab and can throw you off balance. If you hire a porter for a trek with a snow pass or glacier walking, he can wear your running shoes for those sections, unless, like the one man I hired, he already has mountaineering boots with full-length steel shanks!

Insoles. Your feet may become more fatigued than you expect, and a soft cushion beneath them can give some relief. Insoles can also help keep a foot from rubbing when a boot stretches from extensive use. In a pinch, you can cut your own innersoles from the end of your foam pad.

Moleskin. This padding is used to cushion broken skin. Some people prefer Elastoplast or Second Skin to moleskin. Any kind of tape can par-tially protect rubbed skin (if it's clean) from further harm. Be sure to take some sort of preventive measure if you even begin to feel a hot spot.

Gloves or mittens. For chilly mornings and high passes, you'll be glad to have hand protection. Wool, polypro, or pile is best.

Umbrella. That's right, a bumbershoot. Many cognoscenti of the Himalaya would never be without one. It is your best aid against the tropical or alpine sun: with an umbrella you always have shade. Also, in the rain an umbrella is superior to a poncho (which tends to soak you in perspira-tion), and it provides a quick line of defense against charging Tibetan mastiffs. When you take backlit photos, an umbrella is excellent for shading the camera lens. In Nepal, umbrellas are called *chhatris*, and the best presently available come from China. Chhatris are used by *sadhu* (religious renunciates), funky trekker, and Sir Edmund Hillary alike.

Hat. A warm wool stocking cap, pile cap, or down hood is the best instant regulator of body temperature. Because more than 40 percent of the body's heat exits from the head, a thick cap will go a long way toward keeping heat in. If you don't plan to use an umbrella in the sun, take a wide-brimmed hat. Remember that a hat will keep the sun off, but you will sweat like Niagara Falls in one when it's hot. You *must* have something with you to keep the sun off your head.

Money belt or pouch. A thin, sweat-proof money belt that holds trekking permit, passport, immunization booklet, traveler's checks, and currency is most convenient for such valuables. It is the trekker's equivalent of the amulets that Buddhists, Hindus, and Muslims often wear around their necks. Before you get trekking, your money belt should be fastened around you, but on the trail it can be buried in your pack. Your passport (or trekking permit, in Nepal) will be needed along the route at checkposts, so don't become separated from it. At night you can slip your money belt into your sleeping bag.

Handkerchiefs. Hankies are great; take one to two large ones for swabbing sweat, carrying walnuts, and playing peek-a-boo with kids.

Poncho and groundcloth. Sometimes extra baggage, sometimes necessary protection, a poncho may serve as your groundcloth, raingear, or extra padding. Be sure that yours has a hood, grommets in the corners, and snaps along the sides.

Sleeping bag. What makes for a proper sleeping bag is up to you. Don't be awed by Himalayan heights and overequip yourself for trekking. I have used a bag containing 26 ounces of goose down and one that had 42 ounces of goose down. The latter was always too warm below 6,000 feet but fine in colder weather, particularly those winter nights at 16,000-foot elevations. Carry your sleeping bag inside your duffle or pack, if possible: "Not good to tempt fate [rain, damage, or theft], sahib."

Foam pad. A $\frac{1}{2}$-inch-thick or, preferably, $\frac{5}{8}$-inch-thick closed-cell foam pad under the proper sleeping bag will keep you cozy on a glacier. Therm-a-Rest pads are becoming very popular, but if you have one, take a repair kit also. Use a pad everywhere you sleep to keep out the chill and damp.

Sleeping sack. Last in this category, I list a personal favorite. Fold a thin sheet or similar-size piece of cloth lengthwise and sew it closed across the bottom and along both sides to about 10 inches of the top. The sleeping sack that results goes into your bag at night to protect it from dirt and nighttime sweat. Washing a sleeping sack several times is a lot easier than washing a sleeping bag once. The sheet can also serve as a towel.

Camping Equipment

The clothing and gear on the previous list are needed by most trekkers in the Himalaya. You will not need to carry your own shelter if you trek with a group, decide to sleep only in houses or inns, or decide to chance the rain. Most trekkers, though, need at least a tent in order to camp.

Tent. A sturdy, rainproof tent can make all the difference . . . but you know that. Having a tent means you can camp anywhere with a flat spot and reachable water. Your poncho tied up with rope may suffice if need be.

Cooking Equipment

In order to trek fully self-contained, a few cooking implements (in addition to food, which is discussed in the next chapter) are necessary. These items can be bought locally but will be heavier than the lightweight models you can bring with you.

Stove. Using a reliable kerosene stove that you can clean anywhere is preferable to using wood for fuel (unless you are in a remote, heavily forested area like western Nepal). Kerosene is available in Himalayan bazaars; it burns with a hotter flame than gasoline (petrol) and, unlike gas, will not explode. Like many people, I have found the MSR X-GK model to be the lightest and best kerosene stove. (Keep it well wrapped in plastic or in an outside pocket; it can dribble smelly fuel when it is broken down.) Coleman also makes a kerosene stove, and MSR now has another model, called the Internationale. As the wood-fuel crisis spreads and standards of living rise in the mountains, kerosene stoves are slowly coming into greater general use. This helps to assure that you can buy fuel in the darnedest places; ask for it at stores and large homes that double as stores. Local makes of stove are heavier and bulkier than Western models. Also, Asian stoves are less fuel efficient and less well built. Note that white gas, used in many popular models of American camp stoves, is not available in Asia. Carry a filter for the local kerosene, which can be filthy.

Fuel container. Your fuel must not leak away, so think again before waiting until you reach the trailhead bazaar to buy your fuel container. Carry enough fuel, and in a sturdy container or containers.

Nesting cookpots. A minimum of two cookpots, or billies, are needed. Bring some, or purchase a pair in the local bazaar. The Asian variety is heavier but can be given as part of a bonus to your porter when the trek is over.

Stuffbags. To carry bulk rice, flour, sugar, and other foods, you need nylon or cotton cloth bags with drawstrings at the top. In the United States they are called stuffbags; in Asia they have other names, and tailors can make them quickly.

Freeze-dried food. If your style of trekking includes freeze-dried food, bring packets from home. The supply in Kathmandu is spotty at best.

Miscellaneous

This is a long list, but look it over carefully. Many articles are light-weight and might be needed on the trail; others can be omitted. Large and important items are listed toward the beginning. Many are unnecessary (such as a backpack) if you go on a group trek.

Backpack. As with a tent and a sleeping bag, you will have to choose for yourself what you want in a pack. A single-compartment, top-loading pack is the best for me. A broken zipper on an "easy access" pack is quite a nuisance, and that situation can be averted by using a zipperless top-loading model. Try to avoid using a pack that has no sweat-evaporating back panel or webbing, or you will find that both back and pack become drenched with sweat in lower-elevation trekking. If you plan to go by yourself or go long distances with a porter, take a large-volume pack. Mine holds more than 5,800 cubic inches, and it has been quite full several times. Your porter may use a tumpline (called a *naamlo* in Nepali) when he carries your pack. If you go with an organized group, you will need only a duffle bag for a porter or *zopkio* (cross-breed) to carry.

More stuffbags. You will need various sizes and colors to put things in.

Iodine crystals, solution, or tablets. See Chapter 12, "A Himalayan Medical Primer." Some form of water purification utilizing iodine is absolutely essential. Don't leave without it. *Do not use Halazone tablets.* Halazone does not protect against the amoebic cyst that causes amoebic dysentery, a debilitating, sometimes fatal disease. If you drink an iodine solution soon after the ten to twenty minutes needed for the iodine to decontaminate the water, the taste of the water is remarkably unaffected. Treated water that has been standing overnight will have a much stronger taste. The only other way you can treat water to be sure it is safe is to boil it.

Medical kit. A small but complete medical kit should accompany you. A list of recommended items is given at the end of Chapter 12.

Maps. Take the best maps you can. Check Appendix A, "Map Information."

Notebook. Carrying a notebook is almost a necessity for the traveler. Before leaving home you can make notes in it, include addresses and any information needed, and tape duplicated glossary pages to it. After arrival in Asia, you owe to your future memories a record of events and places, even if it is cursory. Use your notebook, or you will forget the color and small touches of your special experiences, despite their vividness at the time.

Day pack or shoulder bag. A day pack or locally made shoulder bag (called a *jhola*) is good for day hikes and while trekking. On a day walk above a town or high camp, the day pack or jhola can carry food and water.

Toilet kit. The toilet kit may include toothbrush and toothpaste, mirror, comb, soap (one bar for washing yourself, plus a laundry bar, available locally, for clothes), washcloth, and dental floss. The floss is important to have, for it is unavailable in South Asia, and a sliver of meat or husk in your teeth can be painful.

Toilet paper. Take it, buy it in the bazaar, or use a current international news magazine for the wild juxtaposition of timeless mountains and ephemeral news stories. Burn the used paper. Or you might do it the way the locals do: with a pebble or the left hand and water (poured from a beer bottle or a small urn with a spout called a *lota*).

Watch. A reliable watch is perfect for knowing when to rise for an early start or for getting an idea how much light is left on cloudy days. Some people keep a few extra inexpensive watches in their packs. They barter their "only" watches and later replace them with others to be used again as trading material.

Enamel cup. Purchase a large enamel cup in a hardware store or in any well-stocked bazaar. If you try to use it at a teahouse, the woman will still pour the tea into her own (perhaps unsanitary) cup first to measure the amount. A cup that holds at least 20 ounces is preferable; some entire meals of soup or tsampa will be eaten from it. (I object to the Sierra-cup style for two reasons: it doesn't hold enough liquid by far, and its metal rim is too hot on the lips.)

Spoon. A large soup spoon will enable you to mix food and eat nearly anything.

Can opener. Weighing about 2 grams, the G.I. or P-38 can opener is the best for the trail.

Pocket knife. A good knife is always necessary; try to get one with a small pair of scissors attached.

Flashlight. An absolute must: for those obligatory nocturnal trips, for the time you find yourself benighted on the precipice trail, and for every other imaginable and unimaginable occurrence in the dark in village or wilderness. Take extra batteries and bulb. Some people prefer a headlamp with a lithium battery (these batteries are rarely available in Kathmandu).

Water bottle. Another sine qua non, your water container should hold 1 to 2 quarts or liters. Don't compromise on quality.

Sewing kit. Needles, light and dark nylon thread, numerous safety pins, and a few feet of 2-inch-wide ripstop repair tape compose a good, minimal sewing kit. You may wish to carry extra clevis pins or eyebolts (for repairing your pack) in the sewing kit.

Thick garbage bags. A garbage bag placed inside your pack, around your sleeping bag, or lining your duffle will provide excellent protection from rain or sweat.

Boot protector. Take Sno Seal, mink oil, or your favorite boot grease if you have leather boots. You will be surprised how much punishment your boots will suffer on a long trek, compared with a shorter outing at home.

Lip balm. Your lips will quickly chap when trekking. Without question, take some form of lip grease with a high sun protection factor (SPF) on any trek.

Suntan lotion. Many people need suntan lotion, although others do fine using only an umbrella or hat. If you burn easily, take lotion with a high SPF (15 or above).

Cord. A 20- to 40-foot length of thin nylon cord has a multitude of uses. And few gifts please a person from the hills more than a nice length of nylon cord.

Photographs. Photographs are great icebreakers. Everyone likes to see "fotos" of your family, buildings where you live, and such places as stores or roads with cars. In the roadless hills, pictures of automobiles can set off wonderful discussions. The favorite photograph I take shows my sister milking a goat, a very large-uddered goat, the sight of which often provokes exclamations of envy and awe.

Sunglasses. These are useful for low and medium elevations; for walking on snow you need more protection.

Spare glasses. If you use prescription glasses, take a spare set in a hard case.

Insect repellent. Insect bites are usually a minor problem unless you trek in the middle of the monsoon. Take strong insect repellent if you are especially sensitive to bites.

Bug powder. Even if you don't cross the threshold of a single dwelling in the Himalaya you may still acquire those tiny things that itch and bite in the night, merely by walking down a path in town or camping somewhere that has recently been frequented by livestock. I have found that for the

Intricate rock carvings like this are found in the upper Buri Gandaki Valley. Milarepa sits in the middle; he listens with a hand to his right ear.

rare times lice or fleas have materialized, lethal powder (available in Asia) has been necessary for dusting clothes and sleeping bag.

Odds and ends. You will always need a candle, large and small rubber bands, plastic bags (available in Kathmandu), tape, and extra pens.

Equipage for the High Snows or Glacier Walking

With a few things more, you can head for the high snows and summits or walk up a high glacier.

Mountaineering or glacier goggles. With nothing about but sun and snow at the teens of thousands of feet, your eyes will fail painfully unless protected from the immense amount of direct and reflected light. Be sure to use goggles with high-altitude lenses. Carry good dark glasses or goggles for your porter if you are going with one, for he, like you, will become sightless without eye protection. (See Chapter 12, "A Himalayan Medical Primer," for more information on snow blindness.)

Glacier cream. Get high-altitude glacier cream or lotion with a high SPF to protect your face from strong radiation and reflection. Be sure to put it under your nostrils.

Extra mittens. Protect your fingers from the possibility of freezing in the heights with at least two pairs of good hand protection made of wool, pile, or polypro.

Cold weather headgear. Carry a thick wool, pile, or polypro balaclava or down hood that will keep your head warm in penetrating winds.

Gaiters. Walking through any deep snow will be a rugged experience unless you can cover the opening between your pants and boots; gaiters accomplish this best. A good stopgap method to keep out snow is to use pieces of plastic or garbage bags held on with rubber bands or cord around your cuffs.

Crampons. Take crampons only if you are quite certain you will be going well above the highest trails onto steep snow slopes. Many people, including me, have naively carried crampons about for weeks in Nepal, returning to Kathmandu with them unused. High passes on almost any intervalley route will not require crampons, because other walkers will have blazed the way.

Ice ax. An ice ax provides a bit of dash, but it weighs a pound or two and is not needed for trekking unless you plan to walk up a steep snow-covered peak.

Climbing equipment. If you are a technical climber, take your gear to the most challenging mountains you'll ever find. Masses of used climbing gear are available for rent or purchase in Kathmandu: caveat emptor.

Rope. Rope is essential if you are walking on the upper part of a glacier where the moraine gives way to snow. Glaciers are often covered with powder snow. To walk high on such a glacier, all members of your party must be roped together and have ice axes for self-arrest.

Optional Accessories

You will want to take along some of the following to record or illumine the world that you step into.

A good book. Most people have time for a good novel when trekking. A paperback with trading potential is best, in case you finish it and want to swap with someone en route. Some people prefer guides to the flora or fauna (see the bibliography). Remember H. W. Tilman on the traditional mountaineer: "His occupational disease is bedsores, and a box of books his most cherished load."

Camera and film. For a few tips about camera equipment and use, see "Photography," below. Some people going to the Himalaya say, "I'm not going to take a camera, because with one, I wouldn't really *see* things there." This notion loses out in the long run, however, as memories fade and nothing is left to remind you, except perhaps someone else's photographs of the place you went.

Cassette recorder. Using a cassette recorder, you can make friends with people by playing music: yours or theirs. When you return home, tapes from your trip will lend great immediacy to a slide show.

Binoculars. Some people prefer a lightweight monocular. Either way, field glasses are required if you want to observe animals or birds.

Compass. Many people find a compass useful, particularly high up in foggy weather. As to using a compass for naming those white peaks on the horizon, I defer again to H. W. Tilman, who wrote, "The identification of very distant peaks is a harmless and fascinating amusement so long as the results are not taken seriously."

Altimeter. Handy for getting approximate elevations when you are wandering the high country or traversing out-of-the-way routes.

Frisbee. Not appropriate for impressing stuffy village elders with your seriousness of purpose, a frisbee can nevertheless be a good icebreaker.

Afterword to the Complete List

From T-shirts to frisbees, this is an exhaustive list, and you couldn't carry everything on it plus food and walk very far (I certainly don't bring everything listed). No matter how you trek, whether funky or fancy, pare this list down to what is appropriate for you. Again, I recommend hiring a porter to haul some of your gear and cook your food. Trekking with a lighter pack will enable you to enjoy, not merely endure, the entire trek and allow you to better assimilate and record the experience. Comparing the many items on this list to the small jhola that many Nepalis carry for days of walking causes me to realize how far we Westerners have drifted from needs to wants.

If you arrive in Nepal with little or no gear, you will have no difficulty equipping yourself in Kathmandu. (See ("Equipping Yourself Locally" in Chapter 3.) For those going to Tibet or Bhutan who do not have what they require on arrival, all I can say is that you will have to be inventive in searching out your needs and be prepared to get by on less than, or something different than, what you might wish to have, for neither Lhasa nor Thimphu has well-stocked clothing or used-equipment shops.

Photography

In the Himalaya, the distance from home and extremes of temperature make special preparation necessary for the photographer, whether beginner or professional. Some of the following hints may be helpful. The nearest qualified camera repair shop will be far away when you are trekking, so take a well-built camera. For most people, a 35 mm single-lens reflex camera is the best to use in Asia. Zoom lenses are handy but heavy. A wide-angle, say a 28 mm lens, and a telephoto of 100 mm or more is minimally good for most people. Beyond these lenses, the sky's the limit, but you will have to carry what you take. Think twice before relying on a camera that utilizes an electronic mechanism unless the camera can also be operated manually. What would you do if the electrical system failed? To preserve your equipment, minimize sudden temperature changes. For example, don't move a camera directly from your sleeping bag into subfreezing outside air. Avoid extremes in temperature if at all possible. Change film in a shaded area, of course, and be very careful that grit does not enter the camera when you replace film or lenses.

To protect your lens, use an ultraviolet filter. Use a polarizing filter to reduce haze, increase contrast and color saturation, and dramatize clouds and sky, but remember to take the polarizer off when not shooting in direct sunlight. If you take only one filter, a polarizer is the best; it will bring out a richness in sky and land colors like no other filter. If you want to compensate for the differences in light between the ground and sky, you can use a split-neutral-density filter. Carry a camel's-hair brush with blower and lens cleaner to clean your lenses. If your camera requires batteries, carry plenty of extras, especially if you will be trekking in late fall or winter. The cold can deplete your batteries' power very quickly. Some people use a lightweight monopod or aluminum camera clamp as a tripod, as a larger tripod can be heavy and clumsy to carry.

When taking pictures of people, put them at ease with a smile and perhaps some soft words. A motor drive can help you catch the spontaneous moment after someone has assumed a typical frozen pose. Some locals do not want to have their pictures taken; please respect this. Other people may ask for payment. This is not at all advisable. If a foreigner took your photograph, would you ask for money? Fill-in flash is good for taking pictures of people in daylight, because dark complexions are very difficult to photograph in the light. Aim your light meter toward your subject's face or the palm of your hand.

When taking scenics, aim the light meter to the ground—never at the sky. It is difficult to get good photographs in the middle of the day because the light is too harsh. Remember that the camera doesn't see things the way we do. The most dramatic photographs are usually taken before mid-morning or after midafternoon.

If you want to photograph frescoes in monasteries, you will probably end up with reflected glare if you use a flash that is attached to your camera; more elaborate equipment with strobes aimed at 45-degree angles to the wall will be necessary. Finally, elaborate camera gear is definitely less important to the results of your photography than care in composition and the indefinable matter of your "eye."

Be certain to carry enough fresh film to last the entire trip. Ektachrome and Kodachrome slide film is now available in Kathmandu, but it is quite expensive. Kodachrome 25 and 64 slide film can be carried for at least a year with no fall-off in image quality. The chemicals in these films are made to last, whereas the chemicals in professional films are meant to be used at the time of purchase. Films utilizing E-6 processing (like Ekta-chrome and Fujichrome) can be developed in Kathmandu on recently imported equipment. If you will be traveling for a long time, expose a roll of E-6 film and have it developed in Kathmandu to make sure your camera is still functioning. Some people like to use Fujichrome 50 or 100 slide film, particularly because of the way it renders greens, while others say the green effect is too garish. Kodachrome 25 has extremely fine grain, but is difficult to use in low-light situations.

Don't let your film or loaded camera pass through the metal-scanning machines at airports, despite what any signs may say about no damage to film. Scanning machines *can* harm your film. Exposed film is at the most risk. You should hand-carry all film on flights. Checked baggage is not only subject to possible loss, but it is very often passed through X-rays at airports: an unadvertised added feature of modern life. Never mail home exposed film from anywhere in South Asia. Hand-carry it only or mail from Japan. Film that is mailed may be exposed by inspectors looking for contraband, stolen by someone who will sell the film as unused, or thrown away by someone who wants the uncancelled stamps on the mailer.

Reaching Asia and Estimating Expenses

In 1973 I flew from New York City to London and traveled overland as far as Kathmandu for a total of $260 in transportation expenses. But of course a price like that is now history, as is the overland route itself for Americans at present. One can still travel overland from Europe to South Asia by taking the southern route through Iran (which, however, prohibits passport holders from the United States, England, and Canada) and crossing into Pakistan. But relatively few people make that still-adventurous trip these days.

Currently, you can fly from either coast of the United States to Kathmandu for $1,000 to $1,500 round trip, depending on the airline. The cost of a flight to Lhasa or Thimphu is somewhat higher. Flights from Europe and Australia to Kathmandu, Lhasa, or Thimphu are significantly cheaper. The 14-to-120-day excursion fare or an around-the-world flight with stopover privileges may be your least-expensive choice. You can find out about the various types of flights by calling a travel agent experienced in international travel. Shop around for travel agents by checking the Sunday travel section of your local paper, or the classified telephone directory. Keep in mind that the cheapest flights to anyplace in Asia can have various riders attached to those low fares. Or you may find that you'll have to overnight for a day or two someplace where the hotel expense will drive up the total cost of the voyage. Remember that you should check-in 2½ hours prior to departure on any international flight because some airlines overbook notoriously. And check your baggage from home to your point of departure for the international flight. Then recheck it for the international flight. Luggage very often goes astray between the internal and international carrier.

Confirm, confirm, and reconfirm air tickets for both in-country and international travel, particularly in Nepal. Before you leave Kathmandu to go trekking, reconfirm your seat home if you are traveling on your own. If you are with a group, your trekking outfitter should do this for you. Check to be sure it will be done. If you don't absolutely ensure that you have a seat, your name may be mysteriously dropped from the manifest.

If you are without reservations for a hotel in Kathmandu, do not be concerned. Kathmandu has plenty of hotel space, from $2-a-day specials to five-star accommodations. Preconfirmed, computer-made reservations are not necessary. The arrival area at Tribhuvan Airport in Kathmandu has a booth with personnel whose job is to assist you with arranging lodging. And your friendly taxi driver will always be glad to take you to a hotel. No matter where you are and what you may be told at first, remember that anywhere in Asia the outcome of a situation is never known until that situation is completely resolved. Information as first stated will be amended, and there is a vacant hotel room.

Estimating expenses is difficult to do, for you can spend vastly different amounts of money in Nepal or Tibet, depending on your standard of lodging and cuisine, particularly while in Kathmandu or Lhasa. An approximate rule of thumb is that your costs will be slightly less than your normal monthly living expenses at home. If you are trekking with a prearranged, organized group (as you must do in Bhutan), most of your in-country expenses will be taken care of, and the only extra money you will need will be for tips, souvenirs, a few meals, and any extras that you buy.

Take sufficient funds with you. Having money sent is difficult, subject to delay, and may produce only local currency. If money must be sent, do it through American Express or the Nepal Rastra Bank in Kathmandu. See "Receiving and Sending Mail," below.

Receiving and Sending Mail

In many a remote village unreachable by road, you will see the round red postbox attached to a tree or post in the square, to be emptied by the mail carrier passing on foot. Look at it, photograph it, just don't use it.

The best kind of mail to send or receive is always an aerogram. It cannot contain anything of interest to anyone who handles it. Further, it does not have any uncanceled stamps on it that could be detached and sold for reuse.

In Nepal, everything is centralized, and you will probably receive your mail in Kathmandu. Advise your correspondents to underline or capitalize your family name when they address your mail, to ensure that the letters held for you are filed correctly. If you are going trekking with an outfitter, you can have your mail sent in care of their address. Should you be trekking with an arranged group, your tour operator at home will direct you where best to send your mail. Otherwise, you can have mail sent to you in care of your embassy. American Express has a centrally located office, and mail may also be sent to you there if you carry their traveler's checks. The address to be avoided for receiving mail in Kathmandu is the general post office, or the GPO. The GPO keeps hundreds upon hundreds of letters in wooden boxes labeled with the letters of the alphabet. The boxes are ransacked daily by travelers, each with complete access to the entire pile of mail in any given box. Some people have told me they always get their mail that way, but I would give Poste Restante, Kathmandu, a wide detour.

If you wish to have mail sent to you in Lhasa, direct it to Poste Restante, Lhasa, Tibet, People's Republic of China. The main post office is located near the Potala, and your mail will be held for you there. Since tourists rarely stay in Bhutan more than two or three weeks, mail sent after you leave will barely arrive by the time you leave Bhutan. If you go to Bhutan, better have mail sent to your next destination or held at home for your return. Mail service out of Thimphu, Bhutan, is quite trustworthy.

Trying to get unaccompanied luggage, even air freight, sent to Kathmandu is next to impossible. It will open you up to an underbelly of bureaucracy, delay, and frustration that you do not want to be exposed to. Customs duties will be 100 percent or more of the object's value if you should receive any freight. If you don't have what you want, buy or rent it in Kathmandu.

Sending mail from Nepal is also tricky. The most certain way of getting your mail actually posted out of the kingdom is to go to the GPO and queue up in the line where letters are hand-canceled. Then you can watch your letters or postcards actually be canceled, rendering them far less valuable. No matter how fancy your hotel or its mail slot, the mail sent from it will pass through the hands of a poorly paid peon (that is his job title) who will be sorely tempted to divert all those tempting uncanceled stamps into extra income. You stand warned. If you want to send a package, it is far easier to have a shipper do this for you. You will probably have to leave your passport with the shipper for a day. The bureaucracy for shipping packages at the foreign post office, next to the GPO, boggles the mind.

When to Go

Himalayan climate is primarily dependent on two factors: elevation and time of year. Because of the great vertical distances involved in most treks, you will have to be prepared to encounter widely varying temperatures. The temperature drops 3.5 degrees Fahrenheit for every 1,000 feet gained in elevation. Be prepared for cold weather after the sun goes down whenever you are above 10,000 feet.

Fall is definitely the best time to trek in Nepal and Bhutan. The annual summer monsoon usually relents by the beginning or middle of October, and temperatures slowly drop from then into the winter. The skies are clearest in the fall and winter, and the mountains gleam like crystals at that time of the year. The height of the trekking season is from mid-October to late November. Some people stay later, however, for even though it's chilly into December, the weather can be clear then. Most years, winter snows begin to close the high passes in December. In December and January the weather is cold and clear except for occasional winter storms. March and April are usually good months for trekking, although the heat can be fierce below 5,000 feet, and deep, wet snow remains on the high passes. Also in springtime, a thick haze that rises from the dry Ganges plain and the middle hills (where ground fires are intentionally set) often obscures the view in Nepal.

Travel to Lhasa, Tibet, can be done any month of the year now that you can fly directly there from Chengdu or Kathmandu. But if you want to visit western Tibet, you had better plan to go between April and October. There is presently no way to fly into western Tibet, and the few roads into the region each cross passes higher than 17,000 feet. Winter is far too cold to consider traveling to west Tibet.

The subcontinent's life-giving monsoon comes from the southeast: it normally arrives in Bhutan about June 5 and reaches western Nepal ten days later. The monsoon causes muddy trails, obscures the view, and brings out leeches, but it also gives rise to a profusion of greenery. Monsoon rain is not continual but should be expected for a few hours daily at least through September and often into October. No matter what the region or season, vicious localized storms can occur anywhere in the mountains, particularly during spring and summer. Go prepared!

3
Into Nepal

None of the books or photographs studied before leaving home had even slightly prepared me for such majesty. Truly this is something that does have to be seen to be believed, and that once seen must be continually yearned for when left behind, becoming as incurable a fever of the spirit as malaria is of the body.

Dervla Murphy, 1967

You never leave Nepal.

Warren Smith, 1984

Kathmandu: A Venerable Enigma

"Namaste." This is the greeting you will hear and use often during your stay in Nepal. Literally, "Namaste" means "I honor the God within you," but like many Nepali words and gestures, the meaning changes in translation and its essence becomes altered.

Most people enter Nepal nowadays by plane to Kathmandu. It has become popular to say that Kathmandu is "ruined," that generic cement buildings and roaring vehicles have inundated the city. But this criticism only peels the onion one layer deep; it does not get to the heart of the matter. Kathmandu remains a mysterious, ultimately unfathomable city, and most of the Kathmandu Valley, let alone the city, is remarkably untouched by the mass tourism that you encounter in a few areas of Kathmandu. Do you want to go to the major squares in town that are usually mobbed with tourists and schlockmeisters? All right, then go at dawn. That's right, set your alarm, get up and go to Durbar Square in the heart of the old city just as the morning light first filters down from above the temples. That is the Nepali time of day. Then you will find the old Kathmandu. It's still there.

The area of town called Thamel contains numerous lodges (with fewer amenities than hotels) where trekkers of all ages often stay. When I first explored Kathmandu in 1967, the inexpensive restaurants numbered precisely four, and as many lodges had a traveler clientele, whereas now scores of eateries and hostelries are oriented to travelers, no matter what their budget may be. Kathmandu presently has four five-star hotels, and more are planned, so you can be sure to find a room in town, whether you want to pay $1 or $100 a night. Remember that the more you pay, the more you insulate yourself from Nepal.

While you wait for a trekking permit to be issued, the sights of Kathmandu's Elizabethan-style wood-and-brick old city await your discovery. Put on those walking boots and roam about the narrow, helter-skelter lanes: you may well be reminded of Shakespeare's London as scraps land at your feet for the onrushing pig, yet you are jolted back to Nepal by the sight of a large pagoda temple with Buddhist and Hindu images adjacent to red peppers drying in the sunlight. Children play games in the street while inches away a new Japanese van edges along. There are many places outside of the city you can explore as well. Here are some suggestions.

The stroll to Swayambhu Temple is an obligatory one: leave early in the morning and go west from the temple-studded Durbar Square past the golden Maru Ganesh Shrine. Across from the Ganesh Temple is a small statue of Ganesh's "vehicle," Muso the Mouse God. Continue between the Ganesh and Muso images down through Maruhity on the narrow brick walkway, past the rebuilt *stupa* (tall votive shrine) and Vishnu Temple at Chibakhel to the footbridge across the Vishnumati River, on by the new brick houses and rug factories to the foot of the steep Swayambhu Hill. In the morning, scores of Tibetan men and women pray at the base of the steps in the direction of the stupa high above. Several minutes' steep walk ahead at the top of the stone staircase is the ancient Swayambhu Stupa, a monastery, and a Buddhist school. As you climb the conical 300-foot hill, soldiers on their morning workouts may run past you while you pass wheezing old folks slowly clambering up the steps. In the morning, Newars from Kathmandu's largest clan gather in an open-faced room at the top of the steps and sing religious songs called *budgen*. Swayambhu is also known as the Monkey Temple because of the legions of rhesus monkeys that make their homes in the trees thereabouts and successfully beg from worshippers and steal from unsuspecting tourists.

You can try out an unimproved path by following the Nagarjun Hill trail up from Balaju Water Gardens, several miles north of the Swayambhu. Be sure to purchase a ticket at the entrance to the water gardens before you head up. The top is some 1,800 feet above Balaju. There, you'll find several whitewashed stupas and an excellent panorama of the Kathmandu Valley. Take some snacks and water for this warm and unshaded half-day walk. You can also reach the top of Nagarjun by walking or bicycling (if you have a mountain bike) up the road that diverges from the paved road leading out of the valley to Trisuli.

Like spokes, roads lead from Kathmandu's outskirts across the valley, and you can enjoy delightful bicycle rides to the Chaucerian towns along the way: Patan, Kirtipur, Bodnath (with its large stupa and Tibetan refugee colony), Sandku, Chapagoan, and the botanical gardens at Godavari. At Godavari you can pedal a mountain bike up the road that goes to Phulchoki, the highest point on the rim of the Kathmandu Valley. Phulchoki, at 9,050 feet in elevation, is fully 4,500 feet above the valley floor. Take liquid and lunch for this one. When I went to Phulchoki in December, it was necessary to push my borrowed bicycle through six inches of snow near the top. Another road for biking that is wide and little used for the most part is the Ring Road, which encircles Kathmandu. The northern stretches of the Ring Road have become Kathmandu's up-scale suburbs. If the day is clear, you can see wide vistas of the snowy Himalaya from the southern reaches of the Ring Road.

On the north rim of the valley is Shivapuri, 8,975 feet, the second-highest point along the hills surrounding Kathmandu. You must walk up Shivapuri, for no road yet climbs its forested slopes. A friend and I thought we could make the climb and return in one day. We did, but just. It is better to think of this walk as an overnight hike. Otherwise be prepared to keep moving all day and don't get lost on the way up (as we did). To climb Shivapuri, take a bicycle or taxi north of Kathmandu to the shrine of Budhanilkantha, the image of Vishnu reclining in a bed of serpents. From here, you must walk northeast up to Naki Gomba, a small cluster of white buildings that is a women's convent. From Naki, just follow the path along the ridgeline several thousand feet up to the top of Shivapuri.

With trekking permit in hand (see "Trekking Regulations," below), you are ready to leave Kathmandu for the trailhead. Transportation will involve a bus, chartered Jeep or other four-wheel-drive vehicle, or a plane. Of the three types, plane travel can prove the most fickle. If your trek depends on a plane to get you to or from the trailhead, don't expect anything to go awry, but do make plans knowing that acts of weather and lack of spare parts sometimes delay or cancel flights. It is always good to have either time at your disposal or "plan B" in your proverbial hip pocket if your trek depends on a flight to the starting point. If you are flying to a busy airport, such as Pokhara or Biratnagar, you can be fairly sure that if weather does cancel your flight, you can always take a land route to your destination. However, if you are going to a STOL (short takeoff and landing) airfield, such as Jumla, Silgarhi (Dipayal), or Tumlingtar, long delays between flights can occur, and you should have alternative plans in mind. If you are going to one of these airfields, you will have to be ready to haunt the Royal Nepal Airlines office on New Road in Kathmandu, or book your air ticket through a major trekking agency or travel agent in Kathmandu. Busy STOL airfields like those at Jomosom and Lukla may receive extra flights when needed, but if your "service," or scheduled flight, to, say, Jumla is canceled, you must scramble for a seat; those people holding tickets for the next flight still have priority for that flight. If your plane leaves Kathmandu but cannot land at its destination, remember that you can get a full ticket refund.

Most of Nepal's well-known trekking routes can be reached by bus, or if there are several of you, vehicle rentals are possible. Alternatively, you can be deposited at Pokhara, Dumre, Trisuli, Panchkhal, or Jiri by bus. Longer rides will take you to *terai* (the flat southern lowlands) roadheads farther west or east. Most bus tickets can be booked from offices near the GPO or at the jammed bus station east of the grassy Tundikhel.

Pokhara

Pokhara is the town where many people begin their first trek, as I once did. The town consists of a long bazaar that extends for more than 2 miles along the western edge of Nepal's second largest valley. Here you are less than 20 miles from peaks that rise up to 4 miles above the 2,500-foot valley floor. The gems to the north are the white *himal*s (snow peaks) of Dhaulagiri, the Annapurna summits, Lamjung, and, off to the east, Manaslu. But Machhapuchhare ("The Fishtail") is the summit we look to first in the morning or evening, when its high, rose-hued triangle gleams with alpenglow.

If you step off a bus or alight from a plane in Pokhara, it may take you a little time to find a porter, but don't worry, you'll find someone soon. People looking to hire on as porters often wait at the bus stop and airfield. Now's your chance to dive in with your Nepali. Open up Charles Gay's "Introduction to Spoken Nepali" (the most valuable part of this book), take a deep breath, and say, "Malaii baariya chaainchha" ("I need a porter"). Off you go on a merry chase. Remember that finding a good porter now can save you time and expense later. Offices of trekking companies are across the road from the airport, and you may be able to locate someone there. You can also try Baidam, the area near Phewa Tal, the largest lake in the valley. Phewa Tal is located a couple of miles southwest of the airfield, and there are many small lodges at Baidam where you can inquire for porters.

Pokhara is best for most trekkers as a rest haven upon return from the mountains. It is a quiet place for nudging toward the hubbub of the outside world again; a place to reminisce, eat continually, finish the journal, and commune once more with the mountains before returning to Kathmandu.

Trekking Regulations

The two primary considerations about walking in the subcontinent's mountains are historic and political. Traditionally, the many Himalayan kingdoms from Chitral to Bhutan were reluctant to admit any outsiders unless a person was a government official, trader, or pilgrim. White foreigners were definitely unwelcome. Present-day Nepal's policies in regard to trekking have slowly evolved from this position but reflect as well the political reality of China's extreme sensitivity to having foreigners approach the Tibetan frontier. Foot travel in Nepal near the northern border is therefore forbidden except where the vertical terrain makes access to Tibet difficult. The only exception is along the road link with Lhasa (see "Today's Routes to Western Tibet" in Chapter 9).

Every visitor to Nepal who wishes to travel off the roads outside the Kathmandu or Pokhara valleys (or in Royal Chitwan National Park in the southern terai) must get a trekking permit. These permits are issued by the Ministry of Home Affairs at the Immigration Office in Maiti Devi, east of Ram Shah Path in Kathmandu. If you are trekking in the Annapurna region or west of there, you may also apply for your permit in Pokhara at the Immigration Office in Ratnapuri, between the airfield and Phewa Tal. It will take from a half to two working days to process your application, depending on the volume of permit requests the day you apply. To apply for a permit you will need your passport, two visa-size photographs, and a bank statement indicating that you have changed the equivalent of $5 for every day you wish to stay in Nepal.

As soon as you have determined your intended walking route, make your application for the permit. List on the application form the principal intermediate places and farthest points you may reach. You might be turned back later if you have not gotten an appropriate permit. Also, when you apply, be absolutely certain to figure in time to take side trips and to rest while trekking. Printed permits are ready-made if you are hiking in the Annapurna, Langtang-Helambu, or Khumbu regions, so you don't need to be specific about where you wish to trek if you are going to one of those areas. Kathmandu and Pokhara are the only places where you can obtain trekking permits. You will have to carry your trekking permit with you at all times while hiking. It is not necessary to take your passport with you while trekking. If you store your passport, however, you must have a secure place to leave it, such as a safe at a hotel or trekking outfitter's office.

Most trekking permit applications also require visa extension applications. You can usually extend your visa up to three months. Difficulty will be encountered in staying longer than ninety days at one time in Nepal. But you can always leave Nepal, then return and begin the three-month cycle again on a new visa.

Trekking permits note on their reverse side that the bearer must remain 25 miles away from the northern border. This warning does not include such places as Kala Pattar near Mt. Everest and the Langtang Valley, where steep mountain barriers make border crossings infeasible. On the reverse side of trekking permits is a list of restricted areas in Nepal. These areas are fairly extensive. Suffice it to say here that special exceptions have been made for some areas, particularly if the applicant has trekking experience and has applied through one of the larger trekking companies. Exceptions are not made for the following areas: Limi, Dolpo District, Mustang District north of Kagbeni, the Nar-Phu Valley, and the upper Arun Valley.

Equipping Yourself Locally

Many people arrive in Kathmandu hoping to outfit themselves. This is indeed possible—for a price. If you lack any item of hiking or mountaineering equipment, you should be able to rent or purchase it in Kathmandu. Many stores in the Thamel area of Kathmandu contain a wide selection of used gear. Often you'll find that it is cheaper to rent rather than purchase what you need. If you are trekking in the Khumbu region south of Mt. Everest, you can rent cold-weather parkas and mountaineering items like ice axes and crampons in Namche Bazaar. Very few items are available in Pokhara. If you are going trekking with an organized group, the chances are that you will be flying directly to Kathmandu with your gear. If your duffle is lost en route, remember that you can purchase or rent all necessities quite quickly.

Many items locally made and available in hill bazaars are appropriate for trekking. The following list covers gear that you can expect to find in every roadhead bazaar and the largest bazaars in the hills.

Kerosene. This is the only fuel you can expect to buy in the hills. So take a stove that uses kerosene if you do not want to burn wood or if you expect to trek where wood is not available.

Cigarettes, loose tea, and matches. These lightweight items are appreciated as thank-you gifts. If you have qualms about giving tobacco, take tea, matches, or sewing needles.

Small-denomination currency. Obtain plenty of 1-, 5-, and 10-rupee notes. With these, you can bargain to the rupee and never need change. You can obtain bills from a bank or neighborhood shopkeeper.

Doko. You can purchase a doko, a conical woven bamboo basket, for your porter. If no doko is available, buy a burlap sack from a merchant for the porter's load. Your porter can also use your pack to carry gear. Depending on who he is, carrying your pack will be considered either prestigious or a nuisance. He may want to use a tumpline (called a *naamlo*) to carry the pack.

Rope. Rope, called *rassi*, will hold together the porter's load. Purchase enough to give some to your porter as a tip.

Fuel and water containers. Sometimes excellent watertight plastic containers for fuel are available in the bazaars. Don't count on finding one beyond Kathmandu or Pokhara, however.

The articles below have already been described in "The Trekker's Complete List of What to Take" in Chapter 2. These items are noted here as well because locally made versions are also available.

Stove. Kerosene stoves are available, but they are less sturdy and much heavier than Western-built models.

Enamel cup. A 20-ounce or larger size gives you an all-purpose cup and bowl.

Nesting pots. Nesting pots are sold by weight; you will need at least two if you are trekking off a major route.

Umbrella. Umbrellas are widely available in Kathmandu and Pokhara. The traditional bamboo style has practically become history, but new Chinese models are now easily found.

Pants. You can get loose-fitting pants made most easily in Kathmandu at a tailor shop. You may have to make it a two-step process by first purchasing cloth, then taking the cloth to the tailor. If you have the tailor make the cuffs small, dust will be kept out.

Food for Trekking

Our own experience coincides with that of Shipton and Tilman, who proved how economically one can live in the Himalayas. . . . Our diet consisted mainly of rice, barley, wheat, and millet. . . . We enjoyed the most excellent health throughout, on an almost strictly vegetarian diet. . . .

Arnold Heim and August Gansser, 1938

Dietary Possibilities

A good balanced diet with adequate calories is essential for enjoyable trekking. Depending on your weight, activity level, and individual metabolism, you are likely to need between 3,000 and 4,500 calories to sustain you each day of vigorous trekking, and these calories should come from a mixture of proteins, carbohydrates, and fats. One pound of pure protein or carbohydrates will provide 1,800 calories, and 1 pound of fat (only for Eskimos) will give 4,500 calories. Carbohydrates (such as crackers, rice, and sugar) provide energy quickly; the energy from proteins and fats becomes available later but lasts over a longer period of time.

A local person eats about 2 pounds of grains each day, which provide about 3,200 calories that are primarily from carbohydrates. The grains are supplemented with *dal* (lentils), milk (if available), and salt. Vegetables, dairy products, legumes, eggs, and sugar are also consumed if they are obtainable. On this meager diet, porters can carry enormous loads through difficult terrain day after day, and many trekkers have enjoyed good health and fitness following the local example. If you rely primarily on local grains, your total dry weight of food per person-day will be about 2½ pounds. The key to a grain-based diet, however, is to eat enough of it. You really have to stuff the food in, and that takes practice.

You may want more variety than the local diet provides, however. From local markets you can add fresh and dried vegetables, canned goods, spices, and even sometimes chicken or other meat. From home, bring packaged sauces; such luxuries as chocolate bars, cocoa powder, drink mixes, dried fruits, and nuts; or other high-calorie, low-weight favorites. But keep in mind that with such additions you may easily end up carrying 3 pounds of food per person-day. If what you bring from home is freeze-dried foods, your total food weight can be lower than 2 pounds per person-day. Bringing freeze-dried rations probably won't be worthwhile, however, unless so much of your trekking route will be through uninhabited country that supplies aren't otherwise available.

These supplements are not essential, however. The local diet is perfectly adequate for nourishment. Indeed, this diet is in line with the theory of protein complementarity popularized by Frances Moore Lappé, who explained in *Diet for a Small Planet* how to get your complete protein requirements without meat protein by using four basic food groups in three basic combinations. Wrote Lappé: "The combination of grains plus beans, peas, or lentils evolved spontaneously, becoming the center of the diet in many different parts of the world—rice and beans in the Caribbean, corn and beans in Mexico, lentils and rice in India, and rice and soy in China. . . . Only recently has modern science truly understood what must have been known intuitively by the human race for thousands of years." The four basic food groups from *Diet for a Small Planet* are:

1. Grains—such as rice, wheat, barley, corn, millet, pasta
2. Legumes—such as lentils, beans, peas, peanuts
3. Milk products—such as cheese, yogurt, butter, *lassi* (similar to buttermilk), milk
4. Seeds—such as sesame, sunflower

The three basic combinations are:

1. Grains and legumes
2. Grains and milk products
3. Seeds and legumes

We Westerners are often surprised that we can trek for weeks eating only the locally available foods and emerge fit and amply nourished. My friend Chris Wriggins and I lived and trekked for ten weeks in western Nepal eating foods entirely from the first three groups (with the addition of eggs when possible) and finished lean but strong: the last full day on the trail I walked 24 miles, ascending and descending a total of 15,000 feet. A high-bulk diet like the locals' in ample quantities is very sustaining, but, again, you must eat enough of it, as they do (and it *is* difficult).

Foods Available Locally

The items on the following lists are not the only foods you will find or can expect to eat while trekking; remember also that not all items will be found everywhere. Some areas are food deficient, and in those places you will have to offer a good price to make the sale of rations to you worthwhile. In regions like Humla and Bajuri where this is the case, I have indicated such in the text. (In this situation you can buy small amounts of food from several families.) When buying food in the hills, check the vocabulary list in "Introduction to Spoken Nepali" for the proper local words. And remember that a porter can be your best help in purchasing food.

If you are going into a very remote area, be certain to carry enough food; the extent of your foot travel will often depend on the amount of food you can carry and obtain in the hills, and people have had to turn around for lack of it.

The most difficult time of year to get food in the hills is early spring before the harvest. Late fall is the best time. Remember to ask about fruits in season, like papayas, guavas, mangoes, bananas, and tangerines. When buying canned food, at a large bazaar or along a major trekking route, examine the tin for signs of expansion, which may indicate spoiled food.

Food Available at Large Bazaars

Whole milk powder. Next to grains, I take more milk powder than anything else into the mountains. Milk is excellent food, whether taken in tea, or mixed with properly treated water. The best way to hydrate the powder (which tends to cake) is to mix it with a few ounces of cool water in a cup. Amul, an Indian cooperative, makes high-quality milk powder that is available in Kathmandu.

Peanut butter. New brands of peanut butter made with only peanuts and salt are being produced in Nepal. Read the label before you buy. Peanut butter makes a good topping for wheatcakes and is an excellent source of protein.

Jam. Most local jams are good. Take plastic containers to repackage jam and any other food that comes in jars.

Butter. You may be able to find canned butter in Kathmandu. If you are in the high pastures during the summer, ask for it fresh. Butter or *ghee* (clarified butter) can be an important source of calories in the trekking diet.

Dry soup mixes. Brought from home or purchased locally, dry soup packets come in handy; they add flavor to soups made on the trail and are a quick topping for grain dishes. You can find locally made dry soup mixes in Kathmandu.

Dried fruit. This is excellent food. Most dried fruit in Nepal is imported from Afghanistan.

Noodles. Instant noodles have reached Nepal, and several competing companies manufacture them. In a pinch, two to four packets make a meal. The cost and bulk of instant noodles can add up, but the weight will not. Long noodles, called chow mein, are often available in large bazaars; if so, you can carry along several meals of them also. Remember to take enough; everyone's appetites will be gargantuan on the trail.

Salt. Moderate use of salt is a necessity when trekking because of the large amount used up in extensive exercise and the limited amount of sodium occurring naturally in the diet. If only rock salt is available, ask the shopkeeper to grind it for you. Pulverizing salt can be very difficult to accomplish en route.

Sugar. Sugar is absorbed rapidly into the blood, providing quick energy when needed; it is usually taken with tea, and it helps make some foods, such as tsampa, more palatable.

Spices. There are two types of spices, hot (like chilies) and sweet. Get four or more of the powdered hot spices to flavor the basic dal and rice; you will find cumin, cayenne, turmeric, and other components of curry powder. Sweet spices, such as cardamom, ginger, cinnamon, and cloves, can be used in tea or curries. Also, check whether your porter wants the astoundingly hot green and red peppers that some locals favor. If so, for a rupee or two you can season food to his particular liking.

Coffee. You can purchase tinned instant coffee from India in the larger bazaars.

Teas. Get lots of high-quality tea; don't buy lesser-grade "dust tea." Nepal's best tea comes from Ilam.

Biscuits. "Biskoots" (an Anglo-Nepali word) are fine for snacks and can sustain you if necessary when you miss a meal, but they are uniformly disappointing when damp. Squeeze the package; if the biscuits don't snap when they break, they are wet. Nepal's own Nebico brand is first class; other brands are available as well.

Candy. A good picker-upper for those day-long uphill tramps. Individually wrapped sweets are safest.

Food Usually Available in the Hills

Grains. Grains in one form or another will form the bulk of your diet on the trail. Wheat flour and rice are the most popular grains, but several others are to be had, and they are available in a number of forms. For example, pounded rice, called *chiurra,* is excellent with tea as a breakfast cereal or snack food. In Tibet and places that are ethnically Tibetan, you'll find roasted barley (most often ground into a flour called *tsampa* or *sattu*). Plan on ½ pound of grain (1 cup) per hiker per meal. Your porter will eat half again that much grain. To determine the total amount of grain needed, multiply 1 pound by the number of person-days (1½ pounds per person-day for each porter).

The accompanying table shows at a glance how the different grains can be prepared and served (*X* signifies forms available).

Dal. Lentils are called dal. With rice, they form an important part of the diet, so be sure to take some. Well-stocked bazaars sell many kinds of dal, and you can also buy it in lower elevations where it's grown. If you will constantly be at high elevations, get a quick-cooking type of dal (orange-colored *masur dal* cooks quickest) or plan to use only flour.

Peanuts. A legume like dal, peanuts combine with grains to form a complete protein, and they are a great snack. Ask for peanuts and you may find them raw or roasted. Also try roasted soybeans (*baatmas*) as trail food.

Milk products. These include milk, buttermilk, lassi, yogurt, cheese, butter, and ghee. Milk products can be purchased seasonally in bazaars near the hills, but you can also ask along the trail and people will tell you where you can buy dairy foods. Remember that eaten with grain, they produce the full protein complement. If you can reach the upland summer pastures, you can trade for, buy, or depending on the circumstances, be freely given delicious fresh milk products. Buttermilk (called *chaiin*) is usually available in the summer.

Himalayan butter is nearly always of excellent quality; it often comes protected in skins. Travelers of yore who have complained of being served rancid butter in salt tea probably were not used to the rich taste of upland butter. Butter comes fresh from the summer pastures and has always been a cash crop, so you will have to pay well for it. Ghee, often misunderstood by Westerners to be inferior to butter, is actually a refined, pure product made by clarifying butter. Ghee is divine: rich and delicious.

Caution: Raw milk may contain harmful bacteria. Before drinking milk, be sure it has been cooked.

Common Ways to Prepare and Serve Grain

	Whole grain, to boil	Flour for fried graincakes	Roasted flour for tsampa	Other form
Rice	X			pounded
Wheat		X		
Barley		X	X	roasted, whole grain
Millet	X	X		
Corn		X	X	roasted, whole grain
Buckwheat		X		
Oats (in tins)	X			
How to serve	rice and millet with butter, dal, vegetables or yogurt	with butter, yogurt, peanut butter, fruit, or jam	eaten in tea or milk with sugar, butter, cheese, yogurt, or jam	from your hand

Eggs. Virtually the most complete protein you can eat comes from eggs. Those you can buy along the trail are from chickens that run around, scratch in the earth, and eat all manner of food. Consequently these eggs, although small, have a deep-orange yolk and a rich, full flavor that is rare in the West. For their weight, eggs are some of the most nutritious food you can carry. In the Annapurna and Khumbu areas, porters carry egg-farm eggs (called twenty-four-hour eggs by the locals) into heavily trekked areas. In these regions, prices have become inflated and egg quality has suffered.

Vegetables. Most vegetables are available only in season, and few are grown extensively. Potatoes, called *alu,* are the principal exception: they are the staple in Khumbu near Mt. Everest and are being introduced in other areas. Squash, pumpkins, and root vegetables will keep into the winter and can be purchased by request when you can locate them. As time goes on and as people begin to realize their nutritional benefits, more and more vegetables are to be found in the hills.

Honey. Sometimes you can buy delicious honey in the hills. Finding honey unexpectedly can lift your spirits—like sighting an ibex or coming across an unmarked spring.

Meals on the Trail

If you have even half the foods listed above, you can eat well while trekking. You may carry additional food from home, but if you or your cook is capable, you will learn that a grain-based diet can be quite adequate. Trail food, though not in endless variety, is usually fresh and can be cooked temptingly with butter and spices. When your palate becomes accustomed to the locally grown food, prepared foods like glucose biscuits (with preservatives) begin to taste suspiciously artificial.

During most trekking days you will have two large meals and one or two additional pauses for tea. The concept of two main meals a day is very deep seated in Nepal. Don't try to tamper with this custom if you are trekking with a porter or staff: what is lunch for the trekking group is actually morning *bhaat* for the Sherpas and porters. *Bhaat* literally means "cooked rice," but its general meaning is "any meal," no matter what the meal is actually composed of. Even office workers in Kathmandu have morning bhaat before rushing to the office by 10 A.M.

A typical day's meals when you are trekking with a porter will begin with a simple breakfast. After arising, you'll have milk tea (or coffee) while striking the tent and preparing to leave. You might supplement this with biscuits, porridge, wheatcakes, rice, or food left over from dinner. After walking a good portion of the distance you will cover that day, everyone stops for up to two hours while bhaat is cooked. This break for the morning meal usually occurs after the day has warmed up but before the afternoon breezes begin. The time for bhaat will vary with the terrain, personnel, time of leaving, and other factors. You can catch up on your journal, wash, explore, or snooze while food is cooking. In the afternoon, tea is made while camp is set up, and dinner comes later. The evening meal may be graincakes fried in butter or oil and washed down with potato soup.

Trekking at high elevations (above 10,000 feet) requires a few meal changes, for dal never completely cooks and even rice is difficult to soften higher up. In the uplands, most meals are of soups, graincakes, potatoes, or tsampa.

Let's let H. W. Tilman have the final word on food: "If one professes and practices living on the country, one must take the rough with the smooth, rancid yak fat and frogs along with buckwheat cakes and rakshi."

Trekking with a Porter

Many people who trek in Nepal on their own need to hire a person who will help carry some of the gear and assist with route finding. The subject of trekking with a porter was introduced in Chapter 1 in the context of choosing your preferred trekking option. This section provides specifics on the who, where, and how of porter hiring and aims to give you an idea of what it is like to trek with a porter.

Who Will Work as a Porter?

A man (or woman) in Nepal who occasionally works for foreign trekkers is usually taking off time from work at home to earn some needed cash. Nearly everyone who has portered and cooked for me has been a

The small Shiva temple at Leguwa village by the Arun River.

farmer, and probably a third have never worked for a foreigner before. Most likely your porter will be a local farmer, but other types of people are also available.

The first person you meet may be an English-speaker who has worked as a sirdar before. He may not usually carry weight himself and may be expensive merely because of his language ability and experience with Angrezi. Despite his usual role, he may have time and be willing to carry for a paid trip into the hills, even at less than expedition salary. Otherwise, he may be a person who can locate the right porter for you.

A younger person who needs income can be a good porter, but try to find out that you are hiring someone who knows the countryside, not a pidgin-English-speaking cowboy type who has no experience in the hills and who may quickly falter.

An older man can be an excellent porter if you can find him and he wants to go. Often older porters are the hardest-working, most reliable companions: wise to the old ways, knowledgeable about the land, and delighted to point out trail lore.

Whom Should You Hire?

Some Himalayan travelers have considered their private porter or expedition sirdar to be a living Buddha, an omniscient titan who can interpret all of nature's wordless hints, signs, and scents. These travelers, through choice or chance, have hired the right person. Others feel differently: "Porters are mostly local men of uncertain occupation and unsteadfast habit, notorious for giving trouble." The author of that statement trekked with a companion so "desperate to get under way" that virtually the first nine people who agreed to carry were hired.

Often the people who happen to be at the roadhead or in the bazaar when you first arrive indeed are not the ablest or sturdiest. The best strategy may be to wait overnight for word to get around and for people to come in from the fields before hiring anyone. This usually saves more time in the long run than does barely slowing down to consider whom you are hiring in your haste to leave. You or your group can move faster and more comfortably with a good porter. A few hours' delay or an overnight halt at the beginning can often save a lot of time and difficulty later.

If you want to hire a sirdar, you must ask to see any letters or chits held by someone claiming this status, as noted in Chapter 1. Many people hire a sirdar through previous contacts or through an outfitter in Kathmandu and make advance arrangements by mail. The sirdar you hire as leader then will enlist his own crew of porters and be responsible for them.

Where and How to Hire

If there are only one or two of you, then wait until you reach the trailhead bazaar before engaging a porter. If you are several people and you need a crew, then hire a competent sirdar. If you are in a tropical climate, you may only be able to hire people who will go partway up with you, and you'll have to change porters. In this case, don't be as choosy in whom you hire initially as you would if you were trying to find someone to walk on a longer haul with snowy passes.

When you reach the place where you will first be hiring someone, you can expect one of two or three situations. First, there may be no one immediately about who is interested in working. Don't be in the least concerned. This is Asia, and the telephone works by word of mouth. Tell whomever you think can help that you need a porter: the Jeep or bus driver on the way, the hotel manager and staff at the hotel, or a nearby shopkeeper or two. If possible, spread the word several days before you need to hire. Think about this process as you would about finding a hotel room: like the inevitable room, a good porter will certainly appear.

In a second likely scenario you may find an accomplished sirdar with a good command of English. If you need him and a crew, you're set. Otherwise, you can ask for his assistance. Drink tea with him and ask him to help you find a person to porter. Given overnight at most, he should be able to refer a friend or two to you.

A third possibility is that a group of people may be waiting at the bus stop or bazaar when you arrive. They will be looking for work and will know that you, as an Angrezi, may want to hire someone. Under these circumstances your best ploy is to feign a lack of interest in the whole affair. Head for the teahouse, keeping any likely prospects in view or nodding to them. Take tea and rest, allowing the scene to quiet down. When my trekking partner Pancho Huddle and I arrived at Trisuli Bazaar with loaded packs, bedlam ensued. We made for the back of the Ranjit Hotel's restaurant and asked the waiter if he would whisper to the person who had impressed both of us. Our choice, Bir Bahadur Lama, proved to be an excellent porter.

Coming to Terms

When you are discussing portering with someone, you need to decide more than just how many rupees per day he will be paid. You might work up to the subject of wages by discussing and agreeing on other points first, as discussed in this section. State your position or offer, then ask, "Teek hi?" ("OK?") If he agrees, he'll answer, "Teek!" ("OK!"), and that will be settled. Keep in mind that wages differ from person to person, as at home. One man will go for 50 rupees per day when another won't budge for less than 60. Salaries will depend on the amount of work to be done, the person's need for money, and many other factors aside from experience and ability, for every agriculturalist can cook local foods and carry. The following list covers the principle terms upon which you will need to agree:

General itinerary. Some people will be able to go with you for weeks, while others will walk only as far up as the next climatic zone. Some men will want only a couple of days' work (in which case you would have to change porters again soon), while others don't want to be bothered unless they are going to earn at least a lot of rupees. To avoid misunderstandings later on, you will want to agree on roughly how many days the person will work for you or how far you will go.

Cooking. In a small group, things go best when everyone eats the same rations (although I avoid the porter's *khursaani,* his red peppers). Your porter is thoroughly familiar with cooking the food you'll be eating: let him do it. If he is Hindu, make certain that he has no caste restrictions against taking his food from the same pot you do.

Wages (including food). Try to learn the local wage scale; then be willing to tamper with it. The person you want to hire is not a top-wage, high-altitude porter, but neither is he an ordinary load hauler, whose work is over the moment you reach camp. If you are not trekking from inn to inn, and you have hired only one person, your porter may be cooking for you: that adds to his responsibilities. In 1974, I paid as little as 15 rupees per day in Jumla, Nepal, but by 1986 I needed to pay 65 (somewhat devalued) rupees in an equally remote region. Expect to pay as much as 80 rupees a day in the Pokhara area during the fall, but wages are inflated near Pokhara and do vary from place to place. Start lower and bargain. Nowadays, you will need to pay about $2 a day plus food for a good porter in Nepal. If the person you are hiring has worked for expeditions and wants a high rate, explain with a twinkle in your eye that your bank is not as big as an expedition's. Offer a higher rate for days on snow.

Don't give your porter a large advance before you leave for any reason or you may well never see him again. Likewise, don't pay him daily as you go, for he may gamble or drink it away. Just cover immediate daily expenses as you proceed. Saving money for the morrow isn't thought of the same way in Asia as it is in the West. Most people nowadays pay for their porter's food. But don't let him take advantage of you. Make it clear that you will pay only for *dal-bhaat* (the national dish of rice, lentils, and vegetables) if you are eating in inns. Some porters may try to take advantage of you and order plates of meat and locally brewed beer or rakshi (spirits). It is proper for you to pay a half day's wages for every day the hiree must walk back to reach the point where you began (unless the return involves going by road, in which case you pay his bus fare). He will make the return trek much more quickly unloaded, but this payment is proper convention.

Clothing. Remember that if you expect to trek high in elevation, you are responsible for your porter. Be sure that he has warm clothes, a coat, and blankets. Ask to see them, for he will not be concerned about the cold when you begin. You must look ahead and anticipate what the weather and elevation may bring. Be ready to camp near shelter at night or bring shelter for your porter. In the Annapurna and Mt. Everest regions on the main trails, there will be inns where you can stay, but there won't always be shelter off the large paths. It is up to you to be responsible for your porter's well-being, just as you expect an employer to be responsible for an employee's at home. Purchase a wide sheet of plastic in Kathmandu or Pokhara for rain protection. Particularly if you are to be on snow or a glacier, you must provide for your porter companion's warmth at all times: shoes, socks, coat, goggles, hat, and gloves are the minimum requirements. If he does not have these six items, see that he borrows the remainder or uses your spares. This should be arranged before leaving for the high country.

Bakshish. The universal Asian term for a gratuity means, in this case, a bonus. If your prospect is going to be working more than just a few days with you, then hint that some of the locally purchased equipment will go his way when you are done with the trek. If by walk's end you have gone several weeks together and gotten along well, there will be no question of giving him gear, extra food, or maybe even your jeans (now that's talking, sahib!), along with an appropriate cash bonus.

Your relationship with your porter may optimally become one of companions on the trail. Using what David Snellgrove has called "a combination of quiet resolution and ingenuous friendliness," you can keep a warm spark within your group and foster good relations with those you meet. Be sure to walk with your porter to get to know him, particularly during the important first few days of a trek.

Your porter is the best lens for you to focus on this world you hope to enter and begin to understand. Remember also that while you are the sahib, he knows the country. On my first west Nepal trek, Chris Wriggins and I thought we could make route-finding decisions, but only one day out of Jumla and one long detour convinced us we had better learn our place and include everyone in such decisions. When I have shown interest, porters have pointed out all manner of flora, fauna, mineral deposits, tracks, and trails, and have told me stories about themselves, their families, and the country we were traversing. These insights can be among the most rewarding aspects of a trek.

Acculturation

The following observations about the culture you will be entering are offered in the hope of helping you get off to a good start and smoothing your way. From the moment you meet the customs *wala* asking you to open your luggage at the airport, you will be forming impressions of who and what you see. Whether observing or taking part in a situation, try to reserve some judgment and set aside preconceptions as much as you can. Try not to fume or be frustrated by inexplicable behavior or situations that cause delay. You are part of the dance and can't always change its tempo.

As stressed earlier, it is very important to learn as much Nepali as you can, particularly if you are trekking on your own. Your time in Nepal, as in any foreign country, will be completely different if you learn as many words as possible. Don't neglect to consult Charles Gay's fine "Introduction to Spoken Nepali" in the back of the book. On arrival in Nepal you'll be able to begin trying words with the customs wala as he eyes your chattels. Don't be concerned with mispronunciation; you'll still be appreciated, and in the process, the invisible barrier demarcating you from him and creating the us-them dichotomy will be lowered. You can easily find English-speaking students, merchants, hotel employees, and others who will be most willing to help you with needed words or pronunciation. Try to trade words with the other person: what you need to know for what he wants to know. Misunderstandings can be ironed out surprisingly often with the right word or phrase. It can often be difficult to use Nepali in Kathmandu because so many people speak English, but you'll quickly find that things are very different on the trail. Often travelers and locals misunderstand each other not through nonagreement but literally from noncommunication. Just a few words can establish connections with shopkeepers, innkeepers, porters, and others who want to make themselves understood but can't, lacking the English.

The word *sahib,* pronounced "sahb," basically has come to mean "sir." It is not reserved for you as foreigner, and it can connote varying degrees of respect in various situations. *Barasahib* is used sparingly and may mean anything from "boss" to "zonal commissioner." Some Westerners fall under the spell of this word, as if by having it used on them, it confers a certain status. Don't become mesmerized by it.

Chai, or tea, the beneficent, deserves a brief paean here. From Istanbul to Tokyo, most people drink black, green, or jasmine tea daily. To the world's billions of tea drinkers, the sipping of a cup is a refreshing break from the business at hand. Chai calms but revivifies; it cools a person in the summer and warms the body in winter, an ever-near balm. Important for the traveler, tea is quite safe to drink, whereas the fresh water it is brewed from may not be potable. Wherever you become involved, you may be asked to "take tea." Always pause to drink tea with officials if they offer it. On the trail in the middle of a long day's afternoon, call an unplanned halt to the walking for a half hour by some inviting stream and brew tea. With every sip, you will appreciate the soothing, restorative value of chai, the traveler's magic catalyst.

Bargaining, like tea drinking, is a venerated Asian custom, but it is a tradition that most neophytes need some time to feel easy with. Bargaining is agreeing on a price or rate of exchange, and this process is usually played out with different mental attitudes on the part of local and visitor. The Westerner often considers bargaining akin to a duel between adversaries, whereas the shopkeeper or porter thinks of bargaining as a social exercise, not unfriendly at all, and at its conclusion, over and done. There is a matching of wits but never a winner or loser, and when the price or rate is decided, that is it: no paperwork, no bad feelings. You may prefer to begin practicing the bargaining process with small things; however, most ordinary items are fixed-price merchandise. For larger purchases, learn the ballpark price first. Think of bargaining as a good way to practice language; you can toss out words and see if they are understood. A polite, firm tone tinged with humor contributes to a good bargaining stance.

When you ask anyone for information, never imply the answer in the question. To suggest in the question the answer you expect is human nature. But Nepalis always wish to please, so they are very likely to agree with you, even if the answer is not in the least bit correct. ("Yes, it's only a half hour to Ghorapani.") In urban or rural Nepal, anyone is likely to go along with you if you answer your question as you pose it. Don't say:

> Are there two buses today to Gorkha?
> Is the next bus at eight o'clock?
> Does this path reach Sinja?

It is better to ask such questions this way:

> Are there buses to Gorkha?
> When is the next bus?
> Where does this trail go?

If the person understands your question and doesn't know your preference, you may hear, "Tah chaina" ("I've no information"), or you will get a more informative answer.

Some of us fantasize about trekking and prepare for it so long that by the time we actually begin we are set askew for a couple of days, experiencing mild fatigue from the outset of walking, minor aches, or a haziness, a feeling of unreality. This is a dose of culture shock akin to what some people feel when they alight from a plane in a new country, almost expecting the clouds to be altered, the air different. Probably the few trekkers who do have these temporary symptoms undergo them not so much because there is a letdown, a leaving go of expectations, but because they experience either an overload of beauty or a repulsion at the lower standard of living. Take things easy for the first few days and let yourself become accustomed to your new surroundings. Nepal is extremely different from home; let its aura enter you slowly.

Finally, also under the heading of acculturation, is readjustment to your own culture. Many people (including myself) find that returning home from such an absorbing experience as trekking involves far more disorientation, more culture shock, than going to Asia in the first place. This disorientation may occur partly because trekking obliges you to become at least somewhat involved in a very different culture, not just be an observer of it. The return home can also be wrenching because of the issues that may still await you. Often people go trekking when they are in one of life's passages: following graduation, between jobs, or after the breakup of a marriage. Sometimes they go trekking to answer a question about their physical abilities or about something abstract. More often the former type of question is answered than the latter. The best thing that you can do when you return home is to keep busy: plunge back into your work. By all means, tell your friends about your trip, show them slides, but remember that they will not be seeing or hearing things exactly as you experienced them. And that's quite all right. Often we find that our reasons for going trekking, or the answers we sought by going, do not crystallize until "reflection in tranquility," as the poet William Wordsworth said. But we can hope to return to our native land with a greater understanding of our own country and an enhanced ability to deal with our complex society at home.

Notes for the Trail

This book does not attempt to mention every trail junction and village along the trekking routes described herein: that would be impossible. Nor does this book tell you hour-by-hour distances. One person's hour is another person's hour and a half. The latter individual has probably gotten more from the experience than the former by stopping to look, talking with people along the way, and smelling the flowers, as it were. My hope (as I mentioned in the preface) is that this book gives an approach to trekking that does away with the desire many people seem to have these days for an exhaustively detailed guidebook. Consider the thought that it's what you experience along the way that is important, not just arriving at the place you will stay for the night.

Treks follow different kinds of courses, and often you will have a choice of possible routes in a given area. You may walk up one valley, climb over a pass, and return down another valley. You might come back to your starting point by the trail you took or by a different path. Or you may return to another roadhead or airfield. If you get off-route, it's all right. Taking the wrong trail may even turn into one of the highlights of the trek or lead you to the best meal of your hike. And never forget that the routes described in this book are only a few of the possible trails that you can follow. I've discussed the most popular treks in Nepal, the ones that now have inns along the way with signs in English, and I've also written about numerous other routes as well. But the possibilities are endless. Try walking into any valley off the main trekking routes and you will have a completely new and different experience.

All the routes mentioned are along established paths, although as you walk, you may become misled by divergent tracks that lead to other villages or grazing pastures than the ones you are attempting to reach. The key is to keep asking people the way, just as locals do who are unfamiliar with an area. Most trails will be in good repair, but there can always be surprises, especially during or after the monsoon. The degree of difficulty from one trail to another will be related to the path's condition and the elevation you gain or lose as you proceed. I have tried to indicate the elevations at valley bottoms and passes or the approximate total elevation gains to reach most passes. If you are walking through particularly high elevations or hilly terrain, your pace will, of course, be slower than otherwise.

Many variables are involved in walking, say, from one valley to another 12 miles away over a 16,000-foot pass. Heavily laden porters or neophyte trekkers might take three days, while those in a hurry might require a single day to traverse the same distance. Rather than setting day-to-day itineraries, I have limited myself to suggesting that a route may take four to six days, for example, or two to three weeks. If you want to plan a trek down to the day, either go with a trekking group, or read a tour operator's catalog and note the number of trekking days allowed for a walk that appeals to you. If the route is easily passable, expect that you will take about as long as the organized group does to cover the same distance. But you won't be leaving yourself any time to follow that interesting side valley or rest at an inn that catches your fancy.

Trails themselves may be used differently from season to season: in the winter during low water, valley routes are often used, whereas higher paths may have to be taken during other times of the year. Always ask directions if you have any doubt at all of the way. Locals are always asking each other directions when unfamiliar with a trail. Nepalis have asked me the way, especially on pilgrimage to Muktinath when they are far from home and obviously uncertain. If you are interested in hour-by-hour accounts of paths in Nepal's main trekking areas, you will find detailed trail descriptions in Stephen Bezruchka's *A Guide to Trekking in Nepal*.

The horizontal distance traveled each day on a trek will not be great unless you are in a relatively flat river valley. The day's distance will not reflect the day's labor if you have just spent ten long hours descending 6,000 feet into a gorge and partially climbing up the other side. To take an extreme example, I have hiked less than a single horizontal mile in a hard day on a faint trail into the Nanda Devi Sanctuary in India. On the other hand, in the Yarkhun Valley of Chitral, Pakistan, I have walked 29 map miles in one day, even with a leisurely start and a lunch break. Your distance covered on any given day can therefore vary greatly. If you eat well, your average will increase after the first few days as your body adjusts physically. Maybe by then you will have slowed down anyway, to take in the interactions with locals along the way and to enjoy the scenery.

Particularly in the first week of a trek, don't set overly ambitious distance goals. Have an easy attitude toward trekking, and don't make it into an endurance contest. Experienced long-distance runners and hikers know that those who go the farthest and remain the strongest pace themselves at the outset. Later on, when your muscles and lungs are stronger, you can push yourself for a day or more. Then, when you ask yourself, "Shall I try for that next ridge?" you can push on for it and know that your aches, parched throat, and empty stomach will not rest as markedly in your memory as the far view you saw by gaining the ridgetop.

An average trekking day's length likewise varies from group to group and person to person but is often some variant of the local schedule. If you are cooking your own food, you can call the shots as you wish, but if you are eating in inns or homes, the two-meal schedule will apply. Rarely in the Himalaya do two days ever unfold exactly alike, but in general the day's journey is geared to the sun: because the cooler hours in the morning are preferred for walking, you will often rise with the sun's earliest light and cover much of the day's distance before the morning meal is cooked. By the time the first meal is over, afternoon breezes or clouds may have arisen to cool the air. After camp is made in mid- to late afternoon and you have had a chance to rest, the evening meal is eaten. Time of year is important to both the length of trail that can be covered and the meal routine. In midsummer, prepare to go to bed before dark so you can walk in the dawn hours before the day's heat builds.

The physical act of walking through the Himalaya (whether or not you carry a pack) may require adaptation because of the scale of things, the order of magnitude involved. In these, the world's highest ranges, river-to-ridge elevation differences can be two or more vertical miles and several climatic zones, not to mention numerous levels of settlements and fields. You will find yourself walking uphill for days at times, and when you have descended halfway down the other side you will discover that going down is as hard on the legs as climbing is on the lungs. Pace yourself when walking, take rests, carry water, and don't forget what you have learned from backpacking at home. A trick to going downhill is to use the bent-knee style of walking. It takes a bit of doing until your upper leg muscles strengthen, but when you can walk down trails in a bent-leg posture you will cushion your upper body, keep your weight directly over your feet, and save your stamina. Westerners who rush heavily down a canyon and later complain of aching knees or, worse, who must remain immobile with swollen knee joints suffer from the malady known as sahib's knee. Only the foreign sahibs are foolish enough to put so much pounding pressure on their legs and knees.

Theft used to be unknown in Nepal, but not now. Thievery, alas, has started to become a real concern, particularly in the Annapurna area any-place within a three-day walk of the road. Trekking groups in this area are now often guarded by their Sherpas, who rotate watches and keep a pressure lamp going all night. You need to be especially careful of all belongings whenever you are in the vicinity of a road. Don't leave your gear scattered about an unlocked room or a dorm in an inn. Just as at home, if you leave something behind when you leave a place, it probably won't be there when you come running back to find it. If the sahib doesn't care enough about his possessions to hang on to them, then someone else who appreciates their value will be glad to relieve him of them. The equipment we blithely carry with us would take most Nepalis all their lives to purchase. Nepal and its people are beautiful and wondrous, but the realities of modern life in the outside world have rapidly come to this special kingdom.

Be as alert as you are able to your surroundings, especially if no one in your group has been on the trail before. Fill water bottles before you leave the vicinity of a stream (especially in upper altitudes) and before climbing passes. And avoid becoming benighted on a narrow trail far from the nearest-conceivable camping spot. In any case, do not head for a pass late in the day without carrying water, fuel, and the know-how to make a high camp. If you are trekking with a porter, give him some voice in any decision to stop or go. In the Himalaya, you always have much to learn; be open to your status as student.

As you walk into villages, remember that you are the best act in town. Imagine for a moment that in the town where you live or in a nearby national forest a Tibetan Drokpa were to pass you. If you live in Kathmandu, you would expect to see lots of tourists in certain parts of town, just as you would if you lived in London or Manhattan. In the sticks, however, unless you are trekking one of Nepal's most frequented routes, a foreigner is an oddity. You can almost gauge the degree to which foreigners are seen in a village by the response to you, especially by the initial reactions of the children. In any remote area, young children who are playing outside will run in fear at the sight of a strange foreigner approaching. Their older brothers and sisters will walk away, to reappear in a

An Indian sadhu *rests during his pilgrimage to the sacred shrine of Muktinath in central Nepal's Kali Gandaki Valley.*

window or on the roof. On a well-trekked trail, however, kids' reactions will vary right on up to nonchalance. Often children will ask for candy, just to divert themselves. (Can you imagine children in the United States asking for candy from strangers!) I have learned that if I camp near a village or stay in someone's home, there may be overly inquisitive people at the campsite (until dinnertime, when the crowd vanishes) or young, crying babies in the house. No matter what my mood when I reach a village, I try not to let myself forget that I am there entirely of my own accord.

Assume goodwill on the part of others. Travelers are often on their guard in new situations, but never do the Golden Rule and its corollaries apply better: expect the kind of treatment from villagers that you would accord a foreign visitor at home (albeit a well-to-do visitor). Better yet, try to imagine how the locals might see you. In cities most people are honest, but in the provinces even fewer people are used to shucking outsiders. Agreed: there will be a fast talker about from time to time. But you will almost always be correct if you do assume that people's intentions are honorable.

When you walk in Nepal, you will be in country that has a human history going back hundreds of years, in a blending of cultures that trace their ethical and spiritual beliefs to events so ancient they disappear into prehistory and have been mythologized. These traditional cultures have elaborate social and, in some areas, caste systems, all of which will be largely invisible to you. As a visitor you are seeing only a slice of time, and much that will meet your eyes, your mind cannot interpret. If you should meet a Peace Corps volunteer, anthropologist, or any local who is competent in English, ask him or her just who is who in town, and you may be surprised: "Oh, he's the mayor and the richest man in town" (an older man in well-used work clothes). "This chap just came back from school and has nothing to do" (a well-dressed man who speaks a little English). "She moved here from down-valley to marry" (a woman with a light complexion). To figure out the cast of characters, and how they might be apprehending you, you'll probably have to be told or must be an acute observer with some language ability.

Keep your eyes open to the interactions about you as you walk. As you become aware of the local customs, respect them, and note the courtesies that you see practiced by people about you. In Nepal (as in all of traditional Asia), public display of affection (PDA) between the sexes is not understood. This is a difficult concept for most Westerners to comprehend, much less attempt to emulate in an attempt to be culturally sensitive. Men or women walking together may hold hands as a sign of friendship, but opposite sexes will never so much as hold each other's hand in public. Remember that in Indian cinema, with lewd and lascivious dancing sequences in every film, the scene is always cut just as the characters are about to kiss each other. Strange (from our perspective), but true. PDA just seems to embarrass people in the East, although this is slowly changing in some urban locales.

In Nepal, one's head is considered to be the most sacred part of the body, while feet are the most impure part. Thus, patting children on the head should be avoided. Likewise, if you are sitting down with your legs extended, pull them in if someone needs to walk by. It is not polite to walk over any part of a person's body. Note also that the cooking fire is considered sacred in Nepal, so it is not appropriate to toss burnables of any kind in the hearth. This is particularly important in Hindu areas.

You will rarely, if ever, see a Nepali defecating. When you need to relieve yourself, go well off the trail and when you are done, bury or burn your toilet paper. You can always carry matches or a lighter for this purpose.

Trekking rarely offers opportunities to acquire things. Take pictures, try to keep a journal going, press some flowers, tape music and conversations, but collect your mementos in the Kathmandu and Pokhara valleys. Often souvenir-meisters peddle wares along the trails near Pokhara, in the Manang region, and in Khumbu, but the discerning eye will note that 90 percent of these goods are carried in from the outside. You can purchase the vast majority of the items for sale cheaper in Kathmandu, and you or your porter won't have to lug them back out. In Namche Bazaar a few interesting items from Tibet are available, and there are ammonites and local woolen scarves for sale in the villages near Muktinath. In Kathmandu the souvenir-cum-collectable industry is alive and well, but few genuine old relics are left in the mountains anymore.

Trekking as Metaphor

You road I enter upon and look around, I believe you are not all that is here,
I believe that much unseen is also here.
Walt Whitman, 1856

A walk is both a sensual and a philosophical experience, a caressing interrogation of nature . . . a metaphor too complex to explain.
Anatole Broyard, 1983

My favorite metaphor is the trail of life. It includes much of life's activities: our observations and experiences, our encounters with friends and strangers, our fantasies and recollections. For many people, walking trails in the Himalaya is an experience all the more powerful because its metaphorical teachings are couched neither in words nor within a system of organized thought. The occurrences of the day, and the days taken together, acquire a connectedness and dimension that is missing in urban Western society.

This palpable realness about life on the trail is called, in the Tibetan tradition, direct perception. Pilgrimage has long been recommended as a means of salvation in both the Tibetan and Hindu traditions, not only for the merit that accrues in reaching a holy shrine or sacred phenomenon, but because of the character and inner strength induced by such travel.

After some days of adjusting to the walking routine, you will begin to pay little or no attention to your hesitant thoughts and will become better acquainted with the milieu of the endlessly changing land that you pass through. You may feel that each day is more intensely etched during these periods of time when the ordinary course of your life is altered. Your initiation may occur when you cross your first high pass: the tough, sweaty, lung-pounding climb with its passing uncertainties and teasing false passes is offset by the growing panorama below, the giddiness of the height, and your exultation at reaching the top. As you stand there between the past and the future, the present can be luminous.

High above the passes are rarely touched places where nature is magnified and visual metaphors abound. Ama Dablam (the mother with two outspread, robed arms) and Machhapuchhare (the fishtail with its double-peaked summit) are two mountains that have visibly metaphoric qualities. So is the sacred, symmetrical peak of Mt. Kailas with its snow-filled couloir, the Stairway to Heaven, etched vertically toward the summit. Glaciers appear dragonlike or riverlike, depending on perspective, and individual glacial features translate immediately into mushrooms, incisors, eyes, and vast amphitheaters. While trekking, we all read meanings into nearby landforms and the human interactions that occur within their aura. No one can fail to be touched by becoming, for a time, part of the Himalayan tapestry.

Recently I was fortunate to walk around Annapurna with a group that included a very sensitive and compassionate man named Gerry Spence. The hike was physically challenging for him, but never was a person more determined to make the most of a trek. Several times during the course of the walk we talked about trekking as a metaphor. Afterward, I asked Gerry if he would be willing to write down some of his thoughts on this theme. He very kindly wrote the following provocative and eloquent statement:

Life, of course, is a matter of ups and downs like any trail in Nepal. When one is going up and the way is steep and tiring and hot, the idea that there will ever be an easier time of it is only a vague belief. It is not real. The trail up and hard is real. The aching bones are real. But not the promised top. That will never come.

Yet when one reaches the top and takes a short breather, one is impressed with how soon the misery of the climb has been left behind. Already I have forgotten the pain of it. The sweat has dried. I see only the way ahead. Where I have been seems immaterial. Where I am going is what engages me.

We learn something, I suppose. We learn that the pain and the sweat are what life is about. It is sweet. It confirms life. It is the heart pounding and the lungs working. The pain confirms existence. The steps are like days. The top is like goals that when achieved seem unimportant, often silly. It is the process, the steps, the getting there, the human effort that is important.

But what are goals about? Well, what is mountain climbing about?

One does not climb a mountain and stay there. One climbs a mountain and comes down in order to climb another. One could get on top of the mountain by merely flying up there in a helicopter. But for what reason? One can easily see that attaining the top is not the issue. The goal itself is not what life is about; rather, it is the process of getting there. Yet the process and the goal cannot live one without the other. If only the process were important, we should just as well never leave the bedroom. We could walk as senselessly and as far on a treadmill.

It seems to me that goals give direction and purpose to life. They give texture and afford closure. They provide satisfaction that one can do what one has set out to do. They reaffirm our worth if the goal is worthy. They prepare us for even greater challenges. In the end it is both the trip and our arrival at the destination that count. One needs the other.

To me trekking provided a goal that seemed slightly beyond me. It is important not to pick easy goals. Trekking as metaphor teaches that goals must be realistic, that they should be set just beyond our expected reach, that they should be carefully planned and thoughtfully executed and that we should utilize the best advice and engage the finest guide available. Otherwise a trek through either Nepal or life can be disastrous.

This business of choosing a guide: what guides are available to us for our trip through life? Our parents have never been where we are actually going. They took their trip, not ours. Our neighbors or friends are not equipped for this trip. They have their own equipment, their own talents that make them ready for an excursion through life quite different from ours. Where do we get a guide? Therein the metaphor breaks down as all eventually do.

There are no guides in life. One must find one's way through this trip alone. Although you may have companions, such as a spouse or children or friends, in the end you take the trip alone and find your way alone. Since no one has been on your trip before, no one can show you the way. They are too busy finding their own way.

The danger in trekking is our expectation that it will provide something for us. Like life, *we* must *take from it*. The problem is that in the end we take only ourselves into the trek. We cannot leave ourselves at home. If we are blind or uncreative, or dead inside or insensitive—if we demand to be thrilled and entertained, then the experience will be only a reflection of who we are.

We will pass many places and see many people who are strangers to us and who, when the trek is over, we will leave behind forever. How we treat them is not so important for them as for us. Our giving is like receiving. We can give little and receive little. Only the very poor who have kept it all for themselves will remain poor on the trek. I say it is important to give a great deal or we risk receiving nothing. If we are truly caring about ourselves, we will see to it that we are richly rewarded by giving freely of ourselves.

This Nepali trader at Taklakot's Humla Bazaar smokes a sulpha *(pipe) of molasses-laced tobacco.*

4
Nepal's Wild West

Nepal is very hilly country.

Chhetra Bahadur, in Jumla,
commenting on the trail to Humla, 1974

That rainbow sits there in the same place on many days.
You may take a picture of it.

Khaptad Baba, 1986

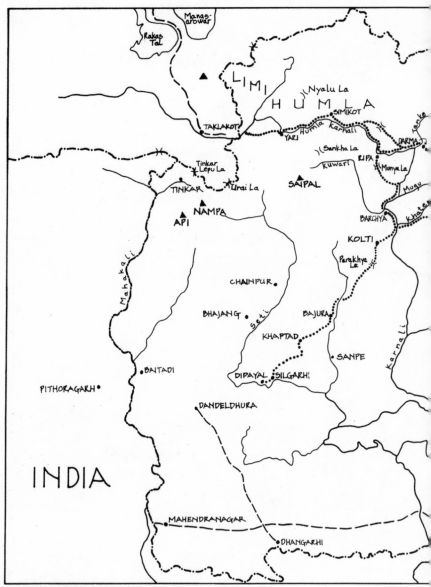

Western Nepal

TIBET

Manza La

MUGU
CHURI
Langu or Dolpo
DOLPO
SHEY
hankeli a
yarnali
MANGRI
WANGRI
Khapre La
KANJIROBA
Phoksumdo Lake
TARAP
JOMOSOM
Rara Lake
PINA
Gurchi La
Dariphya La
NAPOKUNA
RIMI
TIBRIKOT
Barbung
DHAULAGIRI HIMAL
SINJA
JUMLA
Balangra la
DUNAHI
TARAKOT
TATOPANI
Tila
Thulo Bheri
Jeng La
BENI
Jaljala Pass
DHORPATAN
Bheri
Sano
JAJARKOT

DAILEKH

SALLYAN

MILES
0 5 10   25   50

0 5 10   25   50   75
KILOMETERS

SURKHET
Bheri

NEPALGANJ

The Karnali Watershed

The mountainous region of Nepal, a jumble of valleys, ridges, and snow mountains, appears to culminate in a solid barrier of high peaks and vertical ice walls along the length of the northern border. But in fact, Nepal's northern frontier is pierced in six places, from Humla in the far west to the Arun Valley near Sikkim, by rivers that existed before the Himalayan Range was formed. Chief among the river systems that drain Nepal's mountains are the Karnali, the Gandaki, and the Sapt Kosi. In this chapter we will be looking at the westernmost of these large watersheds, the Karnali.

The Karnali River and its tributaries drain the least studied, least trekked, and most remote area of Nepal: its far west. The area discussed in this chapter is bounded on the west by the Mahakali River and on the southeast by the Dhaulagiri massif. This western third of the country is half again as wide from north to south as are Nepal's central and eastern regions. The large and sparsely populated Karnali basin contains vast forested areas and high, winding ridges that are peculiar to the west of Nepal. These long ridges, called *lekh*s, rise from 12,000 to 17,000 feet high, extending from the westernmost spurs of Saipal Himal to the southern ridges of Dhaulagiri in the east. There are lekhs across all of Nepal south of all the main peaks, but the lekhs in western Nepal are larger, more numerous, and less precipitous, offering good pastureland. The north-facing slopes of many of these western lekhs are covered with aging coniferous forests of blue pine, hemlock, fir, and 150-foot-tall spruce. Western Nepal's himals (one Nepali word for "snow peaks") are not as high as peaks in the country's central and eastern areas.

Experienced walkers, tired of the relatively crowded trails in the Annapurna and Everest regions, have enjoyed the differences in Nepal's west: trails that Westerners rarely see lead past rude, widely scattered villages, and the hamlets in Karnali Zone often house a long-haired shaman. Rice fields often extend up to the 9,000-foot level and nourish the hearty red rice that used to be carried hundreds of miles across the hills to Kathmandu for the kingdom's epicurean rulers. Traders who often go into Tibet walk the paths next to the sheep, goats, or yaks that carry their homespun side packs of grain or salt. If you hike in Nepal's wild west, you'll be discovering new country that few trekkers have ever seen. When I was walking in Seti Zone north of Silgarhi, the zonal capital, I met a Dutch volunteer on the trail. He had been installing drinking water systems for two years in villages throughout the area, and he was quite surprised to see me. I was the first trekker (as opposed to development worker) he had ever met thereabouts.

Rough and Ready Jumla

Jumla, on an eastern tributary of the Karnali called the Tila, is the place people often begin trekking if they go to western Nepal. But Jumla is not easy to reach. At present, no roads extend north of the southern hill bazaars of Dipayal (near Silgarhi) and Surkhet. Because of the high temperatures in the lower hill areas, walking to Jumla from Surkhet, the closer of the two hill towns, should be attempted only in early spring or in the fall. You can fly direct to Jumla from Kathmandu, or by way of Surkhet or Nepalganj; be sure to inquire about these alternate flights if those direct to Jumla are booked. Jumla's packed-earth STOL (short takeoff and landing) airfield is usable only if monsoon rains or winter snows do not make the field impossible to land on. Reservations are usually needed long in advance, but you may be able to get on a flight to Jumla by having one of the trekking companies in Kathmandu or an experienced tour operator at home book you a seat.

Jumla (7,700 feet) is the largest upland hill town in Nepal's west, but Jumla's bazaar appears large only to the trekker or local approaching town after weeks in the hills. There may be a few bicycles in Jumla now, but the 200-yard-long stone-paved street has never really known the wheel. Jumla and its nearby villages are populated primarily by dark-skinned people of the Chhetri, Brahmin, and Thakuri clans (who, incidentally, are not known for being good porters). The most visible denizens of the bazaar itself are the *lato*s, the smiling, buffooning "half-wits" who, on further observation, appear to be wise fools mimicking the society they reject. Best known is the ever-smiling "mayor" of Jumla, whose principal job for years has been to unload planes at the nearby airstrip. For all Jumla's frontier-town roughness, however, it is acquiring a tinge of respectability with the arrival of government employees who work in the whitewashed administrative buildings near Naya Bazaar ("New Bazaar"), west of the main bazaar. A new vocational school has been constructed north of Jumla, and numerous foreign development workers now live in town and nearby. The most striking departure from the drab, flat-roofed one- and two-story buildings along the main street are four tall bamboo poles flying sienna-and-white tricornered standards. These banners adorn Jumla's main temple, dedicated to the mythical saint Chandan Nath, whose accomplishments include emptying a lake that once covered the valley, defeating two serpents that threatened Kalangra (as Jumla was once called), and bringing the tasty high-altitude red rice from Kashmir. Loud bell-ringing *puja*s (worship services) take place twice a day at the temple, but outsiders are not invited to observe them. South of the bazaar the Tila River runs crystalline most of the year, and Jumla's flat valley is often traversed by horsemen. The coniferous forests near Jumla are lovely and extensive. Walking in the surrounding area can be very rewarding for the experienced hiker.

If you arrive by plane, bring all but basic grains and pulses with you. Unless a road from the south ever reaches Jumla, shortages of sugar and cooking oil may continue, and the available kerosene will not be of the best quality. Do supply yourself with the delicious local red rice, which may have to be purchased in a nearby village rather than the bazaar. Excellent Tibetan porters can be hired in Napokuna, a long day's walk east of Jumla. A man named Pema Lama (or Pema Tamang—same person), who lives west of the stream in Naya Bazaar, can help put you in touch with these porters.

While you are arranging supplies and porters, several warm-up hikes can be taken from Jumla. A half-hour walk from town, downstream along the north bank of the Tila Valley, is the small village of Micha, 300 feet above and out of sight of the main trail. Next to a house in Micha is a walled burial ground with stone grave markers that were constructed during the Malla dynasty. The powerful Malla kingdom controlled much of what is now central and western Nepal from the eleventh to fourteenth centuries, interweaving Buddhist and Hindu art, architecture, and religious practices. Time's sediment has partially buried the lichen-covered totems in Micha, but these outsized stone stelae, which resemble chess pieces, are quite interesting and unlike any other stelae remaining from the Malla period.

Two high, grass-covered promontories near Jumla are good to scale for acclimatization. Directly northwest of the bazaar is Malika Dara, a hill that reaches to 11,510 feet, with scattered pines for shade along its lower flanks. From the top of Malika, you have a fine view of west Nepal's nearby lekhs and Kanjiroba Himal. Also, you can walk thirty minutes east of the bazaar to the place where the Chaudabise River enters the Tila. Just beyond the Chaudabise confluence, an unforested ridge called Chimara Lekh rises to 12,220 feet. On the top of Chimara is a small shrine, and from there on a clear day you will enjoy a view that spans the distance from Saipal Himal in Humla to Dhaulagiri. Take head covering, water, lunch, and lots of energy.

The Trails to Rara Lake

Oh master divine!
Have you stripped beauty of all her gifts,
And poured them down the shores of Rara. . . .
H.M. Mahendra Bir Bikram Shah, 1964

Rara Lake, a clear oval pool 3 miles in length, is the largest body of water in Nepal. Rara is situated 9,780 feet high between two forested lekhs, a three- to four-day walk north of Jumla. The deep blue lake, also called Rara Daha, is the centerpiece of Rara Lake National Park, established in 1975. Rara Lake must be one of the least visited national parks in the world, next to Khaptad (discussed later in this chapter) and Shey-Phoksumdo (which is restricted and not supposed to be visited at all; this park is also noted later). The inhabitants of both villages on the lake's north shore were moved against their will to Nepal's southern terai, and guards' quarters have been built on the main trails into the area to enforce the parks' status as a game sanctuary. If you want to get away from the hordes, go to Rara Lake (supplied with all foodstuffs you need) and you will not be disappointed.

The view from lake level on Rara's grass-covered southern shore is reminiscent of the Rocky Mountains. The highest point visible is a 13,250-foot ridge to the south, and evergreens dominate the tranquil landscape.

A faint trail encircles Rara, passing through a dense forest of blue pine at the lake's western end and by several chest-high Malla stelae above the north shore. An anachronistic element at the lake is the handsome dwelling used by the park's warden. This Western-style log cabin with its deck, shuttered glass windows, and skylight in a shingled roof was built by Warren Smith, an American who also directed the construction of the guards' huts. When the house was completed, locals would walk for three days just to see it, for it is the only building of its type in western Nepal.

Two principal trails reach Rara Lake from Jumla; each route involves two passes, and the one-way trip from Jumla to Rara requires three to four days of walking. Take porters who will know the way and can help you carry the gear and food you'll need.

The more easterly of the two routes is slightly shorter in distance and has lower passes, but it is more up and down along the way. To begin this route, you have a choice of two alternative paths over two initial passes. These paths then join for the rest of the way to the lake. The longer and lower of these two paths—and the less likely to be snowbound—ascends the Chaudabise Khola (*khola* means "river" or "river valley" in Nepali)

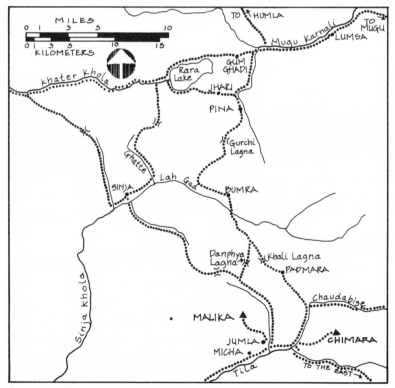

Jumla to Rara Lake

east of Jumla, then continues up the tributary Ghurseni Valley to the village of Padmara. Not far above Padmara is the grass-covered, 11,630-foot Khali Lagna (*lagna* means "pass" in Nepali), and shortly beyond, this path and the higher one join. The higher path crosses the 12,000-foot Danphya Lagna, named for the iridescent impeyan pheasant, Nepal's national bird. This pass offers a sweeping view of Jumla's valley and the flat-ridged Thakurji Lekh to the south, but don't attempt the Danphya Pass in snowy weather, as the southern slope is steep and the pass is exposed to strong winds. The way to the Danphya Pass is a long haul up the left bank of the tributary valley north of Jumla, and the route is not always readily apparent. Let your porter guide you past Charya Chaur, the wide horse pasture below the steep climb to the pass. Here at Charya Chaur, on our first walking day of a nine-week trek, Chris Wriggins and I learned the hard way that "you may be the sahib, but your porter knows the country." We elected to monopolize route finding despite the hints of our excellent porters from Napokuna and got sidetracked onto a herder's trail that disappeared on top of a snowy lekh.

The two alternate paths of the first route join north of the Danphya Lagna, where the higher path emerges from a low forest to join the lower, Padmara path along a gentle meadow. Soon the trail angles out on a ridge and drops 2,000 feet to the Lah Gad Valley. At the bottom of the V-shaped gorge, a wooden bridge rests beneath a pine-studded rock face. Along the Lah Gad River, the right-bank trail rises toward two villages with a heart-breaker drop into a side valley between the towns. Beyond the second village, follow the tributary Chautha Valley northward through a narrow gorge studded with evergreens to a wide upper pasture where the valley branches. Just below this large meadow, a substantial spring issues forth, begetting the stream you have been following. Where the pastureland branches, take the western valley to the grassy area where it forks again. This time bear right along a distinct trail that rises through grasslands to the 11,340-foot Gurchi Lagna. From the pass itself you can see little, but if you climb the steep, grass-tufted slope to the north, you will reach a place above the pines where you can gaze on intersecting ridges that plow into the lower Humla and Mugu valleys, which from here are within several days' walk. Rara Lake is not visible from this ridgeline, but now the snowy peaks north of it appear distinctly closer than they do from the high hills near Jumla.

From Gurchi Lagna, the trail drops into a pine forest, passes a small brook, and descends in short, steep switchbacks to the village of Pina at 8,000 feet. At Pina, paths divide: The northern route leads down-valley to the Mugu Karnali River and trails to Mugu or Humla. To get to Rara Lake, ask for the *maati baato* ("upper track") to Jhari village, which lies along the most direct route to the lake. The half-day trail from Pina to Rara follows a tributary valley west, passes Jhari, then leads up 2,000 feet over a gently sloping ridge that rolls away to Rara's southern shoreline.

The second route from Jumla to Rara is a few miles longer than the first; it also passes through forested country typical of western Nepal. Like one of the first route's alternate paths from Jumla, this trail follows the valley north of town, but instead of climbing to Danphya Lagna, it enters a forest of tall conifers beyond the meadow at Charya Chaur. The path continues some 20 miles over an unnamed, grassy pass to the village of Sinja, passing by many pleasant camping spots beneath immense gnarled pines. Locals accomplish the Jumla-to-Sinja trek between morning and dusk, but Westerners usually require two days. When you see the distinctive Kankasundri Temple on its steep, low knob, you will know that Sinja lies just beyond. The trail passes south of the peaked, white temple and descends to the main river, crossing a thick plank bridge at a place where the water has cut a deep, narrow furrow through bedrock.

Sinja village rests upon a small alluvial plain on the west bank of the clear Lah Gad River, here called the Sinja River. Four stelae beside the main path south are the only standing reminders of what was once the thriving winter capital of the large Malla kingdom. The now-ruined town actually stood on the east bank of the Sinja Khola at a place known as Kotgaon, where you can poke among ancient sculpted stones overgrown with weeds.

Just north of Sinja, stone-bound aeries once used by meditating renunciates are visible along the rock walls. The trail to Rara passes beneath those austere nests as it enters a narrow gorge that continues for several miles to the junction with the Ghatte Khola, which enters from the north. Follow the Ghatte up its left bank past Botan, the last village before Rara. The Ghatte is a beautiful miniature valley that doglegs northeastward past the Rara Lake National Park guards' huts at a place called Ghorasain. The Ghatte Khola trail toward Rara travels through much wilder country than the eastern route through Pina. Above the guards' huts, the path leaves the stream and continues toward Rara, rising onto the Chuchemara Danda (*danda* means "ridge" or "pass"); here the exposed, narrow trail skirts the west-facing Khater Khola basin. The views toward Humla are superb. Eventually you come out onto the last ridgeline before Rara, at 12,500 feet, where you have an excellent prospect of both Rara Lake and the valley leading to Mugu.

From lakeside, to take this route in reverse, south toward Jumla, you initially follow the northern bank of the Khater Khola, Rara's outlet. One and a half miles from the lake, take the side path up the hill south of the Khater. This track climbs 3,000 feet past moss-draped trees to the just-mentioned Humla-Rara-Mugu viewpoint on the Chuchemara Danda.

Nepal's Far Western Hills

The far western hills beyond Jumla are Nepal's widest (north to south) and least known tangle of forests, terracing, villages, and narrow footpaths. Trekkers generally avoid these large regions, and the outfitters in Kathmandu ignore them because of their difficult access. But these hills are alive with history, and if you go, you'll have pleasant, spontaneous interludes with the locals.

Seti Zone's cobblestoned capital, Silgarhi, lies along a low ridgetop above the Seti River in the middle hills of the far west. To the north is the high, undulating Khaptad plateau. In the midst of Khaptad's lush grasslands and forest, the districts of Acham, Bajang, Bhajaur, and Doti join at a single point. This rustic, primeval area has become the fifth of Nepal's six national parks. And like most of Nepal, these lovely far western hills provide excellent opportunities for the intrepid to explore. Only a few places will be mentioned in this chapter, but for additional ideas, on a good map trace the Chamlia, Seti, and Karnali valleys and their tributaries.

To head into Nepal's far western hills you should be both experienced and adventurous, for you will be in valleys that Angrezi rarely enter. Try to get copies of the relevant U502 maps (see Appendix A, "Map Information"), which are quite accurate for most of far western Nepal and particularly helpful with village names. Alternatively, check the better book stores in Kathmandu for a purple ammonia dye map that covers far western Nepal (but don't rely on such a map for much accuracy). Remember that there are virtually no inns or English-speakers on these trails. Hike in low altitudes only in winter, for it is much too hot to trek in low elevations any other time of the year, just as it is in the rest of the country.

You should hire a porter familiar with the area you will be walking in. This means that you will have to hire someone near the trailhead, which will probably mean at or near an airfield. You will have to be patient in this endeavor, but remember that a good porter-companion can be your most valuable asset in these rarely trekked regions. You may have to revise upward your notion of an appropriate daily wage. When I got to Darchula on Nepal's western border with India and needed a porter, I didn't find anyone interested in such work until I upped the wages offered to 65 rupees a day plus food. This was considerably more than I had paid in western Nepal previously, but it was less than most people pay if they start out from Pokhara. And Nandon, my hiree, while initially uncertain about the job, began to quite enjoy himself once he got a couple of days beyond the security of home. He proved to be an excellent cook (when he couldn't foist the job off on someone else) and friend as well as a fine load carrier.

The easiest way to reach Nepal's western hill region is to fly there. Seti Zone (in Nepali, a zone is called an *anchal*, corresponding to a state in the United States) is the westernmost zone in Nepal but one, and each of the four districts (called *jilla*) in Seti Anchal's hilly areas has a small airstrip. These are Chainpur in Bajhang Jilla, Kolti in Bajura Jilla, Sanfe (or Sanphebagar) in Accham Jilla, and Dipayal in Doti Jilla. Dipayal is located just north of the Seti River and is a couple of hours' walk below the large town of Silgarhi, the headquarters of both Doti Jilla and Seti Anchal. (There is even a road to Dipayal from Dhandeldhura, but this track is only passable in the dry season, and there are few vehicles that traverse it.) Dipayal (also called Silgarhi) is probably the best choice if you want to walk in Nepal's far western hills, both because there are more flights there and because Silgarhi is the largest town in the region. Given a few days in Silgarhi, you could outfit yourself completely with food and cooking utensils and also locate one or more porters. Silgarhi is also an easy two-day walk from Khaptad National Park.

Silgarhi and the Way to Khaptad National Park

The grassy runway at Dipayal's airfield is roughly 2,500 feet in elevation and surrounded by a barbed wire fence to keep out the local cattle. To reach Silgarhi (around 4,500 feet), you walk to the northeast. First you cross a river, and then it's uphill all the way, with time out at a teashop or two to rest and "take tea." Silgarhi was once home to a Rana general in days when the country was ruled by the Rana clan. Today's sports fields were the parade grounds of yesteryear, and the high-living Ranas kept their horses in a building that is presently part of a school. Like Dhankuta far to the east, Silgarhi is a pleasant tree-shaded town that lies astride a rounded ridge. Flagstone streets meander through the bazaar, and on-again, off-again electricity has come to town. Silgarhi is the center of Nepal's western development region and home to the large, ambitious Seti Project, a multi-departmental approach to various development projects. Ask a shopkeeper or two and you will be able to find a room to sleep in and dal-bhaat (the national dish of rice, lentils, and vegetables) to eat twice a day. Since there are so many government workers here, you can purchase all necessities you'll need for trekking.

Khaptad National Park is situated at 10,275 feet, and from Silgarhi you'll be walking uphill all the way. Give yourself two days to reach the park headquarters and be sure to take food supplies (although my porter Nandon and I were able to purchase dal-bhaat at a teahouse near the park headquarters). It's easy to find the way to the high, rolling plateau that constitutes Khaptad: just keep walking up the main street out of town and along the ridgeline. Several hours along, you'll reach a small settlement with teashops where you can order a meal and rest. This is the last place where you'll be on a main trail. To the east lies Accham, and above you to the north rises the high, forest-cloaked Khaptad plateau, now part of the national park. From this point, keep to the ascending trail that now proceeds northerly and slowly curves to the northeast, following along at or near the top of the ridge. Eventually the trail drops down into Jhigrano, a small saddle with a few houses. Jhigrano is the last place where you can purchase a meal, so you will want to stop hereabouts for the night. Alternatively, you may be able to stay in a dormitory or camp at the park entrance, a short five-minute walk above, but food will not be available there. Jhigrano and the park entrance are also the last places for some hours' walk where you can be sure to find water, so fill your water bottle here.

Khaptad National Park was created in 1984. Virtually unvisited by either Nepali or foreigner, the 86-square-mile park is unique for its profusion of flora and wildlife. The lofty grass and forestlands on Khaptad are also home to the venerated wise man, Khaptad Baba, who for over forty years has been a multilingual sage to all seekers and to His Royal Highness alike. Be ready for the long uphill walk from the park's entry point to the meadows on the roof of the plateau. Walk quietly, listen, and look, for if you are quiet, your way may pass near such local creatures as musk deer or wild sheep.

You'll probably meet a park official either at Jhigrano or at the official park entrance who will most likely request an entrance fee. Be sure to stop and chat with him, for he's a mine of information about the route and trail conditions. Ask him for a park map, which he should be able to give you—either gratis or for a few rupees. The trail into the park isn't difficult to follow, for it is the only path you'll see until you reach the top of the plateau. The way up is a small trail that rises continually through lush vegetation. About halfway up from the entrance to the top you'll pass Bichko Odar, a small rock overhang. There are meadows en route, but most of the time the path is in forest. Pause from time to time for rests and to look about. If you are quiet, you may be able to see one of the shy, wild creatures that inhabit these dense forests. A small handout of visitor information advises that the following animals are found within the park: leopard, Himalayan black bear, wild dog, musk deer, tahr (a beardless wild goat), jackal, langur monkeys, goral (goat antelope), and wild boar (I saw these last three animals during my brief visit to the park). There are also various species of pheasant and partridge and a wide variety of birds and insects. Additionally you'll see pine, fir, spruce, maple, and birch trees as well as bamboo and numerous medicinal herbs.

The better part of a day's walk up from the park entrance, you will reach the top of the rolling plateau covered with grass and forest. Now you are perhaps a forty-minute walk from the park headquarters, which lies to the north. Again, walk silently, for you never know what animal you might sight as you round the next knoll. It may be something as prosaic as a water buffalo or cow, however, for villagers who live at the base of the plateau are still permitted to graze their animals on these lush meadows (albeit under strict control). The park headquarters and accompanying guards' huts and a teahouse (where food may be available cooked to order) are found on the north side of the high plateau at an elevation of 10,275 feet. I visited with the well-educated and enthusiastic Nepali warden in his quarters nearby and learned he had passed the previous winter right here at the park. I observed that this must have been a lonely experience for such an educated man, but he had obviously relished his time here. Despite the fact that he had been snowed in for weeks at a stretch, he had been able to study the area in depth, which had been most rewarding for him.

Khaptad has also been the home for many years to Khaptad Baba, a well-known spiritual teacher and herbal physician long highly respected in Nepal. For years I had heard of this man who lived on top of a hill north of Silgarhi: a man who was consulted by king and peasant alike, a man who spoke many languages, knew how to heal the ill, and was said to predict the future. Would he deign to speak to us? Would he have matted hair and a loincloth like most sadhus (religious ascetics) I'd seen? It was hard to know what to expect as Nandon and I followed the newly built path through the moss-swathed woods up to the baba's dwelling place. (*Baba* is an honorific title, here loosely meaning "old man.") Nandon picked wildflowers to give him, and I wondered if he would appreciate the dried apricots and apricot nuts I had brought from faraway Kashgar. We reached a gate made of bamboo poles with a small sign to the side that said merely Hermitage. Above, on top of the hill, was a small, square building. We approached expectantly and then noticed a small four-legged wooden platform off below us to the side. On it was what at first appeared to be a pile of blankets. Then I saw that a person was resting or asleep beneath an ochre robe. We hesitated, and then the man looked our way. In one decisive, electric movement, up sat the Khaptad Baba.

With a large twinkle in his kindly, bright eyes, he bade us sit down, and with that we began a conversation, mostly in English, that lasted for several hours, until dusk. Khaptad Baba, slight of build with bushy eyebrows and a piercing, yet compassionate expression, is a member of the ancient Shankarcharya order of *sannyasi*, a sect of renunciate ascetics. Sitting on a deerskin, wrapped in his blanket, he told me that he had made his home right here for thirty-nine years, although sometimes he goes to India on pilgrimage. He often remains at home in the winter, when there can be 4 feet of snow on the ground. And he is obviously good friends with his four-hoofed and four-pawed neighbors. "Yes, the animals remember you, heh heh. Once they see you, they remember you; they don't bother you. Yesterday there were two bears at the watering place just below. Heh." (With this, he smiled and gave me a look as if to ask, "Does that frighten you?") "The birds have remarkable clocks. Each year they come back not more than three to five days apart from before." He spoke with Nandon in Nepali to assure him that he would have no difficulty finding

Khaptad Baba sits contentedly, wrapped in a blanket on top of his hill in Khaptad National Park.

his way home by a shorter route than the circuitous course by which I had directed us here. Baba's bright eyes and keen alertness belied his advancing age. With only two teeth, I wondered how he would be able to eat the food I had brought, but he was obviously very pleased with the gift. As Nandon and I took our leave, we were two more enthusiastic admirers of the wise old man from Khaptad.

From Jumla to Silgarhi via Rara Lake and Khaptad

Another excellent walk in Nepal's western hill area is between Jumla and Silgarhi via Rara Lake and Khaptad, two of Nepal's rarely visited national parks, preserves each rich in untrammeled flora and fauna. This hike—a walk of about three weeks for an experienced trekker—could be done in either direction. But remember that while in either national park, you will have to carry enough food to be self-sufficient.

To briefly sketch the route one way, you could begin at Jumla and go first to Rara Lake, then down the Khater Khola to the Karnali River (see "From Jumla to Humla," below). From the Karnali, you proceed south, then west, passing Kolti village, where an airstrip is located, and cross the 10,000-foot Parakhya Lagna. You could probably resupply at Kolti, but Bajura, like Humla (noted below), is a food-deficient area. In these regions, the best you can do is walk with a savvy porter, be ready to pay premium prices for grains, and inquire often about food availability. From Kolti, it is considered to be a four-day walk to Khaptad. A local would be extremely helpful in guiding you down the Budhi Ganga River west of Kolti, then up the narrow forested track to Khaptad. Only a very few development workers have done this trek, and you would definitely feel like a pioneer trying it. But think of the interesting country you would see and imagine the difficulties and frustrations you might have to overcome along the way. Going on this route would be much more challenging than walking in the Annapurna or Everest regions. Areas like Karnali and Seti anchals are still the real Nepal, with warts and rewards alike for the intrepid hiker who wants to experience trekking away from the well-beaten, well-advertised thruways.

The Northern High Country of Western Nepal

The next four sections describe the high country of Nepal's far west: its snow-covered lekhs and the valleys that are often still trade routes to Tibet. If you have done some trekking already, have a month of time at your disposal, and don't feel the need to ogle 26,000-foot peaks as you walk, consider a walk out of Jumla into the northern hills. You'll meet people who have stepped out of an old book, for time has wrought few changes in these remote valleys. To the many people who say Nepal has become overtrekked, you can stop yelping: here is some different turf.

From Jumla to Humla

The westernmost of Nepal's high valleys is an area known as Humla, situated along the Humla Karnali gorge northwest of Rara Lake. Reachable from Jumla at the end of a ten-day walk, Humla is definitely not on any main trekking circuit. When Chris Wriggins and I arrived with our Tibetan porters at Simikot, Humla's district capital, in the spring, two days before the end of the Nepali calendar year, we were the third and fourth foreigners to register for the year just ending. The two people before us were anthropologists doing extended field studies. Now an airstrip has been built at Simikot, but because flights are infrequent, well booked in advance, and liable to be canceled owing to the elements, the trail from Jumla is still the route you may take for reaching Simikot. Humla is a food-deficient area, and once there, you may have difficulty, as we did, in purchasing food essentials. So stock up well on supplies before departing Jumla, and replenish your grains before crossing the last pass into upper Humla. You can probably find food in upper Humla, but you'll have to be ready to pay dearly for it.

The most commonly traveled path to Humla begins along the already-described trail to Sinja (see "The Trails to Rara Lake," above). (Another route that leads east of Rara Lake, over the Chankheli Lagna, will be referred to later.) From Sinja, walk a mile downriver to Lurkhu village and turn west up the side valley. A steep climb leads to a low pass; on the other side, descend to a tributary of the Khater Khola, the river that drains Rara Lake. Follow the tributary, then the Khater Khola to the Karnali River valley. Along the Khater Khola you will pass lush rice fields, banana trees, and thatched houses quite unlike anything seen in the higher areas you have come from. Descend the Khater Khola to the Karnali itself, here about 4,400 feet in elevation. Some women in this area wear vests or necklaces of old Indian coins. The men smoke pungent *tamak* (tobacco) in their clay *sulpa*s, pipes they light by striking stones with strips of steel to ignite dry, sagelike tinder.

Once on the west bank of the Karnali, after crossing a bridge near the Khater's debouchment into the Karnali, you will reach a main north-south trail with connecting paths to the south and to the far western districts of Bajura, Bajhang, Accham, and Doti. This main trail along the Karnali is used by numerous Thakuri and Bhotia traders who roam from Tibet to the southern hills. The current economic plight of these long-distance food haulers since the strict regulation of trade with Tibet is recounted by Christoph von Fürer-Haimendorf in his thorough book *Himalayan Traders*. Like the American cowboy, these traders have a fanciful reputation in contrast to their hard day-to-day lives.

To reach Humla, however, continue up the Karnali Valley for a day's walk. The trail intersects the narrow, wild Kuwari Khola, which offers a very difficult alternate route into upper Humla. The Kuwari is a deep, forested gorge leading northwest via a summer pass called the Sankha La (15,400 feet) or Rani Kharka ("Queen's Meadow Pass"). South of this pass, the icefall on Saipal Himal's eastern face is a brilliant sight in the early morning. Before you leave the Karnali Valley trail for this side route, however, check at the village of Barchya on the main trail to be certain that the pass is open. With the decrease in the salt trade, the alternate

Kuwari route is seldom used, but its uninhabited upper reaches make a great walk.

The main Karnali Valley trail drops to cross the Kuwari Khola and continues along the Karnali's right bank, passing scree slopes and scattered cacti to a place about a mile below the junction of the Humla Karnali and Mugu Karnali rivers. These two main tributaries of the Karnali drain a 150-mile-wide area north of the Himalayan chain, reaching from the Humla Karnali's headwaters west of Taklakot in west Tibet to the upper reaches of eastern Dolpo above Dhaulagiri, where the eastern branch of the Karnali originates. Near a small stream on the Karnali's right bank, the path rises 2,000 feet directly up a dry spur and angles northward to the fields of two small villages that mirror other terraces across the vertiginous Humla Karnali gorge. Ask in the villages for the trail to the Munya La (*la* means "pass" in Tibetan); the path slants gently upward into the next forested side valley. Cross this tributary and, on the other side, climb the northerly ridge to the Munya La (about 12,500 feet) on the southern border of Humla's traditional boundary. Looking to the south from the top of the Munya La, you see low, forested lekhs and have an overview of the way you have walked from Jumla. In contrast, the northern aspect is topped by snow peaks. From the pass, the trail descends steeply for the most part to Ripa village.

Before trekking on north, note that from Ripa a route leads down-valley to lower Humla, a good way to return later. The alternate route south from Humla crosses the lower Tanke Valley near Darma village and continues south over the Chankheli La (11,700 feet), which is north of the Mugu Karnali Valley. Once at the Mugu Karnali, you take the trail to Pina village and return to Jumla along the eastern route to Rara Lake.

Continuing north from Ripa, the main Humla Karnali trail will follow the left or right bank (depending on the river's water level), passing through groves of rhododendron and bamboo. (Ask locals to show you the trail junction with an alternate upland route leading south to lower Humla, over the high Margor La.) The Humla Karnali River flows generally southeast from its point of origin west of Taklakot. Except for a few stretches, the Humla Karnali plows away at the bottom of a V-shaped gorge from lower Humla right on up to the last few miles before the Tibetan border. When you are in the Humla Valley, be sure to ask for the honey that is produced in hollow-log hives. Humla's honey is some of the best in Nepal, but be prepared to pay well for it.

Humla's most important village is Simikot, situated at about the 10,400-foot level on a spur high above the north bank of the Humla Karnali, a two- to three-day walk from Ripa. A STOL airstrip adjacent to town has been fashioned from the village wheat fields on a gently sloping shelf. Administrative buildings in neat rows sit on a nearby knoll that commands excellent views of converging gorges beneath snowy saw-toothed ridges. Simikot village is largely composed of Thakuris, the same clan found in Jumla. The Thakuris living in and about Simikot are virtually the only Nepali Hindus to conduct transborder trade in Tibet; Nepal's traders are mostly Buddhist highlanders whose ancestors migrated earlier from various Tibetan regions.

Again it should be emphasized that up-valley from Simikot you enter a food-deficient region where you will have to pay high prices for any grains that you are able to purchase. A friend who had put water systems in two villages above Simikot returned years later and was heartily welcomed, but he still had to pay dearly for the rice he bought. This route up the Humla Valley from Simikot is the trail people will take if the border is open to Taklakot in Tibet. See "From Humla, Nepal to Taklakot, Tibet" in Chapter 9.

At several junctures along the main north-bank trail up the Humla Valley beyond Simikot, side paths lead steeply north to two summer settlements. These upper villages, Dhinga and Yakba, are along an upper trail that continues onward, still steeply, to a 16,100-foot pass called the Nyalu La. From this pass, sacred Mt. Kailas is just visible. The region beyond the pass is called Limi: a high, isolated valley with three villages whose inhabitants raise animals and also engage in trade that once extended as far as Lhasa and still reaches to Kathmandu. People from Limi as well as the denizens of upper Humla often go on pilgrimage to sacred Lake Manasarovar and holy Mt. Kailas to the north in Tibet.

Back on the main route through Humla, the frequently restricted trail up-valley from Simikot leads into more steep country, inhabited in the first part by Buddhist Bhotias (people of Tibetan ancestry) and Hindu Thakuris and farther up by Bhotias only. Beyond Simikot this trail passes several villages near the narrow gorge bottom, eventually reaching Kermi, the first all-Bhotia village. Kermi has a 20-foot-long prayer wall and its own *gomba*s (Buddhist temples or monasteries) of the Nyingma and Sakya orders high above the town. West of Kermi, look for the vertiginous Khawa Lungba ravine leading south to Chala village and the Sankha La. Chala was once a thriving trading town in the days of unrestricted transborder trade, but now it is yet another isolated village. The once heavily traveled valley route in northern Humla crosses several flat meadows, continuing by Yangar, Munchu, and Yari. Yangar and Yari once held large summer trade fairs with their neighbors across the Tibetan border. There is a police checkpost at Munchu, and you will not be allowed beyond unless you have a special permit. Near Munchu the valley widens, and beyond Yari the trail negotiates the Nara La (15,000 feet), on a high ridge. Not far up-valley, but beyond the Tibetan border, is a track angling south to the Urai La, a pass that leads into the headwaters of the Seti Valley. To the west of the Urai La is the Tinkar Lepu La, the pass at the head of Nepal's remote Tinkar Valley.

The Mugu Valley

The narrow upper Mugu Valley lies east of Humla and the practically uninhabited Tanke gorge. Mugu's inhabitants have traditionally been limited to trading for a livelihood, because their own valley has little room for fields. The Namja La at the head of the Mugu Valley was once a good route leading to the headwater area of the Tsang Po River in Tibet. More recently, however, many Mugulis have been migrating south into such areas as the lower Chaudabise Valley, where they have taken up agriculture.

From Jumla, two principal routes—one high and one low—lead to the usually restricted Mugu Valley. Each route requires about a week's walk to reach Mugu village, although the higher trail following the Chaudabise Valley may be snow covered for more than five months of the year. If you are going in the autumn and want to try the upper trail, do so on the outbound leg of your trek, for the Khapre Pass at the head of the Chaudabise Valley may be snowed in by the time of your return.

To take the upper route, walk east from Jumla along the Tila Valley to the Chaudabise confluence. Ask for honey at homes along the lower stretches of the Chaudabise, especially near Talphi village. Many Mugulis have built houses in the warmer flat bottomlands near Talphi, and they will know if the Khapre Pass is being used. At Talphi, a less used alternative trail branches north through Maharigaon. This secondary trail crosses three passes and is open slightly longer than the approach over the Khapre La, owing primarily to the Khapre's steep northern slope. Along the Chaudabise

A monk from the Mugu Valley pauses while reading a manuscript on the roof of his relative's home in Mugu village.

route, a two-day walk through a heavily forested and little-populated valley brings you north past the final birch trees to a narrow upper gorge below the 16,600-foot Khapre La. Do not be guided by the U502 map of this area, which indicates that the Chaudabise does not connect with the Khapre, for in fact, below a scree-covered 1,500-foot drop north of the pass, the trail reaches a side valley that leads directly to Wangri village. From gritty, rough Wangri, continue to the bottom of the river gorge. This major tributary of the Mugu Karnali is called the Langu or Namlang on most maps, but the locals call it the Dolpo Chu (*chu* means "river" in Tibetan); it drains the entire area of northern Dolpo. To reach the Mugu Valley, you can take a near-vertical track 3,000 feet over the high ridge to the north, but an easier if slightly longer trail traverses downstream 1,000 feet above the north bank of the Dolpo River. In several miles, this trail drops to join with the lower trail from the south.

Since Wangri and Dalphu, its lone neighboring village across the deep Langu gorge, are the last towns up the Dolpo Valley for many miles, game is sometimes seen up the Dolpo River to the east of the two villages. One of the most interesting endangered species in the Himalaya lives in this area: the Himalayan musk deer. This slight, 30-pound animal has wavy hair that is shiny like plastic, and its hind legs are longer than its forelegs. Always secretive, the musk deer becomes nocturnal if its ways are threatened, as indeed they are, for the *kasturi,* as it is called from Kashmir to Bhutan, is hunted with ardor virtually everywhere it lives. The male deer has the misfortune of carrying a subcutaneous gland near its stomach that holds an average of 35 grams of yellow-grained musk, which also is called kasturi. The best of this substance is called *beautay* in west Nepal. Like rhinoceros horn, this kasturi is believed to have near-miraculous aphrodisiacal and curative properties. Until gold exceeded $500 an ounce in Kathmandu, even its price was exceeded by that of kasturi. Rodney Jackson, the author of the natural history chapter of this book, has studied the hunting patterns of men from Dalphu and Wangri over a period of several years and has estimated that in one year alone, more than a hundred animals were killed for musk in this single remote area. The toll throughout the Himalaya must be staggering. The Himalayan musk deer will unwillingly continue along a path to extinction in the wild unless it can be protected in such sanctuaries as Khumbu in eastern Nepal and Khaptad and Rara Lake national parks.

The second, lower trail from Jumla to Mugu village follows the eastern path to Rara Lake as far as Pina village. A half day's walk down-valley north of Pina takes you far below Gum Gadhi, Mugu Jilla's ridge-straddling district headquarters, and down to the Mugu Karnali gorge. At this junction the trail to Mugu takes an easterly course up the Mugu River and into an area known as the Karan Hills. This Karan region is separate ethnically from the villages of Churi and Mugu in the upper Mugu Valley. There are over a dozen Karan villages. Some, like Lumsa and Mangri, are scattered at around 6,500 feet near the main trail; others lie hidden at the 10,000-foot level on the slopes of northern side valleys. Replenish grains and ask for yogurt (*dahi*) and eggs (*phul*) at the lower villages, as there is little fresh food in the Mugu Valley beyond Mangri.

Eight miles east of Mangri is the confluence of the Mugu and Dolpo branches of the Mugu Karnali River. Several old stupas rest above the vertex of the two streams, as if to announce that all upriver lands are protected by the *dharma*, the Buddhist path. Just above the river junction, the trail from Dalphu and Wangri connects with the main trail up the Mugu Valley.

The first of the two villages in the upper Mugu Valley itself is Churi, 1,700 feet above the river along the rarely traveled upper ridge trail from Dalphu. The valley trail passes well below Churi and continues along the base of the steep valley around two bends where the gorge, now less narrow and U-shaped, aims directly north to the Namja (or Nanza) La at the Tibetan border.

Mugu village sits at the 11,000-foot level on the left bank of the river, a tight collection of a hundred three-story homes constructed of stone, wattle, and timber. The village is windswept and windows are small, but each roof has a protected open porch, and each home has a well-used family room on the third floor. The white Nyingma gomba in its grove of evergreens above town offers a pleasant contrast to the upper valley's study in brown and ochre. The deserted town of Purana Mugu (Old Mugu) lies a two-hour walk up-valley from Mugu near the uppermost groves of white birch trees.

Mugulis, whether met in Jumla, along the trail, or at home, have a vivacity and buoyancy all their own. Ethnically they are Tibetan, with round, bronze faces. The older generation has clung to its ways: the men are often away trading or grazing animals, while the women clean, spin, and weave woolen homespun for clothes, blankets, and animal packbags. Until blue Chinese sneakers became popular, men made and wore the *somba*, a shoe with legging in the Tibetan style that is ingeniously made from leather and wool. Muguli women wear distinctive, circular, 3-inch-wide silver earrings.

Trading between Mugulis and the nomadic Tibetan Drokpas north of the political border has been strictly circumscribed by the Chinese authorities, and as a result Mugu has lost regional influence. In 1976 a Muguli trader who owned fifteen yaks told me that the border was legally open only during September and October. During that time, he and his neighbors made as many trips as possible with their yaks over the 14,020-foot-high Namja La to Pong Dzu village in Tibet, near the headwaters of the Tsang Po (Brahmaputra) River. Taking grains, the Mugulis returned with salt, wool, dry cheese, butter, and the Tibetan tea, which is molded into bricks. These goods were stored in the second stories of their homes until the season was completed. Then travel southward with yaks or sheep could begin. In winter, many Mugulis make at least one trip to Surkhet, ten days south of Jumla. Song Bu, a twenty-five-year-old Muguli who had traveled as far as Calcutta, amazed my friend Chris and me by observing our 1:506,880 *West* sheet of Nepal and without being able to read the

English words, pointing out and naming all the important towns, rivers, and passes.

The Route East from Jumla to Dhorpatan

It is possible to walk between Jumla and Pokhara, scores of miles to the east, in two and a half to three weeks if you don't take side trips or run into bad weather. The route follows the old path used by people carrying Jumla's red rice to Kathmandu during the rule of the Rana family. This section covers the western two-thirds of this trail, as far as Dhorpatan; the Dhorpatan-to-Pokhara stretch is described in Chapter 5 (see "Around Dhaulagiri"). This trek is rarely undertaken because of Jumla's relative inaccessibility. Also, the restricted district of Dolpo has been enlarged to incorporate the former Tibrikot District (through which this route passes), so permits are difficult to come by for this trail. Be sure to get a permit, or you will be apprehended at the checkpost in Dunyer along the Bheri Valley. But this walk is a great one, traversing the forested valleys east of Jumla and primeval forests and spectacular gorges west and south of Dhaulagiri.

Stock up with at least five days' food at Jumla, and expect to replenish basic supplies in Tibrikot and Drikung to the east. The trail begins along the gentle Tila Valley, passing initially through terrain reminiscent of the Colorado high country. In the afternoon of the first day's walk, after climbing a low ridge, you will reach Gothi Chaur, a former sheep-rearing station in a rolling meadow. Just east of the long buildings a small spring emerges beneath a stone Malla shrine. Across the meadow lies an anachronistic, faintly marked STOL airstrip that is no longer used. A short half day's walk beyond Gothi Chaur in the upper Tila Valley is the settlement of Napokuna, populated by rough-and-ready Drokpas who used to roam across the south-central Tibetan plains north of the border. Good porters who are used to high passes can be found at Napokuna.

Several hours' walk east of Napokuna, a low pass called Mauri Lagna ("Honey Pass") brings the trail out of the Karnali River watershed and into the drainage of the Bheri River. (The Bheri is technically part of the larger Karnali system, joining the Karnali just north of the Siwalik Range.) A forested lekh looms ahead, but first the Jagdula River below must be crossed. The path descends to the hamlet of Chaurikot, then proceeds through a large notch and on to the interesting village of Rimi. On either side of Rimi are Malla stelae, but the most intriguing objects in town are the ubiquitous wooden *dokpa* figures, human-shaped protector deities.

Throughout much of Nepal west of Tibrikot are small one- or two-room wooden buildings called *tans*. These humble shrines often contain dokpas and a small, crude altar. The dokpa figures in Rimi and the town's tan represent prehistoric traditions that continue alongside the veneration of Hindu gods and goddesses. Next to the tan, during ceremonies performed several times yearly at the full moon, oracles known as *dhamis* speak in trance with the voice of a local god. Dhamis are often older men with long, roughly braided hair twisted atop their heads who initially gained their position by manifesting *siddhi*s ("powers"—often of divination) and performing *bhit* ("impossible acts"), such as rubbing kernels of rice to produce small green plants. Despite the many carved figures, tans, and dhamis that the trekker can see while passing through, it is the rare foreigner (aside from an occasional Peace Corps volunteer or anthropologist) who ever witnesses a dhami in trance during the full-moon ceremony.

Angling down from Rimi, the path crosses the Jagdula River and continues up toward Kaigaon village. Less than 1,000 feet above Kaigaon, the trail divides: the path south toward Jajarkot heads directly uphill, while the track to Tibrikot and Tarakot goes somewhat more gently to a false pass at 10,800 feet. If you don't have a permit that includes Dunyer or Tarakot, then you should follow the roundabout southern gorge trail to Jajarkot down the Bheri Valley as far as the Sano Bheri Valley turnoff to Dhorpatan. If your trekking permit lists Dunyer and Tarakot, you will be able to continue, through Kaigaon, over the 12,590-foot Balangra Pass to Tibrikot. With its temple above town, Tibrikot rests on a high spur 700 feet above the Bheri River. The area called Tarakot lies two days' walk east. From Tibrikot, the low river trail passes the Dunyer (or Dunahi) airstrip and, farther east, Dunyer Bazaar, the headquarters of Dolpo District.

North of Dunyer, up the narrow, V-shaped Suli Gad gorge, lies Shey-Phoksumdo National Park. This large park is unique because outsiders are not allowed to visit it; the park is located entirely within restricted Dolpo District. Shey refers to Shey Gomba, a monastery in northern or "inner" Dolpo; Phoksumdo Lake is situated to the south of Shey. This cobalt-colored gem lies at the base of steep, towering ridges, a location of exquisite beauty. When the skies are cloudy above the lake, it does not mirror the heavens, but retains its bright radiance. Bharal (blue sheep) and an occasional snow leopard roam the heights above both lake and monastery.

You can find Tarakot on maps, but Dzong (meaning "fort") is the village name used by locals. A prominent fortress town on a knoll south of the Bheri River, Dzong is one of four south-bank villages in the region formerly called Tichu Rong. Dzong's residents once supervised toll collection on caravans traversing Tichu Rong via the Bheri. Above and west of Dzong is Ba, a large village whose inhabitants have the distinction of speaking their own language, a dialect called Kakay. Still higher above Dzong is prosperous Drikung village, populated by Tibetan and Magar Buddhists. From the roofs of Drikung's solid houses you have a grand, 360-degree view of the deep, awesome Bheri Valley. North of you rises a 20,000-foot ridge, which is west of Dolpo's Tarap Valley. To the south are the westernmost summits of the gargantuan Dhaulagiri Himal, a snow-cloaked series of peaks, 40 air miles in length, that reach east to Dhaulagiri I. The Bheri River below you disappears down-valley to the west, but within eyesight the gorge divides upriver to the north and east, where paths lead to the Tarap and Barbung valleys respectively. The Barbung makes up part of the direct route north around Dhaulagiri, described in Chapter 5 (see "Around Dhaulagiri").

Trails leading south leave Drikung and Ba villages and rise more than 4,000 feet to the Jang La (about 14,900 feet). This route from the Tarakot area to the meadowland and village at Dhorpatan takes four to six days (longer if you encounter snow). The path rises and falls almost continuously as it crosses three barren passes and a few low ridges while passing only two impoverished villages. This is very impressive ridge-and-gorge topography, much of it very wild, although some upper meadows are well grazed in the summer. Difficult though the route is, it gets good use in spring and fall from trading caravans that often include pack-carrying horses. Trekking between the Tarakot area and Dhorpatan should be undertaken only with a porter-cum-cook who is familiar with the way. Several pages would be required to describe the route precisely. This is tough, rewarding country, as for days you traverse the western flanks of Dhaulagiri. Look for bharal in the upper meadows. This area is now called the Dhorpatan Hunting Reserve, and wealthy hunters are flown in to take potshots at bharal. Once at Dhorpatan you can replenish supplies from homes that are a half day's stroll from the Kali Gandaki watershed and less than a week's walk from Pokhara.

Dolpo: The Hidden Land

With sweeping, windswept vistas and a traditional Tibetan culture, the northern high valleys of inner Dolpo are some of the Himalaya's most remarkable gems. A book purporting to be a guide must immediately emphasize Dolpo's excessive remoteness, however. The places we think of (and will refer to here) as Dolpo are only the remote northerly part of Dolpo District. Most villages in Dolpo are removed from the rest of the world to the south by one or more difficult passes. The people who live in Dolpo must import grain from the south to feed themselves, and any outsiders who enter the region need to carry enough food to be completely self-sufficient. This is important, because treks to isolated places anywhere are most often curtailed because of low rations. An individual planning to walk into one of Dolpo's valleys north of the extensive Dhaulagiri Himal must have a permit valid for the area, enough food, and a porter-cook who knows the trails and camping places. This can be a nearly impossible order to fill.

The name Dolpo remained unknown to the rest of the world until David Snellgrove and three Nepali companions began to hear the word used in conversation when they reached the region in May 1956. *Himalayan Pilgrimage* is Snellgrove's account of his seven-month journey largely within Tibetan-speaking, inner-mountain areas of west and central Nepal, and it remains one of the most knowledgeable and compassionate of Himalayan journals. It also contains a wealth of information about trails in Dolpo. Snellgrove found that the valleys of the upper Bheri and Langu (Dolpo) watersheds have been divided into subregions called Tarap, Tsharbung, Namgung, and Panzang. These four areas compose the Tibet-like cultural region of Dolpo. Tarap and Tsharbung are valleys of the upper Bheri; Namgung and Panzang comprise the uppermost tributaries in the

Langu watershed. Namgung and Panzang are considered to be "inner" Dolpo, for they lie to the north of Tarap and Tsharbung, beyond additional high passes.

The few hundred people who reside year round in Dolpo's upper villages at 14,000 feet and above are among the world's highest dwellers. The only grain that can grow in the highest valleys is barley, the area's staple food, which is served roasted and ground as tsampa. Although Dolpo has long been part of Nepal, its villagers have looked to Tibet for their culture and are of different south Tibetan clans. Most people are either Rongpas, valley farmers, or Drokpas, seminomadic yak herders.

People in Dolpo wear homespun clothing that is sometimes dyed maroon, and they favor Tibetan-style somba for footgear. Men and women often wear both religious amulets and strings of coral and turquoise about their necks. Women plait their hair in various styles. Older men wear braided hair wrapped about their heads or hanging down their backs, leaving a swath of grease on their wool shirts. In the winter, many people from Dolpo leave home and walk south, with a family member remaining behind to watch the stock. From December to February, you can often see people from these high valleys camped near Bodnath Stupa in the Kathmandu Valley. And at that time you can buy their homespun woolen blankets from merchants at Bodnath or the Thamel area of Kathmandu.

As if to emphasize Dolpo's seclusion from the rest of the world, some villages in the area still practice the pre-Buddhist Bon Po religion. This

Dancers in Dolpo are accompanied by the Tibetan-style guitar. (Photograph by Daniel Miller.)

early sect was almost entirely replaced after Buddhist doctrine began to spread across Tibet in the ninth century. Now, in Nepal, only a few small remnants of Bon Po believers remain: they are largely in and near Dolpo and in the upper Arun Valley to the east. The ideography of Bon and the ritual implements employed during Bon ceremonies are so similar to those of Buddhism that practically anyone not a scholar who enters a Bon Po building will believe it is another Buddhist gomba. Some Bon paintings or gombas are easily identified, however: look to see whether all the swastikas are pointing counterclockwise. Swastikas, the ancient Indian symbol for good fortune, usually point clockwise on Buddhist iconography but are reversed in the Bon Po tradition. Less obvious, but likewise contrary to Buddhist practice, is the way Bon prayer walls are skirted. While Buddhist prayer stones are meant to be passed on the left, people proceed to the right of Bon Po walls. The Buddhist mantra "Om Mani Padme Hum" ("All hail the jewel in the lotus") carved on prayer stones has various levels of allegoric meaning, but the traditional Bon Po invocation "Om matri muye sa le du" is largely enigmatic. Other differences exist, but nowadays Bon Po is effectively a branch of Tibetan Buddhism. The world's most important Bon gomba, where the Bon Po patriarch resides, is located not far from Shimla in the Indian state of Himachal Pradesh.

How to reach Dolpo? The fact is that very few people will be able to summon the energy, time, and permissions required to set foot upon this extremely isolated area. *Himalayan Pilgrimage*, an unintentional but excellent Baedeker, is your best sourcebook for this region. It was reprinted in 1981 by Prajna Press in Boston but is now out of print. If you seriously plan a trek to Dolpo, study that book. If you go, carry it with you. This chapter will tear no more rents in Dolpo's veil.

Bishnu, the best cook in Marpha, holds her young daughter Junie.

5

Around Annapurna
and Dhaulagiri

*Such houses and such men, ragged, tough and cheerful,
both alike reeking of juniper smoke, speak of high valleys
upon the threshold of great mountains.*
H. W. Tilman, in the Marsyangdi Valley, 1949

Central Nepal

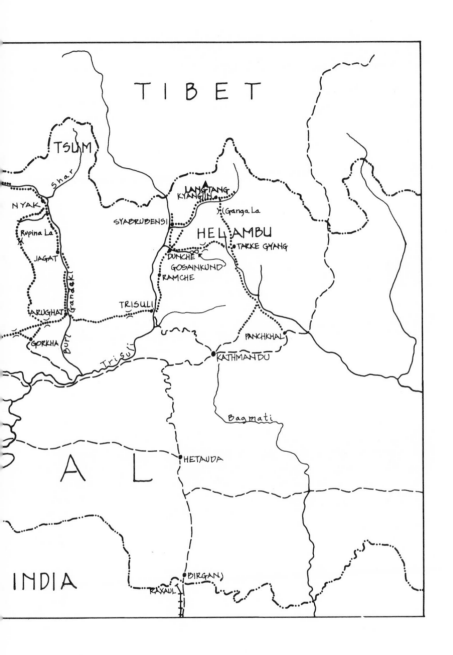

TIBET

TSUM

NYAK

Shar

Rupina La

JAGAT

Buri Gandaki

ARUGHAT

GORKHA

SYABRUBENSI

LANGTANG
KYANGJIN

X (Ganga La

HELAMBU

TARKE GYANG

DUNCHE
GOSAINKUND

RAMCHE

TRISULI

Trisuli

PANCHKHAL

KATHMANDU

Bagmati

A L

HETAUDA

INDIA

(BIRGAN)

RAXAUL

Nepal's Amazing Gorges

In central and eastern Nepal the Great Himalaya Range rises abruptly north of the middle hills. Deep, V-shaped gorges—among the deepest on the face of the earth, and swathed in stone and greenery—carry streams and rivers rapidly into the lower, more southerly Mahabharat Range. Hikers on the roller-coaster paths through these gorges are often surprised by the rapidly changing sequence of culture, climate, and landscape as the trail passes from the warm middle hills to the dry upper valleys. With the exception of the streams in the Kathmandu Valley, virtually all the rivers from the kingdom's mountains empty into one of Nepal's three river systems before penetrating the low hogback ridges of the Siwalik Hills to reach the flatlands of India. Lying between the drainages of the western Karnali and the eastern Sapt Kosi, Nepal's central watershed is called the Great Gandaki. The Gandaki river system includes four gorges that have their origin north of the main Himalaya Range. These four trans-Himalayan valleys—the Kali Gandaki, the Marsyangdi, the Buri Gandaki, and the Trisuli—comprise much of the terrain covered in this and the next chapter.

The valleys of both the Great Gandaki and Sapt Kosi watersheds share a distinctive topography, natural history, and culture. Slowly, a few roads are stretching north along the lower regions of these valleys, for the gentle middle hill areas are both agriculturally productive and easy to build roads into. Once you have reached the Marsyangdi or whichever valley you will hike up, you are in hot subtropical country, 1,000 to 4,000 feet in elevation, where banana and papaya trees shade water buffalo, rice is the principal crop, and the people are Hindu. As you walk up-valley, the ridgelines are replaced by higher and steeper spurs of the Great Himalaya Range. Farther north begins a narrow gorge with stretches of sheer rock walls. Depending on which valley you follow, the gorge requires from one to two days to negotiate on trails that seesaw frequently. While you are passing through the gorge, the river roars alongside, morning temperatures stay cooler, and villages are small and scattered. The path skirts and crosses ribs of the himals above, and in spring and summer the gorge has many waterfalls. Once you are into the Himalaya, the valley floor rises quickly, and the inhabitants you meet are usually Buddhists living near evergreen-forested slopes. Beyond the villages and the last silver birch trees are summer huts in the middle of high grazing meadows. Paths into other valleys continue over rock fields and often through snow toward high, prayer-monument-topped passes.

This chapter primarily describes two circular treks and mentions a few of the many side trails en route. Each of the two circle routes follows a main valley or tributary valley upward from its southern trailhead or a connecting path. By following these routes, you can circumambulate the massifs of Annapurna and Dhaulagiri, two of the world's ten tallest peaks. Remember that you must get a trekking permit before you leave and that permits are nearly impossible to obtain for areas north of Dhaulagiri.

In addition to trekking the circle routes, you can make a number of lower-elevation hikes in the central midlands, as the following short section suggests.

Trekking in the Middle Hills

Central Nepal's lush and well-populated midlands are some of the country's most accessible areas, owing to the roads among the middle hills that connect Kathmandu with both Pokhara to the west and Kodari on the Tibetan border to the north. From April through September, the hills lower than 5,000 feet are too warm to trek in, and from June you have the added problems of the rains and leeches accompanying the monsoon. However, from November through March the hills are neither hot nor muddy. The middle-hill walks suggested here are only a few of the myriad hikes possible in central Nepal. Depending on your time constraints or whim, these treks can be taken only in part or can be extended, and they can be followed in either direction. Some routes are described sketchily, others only suggested. You may devise better ones as you trek or after map perusal. However, there are so many trails in these areas that unless you have a good map and are proficient in asking directions in Nepali, you will have difficulty keeping to any planned course. So do consider taking a porter-guide who knows the area you will be traversing. The U502 map series is helpful for the middle hills in Nepal, although some large villages are misnamed or omitted.

Remember that Nepal's middle hills are largely Hindu and that you will not be aware of many local customs, particularly with respect to the preparation and consumption of food and the matter of sleeping arrangements. Review "Acculturation" in Chapter 3. If you ask shelter from a Chhetri or Brahmin family, you and your porter may be politely directed to the porch or a nearby outbuilding. Your clan (Angrezi) or your porter's may not be considered sufficiently refined! Ancient Hindu principles from the Vedas, dating back thousands of years, determine what is and is not considered pure. The Nepali word *jutho* indicates the concept of something being rendered ritually impure by contact alone. If you touch any piece of unoffered food, it will become jutho and will then be considered fit for consumption only by an animal. People's bodies are believed to decline in sanctity from head to feet. Thus, patting people on the head or stepping over them is not done. When interrelating with locals in or near their homes, watch and follow the lead set by others.

Paths lead to the midlands from the Kathmandu Valley, but nowadays most trekkers leave the valley by vehicle. Hikers bus east out of the valley to Panchkhal and continue from that roadhead to the Helambu region (see Chapter 6). Others take the bus on the winding road to Trisuli Bazaar. Buses to Trisuli leave from Lekhnath Marg near the Gauri Shankar Hotel in northern Kathmandu (on the way to the Balaju Water Gardens) in early morning and early afternoon for the 43-mile trip. Treks of a week or more can be conveniently undertaken from Trisuli Bazaar.

With someone to porter and guide, you can take a ten-day or longer loop walk from the town of Trisuli. Follow the main trail west from Trisuli and then, after crossing the Samri Bhanjang (*bhanjang* is another Nepali word for "pass"), branch off northwesterly and head into the terraced Ankhu Valley. The farther north you proceed up the Ankhu Valley, the closer you will be to the main range and to the upper grazing pastures on Ganesh Himal, populated by Tamang herders. A high jungle route farther up the Ankhu Valley crosses two 12,000-foot passes that lead east to Gatlang and the Trisuli River.

West from Trisuli beyond the Samri Valley lies the old Kathmandu-to-Pokhara trail, a route that leads to the Pokhara Valley in a walk of about a week. This is a good walk to take in midwinter, as I once did, for it follows low hills and rarely exceeds 4,000 feet in elevation. Lodging along this main trail is available in homes that take in travelers for the night, but you will not know which are the correct houses unless you ask, for few people take this trek now that the road to Pokhara is completed. From the ridges on this ancient track, you will have panoramic views of snowy peaks. The historically important town of Gorkha (see Chapter 6) lies on one branch of this trail east of the Marsyangdi River.

Some of the best middle-hill trekking can be found along the southern spurs of the Annapurna-Lamjung massif. This region is approached most easily from the elongated town of Pokhara. From Pokhara, you can take a day walk east-northeast of town to Kahun Danda or north to Batulechaur, the home village of a clan of *gaine*, or minstrel singers, who wander for weeks at a time performing in different locales. A scenic overnight (or day) hike would be to walk from Bindabasini Temple at the high point in Pokhara's bazaar up the ridge to the west to Sarangkot. Another overnight hike from Pokhara reaches Naudanda west of town with its magnificent Himalayan panorama. Along the same trail, you could spend two or three nights out to reach Chandrakot's viewpoint of Annapurna South and Machhapuchhare. Route descriptions of the trail to Naudanda and Chandrakot are given in "Around Annapurna," below.

In the leech-free dry season you can walk north from Pokhara for two to four days and go beyond the villages in the lush Mardi or Seti valleys, which drain Machhapuchhare's vertiginous south slopes. If you follow the Seti Valley far enough on the rough trail, Machhapuchhare will be southwest, towering 12,000 feet above you.

Longer walks of a week to ten days lead along tracks east or west of Pokhara, where you will have excellent exposures to hill life. With a porter who knows the way, walk northeast out of the Pokhara Valley floor from Begnas Tal (*tal* means "lake" in Nepali) to a large town populated by Gurungs, such as Siklis or Ghanpokhara. You will traverse thick jungle and terraced fields and probably meet English-speaking former Gurkha soldiers along the way. On the return you can trek to Pokhara by a different hill route or go east, then south along the Marsyangdi Valley. Another loop route, this one west of Pokhara, begins south of town at the roadside bazaar of Naudanda (a different Naudanda from the one previously mentioned), which you can reach by taking a taxi or the cramped bus from Pokhara for the one-and-a-half hour ride. From Naudanda this lowland course follows the hot Andhi Khola to Karkineta along the trail noted in the first part of "Around Dhaulagiri," below. On the second day of that walk, just before reaching Kusma, turn north along the Modi Khola trail to Birethanti and return on foot to Pokhara by the main trail or the more circuitous but scenic trail through Ghandrung and Landrung.

Around Annapurna

The complete three-and-a-half-week Annapurna circuit is best undertaken counterclockwise, up the Marsyangdi Valley and down the Kali Gandaki. Note that you can do the trek in three and a half weeks, but allowing more time to take side trips is highly recommended. Most trekkers walk up the Marsyangdi Valley to the Kali Gandaki rather than the reverse for several reasons: although the overall time required to walk in either direction is nearly the same, the walk along the Marsyangdi Valley is considerably more gradual in elevation gain, which makes acclimatization easier; the climb to the Thorong Pass between the valleys from the last lodge and camping place on the Marsyangdi side is easier; and going toward the Kali Gandaki Valley you have the good Thakali inns to anticipate. But given the attractiveness of the Kali Gandaki Valley as a destination in itself, the route to the "deepest valley in the world," the 3½-mile-deep Kali Gandaki, deserves first mention.

Before beginning the route descriptions, however, I must mention that when you undertake a trek in the Annapurna region, either around the entire massif or particularly out of Pokhara toward Muktinath, you will be entering the most trekked-in area of the entire Himalaya Range. Because of the region's accessibility and beauty, three times as many hikers visit Ghorapani, northwest of Pokhara, as the number of trekkers who go to the Khumbu region near Mt. Everest. In response to this popularity, the King Mahendra Trust for Nature Conservation under the auspices of His Majesty's Government of Nepal has created the Annapurna Conservation Area, a multiple-use concept for management of the flora and fauna in the Annapurna region. Due to the great number of trekkers, particularly in the Ghorapani-Ghandrung–Annapurna Sanctuary area, several measures are being implemented, with an emphasis on reducing the vast quantities of wood being used for fires. Please respect the ordinances that have been enacted and understand that the rules and restrictions exist to protect the area from further denudation and to preserve it for future use. Thanks to conservation education, great progress has been made in cleaning up trash and slowing down deforestation. Trekkers and villagers alike are learning that environmental protection benefits everyone.

From Pokhara to Muktinath: Up the Kali Gandaki Valley

The ancient salt-trading route from Pokhara that ascends the Kali Gandaki Valley gorge west of Annapurna Himal has introduced more hikers to Himalayan trekking than any other trail in the entire range. Many factors

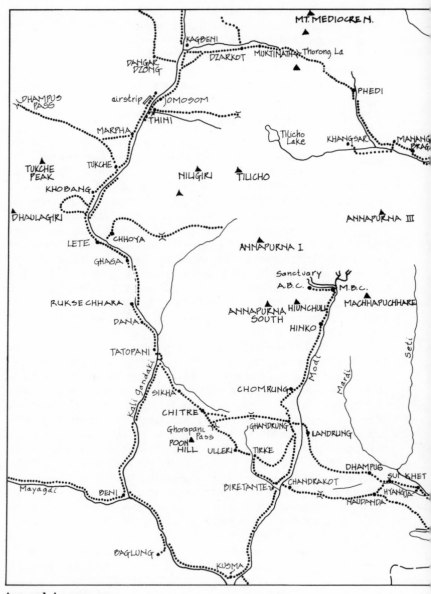

Around Annapurna

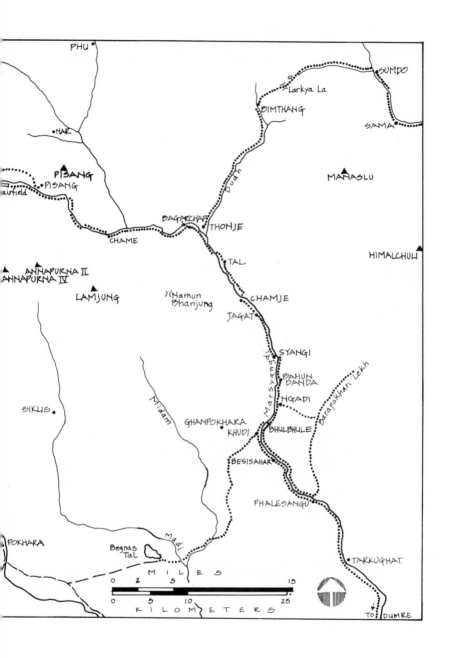

PHU

SUMDO

Larkya La

NAR

DIMTHANG

SAMA

PISANG
PISANG
airfield

MANASLU

Buah

BAGARCHAP
THONJE
CHAME

TAL

HIMALCHULI

ANNAPURNA II
ANNAPURNA IV

LAMJUNG

)(Namun
Bhanjung

CHAMJE

JAGAT

SYANGI

Marsyangdi

BAHUN
DANDA

NGADI

Darapokhari Lekh

SIKUS

Midam

GHANPOKHARA
KHUDI

BHULBHULE

BESISAHAR

PHALESANGU

POKHARA

Begnas
Tal

Madi

TARKUGHAT

M I L E S
0   2   5   15

0   5   10   25
K I L O M E T E R S

TO DUMRE

have combined to make this such a popular region for trekking: Pokhara's accessibility to Kathmandu by road and air, the region's scenic majesty, and the area's well-established inns, run by Thakalis who hail from the region called Thakkhola in the Kali Gandaki, have all helped to ensure this trail's popularity. The inns en route are found in many villages between Pokhara and the ancient shrine of Muktinath a week's walk away. These inns, once traditional bhattis catering to the salt traders and other local travelers, have multiplied manyfold, been adapted to Western tastes, and are now called lodges.

The Kali Gandaki trail begins at the far end of Pokhara's Bagar Bazaar in the north end of town near the quonset huts of the former Shining Hospital (about 2,800 feet). Here, donkey caravans with jangling bells still enter town led by Thakalis or Loba clansmen from Mustang. Also you may see the porters, Sherpas, and *membaars* of a trekking group as they begin or end a trek. And something new has been added: a road. Now you can climb aboard a jammed, rickety vehicle and bounce along for an hour or so to the base of the hill beneath Naudanda. This ride saves you a half day of walking, but can leave you quite disheveled.

If you decide to begin the walk at Pokhara, the main trail leaves Bagar Bazaar through a gauntlet of look-alike shops, passes a new hydroelectric project, crosses to the north of the Yamdi Khola, then begins its long meander past rich rice fields. You'll pass a Tibetan camp, originally set up in the 1950s, where numerous Tibetans sell handicrafts from Kathmandu. Hyangja village spreads out for two miles, and at its end, you'll see the few houses and inns of Suikhet in the distance beyond hundreds of rice fields. Beyond Suikhet, you have two choices. You can stay on the main trail, which continues across the rice fields, then angles slightly south to Phedi. From Phedi (*phedi* means "base of the hill" in Nepali) you climb your first hill to Naudanda (4,700 feet), a ridge-straddling chain of homes and inns where there are stunning views of the Annapurna-Lamjung massif. An alternate route diverges northward near Phedi through the villages of Dhampus and Landrung to Ghandrung, about two full days' walk away. (See "Pokhara to Ghandrung," below.)

The Direct Trail to Ghorapani

From Naudanda (soon to be joined with Pokhara by a road) you need to stay along the crest of the ridgeline as you continue west. The trail proceeds along the denuded ridge gently up to the town of Khare, where you leave the Pokhara Valley. The path then drops slightly down from Khare and carries on to Lumle, where ex-Gurkha soldiers learn farming practices at a large British-operated agricultural farm east of town. West of Lumle and nearly level with it is Chandrakot ("Moon Town," 5,100 feet) with several inns and a sweeping prospect of green hills and scattered villages rising to meet Annapurna South (23,680 feet—now officially renamed Annapurna Dakshin, which means "south" in Nepali) and Hiunchuli (21,135 feet). The distinctive sharp double peak of Machhapuchhare ("The Fishtail," 22,940 feet) is easily seen from Chandrakot (at Pokhara the striking peak is a single symmetrical point). You can walk from Chandrakot to Ghandrung via a trail that heads north out of town and crosses the Modi Khola, then climbs the stone stairway to Ghandrung. But if you are coming from Pokhara, the Dhampus route is better, and if you are approaching from Ghorapani, the route through the forest direct to Ghandrung is more direct and loses much less elevation.

Below Chandrakot to the west you take a steep trail that will probably get the sweat flowing whether you are climbing or descending the hill. At the bottom and a few minutes downstream lies Birethanti (3,400 feet). This large bazaar town sits on the west bank of the Modi Khola, a glacier-spawned torrent that drains the peak-encircled Annapurna Sanctuary. From Birethanti you can walk a day north to the large Gurung town of Ghandrung, along a trail that initially follows the Modi Khola, then rises several thousand feet on wide stone stairways.

The main trail west of Birethanti roller-coasters along up the Bhurungdi Valley, rising 1,600 feet to Hille, then a bit more to Tirkhedhunga. Now the fun starts: get out a handkerchief, unfurl your umbrella, and begin the steep climb up to the clustered, slate-roofed town of Ulleri (6,800 feet), inhabited by the Magar clan (who comprise the largest percentage of overseas British Gurkha soldiers, the famous regiments that are slowly being disbanded). Take the climb one step at a time, keep a slow, steady pace, and you'll do just fine; it's much worse to hear about the walk than to actually do it. Ulleri is far cooler than Birethanti, and the views back toward Pokhara are great. Now you're more than halfway up to Ghorapani.

The path continues up, then contours past fields until it reaches the new settlement of Banthanti. Here the trail enters a forest that continues more or less all the way to the top of the pass. The only other settlement is the few teahouses of Nayathanti about midway up. Nayathanti means "New Place," but actually its teahouses predate Banthanti's larger settlement below. When I first passed this way in 1971, the forest was thick and overhung the path, so that any traveler would feel intimidated and small like a Hobbit, and be inclined to scurry along. The forest has been noticeably thinned out by woodcutters most of the way up, and the path is wider. But now the danger may be greater here and on the trail between Ghorapani and Ghandrung (described later on): individual trekkers have been forcibly robbed along these and other isolated forest trails. The number of incidents have been far fewer than what might take place in any medium-sized town in Europe or the United States, but in pacifistic Nepal, the rumors resulting from such incidents spread as they are passed on over time. Walk with a friend through these beautiful forests. You are much more likely to be pushed off the trail by a loaded mule: be sure to give these tractor-trailers of the Himalaya room to pass, for they don't step aside or slow down.

Once Ghorapani ("Horse Watering Place") consisted of a few bhattis not far below the pass on its eastern side. The old inns are still there, but many more are crammed into Ghorapani Deurali (*deurali* means "pass") at 9,600 feet. The pass used to be a lonely, forested ridge with a single *chautaara* (resting place) that surrounded a tree whose branches were draped with faded white prayer scarves. Now lodge upon lodge are crammed together here, and according to a recent study, Ghorapani is the secondmost impacted place in the Annapurna region (after the Annapurna Sanctuary). The sound of the woodsman's ax has rarely been absent from this once-quiet spot. Southwest of the pass and a forty-five-minute walk above is Poon Hill, named for Major Poon, a retired soldier who first built a trail up to and publicized this excellent viewing place. Now lodges have sprouted along the way up from the pass to Poon Hill, even though all their water must be hauled up. The alpenglow on the peaks is best seen in the evening from Poon Hill, which commands a sweeping view of the Great Himalaya Range from west of Dhaulagiri as far east as Manaslu.

From Pokhara to Ghandrung

You may want to walk past the large Gurung village of Ghandrung and visit the peak-encircled Annapurna Sanctuary, a ten- to fourteen-day round trip from Pokhara. Or you may want to add the walk to Ghandrung or the sanctuary to your trek to Ghorapani or the upper Kali Gandaki Valley (or all the way around Annapurna). The walk through Ghandrung involves about a day's more hiking time than the main trail to Ghorapani, but there is less altitude gain and loss along the way. To take this path, grab a vehicle or walk to Phedi as noted above. At Phedi you want to angle north several hundred yards across the stony valley floor to the point where a trail heads directly up from a rocky outcropping. At first you'll pass through a forest of sal trees, then on up across rice terracing (keep asking if you think you're off-route here). At the top of the hill you'll be at the eastern end of Dhampus (5,700 feet). Now you are one ridge to the north of Naudanda, a little higher than the main trail and closer to the mountains. At Dhampus take the main trail west past the scattered houses and lodges in town and continue on, angling up to the inns at Pothana. By now you're heading northward straight toward the high peaks, but they are out of sight through the foliage. The earth is red here, and the trail can be slippery. You'll always get a laugh from the locals if you say, "Raato maato, chhipalo baato" (literally, "red mud, slippery trail").

Up you go a bit till you reach a clearing where you cross the ridge you've been ascending. Then it's down steeply past some small inns and into the lush, terraced Modi Khola Valley. You want to continue northward here, so ask for the way to Landrung as the trail contours in and out of a tributary valley. Landrung (or Landruk, 5,400 feet) isn't much; have bhaat here, perhaps, and head for Ghandrung. This is easier said than done, for you have to descend 1,500 feet to the Modi Khola, then climb higher than Landrung up to the large stone houses of Ghandrung.

Ghandrung (or Ghandruk) is the second-largest Gurung town in Nepal (Siklis to the northeast of Pokhara is the largest), and it is a wealthy town, since many of its denizens have been employed by the British, Indian, or Nepali armies in the special Gurkha brigades. Ghandrung is also the project headquarters of the Annapurna Conservation Area. The town is in two clusters: the lower village essentially provides laborers and domestics for the upper town. Giving an exact elevation to Ghandrung is impossible, for even the higher town is scattered some 500 feet up and down the hillside. Nonetheless let's call Ghandrung 6,400 feet, a ballpark figure. Ghandrung's solid two- and three-story slate-roofed homes face stone courtyards with tall racks of drying ears of corn and nearby flagstone walkways. There are several lodges in town, particularly at the top of the main village. As you slowly walk upward, you'll catch repeated views of Annapurna South, Hiunchuli, and the top of Machhapuchhare, closer than you've seen them yet.

To the Annapurna Sanctuary

As you look to the north from Ghandrung, you can see the valley of the Modi Khola heading due north into an impossibly precipitous gorge between Hiunchuli and Machhapuchhare. Up this narrow canyon lies the area we now call the Annapurna Sanctuary (or Annapurna Deuthali in Nepali). Before 1956, no Westerner had ever walked up that gorge. Then in 1956, Col. James O. M. ("Jimmy") Roberts, who had long worked with British Gurkha troops and was reconnoitering Machhapuchhare for a forthcoming climbing expedition, went to Ghandrung and asked to buy food and hire porter-guides to take him up the valley. No one would assist him, as the sanctuary was sacred ground for the Gurungs. Finally at the last village of Chumro (or Chomrong), several men reluctantly agreed to guide the Angrezi, and Roberts became the first outsider to enter this remarkable area. On the way, in a narrow slot at a still-existing shrine, he had to leave fifty eggs behind, for eggs and meat were prohibited by the reigning local goddess. When Roberts reached the sanctuary, he was in a 3-by-5-mile pocket of three glaciers, encircled by nine icy summits higher than 21,000 feet. The tiny valley floor rarely receives more than seven hours of sunlight on a clear day, for the surrounding peaks all tower at least a mile and a half above. Ghoral, a wild goat smaller than the bharal, once roamed the high, grassy moraines between the glaciers and can still be seen if you are lucky.

Before you leave Ghandrung, be sure to ask locals and other trekkers about conditions on the trail to the sanctuary. Avalanches regularly sweep the narrow path in the gorge below the sanctuary and the lower parts of the sanctuary itself, especially in the spring and early summer. Early snows in the fall can close the trail, and people have often been trapped in the sanctuary for days at a time because of trails made impassable by snowfall or avalanches. Don't leave Ghandrung or Chomrong without being very alert to conditions up-valley. Allow yourself five to six days north of Ghandrung for a comfortable trip into and back from the sanctuary. And remember that you'll be walking on a path that is at times very narrow and slippery; a path where, in places, a wrong step could lead to a fatal fall into the mighty Modi.

To reach the Annapurna Sanctuary, walk out of Ghandrung, but stay level at first; don't take the upper trail (that leads toward Ghorapani). You'll angle up to the visible notch in the spur ahead of you, where there are teahouses, then drop down into the Kimrong Khola. From there it's up again, keeping to the east. This climb is one of the most relentless, least shady of the entire walk into the sanctuary. Now you descend to Chomrong (6,730 feet) as you enter the last major tributary valley of the Modi, a valley that drains the south face of Annapurna South. From this last village of Chomrong and above, Machhapuchhare clearly shows its twin peaks, looking exactly like a fishtail. Chomrong boasts a forest nursery, some offices connected with the Annapurna Conservation Area, a small electric system (established with the assistance of a Japanese taxi driver named Mr. Hiyashi, who lives here half the year), and a kerosene depot where stoves can be rented. (All trekkers must use kerosene stoves above Chomrong if cooking for themselves.) Chomrong is also the last place where you can purchase bulk foods for the trail.

Beyond Chomrong you soon round a spur and reenter the main gorge of the Modi Khola. Now you can see the Modi's vertical walls stretching ahead, and from various nearby viewpoints you can see the next two days' walk in front of you. Beyond Chomrong is Khuldi, the site of a former sheep-rearing station that is now the largest lodge en route to the sanctuary. The trail roller-coasters down through slabs of rock (be careful here), then up and down through extensive bamboo forests. This is the tricky kind of terrain where, to the eye, the valley doesn't appear to be gaining much altitude. Only when you have practically reached the sanctuary and look back can you see what your aching legs are already telling you: you've really come up thousands of feet.

Soon you'll enter the thick bamboo forest that continues on and off through the wet gorge. Bamboo is a major theme as you travel up the gorge. Everything is bamboo. The mats that form the walls and floors of the hotels, the dokos that the porters carry, the forest you walk through: it's all bamboo. Bamboo is also underfoot, usually lying aimed downhill. You need to be careful not to slip when walking over it, particularly when it is covered with a layer of snow.

At perhaps the most narrow passage in the gorge on the east side of the path and near a multistrand cascade of water is the small shrine to the local goddess, first built years ago by Gurung herders. Just a pile of stones, the shrine (called Panchenin Barha) is adorned with offerings of rhododendron flowers and *dhajo*, the red and white cloth ribbons that are traditional gifts to the goddess. Above this is Hinko (10,300 feet), the large rock overhang that used to be an isolated camping spot where rats scurried about at night. Now Hinko is another in a series of small inns (albeit a unique one due to its location beneath the rock) that stretch as far as Annapurna South Base Camp. Beyond Hinko, both before and after you reach the sanctuary, you encounter the worst avalanche-prone areas of the trek. The snow that avalanches comes from invisible slopes high above on Hiunchuli. If there is any snow avalanching at all, you must wait to cross these dangerous areas.

Finally you enter the sanctuary, walking between rocky ribs that descend sharply from either side of you. The chances are very good that all you'll see when you arrive is fog. The story of the sanctuary is often that of the high peaks playing hide-and-seek above and among the billowing clouds, which usually begin building up by midmorning, especially in the spring. Usually the clouds diminish by sunset, but the first clear view you have of the sanctuary may well be in the morning as you awake.

The first few stone lodges you see are those at Machhapuchhare Base Camp (12,150 feet). Here you are low down, but you have a spectacular view of the west face of Machhapuchhare. This is where Roberts set up his base camp for the first and only sanctioned expedition to Machhapuchhare in 1957. The attempt got to within a few hundred feet of the summit but was turned back by steep, icy slopes. Since then the peak has been declared off-limits to climbers, for it is a mountain sacred to the Gurungs. Note how far up you've come since leaving Chomrong. If you feel poorly, take it easy: you've gained elevation very rapidly the past two days.

The farthest most people go in the sanctuary is to Annapurna South Base Camp (13,550 feet), where the base camp for the successful 1970 British expedition was located. To reach this spot, walk westerly up the narrow gutter between the moraine of the Annapurna South Glacier and Hiunchuli. At any point you can walk up the grassy lateral moraine to the north for excellent views. Carry a copy of Chris Bonnington's *Annapurna South Face* for an excellent description of the 1970 expedition's climb of Annapurna's towering south face. People with adequate rations, technical experience, and climbing gear like to attempt 18,580-foot Tent Peak (its official name is now Tharpu Chuli) north of the Annapurna South Glacier. Most of us, however, are quite satisfied to enjoy the awesome views of the many encircling peaks from the top of the nearby moraine.

The Trail between Ghandrung and Ghorapani

A trail that was once an indistinct collection of forest paths between Ghandrung and Ghorapani Pass has become popular as an alternative to the well-used trail between Birethanti and Ghorapani. You should think carefully about taking this route if there has been much rain recently, for portions of the track follow mossy rocks that can be treacherously slippery and you can also have a dickens of a time with leeches. Further, it is not prudent to walk this trail alone. This route now has two settlements of new lodges along the way, and various other lone inns have sprung up en route at virtually every scenic viewpoint. You can make this lovely hike in either direction in one day, assuming you don't get off-route. But it is much simpler to walk from Ghorapani to Ghandrung, as the pass is 3,000 feet higher than the town of Ghandrung and consequently the path is easier going that way.

To continue in our westerly direction, however, the trail as it goes from Ghandrung to Ghorapani begins at the uppermost part of Ghandrung and heads northwesterly through the fields above the village. Take the upper trail as you leave the cultivated terraces. After you enter a mixed forest the trail drops to cross a stream, then steepens until you reach the first ridgeline. Here is the settlement of inns called Tadapani ("Far Water").

Then it's down and up through a dense forest where you'll pass one or two newly built lodges. The second settlement of small inns along the way is called Banthanti and is clustered in the forest with no views. Here you can stay or eat a meal before heading steeply uphill for a small inn and the pass named simply Deurali ("pass"!) on a trail that is narrow and sometimes extremely slippery. Leading west down from Deurali is a shortcut forest trail to Chitre on the main path west of Ghorapani. But most people climb the ridgeline south through a delightful rhododendron forest. At a meadow with spectacular views of the main range (and, yes, a new lodge) the path descends through forest to reach Ghorapani Deurali (Ghorapani Pass).

From Ghorapani to Muktinath

From the inns at Ghorapani Pass, the main trail leads into the tributary valley of the Ghar Khola, which takes you down to the Kali Gandaki River. When I first set off down the forested path into the green Kali Gandaki Valley, I knew I was entering the deepest valley in the world. And like many others, I could feel a magic about it all. The path descends through rhododendron and oak forest, gradually entering cultivated regions and passing through Chitre, Phalate, and the larger town of Sikha (circa 6,300 feet). You'll enjoy great views of Dhaulagiri as you proceed. To the right of and below Dhaulagiri's main peak is the icefall that will be directly above you in a couple of days' walk. Just north of the trail behind the water spout in Sikha is a level spur with a white temple dedicated to the goddess Sarasvati. Beyond the temple is a flat viewpoint where you can admire the Ghar Valley from its midpoint.

The town below Sikha is Ghara, and from this vicinity you can look up the Kali Gandaki Valley to see an overview of the way you'll be walking the next few days. Ahead on the trail is a rocky notch with a teahouse. At the notch you can first see a glimpse of the Kali Gandaki River itself. The air is warm and damper as you continue down, almost to the main river. To the south is a side trail leading to Beni, Kusma, and the lower route to Pokhara (or the way up the Mayagdi Valley discussed in "From Pokhara to Dhorpatan," below). Near this trail junction on the southern trail are hot springs, which are advertised with signs placed by local lodge owners. Most people cross the short suspension bridge over the Ghar Khola and head north to a larger suspension bridge over the Kali Gandaki River. The sheer, pointed peak you see framed by the valley walls to the north is Nilgiri South.

Just north of the large suspension bridge leading to the west side of the Kali Gandaki River is Tatopani (3,800 feet), a village with three clusters of houses. At the southern end of the northern group of lodges and stores in Tatopani are the hot springs that give the town its name. Pilgrims from India and Nepal on their way to the shrine at Muktinath pause to bathe away sins at the springs, while trekkers from many countries wash away earthly grime at the well-used, recently reconstructed basin of hot water. There are also smaller sources of hot water upstream along the riverbank that can be reached when the water level is low enough.

Tatopani with its tangerine trees and hot springs has been the land of
the lotus eaters ever since trekking began to get popular in the early 1970s.
I was told about Tatopani and one bhatti there in glowing terms in August
of 1967 by Jan Peiper, who had made the walk to Thakkhola. And the first
trekking guide of any sort that I'd ever seen, a Peace Corps informational
bulletin written in March 1967, also described the same inn, the house that
has become the Dhaulagiri Lodge. On a visit to the valley eleven years
after I had stayed at that lodge with two sisters and a cousin (my *teen
buyhini,* "three younger sisters"), I once again met the elder sister of the
family who owns the lodge. She had married, moved away, and was visiting
home. Full of nostalgia, I mentioned to her that I had slept in her family's
lodge eleven years before with my teen buyhini. Without missing a beat,
she pointed up to the third floor and said, "Yes. You and your sisters stayed
in that room."

Some people walk across the hills only as far as Tatopani, but there
are different and fascinating worlds to see up-valley. Not far beyond town,
notice the clear waters of the Miristi Khola entering the Kali Gandaki from
the east. A hydroelectric project is planned for this river, which cuts through
an impenetrable defile, draining the northern flanks of Annapurna I. Above
Tatopani, you'll stay on the western side of the narrow gorge as far as the
waterfall at Rukse Chhara. The main trail used to continue on the west
bank, but now it crosses the Kali Gandaki on a bridge across a narrow
abyss where the river has cut through solid rock. Soon you'll find yourself
climbing steeply out of the tropical world of rice fields and banana trees
into a narrow canyon. Look across to the western side of the gorge in the
narrowest part of the chasm and you can see the old trail cut out of the
sheer rock wall.

As you emerge from the most vertiginous part of the gorge, you begin
to enter an upper zone of long-needle pine forests in the lower reaches of
the area called Thakkhola. This region, which begins at the town of Ghasa
(6,600 feet), is populated by the industrious, congenial Thakali clan, once
the controlling power of the salt trade. Now, many Thakalis have left their
homeland to operate large businesses in Kathmandu, Pokhara, and Butwal,
while other clansmen run the best lodges along the Pokhara-to-Muktinath
trail. Thakali food is renowned across Nepal. Many miles to the west, at
Dipayal near Silgarhi, the busiest bhatti is a Thakali inn serving Thakali-
style food. In Ghasa you are still somewhat hemmed in, but as you climb
through the forest beyond, the valley opens out ahead of you. If the sky
is clear, as you round one ridge you'll begin to see Dhaulagiri and its icefall
high above.

A suspension bridge takes you across the Lete Khola. If you take the
side trail to the east at the inns just beyond the bridge, you can cross the
thundering Kali Gandaki River not far upstream and reach Chhoya village.
From Chhoya a rugged forest trail climbs steeply to cross a 14,500-foot
ridge on the tricky route to the North Annapurna Base Camp, near the
headwaters of the Miristi Khola. The ridge above Chhoya has become
known as the Pass of April 27, since the French expedition to Annapurna

in 1950 first went this way. To take this steep side route, you would need to hire a local from Chhoya (or possibly Lete) who knows the way, and of course you'll have to carry all of your supplies. People from Chhoya do know the path, for they graze their animals in the high grasslands on the upper ridge. The trek to the ridge will take about two days. Continuing down to North Annapurna Base Camp and back to Chhoya will involve up to six to seven days of hard walking. But if you go, you'll have incredible views of Annapurna and Dhaulagiri seen by one trekker in a thousand.

The last time I was in Lete, the following sign was posted:

HOLD ON TREKKERS!
It's a police stations. Please stop here
& ragister your name for your
Safetyness.

From Lete (8,200 feet) to Kalopani the trail levels out. Now you've finished all the climbing you'll do for a couple of days' walk. Along the path between these two villages, you have your best view of Annapurna I (from the main trail) on the entire trek. To the right of Annapurna is the striking peak appropriately called Fang (unclimbed until 1981 and now officially named Baraha Shikhar). At a bridge beyond Kalopani most people cross the river to the east bank. Just above this bridge the valley floor widens, and from here to Kagbeni (as far as you are allowed to travel along the river) the Kali Gandaki flows fairly level and is often braided, flowing through pebbles and sand. After hiccupping over a low spur, the main trail recrosses the river to the west bank on a long suspension bridge. Hereabouts the valley angles to the northeast, and you are in the low point between Dhaulagiri and Annapurna. The peaks are both over 26,500 feet high, 3½ miles above you on either side: the deepest valley on the face of the earth.

At the Ghatte Khola, the next large tributary, trails used by local herders diverge upward to meadows at 12,000 feet and higher. Near the northern extremity of these pastures is the lower terminus of the east Dhaulagiri icefall that you've seen off and on since Poon Hill. If you get near the icefall itself, be careful, because rocks carom off the steep glacier as it melts. You will need a local to guide you onto the right trail to the upper pastures, for the higher terrain is broken and you can end up in some strange culs-de-sac. This should be an overnight walk, for the way is steep. Often by the time you've gotten all the way up, the day's clouds will have arrived and visibility will be nil until late in the afternoon. But what a magnificent viewing place you'll have for the sunset on Annapurna.

Back on the Kali Gandaki trail, the west-bank route passes several interesting Thakali villages, including Khobang, the town you walk beneath, passing between logs that support the buildings above. Now you reach an area that has been electrified by a dam hidden on the east side of the valley across from the large town of Tukche. Poles carrying copper electric wires jut at crazy angles from the ground, and grinning, white-painted skulls on the poles warn you of danger. Tukche was once Thak-

khola's principal town, but many of the town's important families have
migrated to Pokhara or the terai. Still, you can see the large stone homes
with their wooden balconies and stay in one of these houses, many of
which have been transformed into lodges. The field at the north end of the
old town used to be the trading grounds, where the Tibetan wool and salt
were transshipped from yaks to other animals for the trip south.

From either Tukche or Marpha, the next main town beyond, you can
pick up high side routes to the west that follow herdsmen's trails. Assuming
you stay on course high on the ridge (easier in good weather) or go with
the guidance of a local (highly recommended), you will ultimately reach
the 17,000-foot Dhampus Pass. West of the pass is an upper basin aptly
dubbed Hidden Valley by Marcel Ichac during the French exploratory reconnaissance in 1950. Descend into this high valley only if you are well
supplied with food. If you reach Hidden Valley, you will be north of
Dhaulagiri and can try slogging up snowfields to reach French Col (17,500
feet) for a look-see at the Mayagdi Glacier. The walk up to French Col
from the north is nontechnical, but you *must* be experienced in glacier
walking to traverse the dangerous, heavily crevassed Mayagdi Glacier,
which descends south from French Col west of Dhaulagiri I.

North of Tukche on the southern outskirts of Marpha is His Majesty's
Government Agricultural Farm. This demonstration farm is run by Pasang
Khambache, who walked with David Snellgrove through Dolpo in 1956
and who subsequently studied viticulture in France. Pasang is Nepal's
Johnny Appleseed and Johnny Walker, and the ag farm has revolutionized
agriculture in Thakkhola and the villages to the north. Up and down the
valley, apple, peach, and apricot trees grow in former meadows or grain
fields. Until better transport out of the area is available, succulent apples
can be bought in season for a song because of overplanting. As a result
of the ag farm, people also raise cabbages, carrots, and other vegetables
to supplement their diets and sell to trekkers. Ag farm vegetables, when
available, are sold at an outlet on the main trail. And Marpha's world-class
brandies are served at the palace in Kathmandu. (Be careful of the brandy;
it's delicious but lethal.)

Beyond Marpha (8,760 feet) you emerge north of the Great Himalaya
Range. Within a few miles the forested landscape has become transformed
into a dry inner valley with scattered villages of flat-roofed homes adjacent
to fields of wheat and barley. Be prepared for the unusually strong wind
that is likely to blow either up- or down-valley between about 11 A.M. and
4 P.M. from Kalopani to Kagbeni (and north). This daily gale results from
unequal air pressure between the lowlands and the Tibetan plateau. You
will find yourself walking quite slowly unless the wind is at your back.

An often-discussed but rarely attempted high side trail is the route east
from Thini village (Thini is north from Marpha on a low ridge above the
east bank) that leads to a col overlooking Tilicho Lake, also called the
Great Ice Lake (16,140 feet). Note that this route may be restricted. You
should pack at least three days' food to reach the pass and return; take
even more rations if you plan to explore the high plateau beyond. The path

above Thini divides in several places, so you should take a porter-guide to keep you on the direct trail (the general rule of thumb is to take the higher path when the trail branches). The low point of the ridge (16,790 feet) is a technical glacial icefall, so instead you must scramble up a 1,500-foot scree slope to the north that reaches a higher but negotiable col. At the top you will have a spectacular view of Tilicho Lake and the Great Barrier (a long, high ridge ending in Nilgiri Peak) of Annapurna. Be sure to descend at the first sign of bad weather; if not, you could find yourself marooned for days near the lake.

The village of Dzong Sam (or Dzong Sarba) was misinterpreted as Jomosom by early surveyors, and so it retains that name today. With a paved airport, a large army post, bank, government offices, and new hotels, the dusty town (now a district headquarters) has rapidly grown, but it does not have the charm of other towns, like Marpha. However, from Jomosom there are excellent views southward to Nilgiri and the great Kali Gandaki gorge.

There are flights between Jomosom and Pokhara, but it is difficult to get a confirmed seat on these planes. If the weather is bad or the wind picks up early, the flights don't operate. It's best not to count on flying to

"Gurung Daai" and the "Cowboy" have reached the ridge overlooking Tilicho Lake. In the background rises the Great Barrier north of Annapurna Himal. (Photograph by Daniel Miller.)

or from Jomosom if you must be elsewhere in a day or two. The airport and new government offices are on the west side of the river, while the old town is on the east bank. North of Jomosom, trails divide: a difficult route west to Dolpo's restricted Barbung Valley from Dangar Dzong via Sangdak hooks up over the Mu La with trails noted in "From Jomosom to Tarakot," below; a large trail leads north to medieval Mustang; while to the east, a well-trodden path climbs to Muktinath and the Thorong La. These last two trails continue together up the east side of the valley for several miles to Eklaibhatti, noted below.

For years the rumor has circulated that Mustang will be derestricted. Presently, however, this intriguing, parched region that protrudes northward into Tibet will remain tantalizingly close but unreachable. If entry to Mustang is ever permitted, you will be able to hike about three days' distance from Jomosom, past villages with multistoried houses, forlorn monasteries, and crumbling castles, to reach Lo Monthang (12,400 feet), the walled capital of this once-autonomous kingdom. The most striking element of Mustang, as described by those who have been there, is its landscape: sandstone pillars rise near old moraines, and time and again the trail north angles up and down over barren, eroded ridges and high terraces. Mustang's pastel shadings—hues of red, yellow, sienna, tan, and gray—undergo dramatic changes in lighting throughout the day. On the Nyi La (12,600 feet), north of Geling and on the second day's walk from Jomosom, you cross the traditional boundary from the region called Baragaon into Mustang. At Tsarang and Gemi villages, tall castles remind you that, as in Ladakh, here you are in a region of Tibetan culture. If trekkers are ever allowed into this area, they will walk the shortest route to Lo Monthang and back. Perhaps you will seek out for yourself the small, unvisited villages and shrines off the main path, just as you can do now in the rest of the valley.

But back to what's possible. You should by no means consider a trek up the Kali Gandaki Valley complete until you visit Muktinath and the towns leading to it. There is yet another whole new world awaiting you north of Jomosom. From Marpha to Jomosom you've been in the small region called Panchgaon ("Five Villages") with its own local language and four subclans that are different from the four Thakali clans. As you walk north of Jomosom, you enter Baragaon ("Twelve Villages"). By a lone teahouse at a place aptly named Eklaibhatti ("One Inn"), 3 miles north of Jomosom on the east side of the river, the direct trail to Muktinath angles east up the hill.

North of Eklaibhatti and off the direct route to Muktinath (and as far north along the valley floor as you are permitted to walk) is the interesting town of Kagbeni (locally called Kak). In Kagbeni, like the other towns in Baragaon, you are in an area that is culturally and architecturally Tibetan. To see what houses are like hereabouts, see if the Red House Lodge is still operating and check in if so. Frescoes are painted on the walls of what is now a dormitory, and there is a private chapel with a large Buddha image. From the roof you can watch caravans pass on the main street below and look up toward Muktinath and the Thorong Pass above. A trail leads up to the east from the southern edge of Kagbeni and joins the main route to Muktinath a half hour above town in the midst of a flat plain.

As you climb above Eklaibhatti on the main track, walk slowly, for you will probably ascend nearly to 12,000 feet when you head up this side valley. Some distance along on this trail you will angle up and around a bend on the dusty, gravel path and see six scattered towns, like lost cities. These towns along the side valley leading to Muktinath and the Thorong Pass begin at 10,500 feet and extend up to Muktinath's small cluster of shrines at 12,400 feet. Here you are away from the strong winds in the main valley, and you'll be up higher, with correspondingly better views. You may wish to stay in the fortress town of Dzarkot, the second town you'll reach. The Himali Lodge there is run by a local family and has a passive solar heating arrangement designed by an American. Another half hour above Dzarkot is Ranipauwa, where there are several lodges, a check-post, and a large ancient *dharmsala,* or pilgrim's resthouse.

From Ranipauwa it is a twenty-minute walk up the wide trail to Muktinath past the king's helicopter pad (for the king visits Muktinath to perform puja rituals on auspicious occasions). Aside from Pashupatinath near Kathmandu, Muktinath is the most sacred place in Nepal for Hindus. To Tibetan-speakers, Muktinath is known as Chumik Gyatsa (Place of a Hundred Springs).

For us lay folk, at the shrine area there is an even-grander view of this side valley and the hills to the west that hide the inner Dolpo region. But do not confuse sanctity with splendor at Muktinath. The small pagoda-shaped Hindu temple dedicated to Vishnu is well maintained, along with the 108 brass water spouts in the shape of cows' heads behind it that pour the pure spring water. But some of the Buddhist temples nearby are badly in need of repair. The holiness of Muktinath dates from antiquity and arises from the small flames of natural gas within a small Nyingma Buddhist shrine on the south of the temple complex. Behind faded, low curtains is the flickering bluish glow of natural gas above a small rivulet of water, producing a "miracle" conjunction of fire, air, and water. Hindu sadhus (renunciate ascetics) are the only people now permitted to sleep at Muktinath. If you will be walking from Pokhara to Muktinath and returning to Pokhara, give yourself an absolute minimum of two weeks for the hike.

A prominent ridge several miles to the north (that reaches to 17,240 feet at its highest) is an excellent place to take a day hike. Technically the walk is in a restricted area, but the officials won't mind as long as you don't pass the night there. Carry water and lunch and be ready for windy weather as you head north across the valley. You'll go down to the stream below (and curse me if you don't find the small bridge), then head up through the town of Dzong, once the most important village in the area. Continue up above Dzong, then level off and gently ascend to the low point in the ridge that you could see from Dzarkot or Ranipauwa. En route you may be able to find ammonites (locally called *saligrams*) remaining from the era when this region lay on the floor of the Tethys Sea. Saligrams have important religious significance for Hindus, and these fossilized black rocks are displayed in temples as far away as Varanasi on the Ganges River. The best saligrams you're likely to see hereabouts will be sold by locals along the main trail. Standing on the windy low point of this ridge, you won't see much except the himals to the south (yes, that is Annapurna I peeking over the intervening ridges). What you really need to do is climb up to the west to get higher than the ridge to the north. A few hundred feet up, you'll begin to see the basin of upper Mustang. Keep going and you can see the entire Mustang basin with its many-hued pastel colors and wind-sculpted rock. If you walk along the northern branch of this high spur, you can eventually look down to the restricted villages of Thaiee below and Tsum Pak on the far side of the valley. Here you are high on a protruding spur in the midst of the valley, flying earthbound, and you have a spectacular view of the world's deepest gorge. If it is still early enough in the day, you can take an upper trail back by way of Muktinath for the sunset.

Above Muktinath to the east is the trail to the Manang region of the upper Marsyangdi Valley. In season there are now several small inns a long hour's walk above Muktinath at the base of the steep rise leading to the 17,770-foot Thorong La. Water is usually found not far from these inns. You can ask to have dinner cooked for you if someone is in at one of these modest establishments. Try some of their excellent rakshi to help put you to sleep if you will be heading across the pass. Get a very early start if you decide to cross the pass from this side. There are some good campsites about an hour's walk above the inns. Think of the pass as a parabolic curve, with the steepest part of the 4,500-foot climb first. The path levels off as you approach the top from either direction.

The Marsyangdi Valley

Most people walking around Annapurna begin by going up the Mars-yangdi Valley for the reasons noted at the beginning of the chapter. Trekkers often start at Dumre village (about 1,350 feet), roughly two hours' drive east of Pokhara on the Kathmandu-to-Pokhara road. But if the new unpaved road leading north from Dumre is dry enough, you will be able to get a lift as far as Turture, Bhote Odar, or farther. When completed, the road will reach the large district headquarters of Besisahar, and you'll be able to bounce along that far north in a vehicle.

But there are two other ways you can reach the trail up the Marsyangdi Valley. Each of these routes adds a day or two and a few hills to the trek, so don't try either way if it's too hot or you are in a hurry. The correct trail junctions along each of these routes are not easily discernible, so you should plan to keep asking directions, or go with a porter-guide. The first of these options begins with a bus ride from Kathmandu to the hill town of Gorkha. From the old palace above Gorkha, follow the ridge to the west down to the Darondi Khola. Then take the trail to the Luitel Bhanjang, which at about 2,300 feet is the lowest named pass I've heard of in the Himalaya. Continue through lowlands to Chepe Ghat near the mouth of the Chepe Khola. Cross this feeder river and continue on to Tarkughat, where you cross to the west bank of the Marsyangdi. Here, two days from Gorkha, you are a day's walk north of Dumre on the new road.

You can also reach the Marsyangdi trail at Khudi farther north, by walking from Begnas Tal, a short bus ride east of Pokhara. You'll walk along trails that rise and fall through the middle hills by a route passing along the Midam Khola and the bhatti at Baglung Pani. This route definitely requires asking directions or the assistance of a local who knows the way. The hilly, usually unshaded track should not be tried during hot weather. This hill path provides excellent views of Annapurna II and IV and of Lamjung Himal (22,740 feet).

However you begin the trek up the Marsyangdi Valley, prepare for hot going the first few days, carry an umbrella, and get early starts. As you proceed, you will have fine perspectives of Lamjung, Himalchuli (25,895 feet), and Bauda (21,890 feet). For the first couple of days, if you walk from Dumre, you cannot see a breach in the massifs between Lamjung and Manaslu.

A scenic side trek through wild country lasting three to five days (depending how far you go) can be taken out of the lower Marsyangdi Valley along Bara Pokhari Lekh, a spur of Himalchuli. Numerous trails lead onto the flank of this giant ridge, which is east of the Marsyangdi. The most direct route, from the south, branches off the valley trail at Phalesangu, where you can buy last-minute supplies. There is also a trail onto the lekh from Ngadi (see below) north of Bara Pokhari Lekh. The key to correct route finding along the numerous stock trails on this ridge is to go with a local who knows the paths, for no habitation on the lekh is permanent above about 7,500 feet. Most of the way you will be walking on the crest of the ridge, which makes water difficult to find. Bara Pokhari, at 10,200 feet, is a holy lake, a pond really, surrounded by rhododendrons and slowly filling in. The farther you proceed along this spectacular ridge, the closer you will be to Manaslu, Himalchuli, and Bauda Peak, the southern outlier. If you go before May, expect to encounter snow on the upper stretches, where Himalchuli's snowfields seem to lie barely an arm's length away.

From Phalesangu on the main Marsyangdi Valley trail, you can proceed north on either the east or west side of the river valley. The route on the eastern side is higher and slightly shorter, but it doesn't have much to recommend it. If you need any supplies aside from basic foods, Besisahar's large bazaar on the main west-bank route is the last place you can count on finding anything. Besisahar is the large district headquarters of Lamjung District. North of Besisahar is the impoverished town of Khudi, on the north bank of the Khudi Khola. A trail leads up the Khudi Khola to the large Gurung town of Ghanpokhara, high on the ridge to the west. Beyond Khudi the west-bank side trail crosses a long suspension bridge to rejoin the east-bank route at the small town of Bhulbhule (2,800 feet). The onomatopoeic word Bhulbhule means "a place where water bubbles up from the ground," and Bhulbhule's bubbling spring lies not far off the main trail. As you've been walking up the valley, you may have felt as if you are only approaching the mountains, but here at Bhulbhule the ridges finally close in about you. Himalchuli is the snow peak gleaming in the evening light up-valley from Bhulbhule.

An hour beyond Bhulbhule is the new trailside hamlet of small lodges at Ngadi. Dr. Harka Gurung, one of Nepal's most learned native sons, was born in the old town of Ngadi just above the main trail. His venerable mother proudly refers to her son as Harka Bahadur, affectionately calling him by his middle name, which means "the brave." Aama ("Mother") Gurung has reason to speak of her son with pride, for his books, particularly *Vignettes of Nepal,* reveal the remarkable breadth of his knowledge about his motherland.

North of Ngadi the path soon crosses a large tributary, circles a spur and climbs a terraced bowl to the ridge-straddling village of Bahun Danda ("Brahmin Hill") with its checkpost, stores, tailor shop, and shady square. North of Bahun Danda, corn begins to replace rice cultivation, and numerous waterfalls drain unseen snows. Now you enter the narrow Marsyangdi gorge for more than a day's walk. There are inns along the way, but they are often spaced more than an hour apart in this deep canyon. Decent lodges are located at Syange and Tal (5,600 feet). Tal is a pleasant, flat location by a waterfall; a few years ago there was only one house in Tal, but now several large lodges have been built. By now you've ascended past the humid lower regions, and the confining lower gorge is behind you. A new landslide north of Tal brought on by heavy late rains in 1985 caused fatalities, and the trail has been diverted to the west bank for some distance.

North of Tal you will see a few houses in the high notch directly above the east bank of the trail. This is a Gurung hamlet, and from it there must be a trail up the intriguing steep side valley to the east that you see on your map. A Sherpa sirdar I trekked with reported that the side track is small, leading up notched logs at times to the high lake shown on the map. Perhaps one or two intrepid souls among you will try that high side path. It is only one of many byways that may come to mind as you peruse map and countryside. Wouldn't it be fun to get off the main trail for a few days and explore a byway? Trekking is far more than just getting from point A to point B.

The next large settlement beyond Tal, the town of Dharapani, is named for a *dhara,* a spout of spring water that long ago disappeared beneath a landslide. Across the valley from Dharapani is the narrow gorge of the Dudh Khola, a large tributary valley discussed in Chapter 6 (see "The Dudh Khola"). At the Dudh Khola confluence the Marsyangdi Valley turns westward, now north of the Annapurna-Lamjung massif of the main Himalaya range. The dense mixed forest blends into stands of pure conifers beyond Bagarchap village, where the valley's lowest gomba is situated. When I first passed through Bagarchap, the town had one small bhatti. Now the burgeoning village has several stores and lodges and even a brewery.

Beyond Bagarchap the narrow gorge is a pine-carpeted delight, with the river thrashing below. You'll walk through a section of trail that has been blasted out of solid rock, and hereabouts there are good views of

Manaslu back down-valley to the east. This new section of trail has been made to avoid the 1,000-foot climb to Timung, an upper grazing area (where yogurt is often available). Above Timung is the now-unused trail to the difficult high pass called the Namun Bhanjang. Formerly the steep, jungly trail over the Namun was the only route from the south into the upper Marsyangdi Valley during most seasons of the year, because the old path up the Marsyangdi gorge was so dangerous, but today's trail up the valley is the result of much labor and dynamite. Ahead, on the main trail, a waterfall of crystal-clear water pummels large boulders in an area of thick forest. Unfortunately, in several places, particularly near Chame up-valley, trees have been cut indiscriminately. Several new inns at Lata Marang have been built to take advantage of the hot water issuing forth on the far side of the river. Some distance along, near a large spring at a place called Khupar, are a checkpost and several inns. Here you are likely to meet denizens of the Nar Valley.

Across the valley from the checkpost is the narrow entrance to the forbidden Nar Valley, flanked on both sides by vertical rock walls. Nar is a quintessential hidden valley, restricted to the point of having a checkpost here where the Nar Khola issues into the Marsyangdi. Although the valley is currently off-limits, we know that trails enter it from several directions: over a pass reached from Ghyaru village up-valley; from Tange in Mustang over the Mustang La, a difficult pass that is well described by H. W. Tilman in *Nepal Himalaya* but which is probably now unused; over a pass leading from Tibet; and directly from a trail along the valley floor that is said to cross the Nar River fifteen times. Only two villages exist in this valley: Nar Ma ("Lower Nar"), above terraced fields, and Phu, wedged atop an eroded, scalloped promontory. The people of Nar and Phu are of Tibetan descent, and their primary occupations are growing buckwheat, barley, and potatoes; herding; and preparing yak butter to trade. Like Dolpo, Nar and Phu are places far removed from time. If you can locate it, *Cloud-Dwellers of the Himalayas,* by Windsor Chorlton, is an excellent combination of writing and photography about the people who live in this valley.

Not far beyond Khupar lies Chame (8,710 feet), the Manang district headquarters, with its jumble of offices and a bank guarded by a sentry who packs a shotgun. Chame now has electricity, and electric wires run helter-skelter all over town. There is even an Indian-style sweet shop in town. Fluted Annapurna II is the peak you have been seeing high above to the west. Across from town on the north bank of the main river are some hot springs, but their flow has diminished over the years. The trail above Chame continues in and out of forest on the north side of the river and goes by a large walled-in orchard. Here are the last inns you are likely to pass until you reach Pisang. At the west end of the orchard the path used to cross to the south side of the river to a former Tibetan Khampa settlement called Brathang. Now, however, the trail continues on the north bank through a large cut that was hammered and blasted out of the 2,000-foot-high solid rock face, a project that took years to complete. The path crosses the river and rises through a lovely pine forest. You'll pass small, ancient stone memorials built by people from the upper valley when they left home to go on their long overseas trading excursions. Look back as you contour through the forest. You'll begin to see a wide, smooth stone slab that descends thousands of feet on the northern side of the valley. Soon a wall of prayer stones appears, and a panorama of the 15-mile-long upper-valley floor opens out.

Here you enter the wide, dry upper valley that is known locally as Nyeshang but has come to be called Manang. (Strictly speaking, Manang is only the largest village in Nyeshang.) Since 1790, Nyeshangpas, as the locals are called, have been granted special international trading privileges not available to other Nepalis by the king of Nepal. Bell bottoms, large portable cassette-player radios, and golf hats emblazoned with "Thailand" are de rigueur for many. Many of the upper valley's inhabitants now live in Kathmandu, and some have opened hotels in the Thamel and Chhetrapati areas. Local schlockmeisters set out their goods by the trail or come to your camp bringing gemstones and other merchandise from Burma and Bangkok, along with a few, very few, local wares.

Ahead lies the two-part village of Pisang. Most locals live in the upper clustered village north of the river (10,800 feet), but now several families have moved down by the main trail and built lodges there. Be sure to walk up to the old village with its flat-roofed houses, typical of all upper-valley homes. Block-printed prayer flags attached to poles slap in the afternoon breezes as they do from the roofs in the rest of the villages above. The view of Annapurna II to the south is far more dramatic than from the trail below. Once, while visiting the upper village, an avalanche thundered down the slopes of this steep mountain, miles away across the valley. I noticed a few villagers scurrying about and heard some doors close, but didn't think much of it. Minutes later a frigid wind whooshed through town carrying stinging ice particles.

From Pisang, you can carry on along the main trail that hiccups over a narrow spur of Annapurna II and continues along the flat, U-shaped valley bottom past the rarely used airfield at Ongre and by a checkpost. The path passes a large cirque to the south and soon crosses the river to the north bank, where it remains. A longer and higher alternative route that passes through the villages of Ghyaru and Ngawal is one you should definitely consider, however. To reach this side trail, cross the bridge leading to Pisang and take the trail to the west along the fields just above the river. Soon you'll enter a scrub forest and pass a small emerald green lake. Ahead is an old prayer wall and just beyond that a small stream. On the far side of the stream, take the steeper trail that zigzags straight up the hill some 1,200 feet to Ghyaru. Now you are in traditional Nyeshang. Probably no one will know any English, and people speak the local dialect of Tibetan. Their spoken Nepali may not be much better than yours. Saunter around town, and if it's autumn, you'll probably see locals lined up in the squares, thrashing barley with wooden and leather flails.

Walk out of Ghyaru beneath the entranceway and head west. Above town is the high trail to forbidden Nar. High up, east of town, is Pisang

Peak, a steep but nontechnical peak of 19,945 feet in elevation (ice ax, crampons, and some climbing experience are minimal requirements for attempting this peak). As you walk along the trail far above the valley floor, you'll enjoy stunning views of Nyeshang below and, to the south, the Annapurna Himal plummeting directly to the valley floor. Back to the east is the smooth rock bowl you began to see as you climbed up into Nyeshang; ahead to the west are your first views of the Great Barrier above hidden Tilicho Lake. The high point at the end of the Great Barrier is Tilicho Peak. You'll contour in and out, crossing spurs, and reach Ngawal, the second town on this upper route. Do you know the Ngawal View Hotel near Chhetrapati in Kathmandu? Its well-known former owner, an engaging but notorious smuggler, came from this village. People may offer you tea in these towns, but you might be better advised to stick to your iodine water from the water bottle (cleaning glasses is not a fine art hereabouts). The snow peaks to the north are Chulu West and Chulu East, both above 20,000 feet. Beyond Ngawal the trail dips down to cross a stream, then angles out to a point. Not far beyond this place, take the smaller, upper path at a trail junction. If you continue down, you'll end up at the airfield directly below, whereas the upper trail here will carry you along up the valley. You will rejoin the main trail not far east of Braga.

Braga is one of the most picturesque towns in this upper valley. The town lies tucked back just off the main trail above a meadow and beneath carved sandstone walls. It has two temples on the west side of the village: the upper gomba resembles a white wedding cake; the other temple contains a unique double row of images, each nearly two feet high, that extend around the four walls and portray the entire lineage of the Kagyupa sect. For several years Braga quietly resisted the increasing flow of foreigners who traipsed by. At first no signs advertising lodging were hung in front of homes, and trekkers usually proceeded to inns in Manang village not far up the valley. Now, however, new buildings have been constructed on the east side of Braga, and these homes have signs proclaiming themselves to be lodges. As recently as the 1950s, villagers from Braga and Manang fought pitched battles with each other. David Snellgrove was relieved to learn that a truce had just been declared when he passed through in 1956.

The town of Manang (11,600 feet) with its large gomba is the penultimate village on the principal trail. Unlike Braga, the villagers in Manang have never been hesitant about catering to tourists. Signs line the village, and there are several stores. One store does a good business selling Tibetan-style hats of fox or sheep fur. The Himalayan Rescue Association (HRA) has a clinic here. This fine organization also has an older clinic in the settlement of Periche in Khumbu. The Manang clinic is staffed with a physician (and often a nurse also) during the spring and fall trekking seasons, and of course villagers as well as trekkers are treated. You should plan to take a rest day in either Braga or Manang to assist in acclimatization for the 17,770-foot Thorong La ahead if you will be crossing to the Kali Gandaki Valley. During your rest day, you can take it easy or walk back to Braga from Manang, visit Manang's gomba, the glacial lake south of town, or take a walk of several hours to Khangsar village. To reach Khangsar from Manang village, walk down to the river and cross it to the south. Stay low near the river and recross it on a bridge some distance up-valley above the fork in the river. Khangsar (circa 12,100 feet) is the highest permanently inhabited village in the valley, and like other villages off the main trail, it doesn't see many foreigners. Above and to the west lies Tilicho Lake at 16,400 feet, but the trail up to Tilicho is not obvious. If you want to try the scree-covered walk to the lake, you should go with someone from Khangsar and plan to camp near the lake or at the high point east of it.

As you leave Manang village, you get a better view of the large and often-noisy glacial icefall across the valley on Gangapurna. To the west lie the Great Barrier and Tilicho Peak, which are also visible from down-valley and from the Kali Gandaki side. Beyond Tengi, the last village en route in this valley, the trail bends northward, at first rising well above the Jhargeng Khola, the smaller branch of the river that you have been following. Keep looking around when ascending this valley, for you may sight the small local herd of bharal (blue sheep, locally called *nah*). Not many years ago they slept just a couple of hundred yards above our group's camping spot. The path is not steep to Phedi at the base of the pass, but the walk does continue for some distance. Along most of this route you have fine vistas of Gangapurna and Annapurna III. You should think in terms of walking slowly from Manang village only as far as Leder (13,700 feet) in one day, then walking the final three or four hours from Leder to Phedi (14,450 feet) the next day. The better-run trekking groups do this. During the trekking season there will be food and accommodation available in Leder. You can make the long walk from Manang to Phedi in a full day, but you should be well acclimatized and in good shape to do so. If you have brought a tent, camp at the bottomland at Phedi and avoid the crowded inn above.

On a shelf a few minutes above Phedi is an inn (14,650 feet) where "fooding and lodging" (as it is often put) are available. There is a small trickle of water just below the inn, but this source is surely contaminated; use your iodine. The inn at Phedi will not be a high point of the trek if you are without shelter and need to stay inside. The place is usually crowded during the spring and especially the fall trekking seasons. Unfortunately some people think that the secret to successfully climbing the pass is to start walking at 3 or 4 A.M. If any of these ill-advised souls are present, they may wake you as they arise. It is dark and cold at night; the best plan is to leave about dawn. Few trekkers have difficulty with the pass if they are well hydrated, well fed, and well rested. Danger signals are walking hard from Manang to Phedi, not drinking enough liquids, feeling tired at Phedi, but continuing over the pass the next day. If you are experiencing any symptoms of altitude sickness (see Chapter 12, "A Himalayan Medical Primer") at Phedi, think about returning to Leder for the night, then coming up to Phedi again. Figure that the walk from Phedi to Muktinath will take from eight to twelve hours. It's better to wait a day than to attempt the pass in uncertain weather.

The steepest section of the 3,200-foot climb from Phedi to the Thorong La is encountered at the outset, but you are compensated for its difficulty by the ethereal sights that emerge as you rise. Twin 21,270-foot peaks flanking the pass come into view, and simultaneously you have your last glimpses of the Annapurna summits that have been familiar sights for days. The official new names for the peaks on either side of the pass are Yakawa Kang, to the north, and Khatung Kang, to the south (*kang* means "mountain" in Tibetan). The last part of the climb is the gentlest, just like the descent on the west side. When you come to the area where you are right between the peaks, you'll be at the pass. Some years the pass is snowed in by late November. The level, 17,770-foot Thorong La is often swept by penetrating winds, but pause as you cross long enough to toss a stone onto the large cairn, to propitiate the gods.

For the continuation of this walk down the Kali Gandaki Valley toward Pokhara, see "From Ghorapani to Muktinath," above, and follow the route description in reverse. If you plan to walk from the trailhead on the Marsyangdi River to Manang village, then return, you should give yourself at least two weeks to comfortably ascend the valley and return. Allow more days if you plan side trips or a little less time if you are able to ride as far as Besisahar.

Around Dhaulagiri

Just west of Annapurna is the 40-mile-wide Dhaulagiri Himal. Dhaulagiri I, the sixth-tallest peak in the world, towers high above the well-trekked Muktinath pilgrim trail up the Kali Gandaki Valley. The vast massif screens the hidden lands of Dolpo to its north, and to the west of it are Nepal's far western hills. Only to the east along the Kali Gandaki Valley can we easily view the mountain close up, so massive Dhaulagiri with its symmetrical peak and four major outliers remains an enigma along much of its perimeter. Like fabled but restricted Dolpo, the complete month-long trek around Dhaulagiri is only for a handful of hikers. This is because much of the route traverses difficult, remote country and because the trails to the north and west, from Kagbeni to Tarakot and Dhorpatan, are technically forbidden. However, as with other such areas, I will note the restricted part of the route as well.

Let's briefly look at the route around Dhaulagiri, proceeding counterclockwise from Pokhara. The first part of the walk is the easiest: the way leads on well-trekked trails from Pokhara to the Kali Gandaki Valley and up the main path as far as Jomosom. After Dangar Dzong near Jomosom you enter the restricted regions and head west up the forbidding Keha Lungpa gorge, crossing two high passes. Then you descend along the Barbung Valley to Tarakot and head southerly to Dhorpatan, traversing high grazing pastures and rough ridge-and-valley terrain. From Dhorpatan the route leads east over the Jaljala Pass and down the Mayagdi Valley to the large town of Beni. At Beni you have a choice of routes back to Pokhara.

Because portions of the walk around Dhaulagiri have already been covered in earlier sections of this book, the route descriptions will not be presented in a continuous counterclockwise sequence here. Instead, it may be helpful to visualize the route in two arms, each starting from Pokhara and heading around Dhaulagiri in opposite directions. One arm goes west through Beni and south of Dhaulagiri in a clockwise direction as far as Dhorpatan. The other arm goes west as far as Naudanda and Ghorapani, then north up the Kali Gandaki Valley to Jomosom, then west and around Dhaulagiri in a counterclockwise direction to Tarakot, and, finally, south to Dhorpatan.

The clockwise arm of the route is covered below under "From Pokhara to Dhorpatan." The counterclockwise arm is covered in five sections: (1) The walk from Pokhara to Naudanda is described in the beginning of "From Pokhara to Muktinath: Up the Kali Gandaki Valley," earlier in this chapter. (2) The route from Naudanda to Ghorapani continues under "The Direct Trail to Ghorapani," above. (3) From Ghorapani to Jomosom is described under "From Ghorapani to Muktinath," above. (4) "From Jomosom to Tarakot," below, covers the next portion of this counterclockwise circuit. (5) The final portion of this arm, the path from Tarakot to Dhorpatan, is noted in the last paragraph of "The Route East from Jumla to Dhorpatan" in Chapter 4.

From Pokhara to Dhorpatan

Several trails from the Pokhara vicinity lead to Beni at the junction of the Mayagdi Khola with the Kali Gandaki Valley. You will have to pass through Beni's large bazaar to reach Dhorpatan and the high, roller-coaster track to Tarakot. For the southerly route to Beni (all of which is quite hot between April and October), take a bus or taxi south from Pokhara to the roadside bazaar of Naudanda. From there, follow the well-used track west up to the Andhi Khola to the large ridgetop bazaar of Karkineta (5,500 feet). At Karkineta, with its sweeping views and Nepali-style bhattis, descend to the Modi Khola by angling northwestward down the Malyangdi Khola. Ask for the trail to Kusma at or near trail junctions, for there are many paths hereabouts. From Kusma, high above the west bank of the Modi Khola, continue through warm country on the left bank of the Kali Gandaki River past a bridge leading to Baglung. Climb up to Baglung's large bazaar only if you desire lodging or supplies; otherwise continue on by the river to a suspension bridge near Beni. An alternate and slightly longer way to reach Beni is by following the main trail out of Pokhara toward Tatopani as far as Birethanti (see "The Direct Trail to Ghorapani," above), then walking south to Kusma and on to Beni. Another route to the Modi Khola and Kusma angles south from the main trail from Pokhara just west of Naudanda.

At Beni (2,200 feet) the trail to Dhorpatan heads west along the low, green valley bottom of the Mayagdi Khola to Darbang. During two months of trekking in western Nepal in 1974, Darbang's stores were the largest I came across. If you head up-valley to Darbang from the fleshpots of Pokhara and Beni, however, you will not likely be as impressed. Just above

Darbang, cross a bridge to the right bank, where after crossing a tributary several miles upstream, you will rise on switchbacks up a jagged ridge through long-needle pines to Tarapani village. Keep on the trail high above and west of the main river through several villages to Muna, where the valley turns to the west. On a clear day along this stretch, you will enjoy views of Churen Himal and Dhaulagiri I, II, and III (the latter three all higher than 25,000 feet). Muna is a large village, and there is a store in town. If you carry ropes and ice axes and have experience on crevassed glaciers, you may wish to take the rarely used path north up the Mayagdi Valley and attempt the Mayagdi Glacier to French Col just west of and beneath the summit of Dhaulagiri (French Col is noted under "From Ghorapani to Muktinath," above).

On the trail to Dhorpatan, head west from Muna, then drop to cross the Dara Khola (the main river) and pass through Lumsum. Beyond Lumsum you recross the river to the south bank. Here most habitation is left behind, and you begin the steep ascent through buckwheat fields, then a pine and rhododendron forest to Jaljala Pass (about 11,100 feet). A camp near the high point is definitely recommended, for the views of both the Dhaulagiri and Annapurna himals are spectacular from here. There is a small stream not far from the pass on the east side where you can obtain water. This pass is a high ridge, and not far to the west you cross a slight rise that marks the actual divide between the Kali Gandaki and the Karnali watersheds.

West of Jaljala, a gentle but long half-day's walk through enchanting meadow and forest takes you to the several clusters of stolid houses collectively known as Dhorpatan. Not far east of Dhorpatan is a Bon Po gomba north of the trail. One house in the western part of this spread-out town has numerous food supplies available. On my second trip through Dhorpatan, our porter Danu bought grains, cooking oil, and kerosene here from a friendly young Tibetan chap with a pudding bowl haircut. Mastiff puppies licked dry tsampa from a plate underfoot, and their nearby mother, pulling at her chain, barked incessantly. Dhorpatan is in a wide, flat valley where horses graze for three seasons of the year on endless meadows. A rarely used airstrip lies west of town. Here you are approximately six days' walk from Pokhara. West of Dhorpatan is the Uttar Ganga River valley, the route you can take to the Sano Bheri River trail, the large town of Jajarkot, and the southerly route to Jumla.

From Jomosom to Tarakot

Once it is derestricted, the following route should be considered only by experienced trekkers, for beyond Dangar Dzong near Jomosom, you will be in rugged, high terrain with virtually no chance to replenish supplies. The approach for circling north of Dhaulagiri is from the upper Kali Gandaki Valley. Following the route described in "From Ghorapani to Muktinath," above, trek to Jomosom and walk 5 miles north to Dangar Dzong village, which sits above and hidden from the river's west bank. From the tightly packed houses of Dangar Dzong, the trail angles up to a

14,100-foot ridgeline. At this waterless vantage point you have excellent views toward Mustang, Muktinath, and the Annapurna Himal. The path then continues in a westerly direction, into the rugged gorge of the Keha (or Cha) Lungpa and toward Sangdak, a route that should not be attempted without a local who knows the trail.

From the village of Sangdak in the Keha Lungpa gorge, your guide will lead you either by the gorge route or by the high trail toward the wide, flat, 16,810-foot (unnamed) pass at the head of the Keha Lungpa's gray, impossibly convoluted valley. But this is only the first divide to be crossed. Another pass, the 18,200-foot Mu La, leads you to a tributary of the Mukut Khola. Of the few people who have taken this route, most have had to camp between the two passes, for it is too far to cross both in one day. The weather can be fickle: Christian Kleinert (who wrote *Nepal Trekking*) told Chris Wriggins and me of crossing the Mu La two years in a row on the same date, April 19. The first year a flash blizzard swept his camp; the next April, fields of wildflowers smiled beneath a deep blue sky.

The territory between Sangdak village and Dzong and Drikung villages in the Tarakot area (about a week's walk) is considered part of Dolpo. In this desiccated country, yak dung fires urged on with leather bellows have traditionally sustained life. West of the Mu La lies Mukut village. Downstream, the Mukut Khola joins the upper Bheri River, here called the Barbung. Descending the Barbung for several days from Mukut takes you to the Tarakot area, where you can connect with either the trail south to Dhorpatan crossing the Jang La or the path west to Jumla. Expect that the trek from Jomosom to Tarakot will require a week; the entire circle of Dhaulagiri will take a minimum of four weeks from Pokhara and back again. But what a remarkable trek this is. You leave the green lowlands for deep gorges and remote fortress villages recalling Tibet of a century ago, then walk once more into the tropics.

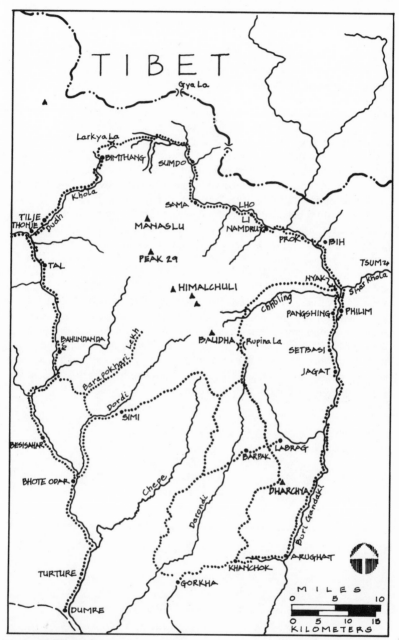

Around Manaslu

6

The Manaslu Region, Langtang, and Helambu

Don't look up until you see down.
Alden Orput, 1983 (on climbing passes)

To the Rupina La

The Manaslu Himal (26,640 feet) is the world's ninth-tallest peak. It rises above central Nepal's Mahabharat Range just to the east of Annapurna, its better-known neighbor, separated only by the Marsyangdi Valley. In many ways the two wide massifs are quite similar, for Manaslu is just 100 feet taller than Annapurna. Each mountain has Gurung villages perched among the hills near its southern base, and each has populated inner valleys to the north that are reached by rivers curling around the peak from the east. These inner valleys are connected north of each massif by a pass over 17,000 feet high. And near the eastern extremity of each himal, a high pass leads toward the inner valley north of the massif. The difficult Namun Bhanjang (circa 18,050 feet) is the pass near Lamjung Himal, on Annapurna's eastern flank. Just to the east of Baudha Peak, Manaslu's easternmost outlier, lies the negotiable Rupina La (circa 15,100 feet).

The trailhead for the route to the Rupina La, a ridge walk that passes through unrestricted terrain, is the town of Gorkha, now connected with Kathmandu by a good road. You can take a crowded bus to Gorkha from Kathmandu's main bus station on the eastern side of the Tundikhel. Alternatively, you might consider going by taxi or renting a vehicle (most easily done through a trekking outfitter or travel agent). Either in Kathmandu through an outfitter, or at Gorkha by asking around, you would be well advised to hire a porter who can also act as guide.

The route from the roadhead at Gorkha Bazaar leads steeply up the hill to the north where the large palace or *durbar* (5,080 feet) built by Prithvinarayan Shah is located. From this hilltop sanctuary, Prithvinarayan Shah built up an army in the mid-eighteenth century that was ultimately able to conquer the many small kingdoms making up the area we know today as Nepal. To this day the Shah dynasty rules the Kingdom of Nepal. The durbar is guarded by soldiers; under no circumstances will you be allowed to enter the inner courtyard, but you can walk around most of the perimeter and enjoy the excellent views. Hopefully you will not arrive at the durbar as I did, right after the Desai holiday. Many water buffaloes are sacrificed then, and the area outside the building reeks of dried blood. The many palm trees around the northern base of the palace were planted by Prithvinarayan Shah to hold the palace in place by their large root systems. The durbar, like the holy temple at Pashupatinath near Kathmandu, is under the guardianship of a special order of men and women called Kanpat Yogis. *Kanpat* means "split ear," and Kanpat Yogis are readily distinguishable by the ochre-colored cloth they wear, the metal whistle hung around the neck, and the thick, round earring that pierces the middle of one or both ears. After a novice has completed his or her apprenticeship, the guru gives the earring that will remain for the rest of the yogi's life. If you are here at the durbar about sunset, you can observe one of the Kanpat Yogis doing a daily bell-ringing puja ceremony at a small cave just south of and below the main palace. This sacred cave was formerly occupied by Goraknath, the founder of the Kanpat order.

After leaving the durbar at Gorkha, the path at first drops down on the northern side of the ridge, then heads up and down to the northeast, generally following the ridgeline. You are walking through terraced hillsides in an area populated by Brahmins and Chhetris. Ask for Khanchok Bhanjang as you proceed. Khanchok (3,600 feet) is the low point on the walk to the Rupina La. From here you will follow a trail to the north that continues along the undulating but rising ridgeline. A half day beyond Khanchok is a small *mandir*, a temple in a lovely grove of chir pine on a round hilltop. A short day north of this grove is the last small collection of stores. All about, the terraces of rice and millet are emerald green. To the west you have ever-changing perspectives of the Annapurna-Lamjung Himal, while ahead is Baudha Peak, and to the east lies Ganesh Himal.

To the north, you have been approaching a 10,000-foot high prominence called Dharchya on the maps. The trail ahead climbs almost to the top of this vantage point, where the locals have made temporary shelters used during the summer grazing season. Imagine the leeches that must be here then! To find water, you'll have to drop down into the forest to the north. Now you have left the midlands behind and are proceeding down through an idyllic rhododendron forest to meadows interspersed with forest. Himalchuli is off to the northwest, and straight north is the Rupina La, the low point in the snow-covered ridge. A half day north of Dharchya a wide path crosses the ridge you are following. Taken to the west, this cross-trail leads you down to the large, prosperous Gurung village of Barpak. To the east, you drop more steeply on stone steps to the clustered town of Labrag. Many potatoes are grown in Labrag; if you come up in the fall (the best time for this trek), you will meet people carrying heavy loads of potatoes south. Barpak is reminiscent of the wealthy Gurung villages north of the Pokhara Valley. Many of its sons become Gurkha soldiers, while fewer people from Labrag achieve this well-paying position. Farther east, in the Gurung villages around a few more ridges up the Buri Gandaki Valley, no one gets into the army, and the towns are jungly and primitive.

Beyond this trail crossing, the route to the Rupina La continues on the ridge for another half day's walk. Then you follow a trail that angles to the west, into the Darondi Valley. You are beyond all habitation now, and a local is essential for route finding. The forest you walk through is primeval, with black moss peeling off tree tunks like spent snake skin and filigrees of light reaching the thick undergrowth.

As you reach the stream that is the upper headwaters of the Darondi Khola, you might like to camp in the last grove of conifers. There are fallen branches for a fire and some almost-level places to pitch a tent. From here you can walk to the Rupina La and back in a day. It is also possible to cross the pass if you are carrying food for several days. The trail up is faint or nonexistent in spots, but be persistent and you'll find it. Above the trees, the path first follows the narrow valley bottom on the west side of the stream. When you reach a place where rock walls rise steeply on all sides, look slightly back for a grassy slope on the west. You can make out a small path angling steeply up this slope. This steep grade continues past a pasture camp and onto a ridgeline to the north. You may have to look a bit, but you'll find a way up that finally leads over a rock-covered slope to the cairn-topped pass. From Gorkha it should take you about six days of walking to reach the pass. Most of this time you will need to carry your own food.

North of the pass you'll see snowy eastern outliers of Himalchuli and glaciers that descend from them to the upper valley floor below. You can continue down the north side of the pass. This slope is not particularly steep, but it may be snow covered and slippery. I have talked to people who have said there is a rarely used nontechnical route that follows a high contour on the northern side of this valley. At one point in the middle of the route there is a cave that can be slept in. Maps call this the Chhuling Valley, and it debouches into the Buri Gandaki Valley not far south of Nyak. The high trail out of the valley leads to Nyak village.

If you return south from the Rupina La, you can continue contouring to the west on high ridges south of Baudha Peak. The first ridge west of the Darondi Valley is called Topche Danda. High on this ridge is a lake called Dudh Pokhari ("Milk Lake"). Be ready to climb to 15,000 feet, at least as high as the Rupina La, before you can expect to reach the lake. There are trails continuing to the west that cross ridges and follow high meadows. With good trail finding, three days' walk will take you to Simi village in the Dordi Valley, the valley at the western base of Bara Pokhari Lekh (noted in Chapter 5). From the Dordi Valley there are fine perspectives of Himalchuli high above the headwaters of the Dordi Khola.

Alternatively, from the Rupina La you can retrace your steps south, perhaps following a route through Barpak village and down the Darondi Valley or along the ridge to the west of the Darondi. Once you are north of Khanchok on this walk, you will probably not see another Westerner the entire time you are trekking. Clouds often build up by mid- to late morning, but they usually dissipate toward evening. If you are camping on a ridge, this can make for a glorious sunset.

Around Manaslu

Manaslu, its high outlier Himalchuli, and Baudha Peak can be circled in either direction to the north by crossing the 17,100-foot Larkya La. This pass connects the head of the Buri Gandaki Valley (which lies north and east of the Manaslu massif) with the Dudh Khola, a tributary of the Marsyangdi. The upper Buri Gandaki has been restricted for trekking, so you cannot be certain of receiving permission to walk there. However, some groups have been permitted to walk as far as Sama, and others have circled the massif. If you ask a trekking company to apply for your permit, you may be lucky. I'll begin with the Buri Gandaki Valley and then describe the Dudh Khola approach to the Larkya La. The entire circle trek will take a minimum of two and a half weeks.

The Buri Gandaki Valley

The best roadhead for reaching the Buri Gandaki River is at Gorkha, described in the previous section. From Gorkha, take the trail to Khanchok Bhanjang (also noted) and continue north up the ridge trail for a few minutes. Ask for the trail to Arughat, which descends to the east down the Mukhti Khola. Arughat Bazaar (1,600 feet) is about a day and a half from Gorkha on the west bank of the Buri Gandaki River. This trail to Arughat saves about a day of walking as compared with the old route, which went to Arughat from Trisuli.

Up-valley from the shops and teahouses of Arughat, you will walk for some four days up into the narrow gorge of the Buri Gandaki. This gorge between the Manaslu and Ganesh himals is longer and more intimidating than most trans-Himalayan valleys in Nepal. Within a few hours' walk north of Arughat the trail begins to climb and descend steep ridges that are not high, but the constant gaining and losing of altitude is frustrating. The second day north of Arughat you will pass the narrow side valley leading to the town of Labrag, mentioned in the previous section. During several days of walking, you wend your way around the base of numerous steep rock ridges that plunge to the valley floor. Within the sheer gorge are a very few scattered bhattis where Gurung women with velveteen blouses serve dal-bhaat. Here you will always have to wait for food to be cooked to order. Along the way, you may see both plastic and old-style wooden water containers being used and men knitting winter sweaters with knitting needles of old umbrella ribs.

As tropical vegetation diminishes in the midst of the gorge, you reach a long uphill stretch followed by a sandy plain, then come to the closely packed collection of well-built stone buildings of Jagat with its police *chaulki* (a chaulki is larger than a checkpost, but smaller than a *thanna*, or police station) and the valley's lowest *stupa* (a reliquary shrine, also called a *chorten*). A half day's walk north of Jagat is the large Gurung village of Pangshing. *Pangshing* means "pine forest," but the forest is long gone, and only grassy slopes surround the town. Squash and millet abound in this town. As you ascend the hill beyond Pangshing, you will get tantalizing glimpses of precipitous slopes above the Shar Khola ("Eastern River"), a major tributary of the Buri Gandaki. The Shar Khola leads to the restricted area called Tsum, a small valley dominated on either side by high peaks. Tsum projects into Tibet like a miniature Mustang. This would be a wonderful side trip if it were not restricted. In the 1950s many Tibetan refugees entered Nepal over a high pass south of Jongka Dzong that leads into Tsum. Nearly nine hundred years ago, the revered Tibetan mystic Milarepa is said to have meditated in a cave not far above Tsum's valley floor.

Beyond Pangshing, before reaching the point where the Shar Khola issues into the main valley, is the mouth of the Chhuling Valley, noted in the previous section. At about this point, the valley usually becomes restricted. On the north bank of the Chhuling Khola is a good camping spot, and not far upriver you can see dark brown honeycombs hanging from an unreachable precipice.

Note that near Pangshing there is a bridge to the east bank of the river and another trail that follows this side of the narrow valley. You can follow this trail, and by crossing several bridges over the Buri Gandaki River it is possible to take a low route up the valley, especially in the late fall and winter, when the waters are low. These bridges near the junction of the main river and the Shar Khola may be washed out, and you should carefully question villagers before going north on the left bank. The sure route is to take either the upper trail from Pangshing or an east-bank trail to a bridge in the bottom of the gorge that is north of Philim village. On the west side of this bridge is a new, steep trail that goes up to meet the right-bank trail near the large Gurung town of Nyak, high above the west side of the river. There are great views up the Shar Khola from Nyak. Stock up on food if you go through Nyak, for the pickings may be slim for a few days up-valley. Descend beyond Nyak and cross the river to the north bank.

At the Shar Khola junction, the Buri Gandaki turns westward. Your perspiration will flow less readily when you have entered this area—locally called Kutang—a narrow, shaded stretch of valley serenaded by the thundering river. Hereabouts you may see a band of monkeys that has come down to the river to drink. The valley trail keeps to the northern bank below the barely glimpsed upper town of Bih, where a narrow high track traverses easterly across the steep ridges to Tsum. Bih is known for its family of master stone-carvers. In Buddhist upland areas throughout the Himalaya, you will see stone prayer walls with Tibetan inscription "Om Mani Padme Hum" ("All hail the jewel in the lotus") chiseled into the rocks. Some places you may also see one or two stones along a wall carved with representations of people or stupas. But in this upper valley alone, thanks to the carvers from Bih, you will see flat stones carved with intricate figures. Some prayer walls off the main trail have stone after stone covered with multifigured images, like rock-carved *tangkha*s (intricately painted scrolls). Often the person portrayed is Milarepa (the nettle-eating saint who holds his hand to his right ear listening for whispered transmissions), for there are several places in the valley where Milarepa is said to have meditated.

Beneath Bih (which is far above the main path), the trail crosses a tributary on a suspended bridge and continues along the left bank of the river until it reaches a new bridge at Prok. The buckwheat flour in Kutang is the tastiest I've ever found, for buckwheat can often be quite bitter. Buckwheat and potatoes are measured out in these villages by the *quak*, Kutang's local measure of volume. Now the valley opens up slightly, and you pass through a few fields and many stretches of enchanting, dense forest. The path steepens again, and on the northern side of the valley you can see the gorge of the Tro (or Tom) River, which holds more water than the Buri Gandaki and somehow forces its way north through a narrow defile into Tibet. The trail crosses and recrosses the river in this forested stretch. One bridge was being reinforced when I passed, and a workman greeted me respectfully, in old Tibetan style, by sticking out his tongue full length.

Puffing merrily along up through the forest, you turn a corner and come upon Namdru checkpost. Above Namdru is the upper-valley region known as Nupri. Kutang, down-valley, has been populated mostly by Gurungs, but people in the upper valley are descendants of Tibetan immigrants. In Nupri the people, language, and culture are essentially Tibetan. During my initial traverse of the valley, my friend Pancho and I found Nupri's inhabitants to be most congenial. At Li village an older man with a *mala* (the Buddhist rosary of 108 prayer beads) showed us the 10-foot-tall prayer wheel in the local gomba and smilingly turned the giant cylinder as we looked over its small room.

Near Lho village the valley opens up, becoming U-shaped, and the summits of Himalchuli and Manaslu emerge as constant companions. A week-long ceremony was in progress at the village gomba the second time I visited Lho, and my Tamang porter Changba and I sat in on some of the proceedings. Twenty people, some of whom were monks but all of whom wore dark maroon chubas (the wraparound Tibetan-style cloak) were seated around the walls of the room. Above them were wall paintings, two sets of the Kenjur (the 108-volume Tibetan canon), and a well-aged joint of yak meat. In the middle of the room, 108 butter lamps burned. The lama, visiting from Rö up-valley, chanted and performed *mudra*s (symbolic hand movements). My friend became so carried away by this auspicious occasion that he performed a lengthy Tamang custom, quite unknown to all present. He honored each participant by placing his hands together at the top of his head, then bowing down in front of each person in turn, his forehead nearly touching the floor. Outside the door, the crows waited patiently for the offerings of rice that the lama's assistant would soon toss to the gods.

A stupa with carved stones stands in a flat meadow above Lho. Manaslu appears quite foreshortened from this glade among pine, birch, and rushing streams. The valley levels out, and soon you reach the last large village: named Sama on the maps, locally it is called Rö. The town is guarded on the east by a large mani (prayer) wall of flat stones; to the north across the deeply cut river lie flat village pastures. The village gomba is not far from town to the west. In the morning sunlight of late autumn, Sama's women spin and weave cloth with furious intensity.

At Sama (about 11,000 feet) the valley turns north, and the path enters a forest of mixed conifers and birch trees that becomes pure birch as you rise toward the treeline. To the west, well above the trail, is a lone boulder capped with white prayer flags. Milarepa once meditated at the base of this sacred rock. The last hamlet of Sumdo is situated near an intersection of trails: south lies Nupri in the main valley, and to the west the Larkya La leads to the Marsyangdi Valley and Nyeshang. Additionally, from both east and north are border passes that connect with the trading village of Riu in Tibet. The high Gya La to the north is the route most often taken by traders to Tibet. Sumdo's inhabitants migrated a generation ago from Riu and continue to trade with their clansmen still in Tibet.

To the west of Sumdo the trail to the Larkya La (17,100 feet) angles upward gently toward the pass. It is a long walk. Over an hour beyond Sumdo there is a lone shelter where you might stay if you want to get a good start on the walk to the top (or if you are coming the other way and have gone far enough for the day). The trail parallels the north side of a long valley glacier, then finally continues onto the glacier's rocky moraine. Hours later, passing a small ice-covered lake near the pass, the path meanders toward the topmost cairn with its faded prayer flags. Here you are between high snow slopes that descend from the Manaslu and Larkya (Cheo) himals. Allow about ten days without stopovers or side walks to reach the Larkya La from Gorkha.

The Dudh Khola

To reach the Larkya La from the west, you must trek up the Marsyangdi Valley to the uppermost part of Dharapani village (described under "The Marsyangdi Valley" in Chapter 5). Directly across the river on the north side you can see the village of Thonje. Just above Dharapani, drop down to cross the Marsyangdi on a bridge to Thonje (once known as Thangjet), where there is a checkpost. The area beyond Thonje has been restricted, so be sure you have the proper permit before you proceed. Beyond the entrance chorten near the school at the far end of town, you'll begin the climb up the wild Dudh Khola ("Milk River"). This region near Thonje is called Gyasumdo ("Meeting of Three Highways"). Here, trails meet from both up- and down-valley along the Marsyangdi, and the Dudh Khola path joins in as well, leading to the Larkya La and the passes beyond, which connect with Tibet.

The only town above Thonje along the Dudh Kola is Tilje. Beyond Tilje, you ascend and just as quickly drop off of a narrow spur. A few homesteaders have begun to build log fences around fields hacked from the more gentle slopes, but most of the valley remains uninhabited. The walk leads easterly higher and higher, through shady glens and past two large, snow-fed tributaries. As you are climbing up through a pine and rhododendron forest, the valley turns to the north, and through the trees you begin to see Manaslu's western flanks. Soon you must cross the rubble-coated glacier that begets the whitish waters of the Dudh Kola.

Set between the glacier and a birch forest 5,000 feet below the Larkya La is Bimthang, an idyllic oval meadow belied by its name, which means "Plain of Sand." A small prayer wall and several tumbledown stone structures are all that remain to remind us of a former era when salt, wool, and turquoise from Tibet changed hands here for the grains, tobacco, and textiles of the south. All these goods were bartered at Bimthang under the eyes of government-authorized tax collectors, for this was the lone trading point for Tibetans from Riu and Gurung traders from Nepal. If trekking becomes derestricted in this area, I can imagine several inns being built here. There are several side walks out of Bimthang that immediately suggest themselves. To the south of the meadow you can walk up into the birch forest for closer views of Manaslu. To the north of Bimthang you can climb the moraine and cross the valley glacier below to reach grass-covered moraines and a deep blue lake. Ah, I will forever treasure my memories of beautiful, solitary Bimthang.

The path's final ascent from Bimthang to the Larkya La continues on a long lateral moraine past a few last camping spots. Then the way steepens considerably, following rock- and snow-covered slopes to the top of the pass. Strong hikers will find the rolling snowfields north of the pass at 18,000 feet excellent to explore for views of several himals.

The Langtang Valley and Gosain Kund

The Langtang Valley is the most easily accessible high mountain valley from Kathmandu, particularly since the new road from Trisuli to Dhunche (and beyond) has been completed. Even in summer you can walk up to the high meadows in Langtang and not have to pass through leech country for more than a couple of days. Treks in the Langtang and Helambu regions north of Kathmandu can be combined by crossing Laurebina Pass near Gosain Kund (*kund* means lake); or if you are experienced in climbing steep, snowy slopes, by crossing the technical Ganga La. Both routes connecting Helambu and Langtang proceed north of sacred Gosain Kund. First, the main paths to the high, narrow Langtang Valley will be noted, then the trail to Gosain Kund. Helambu is discussed in the next section.

To reach Trisuli, you can take an early morning or midday bus from Kathmandu. The buses tend to be very full, so you may have to purchase a ticket a half day in advance, or well ahead of departure. Buses to Trisuli leave from in front of the Gauri Shankar Hotel on Lekhnath Marg, the street in northern Kathmandu that turns into the road to Balaju. The road to Trisuli was built in the 1950s (when the hydroelectric project at Trisuli was being built), so be ready for lots of curlicue twists and turns as your vehicle descends into the Trisuli Valley.

Trisuli Bazaar (about 1,700 feet) used to be the trailhead for the Langtang Valley, but now, with a little bit of inquiry and luck in Trisuli, you can take a truck or bus from Trisuli as far as Dhunche or on to Syabrubesi and save two to three days' walking time. You can still walk from Trisuli, however. If you do, get an early start, for the initial day's walk uphill from the humid valley is often an ordeal by sweat. (Whereas the bus ride will be an ordeal from being crammed into an overcrowded bus.) From the town of Betrawati, almost two hours beyond Trisuli on the east side of the Trisuli River, the trail ascends through scattered villages. If in doubt at trail junctions during the first day's walk, take the upper trail forks. If you reach Ramche (5,870 feet) the first evening, you will be well up from the steamy valley floor and you will have passed the first two grass-covered stupas. At Ramche you have a last view of the lights back at Trisuli Bazaar and can see the main Trisuli Valley disappearing ahead around a ridgeline.

People in the Tamang clan live along this path beyond Ramche and in many middle-hill regions north and east of Kathmandu. Tamangs are Buddhist and often use the word Lama as their last name. They are a large

and extremely diverse clan. Some live in large villages of several hundred
houses near 1,000 feet in elevation, while others live in small hamlets at
9,000 feet in the hills. Some Tamangs carry giant *khukari*s (curved Gurkha
knives) in their waistbands and are as jungly as a person can be, while

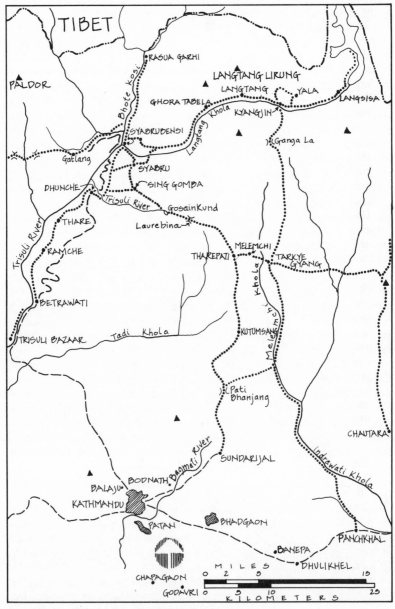

Langtang, Gosain Kund, and Helambu

others are university professors. Several trekking outfitters in Kathmandu employ Tamangs almost exclusively as sirdars and cooks. Tamang women in pairs or groups sometimes hire out as porters with trekking groups, and they usually wear necklaces of old coins for ornamentation. In recent years I have trekked with several Tamangs and found them companionable, strong, and dependable porter-guides.

The stone homes of the Tamang hamlet called Grang (beyond Ramche) have roofs of wooden shingles anchored by rocks, like villages in eastern Nepal and Bhutan. The path up-valley contours in and out of forested ridges and crosses places where landslides have occurred before reaching the large town of Dhunche. The eastern tributary of the main valley north of Dhunche is called the Trisuli Khola. As with the Alaknanda River in Garhwal, India, a side stream here gives its name to the main valley, owing to the importance of a mythical event: Shiva is said to have created Gosain Kund and its two smaller lacustrine neighbors by jabbing his *trisul* (trident) into the ground to form the Trisuli River's headwaters. North of the Trisuli, the main river valley is known as the Bhote Kosi ("River from Tibet"). The trail to Gosain Kund will be noted, but first let's continue north to the Langtang Valley.

Dhunche (6,450 feet) is the headquarters of Rasuwa District and also houses a guardpost of Langtang National Park (you will pay a fee for entering the park just before reaching town). Dhunche rests high on a ridge with a pleasant view, but the town itself is not a particularly appealing place. From Dhunche you may possibly be able to travel northward if a vehicle is leaving soon, or you can begin (or continue) walking. By foot, take the trail east out of town, then, after a half hour, walk downhill to cross the Trisuli Khola. At the trail junction some ways above the river on the north side, take the northwesterly trail toward Barku, not the eastern track, which leads to Gosain Kund. Before you reach Barku the trail forks again; you should take the upper (right) path to Barku. At Barku village you may take either a longer route down through Syabrubesi village (at the junction of the Langtang River with the Bhote Kosi) or a shorter path that leads up over the ridge from Barku and down to Syabru. Syabru (6,950 feet) is a north-slope village of homes built centipedelike in a single line. This town obviously has an industrious resident woodcarver. Every house is decorated with wooden filigree, and some homes have flowerboxes.

At Syabru ask for the correct path leading downward from town to cross the Langtang River. Soon after reaching the river's north bank, you join the longer trail from Syabrubesi to the west. The way then rises for some hours through a thick forest, passing through Ghora Tabela ("Horse Stable," 9,450 feet), where there is a guard station for the national park. Be sure you have kept your receipt for payment of the park entry fee, for it may be rechecked here. When I first passed through Ghora Tabela it was inhabited by Tibetan Khampas (now long gone), and everyone—trekkers and Khampas alike—slept together in a gomba. We were awakened in the morning by the monks murmuring their prayers. The trail continues rising through forest, then emerges from the V-shaped gorge and enters a rounded, formerly glaciated upper valley.

Langtang village (10,850 feet) is the headquarters for Langtang National Park. It is easy to ascend this steep valley too fast, so if you are experiencing any symptoms of altitude sickness, stay in town for two nights and take it easy. This village is the last place inhabited year round, a town of Tibetan-speaking agro-pastoralists whose ancestors have lived in this valley for some three hundred years. The people who live here originally came from Kyirong to the north in Tibet and plant fields of barley, buckwheat, and potatoes. Prior to their arrival, Langtang Valley was considered a *beyul,* a "hidden valley" or refuge that would only be retreated to by followers of Buddhism when the dark age of the Kali Yuga began.

Beyond Langtang village is Kyangjin (12,300 feet) with its small gomba, lodge, and cheese factory. At certain times during the day, you may purchase cheese at the small factory. This summer settlement is the usual base of operations for trekkers in the upper valley. There are several hikes you can take north and east of here, but you will need to be supplied with food and shelter for neither is likely to be found beyond Kyangjin. Depending on transportation from Kathmandu to Trisuli or Dhunche, you will probably get from Kathmandu to Kyangjin in about five days.

One walk you can take from Kyangjin is to Yala. Ask the local herders (whose cow-yak crossbreeds, called *tsauries* in Nepali, provide milk for the cheese-making operation) to point out the hill trail east of Kyangjin that leads to the other cheese-producing location at Yala. Yala, Tibetan for "up," sits some 3,000 feet above Kyangjin. To reach Yala, go east up the main valley and, just after crossing the first stream coming down from the north, start to climb the grassy hill. The path continues, sometimes steeply, past several summer herding settlements to the fairly level plain at Yala. At Yala (or Kyangjin) ask where you can get milk (*oma*—be sure it has been boiled), yogurt (*sho*), buttermilk (*darra*), and dried cheese (*churpee*). From Yala, you can see the high Ganga La to the south and numerous other snow-clad summits that are invisible from the valley floor. Tsergo Ri (circa 16,300 feet), a grassy peak west of Yala, can be climbed for even better views of the mountains, including Langtang Lirung (23,770 feet), the highest peak in the area. It is possible to make the walk to Yala and back a long day trip, but camping for the night would be the best way to enjoy the alpenglow on the high peaks and the serenity of the high country (serene if yaks aren't clomping around your tent).

A shorter day hike from Kyangjin is the walk to a small lake near the base of the steep glacier that descends from Langtang Lirung. From Kyangjin Gomba, a small trail winds up along the bottom of an old lateral moraine. Follow this trail for a couple of hours until you reach the lake, where there is a temporary yak-herding settlement. If you want, you can carry food and shelter and walk up to the east, crossing a small pass at about 15,000 feet, and emerging just to the west of Tsergo Ri. From here you carry on easterly to Yala.

Another day hike from Kyangjin would be to explore the birch-and-rhododendron forest across the river to the south. With luck you might even see a musk deer.

East from Kyangjin you can take day or overnight hikes to the interesting upper valley. In the summer the valley floor and the pastures above are covered with wildflowers, lending a blanket of color to the often-cloud-covered valley. To walk up-valley from Kyangjin, hike past the STOL airstrip to the shepherds' huts collectively called Noom Thang. Just past the last hut at Noom Thang, a spring flows from beneath a rock. Check out the cliffs above, for Himalayan *tahr* (wild goats) are often sighted hereabouts.

Going up-valley, keep to the low ground and don't get caught in the high moraine protruding from the north, as I once did. It is exciting to stride onward and see new stretches of the valley come into view as you proceed around additional talus slopes. The upper-valley glacier begins beyond the single hut named Langsisa ("Place Where the Bull Died"). If you want to explore the glacier and surrounding high country, take food and a tent with you when you leave Kyangjin, for the distance is too great to be covered in a single day. You will see the beautiful fluted peaks of Langsisa Ri and other peaks in the eastern end of the valley to best advantage if you climb up a south-facing valley slope. The uppermost part of the glacier, although many maps do not show it, bends due north like a crooked little finger north of Langsisa Ri. There is one more herder's hut a few hours beyond Langsisa. Not far beyond this last hut, if you want to keep going, you will have to thread your way onto the slippery moraine of the valley glacier. Across the river to the south of Langsisa a difficult track leads over a pass known as Tilman's Col. By following this trail you can reach the lakes at Panch Pokhari in the Helambu region to the south, but you will definitely have to travel with someone who knows the way, for the glaciated route is by no means obvious.

The 16,800-foot snow-covered Ganga La south of Kyangjin leads to Tarke Gyang village in Helambu. Some mountaineers have successfully made their own way across the pass and others have found the path, but the approach route is not easy to locate (particularly on the southern side), so you should definitely hire a local to guide you. Take shelter and enough food for four days. This is a difficult pass that may require technical aids and should be attempted only by people who feel comfortable on steep, snowy slopes. If you leave at the crack of dawn and climb like a mountain goat all day, you may be able to cross the pass the first day from Kyangjin. If you do cross the pass the first day, you'll probably have to camp on a high, uncomfortably rocky place. Most people make their first camp on the north side. The steep descent to the south takes at least two days, following a route that is not always easily discernible. The trick to descending is to head for the upper shelters you'll see (if the weather is clear) near the headwaters of the Yangri Khola. But then you must follow the stone markers to regain the ridgeline to the west and follow the ridge down a long day to Gekye Gomba and Tarke Gyang.

The Way to Gosain Kund

A lower pass, called Laurebina, east of Gosain Kund, also connects the Trisuli and Langtang valleys with Helambu. This is the pass most people take if they want to connect a visit to Langtang with the walk to Helambu (or vice versa). Alternatively, of course, you can walk up to Gosain Kund from the Trisuli Valley side and then return. If you are coming back from Langtang, you can reach Gosain Kund by walking south, up a pleasant forested trail from Syabru village. Keep going to the ridgeline, always taking the upper trail. After you reach the ridge trail and proceed east, you'll get to Sing Gomba (10,680 feet) at a place called Chenchen Bari, where there is another cheese factory. You can also ascend to Sing Gomba from Dhunche. If you walk from Dhunche, you leave town as if going to Barku. Then at the trail junction above and north of the Trisuli Khola, turn east and follow the path up the ridge. Beyond the halfway point en route to the lake is Sing Gomba, where you can obtain food and lodging overnight during most seasons. Remember that no food will be available beyond here until you reach Melemchi in Helambu, two days to the east. You don't leave the national park until reaching Tharepati, so you must also carry enough fuel to be self-sufficient.

Above Chenchen Bari, the trail follows a ridgeline that is great for views but poor for good sources of water, so be sure to stock up on water before leaving Chenchen Bari. On clear days, the himals in central Nepal from Annapurna as far east as Langtang are visible from this high ridge. You can even see the flat meadows of Kyirong not far north in Tibet. When the trail drops off to the south side of the ridge, you know that you are nearing the lakes. Far below lies Saraswati Kund, the first small lake. Above it some 700 feet higher is Bhairav Kund. Soon you see the large Gosain Kund (14,200 feet) ahead. During the full moon of August, when the monsoon is at its height, a large pilgrimage called Janai Purne is made to Gosain Kund in honor of Shiva. Most of the year only occasional herders or trekkers pass this way. But during this festival the northern shores of the lake are alive with shivering lowlanders who come to pay homage to Shiva by tossing coins in the lake and taking a dip in the sacred waters. There are small shelters here and a stone Shiva lingam.

To reach the 15,100-foot Laurebina Pass, which connects with Helambu, take the narrow trail along the north side of Gosain Kund. Follow this path as it rises to the southeast in view of several other small lakes that feed into Gosain Kund. When I took this route alone toward the end of October, I was glad that people had preceded me the previous day. In the snowy landscape the route can be difficult to locate without tracks to follow. Beyond the pass cairn, the path drops precipitously at first, then angles northeastward down rocky slopes, eventually passing a couple of streams and then two separate overhanging rocks, called Ghopte, that are good for overnight shelter. Finally the track gently ascends to several shepherds' huts at Tharepati (11,400 feet), a waterless ridge with splendid views of nearby ridges and the dusky Helambu region below.

If you are approaching the pass from Helambu, note that the trail at first

Hindu pilgrims at the Janai Purne Festival on the bank of Gosain Kund Lake. (Photograph by Kevin Bubriski.)

descends from Tharepati, then begins to rise. And don't underestimate the distance involved up to the pass. You may have to make a last camp before reaching the pass, either near one of the overhanging rocks or on the gently sloping ground close to the last stream.

Helambu

The region called Helambu (or Helmu) is situated about three days' walk northeast of the Kathmandu Valley. Helambu, like Langtang, is popular with people having a very limited time to trek, for it is quick of access, inns are scattered along the main routes, and the area is picturesque but not high in elevation. Helambu is populated by people called Sherpas, but although they have the name in common with the well-known clan of the Khumbu area near Mt. Everest, the two clans have different language, dress, and family lineage. Most inhabitants of Melemchi and Tarke Gyang, the two large villages in upper Helambu, are well-to-do and have homes decorated with copper and brass cookware, like the prosperous Thakali bhattis west of Pokhara. Handsomely maintained gombas, particularly the large one in Tarke Gyang, are additional evidence of Helambu's thriving economy.

The hotter, quicker route into Helambu begins at the roadhead of Panchkhal on the Kathmandu-to-Kodari road, the road to the Tibetan border. You can reach Panchkhal by taxi, or by bus from the busy bus park east of the Tundikhel in Kathmandu. The trail north of Panchkhal is actually a rarely used Jeep road for the initial day's walk along the valley bottom. At Melemchi Pul village, about six hours from Panchkhal, you enter the Melemchi Khola, the valley in which Helambu is located. The trail continues past Talamarang, finally gaining elevation as it ascends the ridge to the east. This path takes you past several towns to Tarke Gyang (about 8,500 feet), the largest village in Helambu and the starting point, from this side, for the walk over the difficult Ganga La. If you do the climb of the Ganga La, take a porter-guide, no ifs or buts about it. At Tarke Gyang consider making a side trip overnight past Gekye Gomba onto the ridge to the east, to take in the excellent view of Nepal's central Himalayan peaks. A trail leads west from Tarke Gyang down to the river and up again to Melemchi village across the valley. Melemchi is as spread out as Tarke Gyang is clustered. If you visit Helambu in fall or winter, ask whether the excellent local apples are available.

The higher trail to Helambu leaves from Sundarijal in the Kathmandu Valley. Much of the capital's water supply reaches the valley floor by means of a large pipe that descends from a reservoir above Sundarijal. Hire a taxi to Sundarijal, or take a bus from Ratna Park in Kathmandu to Bodnath and hire a taxi from there to Sundarijal. Stop for a cup at the local teashop before you start on your way up. The 3,500-foot ascent, initially paralleling the large water pipe, takes you to a point on the rim of the valley called Burlang Bhanjang (about 8,000 feet). Beyond Burlang Bhanjang you can follow a ridge trail for two days to reach Tharepati. There are several villages along the ridge during the first part of the walk, but from not far beyond Kutumsang you will encounter only temporary shepherds' quarters. The path rises and falls, often passing through rhododendron forests, and reaches 12,000 feet in places. From Tharepati, either drop down to Melemchi in Helambu or climb to Gosain Kund. (Or at Pati Bhanjang, not far north of Burlang Bhanjang, you can take a rocky trail leading off the ridge down to Talamarang in the Melemchi Khola and follow the valley route up as noted in the previous paragraph.)

The ridge leading from Pati Bhanjang to Tharepati marks a significant divide: it is the boundary between the Great Gandaki watershed, which extends west to the southern slopes of Dhaulagiri, and the Sapt Kosi river system, which drains Nepal's mountainous regions all the way to the country's eastern border with Sikkim. The ridge trail ends at Tharepati, on the path between Gosain Kund higher up to the west and Melemchi to the east in Helambu. Melemchi village (8,500 feet) is reached from Tharepati by a forest track with many side paths that is used by shepherds and woodcutters. If in doubt, take the northerly trail forks as you descend from Tharepati. Melemchi's large homes are scattered on a level shelf at about the same elevation as Tarke Gyang, across the valley. The ridge route from Sundarijal takes about three days to reach Melemchi; the hot valley route from Panchkhal to Tarke Gyang is slightly shorter.

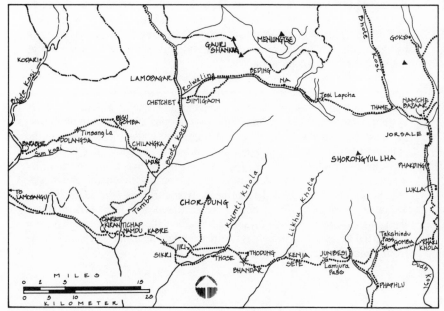

Rolwaling and the trail to Khumbu

7

The Trails to Khumbu and Mt. Everest

Just hap hour more. Just hap hour more.
Sherpa cajoling tired hiker
up the hill to Namche Bazaar

The Verdant Eastern Himalaya

Excepting the southern slopes of Dhaulagiri and Annapurna, the area encompassing eastern Nepal, Sikkim, and Bhutan reaps more of the monsoon's life-giving rain than any other portion of the Himalaya. During late summer the seven large tributaries called the Sapt Kosi (the "Seven Kosi") rivers in Nepal and the Tista River in Sikkim resound with the thunder of runoff. Thanks to this abundance of rain, terraced, irrigated cultivation is especially widespread in eastern Nepal, and these hills are the most densely populated in the kingdom.

The weekly or biweekly market days called *haat* bazaars are unique to the region of eastern Nepal's fertile hills. *Haat* means "hand," signifying trade from hand to hand. Stretching from Dolakha by the Tamba Kosi to Pashupati near Nepal's eastern border, the haat bazaars are a bright, multiclan spectacle. Most bazaars are held at specially cleared areas on the edge of towns, but in some places, like Ilam, they take place in the central square. Usually people travel no longer than a day with goods to trade, but sometimes they travel up to five days to trade or sell a single doko (basket) load of grains, produce, manufactured goods from the south, or a few khukaris (curved Gurkha knives). Other goods exchanged often include local fruits in season, butter, pulses, salt, spices, raw tobacco, cigarettes, sugar and candy, chickens, piglets, brassware, plastic bracelets, combs, beads, and other trinkets.

A haat that is atypical but far better known than most others occurs every Saturday at the important Sherpa town of Namche Bazaar, the southernmost town in the Khumbu region. Due to the prosperity wrought by tourism thereabouts, it is often said that the Sherpas have learned to mint their own money. With this in mind, people often walk for the better part of a week to sell goods at Namche Bazaar. As the morning sun first reached the trail leading to Namche one Saturday, I climbed to an overlook and watched as scores of people walked up from the lower valley trail with loads to be sold in the market. Simultaneously, Sherpas descended on three paths from above town. Later, at the multilevel bazaar grounds just south of town, Sherpas (dressed in both traditional clothes and the latest in down wear) bought food from thinly clad vendors of the Rai and Chhetri clans. As their goods were sold, the down-valley people usually had a cup of tea and left in groups with their friends on the homeward trail, often whooping it up on the way down. The Sherpas, some redolent of chang (beer), gravitated toward Namche Bazaar, or farther up-valley to their villages. Like all markets, which are social as well as commercial, Namche's bazaar day involves an exchange of both goods and recent local news.

This chapter takes up the principal trekking routes in the often-visited Khumbu region south of Mt. Everest. First described, however, are two treks west of Khumbu. Visiting the Rolwaling Valley, a narrow, little-populated region, can make for an excellent hike. The second of these walks will take you to Khumbu by foot from the roadhead at Jiri.

The Rolwaling Valley

Rolwaling is a sparsely populated, east-west valley near the Tibetan border that is west of the Khumbu region and just south of the magnificent Gauri Shankar Himal. You can walk into the lovely upper part of this valley and return in a minimum of about two weeks. If you have sufficient equipment, mountaineering experience, a local guide, and a permit, you can attempt the technical Tesi Lapcha Pass at the valley's head, reaching Namche Bazaar in the well-trekked Khumbu region a day and a half after crossing the pass. However, this is an extremely difficult route and is not recommended. Because the route into the Rolwaling Valley has no inns and because there are many trail junctions before you reach Rolwaling, you should take along a porter who is familiar with the region, or who can ask the way to it. Recently the Rolwaling Valley (or at least the pass area at the head of it) was closed to trekking. You may be able to get a trekking permit to walk into the valley, particularly if you apply through a large trekking outfitter, but you probably won't get a permit to cross the Tesi Lapcha Pass unless regulations have changed.

To reach the trailhead* for this trek, take a bus from Kathmandu to Barabise, beyond Lamogsangu on the Arniko Rajmarg, the road that leads to the Tibetan border. You can more than halve the driving time by renting a taxi for the drive to Barabise. En route you will ride through terraced middle hills much of the way. Barabise (2,700 feet) is a large bazaar in the Bhote Kosi gorge just beyond a bridge where the road crosses to the river's east bank. In Barabise, have dal-bhaat, get any last-minute supplies, and hire a porter if you still need one.

The trail begins right in Barabise by a water spout on the east side of the road. Fill your water bottle now, for water is scarce initially and you will be walking several thousand feet right up the unshaded ridge to the east of town (get an umbrella in Barabise if you don't have one yet). After some time, you'll round the ridgeline and begin contouring gently into the Sun Kosi Valley. There are several villages, and after asking the way, you usually need to take the upper trails. Up and up you go. If you leave early in the day and walk hard, the first day you may be able to reach the scattered white houses of Dolangsa, the valley's last village, with its small gomba above town. Above Dolangsa, you pass through a lovely mist-filled forest with many rhododendrons, then you'll encounter a steep climb before reaching the Tinsang La (10,900 feet), where there are several old stone stupas.

---

* Note that there is an alternate trailhead for this trek that reduces the walking time by a day or two, but the path from this roadhead misses the scenic Tinsang La and Bigu Gomba. The other trailhead begins at Charikot (see the *Rolwaling and the Trail to Khumbu* map in this chapter) on the Lamosangu-to-Jiri road. From Charikot, you walk north, high above the Tamba Kosi River until reaching the Sangawa Valley. Cross the Sangawa Khola, then join the trail to Rolwaling near Laduk north of this tributary.

The beginning of the forested path on the east side of the Tinsang La is as gentle as the west side is steep. From clearings near the pass you can see Gauri Shankar to the east in clear weather. Soon the trail descends more steeply, and in several places you have to be careful not to get off-route on woodcutters' trails. At the point where you meet a stream from the left (north) joining the valley you've been descending, you have two choices. You may either continue down-valley or climb a thousand feet to see the convent called Bigu Gomba (8,240 feet). Bigu is an interesting place to visit, and views from it to the east are superb. The square, white gomba is fronted by a long, low, whitewashed dwelling that serves as a sleeping quarters for the nuns. When I arrived with a friend and two porters in December, no other Westerners but one had been to Bigu for at least a week. We were given a dusty room in an empty building. I swept the floor with fern fronds and wedged my open umbrella in the window to keep out the cold air.

Whichever way you go, either through Bigu or by the lower route, you'll have to walk onto the northern slope of the Sangawa Valley. Heading east along this valley, you pass scattered homes, terraced landscape, and three large tributary streams as you continue, well above the northern bank of the Saun (or Sangawa) Khola. Several hours' walk beyond Chilangka, above the village of Laduk, you round a ridgeline and enter the Bhote Kosi Valley. Here are excellent views of Gauri Shankar; by now you are some four days' walk from the roadhead. There are numerous trails in this area, and you'll just have to keep asking the way. Inquire the way to Deolang when you come around the ridgeline. Then begin asking for the trail to Chetchet as you carry on up the Bhote Kosi Valley. Like the other Bhote Kosi, to the west where you began the trek, this river is so named because it originates in Bhot: Tibet. These rivers take on different names (Sun Kosi and Tamba Kosi, respectively) when each is joined by a large cis-Himalayan tributary (a tributary that enters from the Nepal side, south of the main crest).

To the north up the Bhote Kosi, farther than you will go, is Lamabagar with its checkpost and wireless station. Beyond Lamabagar, near the tip of a tiny finger of land belonging to Nepal, lies the small Lapche Gomba. For an interesting account by an extremely observant scientist who was allowed into that restricted area surrounded by Tibet, read the "Kang Chu" chapter in *Stones of Silence,* by George B. Schaller.

Just north of Chetchet, cross a suspension bridge (3,500 feet) to the east bank of the Bhote Kosi. Here you climb steeply for thousands of feet, passing only the village of Simigaon (6,600 feet), the last village for some distance. Continue up to two shelters called Shakpa (the Sherpa word for soup). The main trail crosses over to the north side of the ridge from here. If you have a porter who knows the route, you might consider taking an upper path that divides from the main trail above Shakpa and ascends to cross the Daldung La (about 13,000 feet), passing through several high summer pastures. This upper path has an excellent view of Gauri Shankar's double peak (23,439 feet). The main trail angles into the Rolwaling Valley, passing through mixed forest and eventually crossing to the north (right) bank of the river near an old covered bridge. The path is sometimes narrow as you continue up through forested and uninhabited terrain.

Two long days' walk from the Bhote Kosi bridge, you reach Ramding, one of several winter villages used by the valley's Sherpa inhabitants. The small community of Sherpas in this spectacular, narrow valley moves up to Beding and farther along to Na, depending on the season. Up-valley from Ramding, the stone houses of Beding (12,000 feet) rest on a hill above the small, square village gomba, which contains an 8-foot-tall prayer wheel. At Beding you can see the upper slopes of Gauri Shankar, but not the main peak. If you need food supplies in this valley, start asking as soon as you see locals. You may not encounter many people because the locals scatter out among the various settlements and high pastures, and it can be difficult to purchase food.

Do walk on beyond Beding to the summer settlement of Na (13,700 feet), where there is the partially dismembered skeleton of an Alouette helicopter. Farther up-valley the meadows become nearly flat, and you have excellent views of Chobotse, the fluted peak to end all fluted peaks. After we had finished a meal in this part of the valley, our Sherpa porters performed an interesting ritual. They took some of the fragrant plant called *sunpati* ("goldleaf"), which highlanders use as incense, and put it in the glowing coals of the fire. Then they placed a round stone over the smouldering, pungent embers. This is an auspicious offering of smoke to the deity; a pre-Buddhist ritual involving the concept of ascension to the godhead.

Numerous other side excursions in and about Rolwaling will become evident if you have a copy of the Schneider *Rolwaling Himal* sheet (see Appendix A, "Map Information"). One possible way to leave the valley, but only for the intrepid and well-provisioned person, is by the long route that crosses the Yalung (17,420 feet) and Honobu (14,600 feet) passes, eventually reaching Jiri on the roadhead. For this out-of-the-way route, you will need food for *at least* six days, a strong porter-guide who (without doubt) knows the way, and the *Rolwaling Himal* sheet (which does not always accurately portray the route). Sometimes locals will claim to have experience on a rarely traveled route such as this one, then admit along the way that they do not. Try very carefully to determine that your guide knows the way before you leave on this difficult walk.

Attempt the Tesi Lapcha Pass (18,875 feet), which separates the Rolwaling Valley from Khumbu, only if you have a permit and are a well-acclimatized person who has engaged in technical mountaineering. You need to be equipped with ice screws, ice ax, crampons, and rope and should know how to cut ice steps. The best help you can obtain for crossing the Tesi Lapcha is a Sherpa from Khumbu (if starting from that side) or Rolwaling who has already been over the pass, but he cannot do the walk for you. He can only help to show you the best route past the rockfalls and other dicey spots along the way.

For the pass route, walk past the last pastures at Sangma beyond Na to the north side of the Trakarding Glacier. As you skirt Tsho Rolpa Lake (Chu Pokhari), rockfalls are the first objective danger on the way. At first you must walk high up on the lower portion of the glacial moraine, beginning at dawn, before the sun's heat loosens the rocks above. Continue along the Trakarding Glacier for the better part of a day's walk. The route does not follow the dashed line on the *Rolwaling Himal* map but now goes farther east, to the east of the most active part of the Drolambo icefall. Climbing onto the Drolambo Glacier from the Trakarding is one of the most dangerous parts of the entire route over the pass. You will need to use a rope and may have to cut steps here. Be very alert for falling rocks, particularly in the afternoon. Do not try to climb or descend this hazardous section if any melting has begun, because rocks can come hurtling down on you from above. This area where the two glaciers join has become progressively more dangerous over the years. (The night noises of avalanches and of glaciers rumbling and creaking are enough to give anyone the jitters.) Take a last look at Gauri Shankar as you ascend onto the Drolambo. After you are above the Drolambo icefall, walk north along a medial moraine on the glacier's eastern side. The pass is high above to the east up a diagonal, snowy ramp. Be careful as you climb toward the pass; there are crevasses along the way that may be covered with a dusting of snow, and your entire party should be roped along this stretch.

The views toward Khumbu are superb at the pass. A steep descent east of the pass follows first a snow- and rock-covered slope. Stay to the north side of the valley, pick your route carefully, and again be alert for falling rocks from the north. You will eventually pass Ngole, then Tengpo, the highest two small clusters of huts (expect these huts to be locked) used by yak herders. Once below the rockfall and the permanent snow line, you are one very long day's walk from bustling Namche Bazaar. Note that you can approach the high Tesi Lapcha Pass from the Khumbu side more easily than from the Rolwaling Valley. This is because the pass is much closer to the villages of Thame and Namche Bazaar, where there are excellent high-altitude porter-guides available. You also have a much better fallback position if you have to return for any reason than you have if you walk back down the long, cold Trakarding Glacier to Rolwaling.

The Walk to Khumbu

Since 1953, when descriptions and photographs began to circulate about the successful British expedition to Mt. Everest, many people have been fascinated by the thought of walking to the base of the world's highest mountain. By now, thousands of trekkers have discovered for themselves the steamy, many-hilled trek to Khumbu, the Sherpa-inhabited region south of Mt. Everest. This section briefly describes the walk to Namche Bazaar, the first village in Khumbu.

The construction of new roads has changed the nature of the walk in to Khumbu. For many years this trek began at Banepa in the Kathmandu

Valley. Then, for many years after the road to the Tibetan border was completed, the trailhead lay at Lamosangu, 50 miles from Kathmandu along this highway. Now a spur road has been completed to the town of Jiri, 68 miles farther, and you can now take an all-terrain vehicle, a truck, or a bus to Jiri. Sometimes there are buses direct from the Kathmandu bus park to Jiri, or you can take one of the more frequent buses or a taxi to Lamosangu and change vehicles there. The road to Jiri begins at the metal bridge that looks like an outsize erector set and lies across the Sun Kosi 2 miles north of Lamosangu. If you ride to Jiri, pick up the trail description at that point below. If you wish to add several days to your trek, you can still begin at the footbridge right at Lamosangu.

This trek can be done alone or with a porter to carry gear, and you can stay at the small inns called bhattis along the path. In Kathmandu you can get a locally produced trekking map that will give a good approximation of the distances involved. Most people take from ten to fourteen days to reach Namche Bazaar from the roadhead at Lamosangu, although some have made the walk in less time by hiking very long days. If you begin walking at Jiri, expect that it will take you about a week to reach Namche. Or during the spring and fall trekking seasons, you can fly all the way to Lukla, still farther east. This is the way the majority of trekkers reach Khumbu. At Lukla you will be only a day and a half by foot from Namche Bazaar. Flights to Lukla can be quite difficult to book in season. The best way to assure that you get on a flight is by booking your ticket through a travel agency or trekking outfitter in Kathmandu.

To begin the trek at Lamosangu ("Long Bridge," 2,525 feet), cross the Sun Kosi River by the suspension bridge (for foot traffic only) near Lamosangu's bazaar and begin walking up the first long hill. This trek is characterized by up-and-down crossings of five major ridges before you reach the Dudh Kosi Valley below Namche Bazaar. Use an umbrella brought from Kathmandu for sun protection, and plan your uphill walks for the cooler morning hours if at all possible. Backlighting is beautiful in the mornings as you walk east through country that appears increasingly vast as you progress.

The first hill seems interminable; you pass Kaping, Perku, and Pakha villages amid terracing and scattered trees. On your second day out, at the hamlet of Muldi (more than 6,000 feet higher than Lamosangu), you will have a brief but tantalizing glimpse north to the Himalaya Range. Here, along the top of the ridge, you can either follow the new road, which contours along a fairly level course to the north, or take the trail. By either route, you then descend to Surkhe and follow the northern bank of a tributary to Shere (also called Serobesi). Cross another bridge to the northern bank of the Charnawati Khola and continue down-valley. Then climb slowly through terraces, using your umbrella for shade, until you reach Kirantichap. Above you the road passes through Charikot, and you could head up-valley toward Rolwaling from there. The road passes through Kirantichap also, but whichever way you have walked thus far, you will probably want to take the shorter route, the trail, down to the suspension bridge over the Bhote Kosi River. At the Bhote Kosi, you have descended nearly to the elevation of Lamosangu, where you began.

Climb steeply onto the ridgeline east of the river, then pick up the road as it gently rises through Namdu and Kabre villages south of the ridge. You may see a cluster of villagers approaching: is it a wedding or a funeral? If only men are hurrying along, dressed in white (the color of mourning), carrying long sticks of wood, and two people are carrying a swaddled body, they will be going to a burning *ghat* (a cremation platform) beside the river. But if there is singing and one well-dressed youth walks bedecked in flower chains (the bride may not be present), then you are watching a *bibaha,* a wedding procession.

Beyond Kabre, leave the road for the trail and cross the Yarsa Khola, then begin climbing the wooded ridge you have been approaching. Above the small village of Chisopani ("Cold Water"), ascend to the pass at 8,240 feet. From here you can see the impressive summits of Gauri Shankar (23,439 feet) on the border and Menlungtse (23,554 feet) inside Tibet. Follow the trail down to the village of Sikri 2,000 feet below, or if you wish, follow the road as it contours northward to its terminus at Jiri. If you have taken the path to Sikri, you can continue on one of two trails: the shorter path goes down-valley, crosses the southeast ridge, passes through Kattike village, and then goes up the Khimti Khola to Those, the largest bazaar town between the main road and Namche Bazaar. At Those, iron was once produced for locks and bridge chain links, but the town's output has now declined greatly.

To reach Jiri (6,200 feet) from Sikri, cross the upper bridge northeast of town and climb a ridge where you will pass a flat area used for the haat bazaar on Saturdays. Not far below lies Jiri, with its airstrip, hospital, lodge, restaurant, and large agricultural project. From Jiri, you may want to take a side trip north to Chordung, a 12,105-foot high point, for excellent views of the main peaks. Allow a day and a half for this dry-ridge walk. To continue to Those from Jiri, walk among fields south along the east bank of the river to Kune. Then climb slowly through pine groves to meet the trail from Sikri, where you turn east and reach Those by way of Kattike. After exploring Those's bazaar with its whitewashed homes, continue up the left bank of the Khimti Khola to a suspension bridge beyond Shivalaya. A different eastern path from Jiri climbs in a southeasterly direction over the ridge called Patashe Danda, descends through Mali village, crosses the Yelung Khola, and joins the main trail at the suspension bridge over the Khimti Khola.

At the suspension bridge (5,905 feet), climb past Sangbadanda village to an 8,850-foot pass with double main walls. Alternatively, you could continue along the crest of the spur from Sangbadanda through the town of Buldanda to a small cheese factory near the ridgetop (10,250 feet). In summer and fall you may be able to purchase milk, yogurt, butter, and cheese at the factory. Not far south of the cheese factory is Thodung Gomba. The gomba and cheese factory are connected with the pass by a trail that closely follows the ridgeline. East of the pass, descend to the large stupas and small gomba at the Sherpa village of Bhandar (also called Changma) on a shelf less than halfway to the valley floor. High on the eastern ridge you can see the Lamjura Pass, which you will cross. From Bhandar descend gently, then steeply eastward beside hulking ridges, and cross the tributary Surma Khola to reach the Likhu Khola. Pass over the Likhu Khola on a suspension bridge and continue along the east bank to the small village of Kenja (5,350 feet), with its several modest bhattis, on the northern bank of the Kenja Khola.

Kenja village marks the beginning of the 6,200-foot ascent to the trek's highest point prior to Namche Bazaar. Break up this climb, if possible. You can stop overnight at Sete (8,450 feet), a small settlement with a gomba. To reach Sete, take the right-hand trail fork several hours' walk above Kenja. From Sete you need an early start for the next day's long hike over the pass. Be certain to stock up on water, because none will likely be found above town. Climb to the top of an east-west spur above Sete and continue to a trail fork; take the northerly path through rhododendrons to the cairn- and flag-bedecked top of 11,580-foot Lamjura Pass. Two hours' walk north of the pass is a magnificent 13,160-foot viewpoint.

Since reaching Bhandar you have been in Sherpa country and will continue through land populated by this hardy clan as far as the uppermost pastures beneath Mt. Everest. Sometime in the mid-sixteenth century, the group of people that have come to be called Sherpas ("People from the East") migrated to their present homeland from Kham in eastern Tibet. Buddhists of the old Nyingma sect, Sherpas speak an unwritten Tibetan dialect that is often translated directly into spoken English with a delightfully scrambled word order.

The Sherpas were once exclusively agriculturalists, animal breeders, and transborder traders. Today the livelihood of many Sherpas depends on the visitors who flock to their homeland. The men of the clan first became known to English visitors in 1907 as strong, reliable mountain porters and guides. Once Sherpa porters were paid 5 rupees (about half a dollar) a day plus food. Now some high-altitude Sherpa porters have been paid hundreds of rupees for carrying loads up a single stage high on Mt. Everest. Until recently, every recognized sirdar in Nepal was a Sherpa. Many of the clan who work for trekkers and mountaineers are young men, and some are young women (called Sherpanis). But you may still see an occasional older Sherpa man with turquoise earrings and the traditional long braid who looks at photographs or maps through curled fingers as if scrutinizing the printed image with a magnifying glass. Some Sherpas have second homes in Kathmandu, and others have become quite wealthy working as guides, sirdars, and hoteliers.

The trail on the eastern side of Lamjura Ridge descends through evergreens that hug plunging slopes. Here you enter the region Sherpas call Shorong, but the area is more widely known as Solu. Until trekking became big business, the Sherpas of Solu were better off than those in Khumbu, for the cropland in Solu is lower and its pastures are more verdant. Solu butter is still carried to the market at Namche Bazaar and commands a good price. The first village reached in Solu is Tragdobuk. Another 2 miles takes you to Junbesi (8,755 feet) with its gomba, new school, and large homes typical of the prosperous, almost Swiss-like houses found hereabouts. Above the head of the valley is the peak called Shorong Yul Lha ("Country God of Solu," 22,826 feet), also called Numbur. Two miles north of Junbesi, near Mopung village, is the active Thupten Choling Gomba, under the direction of Tulshi Rimpoche, who was formerly one of two abbots at Dzarongphu (Rongbuk) Gomba in Tibet, north of Mt. Everest. An excellent book by Hugh R. Downs, *Rhythms of a Himalayan Village,* depicts life in Solu from an insider's perspective.

From Junbesi you can walk southward to reach Phaphlu's recently lengthened STOL airstrip, its busy hospital, or Chiwong Gomba high on the ridge northeast of Phaphlu. Farther south, off the main Khumbu trail, is the large administrative town of Salleri. From Junbesi on to Namche, you are walking through the area depicted on the Schneider *Shorong/Hinku* map, but note that some of the route along the Dudh Kosi Valley has been changed since the map was completed.

To continue toward Khumbu from Junbesi, cross the Junbesi Khola and take the upper trail heading southeast and up the ridge. As you round the grassy ridgeline 1,200 feet above Junbesi, you have your first view of both Mt. Everest and Makalu. Descend through Salung, cross the main river below, and walk up through Ringmo village. The direct southern trail from Phaphlu and Salleri joins the trail at Ringmo. Above Ringmo is a one-building cheese factory. Proceed along a gentle slope, and not far beyond you'll cross Takshindu Pass (10,075 feet), marked by a large stupa, here called a chorten. This is the last east-west pass on the trek, but you still have a couple of high spurs to cross before walking up to Namche. Proceed on the middle trail east of the pass for the fifteen-minute walk to Takshindu Gomba; you can stay the night high on this ridge in a nearby inn with views of snow-topped peaks to the east and north. The low point of the ridge directly across the valley is the pass leading to the Hinku Valley and eastern Nepal.

When leaving Takshindu Gomba, take the trail toward Manidingma that angles southeast. Don't take the northeast path, or you will end up in a cul-de-sac below several villages. Continue down, at first through a forest, 2,400 feet to Manidingma and another 2,300 feet to cross a bridge over the Dudh Kosi ("Milk River," 5,100 feet). You have glimpses of the bridge as you approach this large river, which drains all of Khumbu. On the eastern bank, angle northeasterly through scattered terraces past Jubing and several smaller villages. You cross over a notch to reach Kharikhola village, with its few shops and inns, just south of the stream known as Khari Khola. The lower branch of the trail leading uphill to Pangum and on to eastern Nepal leaves from Kharikhola (see "From Khumbu to the Arun Valley" in Chapter 8). This region, from Kharikhola to Namche Bazaar, is inhabited almost exclusively by Sherpas and is called Pharak. Pharak ("the area that connects") is the region that joins Solu with Khumbu.

Have a good meal in Kharikhola, for now you'll be doing some uphill walking. First you head for the small village of Bupsa (avoiding the old route through Kharte). From Bupsa, continue uphill through forest on a recently built trail that angles upward, but not as far up as the old trail (the path depicted on the Schneider map). When you reach the ridgeline you will have imposing views up and down the precipitous Dudh Kosi gorge. Now you head into the side valley, the Puiyan Khola, on a trail that goes level and down until you reach the stream itself. Then you walk away from the stream, passing the small village of Puiyan, which you could see before from the ridgeline. From the stream to the village, the trail is level, but now it ascends until the next ridgeline. If it's not cloudy at the ridge, you can see the numerous large buildings at Lukla, even though the airstrip itself is not obvious. The trail lies ahead and drops well below. At the bottom of the steep river valley, many ominous landslides have torn apart the slopes just above the Dudh Kosi. You'll walk across some similar landslides up-valley, the cause of which will be explained below.

Now you must descend about 1,600 feet from this ridge to the hamlet of Surkye (7,250 feet) at the stream of the same name. Again you angle upward, toward the steep slopes above the Dudh Kosi. The trail rises for a few minutes' walk, then you'll see a side path heading directly up to the east. This way leads to Lukla, about a thousand feet above. If you are heading for Namche Bazaar and Khumbu, there is no reason to take this side trail to Lukla, and you can continue on the main route north. As you rise, you'll see that the peaks on either side of the trail are either frosted or covered with snow. Chaunrikharka, with its several old stupas, is the next large village. Now you are temporarily out of the bottom of the gorge on more level ground. At Chaplung, the principal side trail from the airstrip and settlement at Lukla angles down to meet the main path we've been following from the south.

Flying into Lukla (9,300 feet) is the way most trekkers reach Khumbu. Many are aghast when the small twin Otter's engines make strange popping noises as the plane slows down for the approach and the upward-sloping runway comes into view. At least the old fuselages have been removed from sight (unless you go looking for them). Lukla has expanded greatly in recent years and has become a world unto its own: the runway has been lengthened somewhat, a control tower has been built, and there are many new lodges. During trekking season, people carrying goods for the haat bazaar at Namche often stop at Lukla; if they can sell their wares, they gleefully head homeward, avoiding the rest of the walk up to Namche. On arrival at Lukla, most trekkers barely look around. It's on the way back that the waiting begins.

Yes, all the stories and more you've heard about Lukla are true. The typed waiting list of trekkers and locals waiting for flights to Kathmandu can be over three hundred names long; there have been large demonstrations attempting to force RNAC (Royal Nepal Airlines Corporation) to add flights; planeloads of police have arrived to restore order; seventeen flights have landed in one day to clear people out; and much, much more. The hard-pressed RNAC staff does its best, given the limiting factors. Everyone is at the mercy of wind and clouds (instruments aren't used here) and the small number of sixteen-seat aircraft available. If you don't have a dated ticket, be ready to either walk to Phaphlu (two or three days) or Jiri (about five days) or be patient. Lukla can be very crowded from the end of October until the second week in December, when the crush usually diminishes. If you have a dated ticket, be sure to arrive at Lukla by about 4 P.M. the day before your flight. The RNAC office is open for only an hour a day sometime in the late afternoon (the exact hour is always posted). If you are not at the office the day before your flight to reconfirm, you will be dropped from the list. You can ask your hotel manager (or the local agent of your trekking outfitter) to assist you. If your flight comes, all well and good. If the plane does not come, you will go to the bottom of the waiting list of confirmed passengers. Then the wait begins for extra planes to arrive. Be patient; be calm: you came of your own accord, you were warned, and you've probably just finished a wonderful trek, so don't let a few days at Lukla get to you. You can always walk out.

If you want to get away from the charged atmosphere that often pervades Lukla during trekking season, here are three short excursions. Near the north part of the runway (walk uphill from the control tower), follow a steep trail that goes high above the landing strip. Climbing this hill helps put things in perspective. So does the walk to the grazing pastures southeast from Lukla. Find the trail that goes between two of the lodges just south of the upper part of the airfield. Follow the path as it winds in and out, rising and falling, until you reach a series of grassy meadows some fifteen minutes from Lukla. Suddenly you're back in Pharak again (and en route to the Chhatara Teng Pass, noted below). Finally, if you're tired of walking and want to succumb to drink, there is always the excellent rakshi at Tamang Tole ("Tamang Street"). Tamang Tole is the northernmost group of houses five minutes' walk away from Lukla on the main trail north. Two to three full glasses here will guarantee you an altered outlook and a good night's sleep.

East of Lukla and almost visible from the airfield is the 15,100-foot Chhatara Teng Pass, which connects with the upper Hinku Valley, the 17,765-foot Mera La, and the upper Hongu Valley. Only attempt this route if you are experienced, well provisioned, and with a knowledgeable porter-guide. The Schneider *Shorong/Hinku* map shows all of this area.

Now it's time to walk north and begin to see the high country of Khumbu. Follow the wide trail that angles downward from Lukla. You pass a gigantic tree that bends protectively over the path and has small, ancient shrines at its base. Below and to the west is Chaunrikharka. Be careful. Look when you look and walk when you walk. An experienced group leader once started hiking (wearing running shoes) and became immersed in birdwatching. Fifteen minutes out of Lukla he fell, twisted his ankle, and that was the end of his trek.

North of Lukla the going is easy and the trail quite wide. If you have flown into Lukla, you may possibly feel the altitude, but if you have walked in, you will be an old hand and this will be the easiest part of the trek thus far. The path continues near the bottom of the steep, forested gorge on the east bank of the Dudh Kosi. Now you can't help but see that the river has recently gone wild. In fact, two catastrophes have taken place within ten years.

During the monsoon of 1977, part of a steep hillside beneath Ama Dablam broke loose (the white scar is still visible up-valley) and dammed up a stream. The lake that formed washed over the avalanched soil and sent a wall of water down the valley that ruined several bridges and killed three people (for this happened on a Friday night before bazaar day, and many people were camped with their loads near the bottom of the Namche hill). Then in August 1985, just before the expeditions for the fall season were ready to head up the Dudh Kosi Valley with hundreds of porter loads, a more devastating natural calamity occurred (although there were no fatalities this time). In the Bhote Kosi Valley beyond the village of Thame, a large chunk of glacier broke off into a high lake, causing the water to pour over the moraine that contained it. The resulting flood sent a 30-foot-high tidal wave of mud coursing down the valley. The noise from this cataclysm sounded like thunder thousands of feet above in Namche. People in low-lying villages along the Dudh Kosi must have thought the world was coming to an end. This wall of muck tore out every bridge in the entire region of Pharak and decimated considerable portions of the trail along the valley.

A new route was quickly pieced together, bridges were built, and the path has since been improved, but by the time you read this, the exact route may well be different for the walk between Lukla and Namche Bazaar. There are reports, for instance, that a completely different high trail may be constructed on the east side of the valley. Never fear: this is a very well used path, and you'll surely be able to find the way. Just look for the Vibram prints on the path.

The trail north of Chaunrikharka angles downward, crossing the Kusum River, which drains the western slopes of Kusum Kangguru. This mountain's double peak is visible for a few minutes' walk. You pass through several small settlements and cross the river to the west bank at Phakding (8,650 feet). Many groups camp at Phakding because of the level ground hereabouts, so it can be crowded and you might want to stop before Phakding or carry on to an inn farther along if you are on your own. Pharak's largest gomba is located several hundred feet above Phakding on the west side of the river. Be sure to watch the trail carefully as you walk and stay away from the edge, which can overhang the embankment. The long-needle pine forests are lovely in Pharak. Unfortunately these trees are rapidly being cut south of the national park boundary. At the small settlement of

Benkar is a large boulder entirely covered with the sacred words "Om Mani Padme Hum." You may be proceeding a bit diffidently, but when you return back down this valley from Khumbu you will feel like Super Trekker: you'll be able to leap up the few hills with legs of iron and altitude-strengthened lungs.

North of Benkar you cross to the east side of the river. Now you are at Chumoa and the Hatago Lodge, formerly run by a bewhiskered Japanese gent who liked to pretend he was Nepali. His establishment was originally built to provide fresh vegetables for the now-defunct Hotel Everest View above Namche Bazaar. You'll see many kinds of fruit trees here, each donated by a person whose name is noted on a small sign. Just north of Chumoa the trail dips in and out of a clear stream that drains the Kyashar Glacier at the base of Thamserku and Kangtega himals. The small path leading into this inviting cleft is most intriguing. If you took two or three days and walked up this side valley, you would walk along a ragged moraine by the Kyashar Glacier in a deep, narrow basin below those two high peaks: so near, yet so far from the well-traveled trail. North of here is the hamlet of Monzo. Recently one small teahouse there (indistinguishable from scores of others) had a piece of paper tacked onto the front wall that read: "One of the World's Best Hotels is in Monzo."

Just north of Monzo you enter Sagarmatha National Park, then immediately descend by large boulders covered with the sacred "Om Mani Padme Hum" through a narrow notch to the park's entrance station (this location will change if the trail is relocated). At the entrance you pay a modest fee and will be given a receipt (save this in case it is asked for later). From here on, foreigners are not allowed to build fires, although you can eat food cooked over fires in lodges (if current regulations remain unchanged). All trekking groups must carry kerosene from below or purchase it from a nearby depot; kerosene alone must be used from here on.

North of the national park entrance the trail seesaws up and down along the wooded east side of the river. Now you can see the V-shaped Bhote Kosi Valley joining from the northwest. The debris-strewn floor of that valley as compared with the main Dudh Kosi Valley makes clear the havoc that was wreaked during the 1985 inundation. Eventually you drop down to the Dudh Kosi Valley floor, cross a bridge (which may be replaced by a higher suspension bridge), and begin the 2,100-foot climb to Namche Bazaar. Since the junction of the two valleys you have been in the area depicted on the *Khumbu Himal* sheet of the Schneider map series.

The trail is narrow and steep at the beginning, so take it slowly and you will be much less likely to have a headache in the evening at Namche. After some time you emerge at a ridgeline, where you can see up the Bhote Kosi Valley. To the north you can also see Mt. Everest just peeking out behind the Nuptse-Lhotse wall. The trail now widens and becomes less steep for the most part. Water is probably available here at the ridgeline and definitely can be obtained not far above. At a trail junction just below Namche, keep to the higher path or you will end up at the clothes-washing spot below town. Now you can pinch yourself and say, "I have arrived in Khumbu."

Khumbu: Land of the World's Highest Peaks

Namche Bazaar and Vicinity

Namche Bazaar (11,300 feet) is a large town built in the shape of a horseshoe. Namche consists of several-score homes, stores, hotels, and a gomba. The new game in town for the lodge owners is to enlarge their houses-cum-hotels, and the owners of the large hotels seem to be in competition to see who can build the tallest building. Photographs of Nepal's king and queen, the Dalai Lama, and the lodge owners adorn the walls of these large inns. But, wait, there are also framed photos of Robert Redford and Jimmy and Rosalynn Carter. Namche *has* changed in the past few years, hasn't it? Below the main trail in town a large spring pours forth. The water from this source makes the town's existence possible and also supplies the energy for Namche's new small hydroelectric system (located just out of sight below town). At night, each of the buildings hooked into the system is permitted to have two light bulbs, making Namche quite lovely from above. During the day, food is cooked on electric hot plates to conserve scarce firewood. At one lodge I saw the hot plates in use, but the large wood-fueled fireplace was also blazing away distilling *arak* (as rakshi is called locally).

You can help yourself acclimatize if you stay two nights in Namche on your way up-valley. There are day hikes you can take above town, but then it's best to return to Namche for the night. This will greatly help you higher up with adjusting to the elevation. Namche (Nauche in the Sherpa dialect) is the best place from here on to stock up on food, fuel, and warm clothing; many shops offer used expedition and trekking gear for rent or purchase. The Cadbury's chocolate is from England, and the expedition gear is as new as the most recent expedition to Mt. Everest. Remember the bustling Saturday market for buying bulk food or fuel. You will be able to find canned or freeze-dried food and hot prepared meals as far as Lobuche, or even Gorak Shep, up-valley, but the quality and array of packaged food, and particularly hot meals, will lessen the farther you go.

The shortest hike from Namche is a ten-minute walk east of town up to the Sagarmatha National Park headquarters on a rounded prominence above the police station. Here is an interesting museum that tells about Sherpa culture and the natural history and geology of Khumbu. After you've seen the museum, stroll out to the eastern edge of the shelf beyond the buildings. Here you can see the sweep of the valley you have been ascending, both down-valley where you've been and up past Tengboche Monastery to the massive Nuptse-Lhotse wall with Mt. Everest peeking above. It's best to walk up here in the morning before the day's clouds begin to build and obstruct the view.

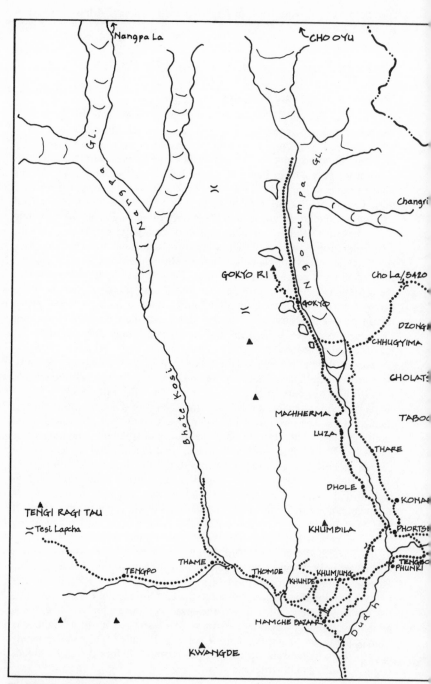

Trekker's Khumbu

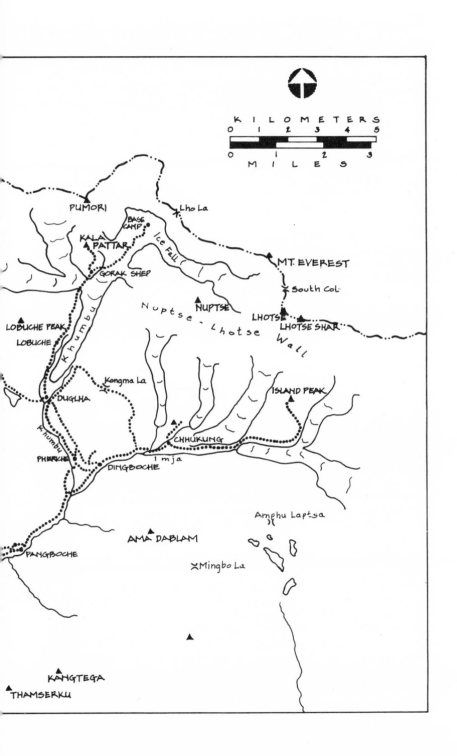

KILOMETERS
0 1 2 3 4 5

MILES
0 1 2 3

PUMORI

Lho La

BASE CAMP

KALA PATTAR

Ice Fall

MT. EVEREST

GORAK SHEP

South Col

Nuptse - Lhotse Wall

NUPTSE

LHOTSE

LHOTSE SHAR

LOBUCHE PEAK

LOBUCHE

Khumbu

Kongma La

DUGLHA

ISLAND PEAK

Khumbu

CHHUKUNG

PHERICHE

Imja

DINGBOCHE

Amphu Laptsa

AMA DABLAM

Mingbo La

PANGBOCHE

KANGTEGA

THAMSERKU

For a longer walk, head up the steep trail north of the park headquarters (the path begins by a large boulder near some inns) or the trail that angles north near the village gomba. You will climb up to the top of the basin where Namche is located and then cross the rarely used landing strip called Shyangboche. From Shyangboche you can walk twenty minutes northeast of the airfield along a path that slowly gains elevation to the Everest View Hotel at about 12,800 feet. This hotel once offered bottled oxygen in each room and spotless tablecloths in the dining room, but it floundered for lack of supplies and customers. You may still be able to take tea or coffee in the dining room as you gaze up-valley where you'll be going. It's also fun to walk out on the ridge as far as you can go just beyond the hotel. You stand on a high promontory with the wind enveloping you. The 10,000-foot-high Nuptse-Lhotse wall appears far closer than the two days' walk it will take you to approach it. This Nuptse-Lhotse wall is a sheer mountain barrier extending some 10 miles from west of Nuptse to east of Lhotse. The ridge is never lower than 24,900 feet and connects two of the world's ten highest peaks.

Another direction you can walk from Shyangboche is over the low ridge to the north to the two villages of Khumjung and Khunde (about 12,500 feet). These villages, unlike Namche, have remained determinedly traditional in their outward appearance. You can certainly find food and lodging in a home here, but you may have to inquire around a bit; there are very few signs in either of these towns. Once you find a home to stay in, you'll definitely feel more a part of the family than you would in commercialized Namche. Have some *shakpa,* the basic "Sherpa stew," a thick soup that will be different every place you try it. Shakpa always includes potatoes, the ubiquitous local ingredient, and wheat; then it also has whatever's available, from turnips to tender yak meat. Remember that you are a thousand feet higher here than in Namche, so consider staying in Khunde or Khumjung only after passing at least one night in Namche or on the way back down-valley. These two villages are much closer to traditional Khumbu than the busy bazaar town below. Seek them out, linger in one or both of them, and you'll be glad you did.

Khunde, the more westerly and higher of the two villages, is the home of the long-established Khunde Hospital, funded by the Himalayan Trust, a philanthropic organization founded by Sir Edmund Hillary. The Western-staffed Khunde Hospital is the largest of the Himalayan Trust's several health posts in Solu-Khumbu. Khumjung, the larger village, is the site of a Himalayan Trust–financed primary and secondary school. The trail angling up to the east from Khumjung leads to the village water supply, situated around the ridge quite some distance from town.

Khumbu's sacred mountain Khumbila (an abbreviation of its full name, Khumbui Yul Lha, which means "Country of God of Khumbu") has a climbable spur above Khunde. If you ascend this high ridge, you will have excellent perspectives on such peaks as Kwangde to the south, fluted Thamserku, Kangtega's double summit, and heaven-seeking Ama Dablam. Khumbila is actually named for the deity Khumbila Terzen Gelbu, who is pictured riding a red horse and wearing all-white clothing. The sacred peak is off-limits to climbers, and its summit can be seen from nearly every village in Khumbu.

The remainder of this section on Khumbu first describes the side valley of the Bhote Kosi to the west of Namche. Then you will travel along the most direct route to the base of Mt. Everest. Finally, I'll mention the principal side treks you can take in this well-visited region. Your best possible guide to this area is the 1:50,000 *Khumbu Himal* map noted in Appendix A, "Map Information." With that sheet, you can pick your own routes and embark on climbs or side hikes that you choose yourself. Note that there are many additional trails in Khumbu that are not depicted on this map.

The most important precaution about trekking in Khumbu is to avoid going too high too fast, particularly if you have flown into the region at Lukla. Unacclimatized people have become quite ill, and a very few have even died from walking too rapidly into the upper valleys. If you begin to develop symptoms of altitude sickness (see Chapter 12, "A Himalayan Medical Primer"), descend immediately and rest before attempting to trek higher.

The Bhote Kosi Valley

The only valley in Khumbu west of Namche Bazaar is the Bhote Kosi Valley (also called the Nangpo Tsangpo). To begin walking up this valley, follow the wide trail that angles out of Namche's basin from the village gomba. At first you proceed on a gentle path that rolls along in and out of mixed forest. Not far beyond Namche, a side trail angles back uphill leading to Khunde village. On the valley floor below, you can see the destruction wrought by the tidal wave of muck that thundered down this valley in 1985. Somewhere below the debris is the ruined foundation of a hydroelectric project that was to have provided all of Khumbu with electricity. In less than two hours from Namche you will reach the scattered houses of Thomde village; its gomba rests high above town. Beyond Thomde the path descends to the devastated valley floor and crosses to the Bhote Kosi's right bank, then rises, crosses the tributary stream draining the basin below the Tesi Lapcha, and continues ascending to lower Thame village (Thame Og). Thame is three to four hours from Namche Bazaar and the farthest you are permitted to proceed up the Bhote Kosi Valley. In the restricted area at the head of the long valley is the wide, glaciated Nangpa La, the 18,750-foot pass on the border with Tibet. Several days' walk beyond the Nangpa La to the north is Tingri village, the town traditionally visited for trading by the Sherpas of Khumbu. A few traders from both Tibet and Khumbu still use the Nangpa La with official permission, but the pass is less frequented than it used to be. Certain kinds of cow-yak crossbreeds from Khumbu are very much in demand now in Tibet, for the Sherpas have kept up their breeding programs, while the herds in Tibet have dwindled.

At Thame you can see the gomba above town on its steep hillside near a few stunted conifers. The Mani Rimdu masked dances take place at Thame Gomba during the full moon of May. (The same scenes are enacted at Tengboche during the November-December full moon). Tenzing Norgay, one of the first two people to climb Mt. Everest, grew up in this village. A trail up the side valley to the west leads to the 18,875-foot Tesi Lapcha Pass. (For information about this difficult pass crossing, see "The Rolwaling Valley," above.) You can walk from Namche to Thame and back in a day. But you should consider staying the night in a home at Thame and enjoying the evening light on Thamserku and Kangtega. Savor your experience in these unique places; don't always touch base and leave. As much as any town in Khumbu, Thame is off the tourist route, and you may be the only foreigner in town.

The Direct Trail to the Base of Mt. Everest

The trail up-valley from Namche Bazaar ascends east of town, just to the north of the path to the Sagarmatha National Park headquarters. Then the route begins a level traverse toward and high above the Dudh Kosi River. Cattle and cow-yak crossbreeds graze on the precarious slopes above and below the trail, indifferent to the sweeping mountain views. Wild animals are rigorously protected in Khumbu, and from this section of trail until you reach Pangboche village, you may be lucky and sight Himalayan tahr (wild goats) with their dark brown coats. If you round a corner and see one close by, it will bound away either up or straight down the hill. The places you are most likely to see tahr in Khumbu are along this section of trail north of Namche, in the semiwooded areas on either side of Tengboche Monastery, and along the steep hill on the side path between Phortse and Pangboche villages.

The path angles into a wooded fold in the hills where there are a few small houses and, during the trekking season, several Tibetan souvenir sellers (with their wares mostly lugged up from Kathmandu). The path to Khumjung joins the main trail at the innermost V of the trail just south of these houses. Along this side trail to Khumjung you are very likely to see Nepal's national bird, the protected impeyan pheasant, called a *danphe* in Nepali. The males of this species have iridescent feathers that shine with every color of the rainbow. You may also see danphe and hear them chuckling near Tengboche Monastery. On the main path, between the trail junction to Khumjung and the small Tibetan settlement, a narrow path angles upward to the northeast (in the opposite direction of Khumjung). This trail climbs to join the route from Khumjung that goes to the Gokyo Valley, a path described later on.

The main path now angles out again toward the Dudh Kosi Valley. Just below the trail is a forestry department nursery, and above lie the scattered houses of Trashinga. Now the track descends steeply to the roaring Dudh Kosi River. On the east bank of the river lies the small settlement of Phunki (10,700 feet), where there are two inns. People with bad cases of altitude sickness are sometimes brought here from up-valley because this is the lowest place in the area. Several water-powered prayer wheels, one above the other and each in its own small abode, help make Phunki a charming location. From Phunki you enter a forest and begin the 2,000-foot climb to Tengboche Monastery. The steepest part is first, so take it slowly as you ascend through the trees. After a while, the path adopts a steady angle, as it climbs to the east. This part of the trail is visible from the lookout points near Namche. If you are walking here in the early morning, you may possibly see a musk deer. This strange, fanged animal with its long rear legs may be seen by the quiet and observant hiker from this forest as far as the next bridge across the main river.

The square, red Tengboche Monastery ("Great High Place," 12,700 feet) sits on a spur at what is possibly the most picturesque location in Khumbu. Thirty-five monks of the Nyingma order resided at Tengboche when the first Western mountaineers reached the monastery in the fall of 1950. Presently, after a drop in the size of the order, the population of maroon-robed monks has risen again almost to what it was a generation ago. The lama at Tengboche, Nawang Tenzing Zangbu, was born in Namche and came to be recognized as the reincarnation of the lama of Tengboche via a pilgrimage that took him to Lhasa (in the arms of his mother), to Rongbuk Monastery north of Khumbu, and back again to Tengboche. Rimpoche ("Precious One"), as he is called, has studied intensively for a total of eight years at several monasteries in central Tibet. He has started a school for young monks at Tengboche and has also guided the construction of the new Sherpa Cultural Center just behind the monastery. The stone, two-story cultural center has displays on Sherpa religion, customs, and culture. At the cultural center or one of the nearby lodges, be sure to purchase the locally written, informative booklet *Stories and Customs of the Sherpas*. You will also want to visit the gomba itself, and if you arrive at the right time, you may be able to attend a prayer session. Tengboche's annual Mani Rimdu festival takes place at the full moon of November-December (the ninth Tibetan month). There can be as many Westerners as locals at this affair, so be ready for a bustling event.

Tengboche rests not far beneath the spreading arms of Ama Dablam ("Mother's Charm Box," 22,494 feet), considered by many people to be the most striking peak in the area. The mountain's name refers to the large, squarish clump of snow near the summit that resembles a *dablam,* a charm box worn by women in Khumbu and Tibet. Here you can also see the tip of Mt. Everest peeking from behind the formidable Nuptse-Lhotse wall. At Tengboche, you may camp, stay in a dormitory room provided by the monks, in a lodge, or in a nearby New Zealand–built, glassed-in dormitory. Staying for at least a day in this exquisite location would be time well utilized. Be sure to walk out to the end of the ridge where you can see Cho Oyu Himal far to the west at the head of the Gokyo Valley.

North of Tengboche the path angles down through a moss-draped forest that is often coated with frost in the early morning. This stretch of trail near Debuche Convent passes several old mani walls and rambles through forest and meadow. It is a lovely, tranquil part of the walk, traversing the last thick forest you'll pass through until you return. If you are walking here in autumn, you may pass a Sherpani carrying a towering load of *soluk*—the dried leaves and pine needles used to carpet the ground floor of all Sherpa homes, where every family's animals are domiciled. All too soon, you cross to the west bank on a short bridge suspended high above a thundering cataract of the river, now called the Imja Khola.

The path ascends past an old-style chorten and beneath an entranceway to a notch where there is a prominent boulder. Just beyond this place the trail divides. The more direct route is the lower trail that passes among the small houses of Pangboche, Khumbu's highest permanent village. The higher trail leads you to "upper" Pangboche, where you can visit the gomba, red and squarish, with a pagoda-style roof like the one at Tengboche. Pangboche's gomba, like the gomba at Khumjung, has a scalp said to have come from a yeti, and you can see it and the accompanying skeleton of a yeti hand if the keeper of the gomba is present. I found the old guest book at Pangboche (there is a similar book at Tengboche) of greater interest. Perusing the pages of the oldest of these guest registers (if they are still about) is like reading a history of the foreigners who have traveled to Khumbu.

Tall, stately juniper trees rise near Pangboche's gomba. These trees, like half the forest cover in Khumbu, are considered to be "closed," or protected. There are twenty of these sacred forests, called *khakh shing* in the Sherpa dialect. In traditional Sherpa culture, such trees are thought to be inhabited by strong *lu,* or spirits. Formerly these khakh shing were overseen by men called *shingki naua,* "guardians of wood."

Near Pangboche, Ama Dablam rises high above, as if protecting the village beneath its perpendicular west and south ridges. Beneath the peak, in one narrow ravine you can see the white scar where an avalanche set off an inundation in 1977. The trail contours along north of Pangboche across the valley from Khumbu's highest forest (of birch); then the way ascends to a meadow. At the most southerly part of this gently rising grassy area, you can just spy the very tip of Mt. Everest, but by the time you have passed a lone teahouse at Orsho, only the massive Nuptse-Lhotse wall is visible. Ahead you can see that the river divides. The larger trail that drops to cross the western fork, the Khumbu River, goes east to Dingboche in the Imja Valley. This route is described later.

Now you will follow the most frequented path above a couple of huts and up the hill toward the Khumbu River in the wide valley to the west. Not far ahead on the north bank of the river is Pheriche (14,000 feet), a mile beyond the river junction. Pheriche consists of several low stone buildings and is considered a *yersa,* or summer settlement. Trekkers should halt for two nights here, as at Namche Bazaar, for acclimatization. Alternatively, you could go to Dingboche in the Imja Valley to the east and pass the second night (or two nights) there. Experience has shown that two nights passed at this elevation will greatly help with acclimatization as you go higher.

Most people find that as they walk above about 13,000 feet, something quite difficult to define changes in their consciousness. This is not the temporary crankiness or euphoria associated with adjustment to high elevation. It is longer lasting than a temporary mood. We begin somehow operating on automatic. It's almost as if you are outside your body and watching yourself. Mountaineers experience this shift in consciousness to extremes at higher elevations, but those of us who haven't had time to fully acclimatize often notice it at these "lower" altitudes. Is it super or diminished consciousness? People have different interpretations of it, depending on the individual. You may best be aware of this subtle shift in consciousness in retrospect, after you return to a lower elevation and suddenly think, "Oh yes, here 'I' am again."

While at Pheriche you can climb the northern ridge to visit the small, usually locked Nangkartshang Gomba. This gomba offers excellent views of Ama Dablam and Makalu, the world's fifth-highest peak, to the east. From this perspective to the north of the mountain, Ama Dablam looks like an entirely different peak; its ridges no longer look like robes but appear razor sharp. You might also walk to Chhukung from Pheriche: see "The Imja Valley," below, for a description of this walk. A Trekker's Aid post at Pheriche is staffed in the spring and fall by a physician who works with the Himalayan Rescue Association. If you have any questions at all about how you're doing, stop by the Trekker's Aid post. The physician is there to assist you.

Beyond Pheriche, most people walk toward Lobuche Peak along the main trail on the wide bottomland. I have always enjoyed taking the smaller path along the wide shelf located north of and some 600 feet higher than the usual route. After all, you have to gain the elevation before Duglha, the next settlement, and now is as good a time as any to go up. You can reach this trail by angling northwest up one of the small stock trails behind Pheriche. What fabulous views there are along this higher path. The entire valley seems to expand. Taboche and Cholatse's sheer faces and Ama Dablam's ridges grow higher as you ascend. Below you is the "yak" route, the main trail with trekkers and locals marching determinedly upward or charging merrily down the valley.

Whichever way you go, you will reach the small buildings at Duglha (15,150 feet) just beyond the stream that issues from the Khumbu Glacier above. Here you are on the terminal moraine of the Khumbu Glacier. At Duglha you will welcome lunch, or at least a rest and cup of tea. Now your rest days begin to make themselves felt. If you have been acclimatizing properly, you should feel all right even though you walk more slowly from here on up. If you are a "Type A" who has been charging up the valley, you may have to return to Pheriche to give your body time to adjust to the thin atmosphere.

From Duglha, you must climb the terminal moraine of the as-yet-unseen Khumbu Glacier. The altitude slows your steps on this hill, but it is the last ascent of the day, so walk *bistaari-bistaari,* "slowly-slowly." The long row of stone monuments at the top of the hill has been built in memory of various high-altitude porters and climbers who have died on Mt. Everest. After you turn the corner and begin walking up the level valley, the round-topped peak to the north with the slanted ridges is Pumori ("Daughter Peak," named for George Mallory's daughter). A mile beyond the top of the hill lies Lobuche (16,200 feet), another yersa, hidden away between a hill and a rocky moraine. Lobuche, like Pheriche, has a large pure spring (whose water rapidly becomes contaminated as it leaves its source, so keep purifying your water). There are several smoky and often-crowded inns at Lobuche. Don't expect to have the best sleep of the trek here, although the second night should be better than the first. Keep drinking water or sweet tea; it is extremely helpful for your acclimatization and strength. Climb one of the hills above Lobuche for excellent perspectives of the tan-and-gray granite webbing on Nuptse, where you'll see bright golden alpenglow at sunset. Most people take about four days (allowing acclimatization time) to reach Lobuche from Namche Bazaar.

The path above Lobuche traverses nearly level alongside the Khumbu Glacier's lateral moraine. Then the way zips up a moraine and proceeds for some distance across rubble of the active Changri Glacier. (If you are thinking of walking to the area called Everest Base Camp and you don't like this part of the walk, then don't plan on walking for six hours on even worse terrain than here.) After some rocky scrambling, you can look ahead and see Kala Pattar ("Black Rock") and, below, the sandy basin called Gorak Shep ("Crow's Death," 17,000 feet). At Gorak Shep a small tarn provides water. The source for this water is near the base of the hill. Be sure to keep drinking enough liquid to avoid dehydration at this high elevation. There are usually two small, drafty inns operating here during the spring and fall trekking seasons. If you intend to walk to Everest Base Camp on the Khumbu Glacier, you should probably stay here at Gorak Shep the night before you leave (to ensure that you can get back before too late). If you aren't going to base camp, you can easily walk from Lobuche to Kala Pattar and return to Lobuche the same day. But remember that the 900-foot rise in elevation between Lobuche and Gorak Shep (not to mention the lower temperature) makes a lot of difference in your ability to sleep.

Kala Pattar is the hill above Gorak Shep. The high point above Gorak Shep you see as you approach is not the best vantage point, however. It is best to walk up from Gorak Shep until you reach the wide, grassy shelf some 500 feet up; then traverse northward along the nearly level but bumpy ground for half an hour until you see a higher point to the north with a distinct trail leading up to it. From this upper Kala Pattar (18,450 feet), you can see the famous South Col (26,195 feet), where most expeditions to Mt. Everest have their highest camp. Here you have the classic view of Mt. Everest. At Kala Pattar, you are on a spur of Pumori, directly below its slanted light granite and snow channels. To the east and south, the Khumbu Glacier sweeps below you; above it is Ama Dablam from yet a new perspective. Northward rise several border peaks and the vertical Lho La, reached in July 1921 from the Tibetan side by Mallory, the first time a foreigner had seen any part of Khumbu. The surroundings have an awesome brilliance and clarity. Truly this is one of the world's most majestic mountain panoramas.

Stolid and monumental, Mt. Everest (29,028 feet) rises above all. Known as Chomolungma ("Lady Goddess of the Wind") by Sherpas and Tibetans and named Sagarmatha ("Churning Stick of the Ocean") by Nepalis, the mountain was initially called Peak XV by surveyors when it was first identified from the plains. In 1852 it was recognized as the highest peak on earth and four years later was given the name Everest in honor of Sir George Everest, the early surveyor general of (British) India. The mountain was first climbed on May 29, 1953, by Tenzing Norgay and Edmund Hillary. Since then, its summit has been briefly surmounted by over two hundred people. Chomolungma is by no means the most difficult peak in Khumbu to climb, but since it's the highest mountain on earth, the various routes to the summit are "booked" years in advance.

On a recent walk to Kala Pattar in early December, I was most fortunate to reach the top with four monks from Tengboche Monastery. It has become a recent tradition for several monks from Tengboche to do a *kora,* a circumambulation, of the upper valley each year. One monk, a friend from my previous visits, wore the hat popular with many Sherpas: a baseball cap with "Captain" emblazoned on the front amidst gold braid. Wearing sweaters, maroon robes, and low canvas shoes, the monks sprightly passed us foreigners in our high-tech gear as they scampered up Kala Pattar. They had crossed the Cho La (noted below) and would cross the Kongma La (a tricky col east of the Khumbu Glacier) the next day. Kora is good karma.

The second walk from Gorak Shep, should you choose to do it, takes some five or more hours to complete round trip. This hike to Everest Base Camp (17,400 feet) on the Khumbu Glacier can be done round trip from Lobuche in a long day, but only by the fit, and it will be a long, tiring trek. Remember that the best views are to be had from Kala Pattar. Go to base camp only if you are feeling fit and want to see rocks, ice, expedition trash, and the famous location across from the Khumbu icefall. Beyond the memorial stone (to Jake Breitenbach of the 1963 American expedition and others) at the far end of Gorak Shep, a narrow trail leads onto the Khumbu Glacier. Once on the glacier, your route will not always be apparent. Try to follow any cairns or dung (always a good trail sign in such places) and keep heading along the moraine toward the Lho La past tall incisor-shaped seracs. After you reach the area across from the base of the Khumbu icefall (the scene of the greatest number of fatalities on the entire mountain), you see trash piles and other signs of humans. You have reached the area called Everest Base Camp, where you are out of sight of, but as close as you can get to, Mt. Everest.

The Gokyo or Dudh Kosi Valley

Some people consider trekking up the Gokyo Valley to be the high point of their experience in Khumbu. The valley is less frequented than the busy route to Kala Pattar, and there are excellent mountain perspectives along the way. This side valley has only one large permanent village, Phortse, which is right at the mouth of the valley. A house at the uppermost part of Phortse acts as the local inn. The path from down-valley to Gokyo begins from Khumjung village. At Khumjung, the trail toward Gokyo angles northward from the larger track near the stupa at the eastern end of town. The path then seesaws up and down beneath a sheer stone face, then slowly rises to a stupa at 13,030 feet. From this point the views are superb, particularly of Tengboche Gomba directly across the valley. The path then descends more than 1,000 feet to the right bank of the Dudh Kosi River, where it meets a trail leading downward from Phortse. From this junction the trail begins the long traverse up-valley. You may also reach Phortse if you are coming from the north by taking a narrow trail that leads along steep, rocky slopes (keep your eyes open for tahr here) from the upper part of Pangboche village.

After you begin the ascent up the Gokyo Valley, you have excellent views to the southeast of Kangtega ("Snow Horse Saddle") and Thamserku, the two summits over 21,500 feet that tower over Tengboche Monastery. Soon you will see Cho Oyu (26,750 feet) emerge (then disappear again) at the head of the valley. Note any signs of altitude sickness among your party as you proceed: it is easy to ascend too quickly into this high valley. The third small settlement you reach is Dhole (13,400 feet), where there is a modest inn or two during trekking season. If you question how well you are acclimatizing, halt early in the day or take a day's rest. A couple of miles beyond Dhole is Luza. At Luza you can begin to see the steep south face of Mt. Mera sandwiched between Kangtega and Thamserku.

One of the most beautifully situated yersas is Machherma (14,470 feet). Machherma now sports two inns in use during trekking season. Above Machherma's level side valley is the steep snow peak you can see from Tengboche. Across the valley to the east are the high peaks of Taboche and Cholatse that you can also see particularly well from Pheriche and Duglha in the Khumbu Valley. After you climb the ridge on the trail north of Machherma, you have a particularly good view of this part of the wide Gokyo Valley and the large terminal moraine of the Ngozumpa Glacier, the longest glacier in Nepal. The next yersa is called Pangka, closer to the glacier. Soon the path leads up a rocky slope next to a steep wall west of the glacier's lateral moraine. To the side, you can see the clear water from the lakes above mixing with the headwaters of the Dudh Kosi, the milky water from the glacier.

The path is rocky now, and you pass a small pond, then a larger one, and finally reach the third lake. Here are a few small inns and other buildings and the walled pastures collectively called Gokyo (15,700 feet). Be sure to walk a few feet up to the top of the moraine. From here you can see Cho Oyu, the world's ninth-highest peak, and the wide Ngozumpa Glacier, an undulating mass of gray rock. Some two to three hours' trudge directly uphill from Gokyo is Gokyo Ri (ri means "mountain" in Tibetan), one of Khumbu's most spectacular viewing locations, the peak marked 5483 (its elevation in meters) on the Schneider Khumbu Himal map. At this point you have great perspectives of the vast Ngozumpa Glacier, Cho Oyu with its neighbor Gyachung Kang, Mt. Everest rising above a fluted ridge, Lhotse, and Makalu: four of the world's ten highest peaks. Some call this the finest mountain panorama in Nepal. If you are feeling the altitude, don't make this steep climb. Rest is the better part of valor here. If you will be walking from Gokyo to Lobuche, the latter will be a piece of cake after this acclimatization (assuming you have kept yourself well fed and well hydrated).

On my first trip to Gokyo I dutifully slogged up Gokyo Ri, but the second time, I took a friend's advice and headed up the valley floor, carrying lunch. This short day hike was a pleasant, fairly level ramble, and I was very impressed. Walking along a path that is barely discernable at times, you eventually pass two more lakes. By the time you are near the second lake above Gokyo, you can see Mt. Everest from a unique perspective. Here the world's highest peak really stands out like a separate mountain, looking for all the world like a giant pup tent. Everest's north slopes, in Tibet, are too steep to hold the snow and stand out like burnished ebony. Cho Oyu and Gyachung Kang rise closer above, and the feeling of being in utterly deserted alpine splendor is intense.

A 17,780-foot pass variously called the Cho La or Pass 5420 (its elevation in meters on the *Khumbu Himal* map) connects the Gokyo Valley with a secondary path that emerges near Duglha in the Khumbu Valley. To reach this pass from Gokyo, walk back down-valley until you almost reach the lowest lake. From here there is a small path marked by cairns that takes you onto the glacier. You'll have to find your way across the glacier to the eastern side, then proceed above the small settlement of Dragnag. (Alternatively, there is a longer route below the glacier that requires more down and up-going.) After walking up from Dragnag on rolling pasture and moraine, you will reach the area called Chhugyima. Climb steeply above Chhugyima on scree or snow to the low point in the eastern ridge, the place marked 5420. The eastern descent follows a nearly level glacier at first, but you must keep to the south side of this glacier and cross onto the rock before too long, for the lower part of this small glacier is crevassed and shouldn't be attempted. Traverse to the east of the streams you meet and walk to the yersa of Dzonglha, situated on a low knob. From Dzonglha, you can follow a trail down-valley past Cholatse's steep, leaning face and above the lake of Tshola Tsho, continuing to the main Khumbu Valley path. You will join the main trail at Duglha.

If you try this pass from the Khumbu side, carry supplies for at least two days. On the ascent from Khumbu, keep left on low ground beyond Dzonglha and, as you approach the glacier, angle to the left (west) on moraine. Remember to ascend on rock at the south side of the glacier; then, where the rock becomes too steep to climb, cross onto the snow.

Note that you can descend the Gokyo Valley on a small path that angles along above the northern (left bank) side of the valley. You can reach this route by crossing the Ngozumpa Glacier or skirting below it, as noted above. Instead of heading up for Chhugyima, aim down-valley and cruise. This less-traveled route has fine views of the settlements you passed on the way up and also the sharp peaks above the valley to the southwest, including Khumbila. You can make good time heading down and may possibly find tea or shakpa (stew) available at the small settlements of Thare or Konar. There are several trails south out of Konar: take the middle one, or better yet, ask a local to point out the way to Phortse. This lowest part of the trail is lovely—it rises to a chorten, then descends through forest to the upper part of Phortse, right near the town's small inn.

The Imja Valley

The gentle Imja Valley lies to the east of Pheriche and the Khumbu Valley. You can reach the Imja Valley by walking easterly from Pheriche over the ridge. Or, when walking up from Pangboche, follow the Imja Khola's right bank to the east at the point where the Imja and Khumbu rivers join. The first habitation in the Imja Valley is the spread-out village of Dingboche (about 14,200 feet), where potatoes are raised in abundance. Inns are open here during trekking season. A trail leads up from Dingboche to Nangkartshang Gomba (which can also be reached from Pheriche). The Imja's unique allure is visible in the views of steep walls to the north and south as you proceed up the slowly rising trail along the main valley. To your right are fine perspectives of Ama Dablam's northern face.

As you continue walking up-valley in an easterly direction, the Nuptse-Lhotse wall comes into better view, towering nearly two miles above. About an hour's easy walk beyond Dingboche is the Imja Valley's last settlement of Chhukung (15,250 feet), where there are two inns. You reach Chhukung after jumping streams from the Nuptse, Lhotse Nup, and Lhotse glaciers. From Chhukung, the view of the Nuptse-Lhotse wall is excellent, and you can also see 20,305-foot Island Peak to the east-northeast. For a much better view of the area's panorama, stroll up the grassy hill to the north (toward the point marked 5043 on the Schneider map). Here you are even closer to the Nuptse-Lhotse wall and have a better look at Island Peak, now officially renamed Imja Tse Himal. This peak has a consuming fascination for some who wish to ascend a minor peak in the Khumbu area. It can be climbed from the south if you are equipped with crampons, rope, and ice ax and have some technical experience.

When I last strolled up to Chhukung, I met Ron Giddy, a tough, grizzled Englishman who had just walked with three hardy Sherpas in four long days from Makalu Base Camp over Sherpani Col, West Col, across the Panch Pokhari area of the uppermost Hongu Valley, and over the sheer Amphu Laptsa. This difficult, bitter-cold, technical route is not recommended for the likes of most of us. Nonetheless, there are numerous nontechnical routes here in Khumbu that I have not described. Using the *Khumbu Himal* map, strike off for a distant high place or a small side valley you can call your own.

8
Eastern Nepal

*I turned to the intricate terrace fields that represent the
honest toil of farmers. Mechi to Mahakali they are the stuff
and substance of the country.*

Harka Gurung, 1979

Oh that pork meat—
Chews like bubble gum and tastes like bacon!

Peace Corps volunteer
in Limbuwan, 1974

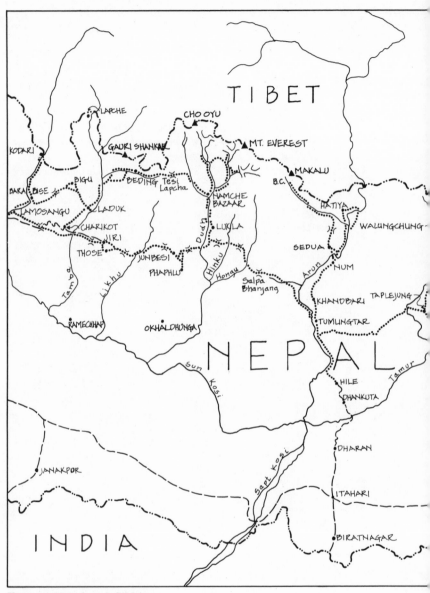

Eastern Nepal and Sikkim

MILES
0 5 10   25   50
KILOMETERS
0 5 10   25   50   75

LHONAK
GHUNSA
JANNU
KANGCHENJUNGA
LACHEN

CHOMOLHARI

Goechi La

S I K K I M

Tista

Natu
La

DRUGYEL
DZONG
THIMPHU
PARO
DZONG

RUMTEK
GANGTOK

Ha

BHUTAN

Rangit

DARJEELING
KALIMPONG

ILAM

PHUNTSHOLING

KAKARBHITTA
BAGHDOGRA
SILIGURI

BANG-
LADESH

Home to Rai and Limbu

Eastern Nepal from the Arun Valley to the border with Sikkim is a fascinating region visited by few foreigners. If you want to get away from the many trekkers in the popular hiking areas, consider the verdant eastern hills. The hilly areas in this part of the kingdom are more easily reachable than in the far west. This is because Nepal is narrower north to south in the east than in the west and because transport is good: by air to Tumlingtar and Biratnagar (Nepal's second-largest city) and by night bus to Biratnagar.

Eastern Nepal is also more populous than the west, and as anywhere in the kingdom, you never know whom you'll meet. The redoubtable trekker K. Garnay made the acquaintance of a man belonging to the Limbu clan who had gained an exceptional grasp of global geography and spoken French and English during the two years he had passed in a prisoner of war camp during World War II. Another time Garnay was far up the Tamur Valley when he met a Limbu gentleman who spoke impeccable English. This man, hunkered on his porch, divulged that he had perfected his British accent while on guard duty at Buckingham Palace.

The Limbus are a large clan in Nepal's easternmost middle hills, an area called Limbuwan. They are related to the more numerous Rai, who live to the west of them. Limbus are known for their *dhan nach,* the "rice dance," a mating ritual that adolescents perform from evening throughout the night until past dawn. In preparation for this dance, the men dress in Western-style dark coats, light cotton Nepali trousers, and new, colorful Nepali *topi*s, the national hat. Women wear the finest of their magenta wraps and carefully fix their hair with flowers. The dance itself is done in a line or circle with men and women alternating and, get this: holding hands, something practically unknown in the entire subcontinent. The songs are a strange stuttering, guttural series of vowel sounds, and the footwork can be minimal. Surely the niceties of this subtle dance totally elude the Western observer.

Gundruk is an important part of diet in the eastern hills. This is a spicy vegetable of pickled radish greens that are fermented for several weeks in underground pits, then sun-dried and stewed. And what mention of the eastern Himalaya would be complete without noting *tungba?* From the Arun Valley to Bhutan, tungba is a popular alcoholic beverage that is not always as mild as it tastes. Tungba is made by placing a couple of handfuls of fermented millet kernels in a 10-inch-high cylindrical wooden or bamboo cask. Boiling water is then poured over the grain, and a bamboo straw and wooden lid (with a hole to accommodate the straw) are added. The hot beer is then sipped through the straw, which keeps the millet kernels in the cask and out of the drinker's mouth. When the liquid is finished, more water is added (to a total of two refills) to bring the tungba back to life. The potency of this delicious, smooth beverage isn't always appreciated until the imbiber tries to stand.

We'll be looking at several areas of eastern Nepal in this chapter. You'll read about walking from Khumbu to the Arun Valley; up the Arun to its Lhomi-populated regions; and also along the Tamur and Ghunsa valleys as far as you can go into the northeastern corner of Nepal. There are also high trails between the Arun and Tamur valleys that aren't covered here, and these routes make for fine trekking too. Ah, with world enough and time, a person could walk forever and beyond.

From Khumbu to the Arun Valley

To begin, we'll walk from the well-trekked Khumbu region to the Arun Valley. But note that you could easily do this hike in reverse, going by plane or bus to Biratnagar, then taking a bus or renting a vehicle to carry you to Dhankuta or Hile. You would then be proceeding from the tropical lowlands to the top of the world in Khumbu.

This little-trekked route (referred to in Chapter 7's "The Walk to Khumbu") leads to eastern Nepal's Arun Valley from the small hamlet of Kharte, a long day's walk south of Lukla airfield. Kharte is off the main trail not far above the village of Bupsa on the current main path. The path from Kharte is not obvious, for it leads over a sty near the top of the few houses here. You'll have to ask a local in Kharte to get you onto the correct trail. Better yet, take a local as porter and guide unless you want to carry a medium-to-heavy pack and are somewhat familiar with spoken Nepali. You will often encounter confusing trail junctions on this route and may have difficulty finding your way from the Irkhua Valley to the Arun. You will need to carry several days' worth of food for this walk. Few bhattis are maintained along this route, so be ready to camp. At some places you can seek accommodation in the rude dwellings that are scattered along the way. This trail is mostly used by people transporting grain to Namche Bazaar from the neighboring valleys to the east. Expect to walk for a week from the time you leave the trail at Kharte until you reach the Arun River.

This trail was first negotiated by Westerners when the 1950 Mt. Everest reconnaissance expedition (which included H. W. Tilman) walked it from the east. In 1951 a group that included Eric Shipton and Edmund Hillary hiked the trail and explored some of the passes at the head of the Hongu Valley. Even today you might trek the entire distance to the Arun Valley and see only one or two Westerners as you cross high, forested ridges and pass isolated Sherpa, Rai, and Chhetri villages.

From Kharte village (8,800 feet) you follow a trail that seesaws along for several hours' walk to the Sherpa village of Pangum, situated on a high, nearly level shelf. Several hundred feet above the village, its gomba sits alone surrounded by forest and with a wonderful view of Pharak. When I visited the gomba, an elderly nun with a delightful sense of humor appeared to be in charge of the otherwise-deserted building. Pangum can also be reached from lower elevations by a trail from Kharikhola village far below. You can find food and lodging in Pangum at a house.

The trail from Pangum climbs gently to the Pangum or Satu La (10,405 feet), 1,000 feet above the village. Beyond this ridge, the path angles to the north, then descends to a small settlement in which you'll pass the last inn for over a day's walk. Now you are in the narrow Hinku (or Inukhu) Valley. Not far away you can see the next pass, the low point in the ridge to the east. Out of sight to the north, the high trail over the Chhatra Teng Pass from Lukla heads to the glaciated Mera La (17,760 feet) north of 21,200-foot Mt. Mera. That peak is considered a "walk up," but only in good weather and if the snow conditions are not too soft. Below the last houses in the settlement, the trail drops off (almost literally) the ridge and switchbacks down to the Hinku River (6,090 feet) on one of the steepest slopes you'll encounter anywhere. Go slow and watch your step here. One trekker was not careful; he was buried where he fell. A suspension bridge takes you to the east bank, and the path then begins climbing through forest. Finally you have a breather as the path reaches the rolling pastures of Gaikharka ("Cow's Meadow"). There are some abandoned buildings and ancient prayer walls here, and it may be a bit difficult to pick up the proper trail at the end of the meadow. Soon after you cross a stream and leave the meadow, you should be heading upward. In the forest above are rhododendrons with trunks so thick you can't wrap your arms around them. Now you have a final steep climb to the Sipki Pass (10,120 feet).

Well-equipped, adventurous groups with experienced Sherpas have trekked north into the upper Hongu Valley, departing from the regular path described below, not far east of this pass, or reaching the upper valley via the Mera La. To walk north, you should go with a well-provisioned, organized group of porters with a guide who has been there before. Only a few Sherpas have experience in this area, and they will probably have to be engaged through a Kathmandu-based trekking outfitter. Another difficulty about trekking in this formidable region is that you must carry all your food for the time you will be there. Storms have dumped great quantities of snow into the Hongu's high, trackless basin, making escape precarious. If you go there, however, you can see Mt. Mera, Chamlang (24,010 feet), and from a distance, the tip of the rarely seen east, or Kangshung, face of Mt. Everest. From the upper Hongu, technically proficient parties have exited into Khumbu over the Mingbo La south of Ama Dablam, or the Amphu Laptsa into the Imja Khola.

Continuing on the main route from the Sipki Pass, take the trail that angles to the south not far below the pass. You'll ramble through oak and rhododendron forest that turns to meadow and passes by mani walls, finally reaching a tall stupa on a ridgeline. The path drops down, and you can see an intriguing circle of conifers below to the east. Do walk off the path and circumambulate this unique grove of spruce and pine. Beneath the trees and completely encircling them is an unbroken wall of old, lichen-covered mani stones, rocks carved in varying patterns with the sacred mantra "Om Mani Padme Hum." The gomba in the midst of this ring of trees is surrounded by ferns, but the building seems ill used, and this lovely place has a mysterious, checkered history.

The trail angles high above the valley floor (keep to the upper, main path), passing well away from most houses in the Sherpa settlement of Kiraunle. Eventually you reach the large Rai village of Bung, where the homes in the upper part of town are about 1,500 feet above those at the bottom of town. Across the valley is the village of Gudel, but you must descend and then climb a good way to reach it. Rude signboards at both the upper and lower parts of Bung suggest that at least two erstwhile entrepreneurs have set up inns. Bung is interspersed with millet fields, and

A Rai woman sells tangerines at Tumlingtar in the Arun Valley.

you can imagine the rivers of tungba that must flow on festival days or during wedding celebrations.

At the base of the V-shaped Hongu gorge (4,310 feet), you cross the river on a sturdy bridge replacing the bamboo span that needed to be rebuilt each year after the high waters had receded. When one trekker reached this torrent farther north on his way to the upper Hongu basin, he crossed the river on a dilapidated bridge that lacked many planks and railings. On the far side, he met a toothless old gentleman who motioned silently toward the skewed bridge and broke a twig between his fingers.

The steep hills west of the Arun River including the Hongu Valley are the homeland of the Rai clan, the largest ethnic group in eastern Nepal. Rais are of Mongolian extraction and are easily recognizable by their distinctive almond-shaped eyes. Most Rais live between 3,000 and 6,000 feet in elevation, but many have migrated to flatter land. This large clan has about eighteen divisions called *thars*, and the dialects that Rais speak number nearly as many as these subgroups. Although primarily agriculturalists, many Rai men, like their Limbu cousins, have bravely distinguished themselves in Gurkha regiments of the British and Indian armies. Strictly speaking, Rais are not Hindu but worship local deities according to ancient custom. Unlike Hindus or Buddhists, they bury their dead, often beneath stone memorial platforms. Many Rai women wear nose rings (as do Limbu women), large round earrings, and necklaces of old coins.

Ascending out of the Hongu gorge, the path climbs steeply past rice and millet fields to the large village of Gudel. From here you angle into the side valley to the south and keep climbing through open, then forested, country. Then the way rises steadily to the first of three small villages inhabited by Sherpas. In the upper section of this walk is a forest of old, weathered trees that you walk through to reach Sanam, the last Sherpa town. At Sanam, you can purchase tasty milk products and excellent arak. I particularly liked the soft, white cheese, which is similar to cottage cheese. In the Hinku and Hongu valleys, the Sherpas, who raise wheat and potatoes and have cattle, always live higher than the Rais, who grow corn, millet, and rice. After Sanam, the track continues up in a steep pine-and-rhododendron forest with all shapes, sizes, and colors of green. The path finally rises steeply to the Salpa Bhanjang, crowned by a 12-foot-high stupa. At 11,200 feet, this is the highest of the three passes you cross east of the Dudh Kosi Valley. The peak you can see to the west from all three of these passes is Numbur, Solu's sacred mountain. Walk a little way up south of the pass for better views. The Salpa Bhanjang marks the watershed between the Dudh Kosi and the mighty Arun River. North of the Salpa Bhanjang is a small lake called Salpa Pokhari ("Salpa Pond"), where fairs presided over by shamans are held twice yearly.

The descent from the pass is forested at first, then becomes nearly level as you cross some high meadows. Don't take the trails that descend, but stay on the ridge, following a path that jogs slightly up past some large boulders. You'll continue on a high forested ridge, then start to lose elevation as the ridge descends to the east. The views to the east are great, and you may possibly be able to talk one of the Sherpa women in the high temporary shelters into feeding you. Water is available from a small spring to the north of this temporary settlement. If you don't stay here, follow the path that goes down and down with a vengeance off the eastern end of the ridge until you reach the Rai village of Phedi (circa 6,000 feet).

Now you are in the Irkhua River Valley, which ultimately debouches into the Arun practically due east of Phedi. This is a totally new lowland world from the scattered villages and forested areas where you have been. Continue by following the Irkhua Khola, crossing and recrossing it several times on bamboo bridges. At some point the better part of a day's walk down this valley you'll have to begin angling up southward near the villages of Petini, Dandagaon, and Dangmaya. It would be futile to describe an exact route in this area crisscrossed with trails. Just ask for the paths to these villages and tell people you want to get to Tumlingtar. You'll have a merry time of it. Here, walking through scattered sal trees and terracing, you will pour sweat at every uphill stretch, but the views up the green Arun Valley are splendid as you rise. You round a ridge and hike down to the Chirkhuwa Khola, a tributary that flows south of and roughly parallel to the Irkhua Khola. South of the Chirkhuwa Khola a low trail near the Arun River shortly leads to a suspension bridge, which you should cross. Now you are below 900 feet in elevation.

Once you are on the Arun River's east bank, walk south for nearly a day to the wide red terrace where Tumlingtar airstrip is situated. At Tumlingtar, you reach the main north-south Arun River trail, which is discussed under "The Arun Valley," below. Here are stores and bhattis. Now you are a hot three-to-four-day walk north of the roadhead at Hile or Dhankuta. If resting is in your blood, you can wait until the next plane arrives. Check with the RNAC station manager, who can be found by asking for him at a store or even his office near the airstrip.

The Arun Valley

The Arun River originates in Tibet north of Mt. Everest, where its northern headwaters are called the Phung Chu (see "Today's Routes to Western Tibet" in Chapter 9). This mighty waterway predates the Himalaya and carves a deep gorge where it cuts through the range on its way to the Ganges plain. The Arun is one of Nepal's two largest rivers, along with the Karnali, and it flows rather directly from north to south. Near Nepal's northern border, the Arun passes through country that is sparsely inhabited by Bhotias called Lhomis, who practice Bon Po. The river descends through deep, thickly forested gorges and continues for many miles through hills that are well populated by Rai, Limbu, Chhetri, and Brahmin villagers. This valley is a naturalist's delight, supporting an abundance of flora and fauna. *The Arun,* by Edward Cronin, is a good natural history sourcebook for the area.

The Arun Valley is rarely visited by hikers for several reasons: it is not well known to most Westerners; it can be very hot in its lower areas;

it contains several steep portions of trail; and permits to visit its most culturally interesting northern regions are granted infrequently. Still, you can request permission to trek to Makalu Base Camp, which is considered open. That most sporting route (briefly described in this section) leads up from Sedua over the high Shipton Pass into the upper Barun Valley. Or you can get a permit for the Makalu Base Camp, then try your luck with the rigid authorities at checkposts in the upper valley. If you must return back down-valley from as far south as Num or thereabouts, you will miss the Arun's most fascinating regions. Plan to take a minimum of three weeks from the southern roadhead if you want to trek into the Lhomi-populated northern area. You will need more time if you take any side treks or plan to walk to the base of Makalu. Since the southern part of the valley is very hot most of the year, you may prefer to trek here between November and March. In midwinter, however, the upper pass areas will be closed. The extremes of heat in the lower regions and cold higher up are one of the reasons this is a tricky area to trek in. We'll begin in the lower Arun Valley and head north.

A good place to begin walking up the Arun is from Tumlingtar airfield. Owing to the low number of flights scheduled there, however, you may start this trek from Dhankuta, which is on a ridge about three days south of Tumlingtar. The first leg of a trip to Dhankuta from Kathmandu is either a dusk-to-dawn express bus to Biratnagar or a forty-minute RNAC flight from Kathmandu to Biratnagar. If you take a bus, try to get off (if possible) at Itahari, a throbbing, major intersection 13 miles north of Biratnagar. If you switch vehicles here, you won't have to travel this stretch of road twice. Biratnagar, Nepal's second-largest city, is in the terai near India. It is a steamy place teeming with rickshaws and lorries and has many jute mills and other industries. Once you are at Biratnagar, rent a vehicle or take the first available bus north to Dharan (1,350 feet), a town situated on the southern slopes of the Siwalik Range, here called the Churia Hills. Dharan was partially leveled by a major earthquake in the summer of 1988. At Dharan you can continue by bus or hired vehicle north to Dhankuta. After you cross the ridgeline north of Dharan, you may have a hazy view of Kangchenjunga (28,168 feet) on Nepal's northeastern border with Sikkim.

Dhankuta (3,900 feet) lies across the Tamur River on the first ridge to the north of Dharan. Dhankuta occupies a wide spur and is a large, attractive town with a main street of flagstones, scores of shops, administrative offices, and several schools. The town's haat bazaar is on Thursday. I was surprised to find a large hotel here, several stories high with separate rooms and good dal-bhaat. In Dhankuta you should be able to find someone who can porter for you, because people often come here (or to Hile) looking for load-carrying work. You may find someone who will only go a few days and then have to replace him in, say, Khandbari. Ask a friendly shopkeeper or the folks who manage the hotel you're in if you need any assistance getting started. A bumpy road leads from Dhankuta to Hile directly up the ridge to the north. You may be able to find a vehicle, but you may just as likely have to walk.

Hile (6,200 feet) lies on top of the ridge. The population of Hile increased considerably when Bhotias from Walungchung in the upper Tamur watershed moved into town after a disastrous landslide ruined part of their prosperous village. This accounts for the gomba near the southern end of town and the fact that Hile is known for its excellent tungba: ready at a moment's notice from several stores. The trail from Hile to the Arun proceeds inconspicuously at first down out of the west side of the bazaar. Soon you'll pass Pakribas, a large agricultural demonstration and experiment station. The atmosphere will probably be hazy, but you might possibly have good views to the north. These views will disappear as you descend to the torrid Arun Valley floor. Ask the way to Mangmaya. The trail follows a ridge, then angles thousands of feet down to the small cluster of bhattis at Mangmaya on the valley bottom.

Continue to the north near the eastern bank of the Arun, where porters carry all manner of goods for the large bazaar towns to the north and west. Tangerines *(suntala)* are plentiful in the lower Arun during fall and early winter. Just east of the trail at the village of Leguwa is a small brick Shiva temple. A gigantic pipal tree (a fig) has grown from its midst, and the temple walls are bulging and threatening to burst. Farther along, on a recent trek, I noticed a new chautaara by the trail on a low ridge. I didn't think much of the chautaara until I reached the nearby village. There, a week-long celebration was approaching its climax. It seems that the two wilted young trees on the chautaara were the traditional pipal and banyan. This ceremony was to marry the male pipal to the female banyan! A fire was burning in a large pit, and the women present began circling the pit while a priest chanted and directed several elders to toss a grain mixture on the fire. From the roof of a house, two people slowly poured liquid ghee into a long bamboo channel that reached just over the fire. The dripping ghee caused the flames to flare up. Then a burly woman wafted handfuls of violet powder over all the male participants. Scores of children watched. The pipal and the banyan were being given most auspicious nuptials. I just hoped someone would water them so they might live beyond infancy.

You cross several tributaries as you walk toward Tumlingtar's red clay airstrip. The dusty hill people you see coming from the north may be Lhomis from the upper valley carrying cinnamon in their sturdy dokos. At night in this area you may hear jackals howling or even see them running about on the wide, stony shores of the Arun. At Tumlingtar airfield, trails divide. If you are walking toward Khumbu, you must soon angle down toward the river from the flat plain. For that route, read the previous section's trail description in reverse.

If you are heading up the Arun Valley, however, you must ask for the path to Khandbari. Now you begin climbing to the valley's last bazaar town of Khandbari with its small hotel, whitewashed houses, cobblestone main street, and its own Saturday haat market. Stock up on food in Khandbari; many basic rations will probably be difficult to purchase in any quantity farther north. Continue ascending as you draw parallel to the Irkhua Khola

across the Arun, where the trail to Khumbu disappears westward. From
here north into Tibet, the Arun gorge is particularly deep. Enjoy the cooler
air, and in response to the children who say, "Whaat ees zoor name?" ask
where you can get drinking water, for streams are few on this ridge.
Spectacular views of the northern peaks are seen through the rhododendrons, especially at the Sherpa town of Munche (or Munde).

Descend to Num (checkpost here), then continue steeply down through
jungle to the Arun. Once the trail crosses to the west bank of the river, it
climbs again. To the west is the tributary valley of the Kasuwa Khola and
the beginning of the route north toward Makalu Base Camp in the upper
Barun Valley. With one or more locals who know the way, you can descend
into the Kasuwa and trek up through Sedua and Tashigaon villages to the
Keke La and Shipton La, which provide entrance to the upper Barun Valley.
You can hire porters who know the area at either Sedua or Tashigaon. Five
to six days' walk from Sedua through rugged terrain takes you into the
Barun Valley and past the lower Barun Glacier to the place known as
Makalu Base Camp. If you have the determination to reach this isolated
place, you will be rewarded with the sight of Makalu's 8,000-foot "pink"
granite south face and a great deal of solitude.

On the main west-bank trail of the Arun, continue past the permit
checkpoint at Hedangna and through scattered Rai villages as you plow

*These men are celebrating the marriage of the pipal and banyan trees they have
recently planted at the edge of their village in the Arun Valley.*

along near the base of the valley's deep furrow. Beyond Uwa, climb to a notch, then descend to the valley floor. (At a nearby bridge you can cross the Arun on the way back, having made a circle walk in the upper valley.) North of the bridge is the hamlet of Lamobagar Gola and the mouth of the Barun Valley, its pine-forested lower gorge too steep to negotiate. Now you are beginning to reach the area populated almost exclusively by Lhomi Bhotias, most of whom are Bon Po. Here, about four days' walk north of Tumlingtar, most nearby villages have both local and Nepali names. Beyond the village of Sempung, you cross a high spur that has dramatic closeup views of the border peaks. Clinging to such spurs high above the Arun are the few villages hereabouts: Hatiya, for example, the next right-bank town after Sempung.

Hatiya (5,200 feet), locally called Damdong, is a large Lhomi village set above a sweeping bend in the Arun and ringed by high, forested ridges. Most houses are stonewalled, with woven bamboo roofs. Many homes have five bamboo wands spread in a fan shape and topped with prayer flags to protect against malevolent spirits. Small yarn cages called spirit traps are also in evidence. People wear homespun, vegetable-dyed clothes, silver jewelry, and necklaces of coral and turquoise, and some have squarish pillbox hats or Tibetan-style hats with large earflaps. Hatiya is Bon Po like most nearby villages: prayer wheels are turned counterclockwise, and prayer walls are passed on the right. When Chris Wriggins arrived in Hatiya, he was just in time for an inebriated three-day marriage celebration. Tungba and rakshi were flowing freely. Unrestrained dancing continued for hours; some of the participants wore masks depicting animals, skulls, or demons. Later in the day, an intoxicated priest wearing a bandolier of bone carvings and a round black fur hat began a ceremony. The finale involved an exorcism that ended with the shooting of an arrow into a small pile of burning straw decorated with small symbolic figures.

Crossing the Sursing tributary just up-valley from Hatiya, you can continue to the large village of Honggaon (Pangdok) high above the Arun. From this town of nearly a hundred houses, a path leads through dark, vine-tangled jungle up to the border pass, the Popti La. If you have been able to pass the several checkposts and get this far north with your permit, you may be able to walk to the pass and back. It will take a very long day or more from Honggaon. When Chris Wriggins was camped along this trail there was a light snowfall during the night. In the morning, he and his porter emerged from their tent to see a series of extremely large footprints in the snow. To this day, Chris speaks of that sight with awe, and he has no doubt about the existence of the yeti.

You can make a small loop in the upper Arun by taking the path below town to the east. Traverse crudely terraced fields to a bridge across the Arun River. At the bridge you begin the walk down-valley by climbing a steep, 4,000-foot ridge cloaked in pine and eerie damp jungle of rhododendron and bamboo. Beyond a 9,100-foot pass, descend sharply to Namoche village. Some of Namoche's homes and all its granaries stand on bamboo poles. Chickens and eggs will probably be available. A relatively gentle downhill trail below Namoche carries you back to the Arun River bridge south of the Barun Valley. From the bridge crossing, the path down-valley to Tumlingtar or Dhankuta is the same path you took north.

To the Base of Jannu and Kangchenjunga   by Anne Frej

[Over an eighteen-month period during 1985 and 1986, Bill and Anne Frej of Oakland, California, took that long trip to the mountains of Africa and Asia about which most of us only daydream. During the course of that sojourn (a pilgrimage, really) they did something that has very likely never been done before: they trekked to the base camps of the world's twelve highest peaks. In this section, Anne Frej has kindly provided a description of the walk up Nepal's easternmost major valley, the Tamur.]

The trek to the Yalung Glacier at the base of Jannu Peak and the longer walk to the Ghunsa Valley north of Kangchenjunga make for a fine hike, well off the beaten track. But you will need time, that magic ingredient, for this route. You should figure *at least* twenty-five to thirty days for this trip if you want to reach both Ramser Lake near Jannu and Pang Pema north of Kangchenjunga. You may be able to shave a few days if you can manage to fly in and/or out of Suketar airfield (near Taplejung) or to take a vehicle on the new road to Taplejung (a dubious proposal). The most culturally interesting villages and the best views of Kangchenjunga and Jannu (now officially named Kumbakharna) are to be had only when you reach the meadows and glaciers at the base of the mountains. Much of the rest of the route is pleasant enough, but it is a series of ups and downs with few views. Several groups that have gone into this area have gotten bogged down in the hilly sections with not enough time to reach the upper regions. Be sure you give yourself enough time.

This route can be started at either Hile, noted above, or from the tea-growing center of Ilam (1,960 feet). Ilam is connected with Nepal's east-west highway by a dry-weather road, and bus service is available on this route when the road is in good condition. The turnoff for Ilam is at Charsli, east of Birtamod. On the way to Ilam you pass hillsides covered with tea bushes, and you won't be far from Darjeeling, just south of Sikkim. A road is being built north of Ilam to Taplejung, but don't count on this route being finished. Whether you start at Hile or Ilam, figure almost two weeks' walk in to Ramser Lake, south of Jannu. Then add on time to walk north to the upper Ghunsa Valley. Remember that there is a blue ammonia dye map of this entire route that you can purchase in Kathmandu for less than $1 and which will help orient you on this trek.

From Ilam, not far west of the Nepal-Sikkim border, the trail follows a jeep road for several miles and then winds north toward the village of Rakshi, a good stopping point the first day. After leaving the jeep road, you may find the trail confusing and difficult to distinguish from local paths. Tell the people you encounter that you are heading for Nagin, and they will direct you. For the next several days you pass through lush valleys, forests, terraces, and villages where pumpkins, squash, and radishes are available in the fall.

Nagin is three days from Ilam. North of Nagin, descend to a rough bamboo bridge, then climb uphill on a narrow trail. A schoolyard about two hours up the hill offers a good spot for camping. Two hours more brings you to the top of a ridge with good views of Kangchenjunga. From this ridge, the trail descends gradually to Gopetar, a small Sherpa village. The path then continues downhill to the Kobeli Khola, following stream-beds and the edges of terraces. At some points you will be able to see the river below or look across to the village of Sinam in the distance. At the bottom of the hill, cross a fork of the river on a bouncy bamboo bridge and scramble up a steep hill, using rocky handholds to pull yourself up. Proceed downhill to another fork of the river, which you cross on a long, wooden slat bridge. After the river you go uphill to Sinam, where such supplies as rice, flour, and kerosene are available.

From Sinam the trail generally follows the west side of the Kobeli through steamy, green hillsides of flowering trees and rice terracing. Approximately six hours beyond Sinam, before Tellock, it is possible to turn downhill on a narrow, seldom-used path to avoid the police checkpost high on the hill. There is a pleasant place for camping at the junction of the Tada and Kobeli kholas.

Cross the river to the east side and follow the trail as it climbs steeply for 3,000 feet to the village of Khewang. Try to stop near Khewang because there are few appealing campsites beyond. When we walked through this area in late October, it was Desai, the biggest festival of the year in Nepal, and every house was newly painted in violet, orange, beige, and white. For several days the people we met on the trail were likewise spattered with the same colors.

From Khewang, climb several hours to a ridgetop and cut steeply downhill for an hour. Then climb up a canyon filled with tropical foliage and a variety of birds, including parrots. You then descend again to the Kobeli Khola, now a wide and fast-moving river.

Cross the Kobeli on a plank bridge, follow the river upstream, cross another tributary on two suspended logs, and then begin the long uphill hike to Yamphudin. After Yamphudin you continue climbing, but now through forests of bamboo, rhododendron, and hanging moss. You reach a grassy point below the top of the ridge and cross a saddle with views to the rivers below on either side. Then it's a heartbreaking descent after a full day of uphill climbing. The trail drops until you reach the Simbua River, where you cross a log bridge to reach the right bank. Now you are in the valley that leads you to the Yalung Glacier at the southern base of Jannu and Kangchenjunga. Hereabouts you begin to notice a change in vegetation and start to feel that you are finally getting nearer the mountains.

Now you follow the north bank of the Simbua to Yalung. This place is shown on maps as a village, but it is really only a small settlement with a couple of families and their assorted dogs and yaks. Continue on to Ramser (Ramjar) Lake, less than an hour away, for a spectacular campsite. Your porters may try to convince you, as ours did, that there is no Ramser Lake, because Yalung is warmer and more to their liking. In fact, Ramser is a beautiful shallow lake reflecting many of the spectacular peaks leading up to Kangchenjunga, including Kabru Dome, Kabru, and Talung.

From Ramser Lake camp it is possible to take a day hike up to Oktang, a staging area for the base camp southwest of Kangchenjunga, several hours beyond. To reach Oktang, walk beyond the lake about five hours up the west side of the Yalung Glacier and climb the ridge where you see a small stone cairn with prayer flags. Here is an excellent view of Jannu and the southwest facade of Kangchenjunga.

For a different, less-seen, and even more spectacular view of Kangchenjunga, you can hike for another four to six days around the west side of the massif along the Ghunsa Valley to Pang Pema, the north base camp. There are two trails heading north, and each one descends into Ghunsa village. The first route is the higher, easterly path leaving from Ramser Lake that crosses the high, rocky, snow-covered Lapsang La. We chose the lower, westerly trail because of a recent heavy snow. This path crosses three lower ridges, the Mirgin La, Sinion La, and Tamo La. Starting from Yalung and hiking through three feet of snow, we were able to reach the southern base of the Tamo La before dark.

As you descend through forest along the last stretch of trail above Ghunsa, you will see prayer flags on poles and wooden houses with flat slate roofs. In the village, there is a gomba on one side of the trail and a police checkpost on the other. North of town are excellent camping sites, or you can stay with a Sherpa family, as we did.

The round trip from Ghunsa to Pang Pema takes at least five days. The beautiful forest trail from Ghunsa follows the left bank on the Ghunsa Chu for several hours, then crosses the river on a slat bridge. From this place it is two hours farther to Kambachen, one of the most primitive places we encountered during sixteen months in the Himalaya. The people we met in the cold, damp village spoke only Tibetan and existed on a meager diet of potatoes and a little rice.

The walk from Kambachen follows the river north, passing tundralike fields of rough grass and boulders. As we walked, our guide pointed to a large herd of blue sheep (bharal) in the distance. Five hours above Kambachen you cross a stream and follow the trail downhill to a wide, flat meadow. The small stone shelter with a wood slat roof is the place called Lhonak. Here you are barely a 10-mile walk from the Tibetan border.

From Lhonak to Pang Pema and back is approximately a 12-mile walk, so this hike can be done in one day. If the trail is snow covered, it may be difficult to follow. The route follows the top of the lateral moraine north of the Kangchenjunga Glacier until you reach a large flat area that serves as base camp. From here the northwest face of Kangchenjunga looms high above. This view, from within the high snow-covered basin you have entered, is even more impressive than the panorama at Oktang to the south. Several side walks from here suggest themselves if you have time.

Return by the same trail through Lhonak and Kambachen to Ghunsa. When we reached Ghunsa after our trip to Pang Pema, our Sherpa hosts were ready to join us on the next leg of our trek to Khumbu. As our larger group walked out of Ghunsa, many people from town met us at the gomba and presented each of us with a *kata* (prayer scarf) to wish us well on our journey. We did not know it then, but the eventual destination of our Sherpa companions was the same as ours. Two months later we met them again in Bodh Gaya, India, where over two hundred thousand Tibetan Buddhists had gathered to participate in the Kalachakra ("Wheel of Time") ceremony led by the Dalai Lama.

Heading down-valley from Ghunsa, you cross the Ghunsa Chu and soon pass through the village of Phere, also known as Poli. This small village (located on a historic trade route to Tibet that passes through the town of Walungchung) has an active gomba with colorful tangkhas and many religious artifacts. Below Phere, you enter a forest with many waterfalls, stands of bamboo, and dense foliage. In this forest we spotted a small Himalayan black bear feeding in a nearby tree.

Two days from Ghunsa down the Ghunsa Khola you reach the bridge below Hellock, where many trails and three valleys converge. To the north is Walungchung up the Tamur Valley, to the east is the way to the Yalung Glacier, and down-valley are trails on either side of the Tamur Valley to Taplejung. You could head up the Simbua Valley, then cut south to reach Ilam, or you could continue down the main valley toward Taplejung (and Hile), as we did on our way to Khumbu.

Sikkim

This book does not describe the hills of India. You'll have to look at the companion volume on trekking in India and Pakistan to learn about routes in the Indian Himalaya. But the tiny Indian state of Sikkim lies wedged between Nepal and Bhutan, so it does seem appropriate to include mention of Sikkim here.

The only place you can cross the eastern border of Nepal into India near Siliguri and south of Sikkim is at Kakarbitta on Nepal's main east-west road. The Indian border point is named Raniganj. If you are crossing from India into Nepal, two photographs and $10 should get you in. But if you want to cross from Nepal into India, you may well have to have a special stamp in your passport that you can get at the Indian High Commission in Kathmandu. Don't try to get this stamp overseas, or you could be dragged into an application process that might be endless.

Sikkim measures only 40 by 80 miles and is isolated from both Tibet and the rest of India by high ridges. Smaller than Yellowstone National Park, Sikkim was joined to the British empire by treaty; its northern boundary was demarcated in 1890. It became an Indian protectorate in 1947; more recently, it was made into a state. Sikkim is composed of the

Ranjit and Tista river basins. These two river valleys are immensely luxuriant, with thick forests ranging from sal in the deep southern gorges to conifer in the upper tributaries. Sikkim's varied vegetation includes literally thousands of plants, among them magnolia, tree fern, lily, wild strawberry and raspberry, woody creeper, primrose, bougainvillea, crimson and yellow rhododendron, poinsettia, and hundreds of orchid varieties. Sikkim's "endless diversity of green" is best seen during the monsoon. Butterflies and leeches also abound in the wet summers. Cardamom plants provide Sikkim with one of its largest export crops. Tiny and black, cardamom seeds have become a very popular spice in Asia, Europe, and North America.

Sikkim's population of just under a quarter million is largely ethnic Nepalis. Nepalis were urged to emigrate to Sikkim by the British, who required administrators and cultivators. Until Sikkim became an Indian state in 1975, it was ruled for five centuries by the Buddhist Namgyal dynasty. The Namgyals are Lepchas, traditionally the region's most powerful clan. More than fifty Buddhist monasteries are scattered across Sikkim, primarily in the more densely populated south. Rumtek is the area's best-known monastery, situated high on a ridge not far southeast of Gangtok, Sikkim's capital. This monastic community was home to the late Gyalwa Karmapa, leader of the Kagyupa branch of Tibetan Buddhism. Each May at Rumtek, masked ritual dances are performed. These dances are similar to those that take place at Hemis in Ladakh, and in Marpha, Thame, and Tengboche in Nepal.

To reach Sikkim, you must first travel to Siliguri in the Indian state of West Bengal. Siliguri can be reached by train from Calcutta, but fly to Siliguri's Baghdogra Airport from Calcutta if at all possible; the train ride, which includes a boat trip across the Ganges, is only for hard-core travelers. From Siliguri, the best way to get to Darjeeling is by shared taxi or rented four-wheel-drive vehicle. A narrow-gauge train goes from Siliguri to Darjeeling, but soot from the coal-burning engine makes it a very gritty ride that is not recommended. Once you have your permit to enter Sikkim (see below), you can travel by jeep from Darjeeling to Gangtok. Your permit will be inspected at Rongphu on the border before you are allowed to enter Sikkim.

Permission to enter (let alone trek in) Sikkim has been difficult to obtain, and because of this, those who can afford to usually go with an organized group. Since 1980, a few groups consisting of at least six trekkers and accompanied by a liaison officer have been permitted to trek from Yuksam village up the Rathong and Prek tributaries of the upper Ranjit Valley to Dzongri ("High Fortress") in southwestern Sikkim. The country is superb. You walk in a narrow north-to-south valley toward Kangchenjunga (28,168 feet), the world's third-highest peak, through Lepcha and Bhotia villages. Less than 2 miles north of Dzongri is Kaburlam Tso, a high lake. Some people have reached the Goechi La at the valley's head, which commands an unparalleled closeup view of the Kangchenjunga massif.

To initiate the trekking permit procedure, write to the Indian embassy or the nearest Indian diplomatic mission and request an application form for entry into Sikkim. When you return this form, it and your photographs will be forwarded by the Indian embassy to the Home Ministry (Section S1) in New Delhi. Your application should be submitted at least three months in advance of your expected entry into Sikkim. When the application has been processed, you will receive a letter; if your application has been approved, you can present the letter to the deputy commissioner in Darjeeling, who will issue you the permit for entry to Sikkim (and a trekking permit, if requested). The procedure is lengthy and subject to change, and the application must go through the Home Ministry in New Delhi; don't expect to receive a permit if you should arrive in Darjeeling without the advance paperwork. Areas other than the route to Dzongri may also open up to trekkers; inquire when you are requesting the permit application.

These two Drokpa men in west Tibet thought the camera was a telescope; the man on the right holds wool thread he has been spinning.

9

Ngari: Tibet's Wide Open West

Naykor yakpo yakpo.

"Pilgrimage is great," in Tibetan

Western Tibet

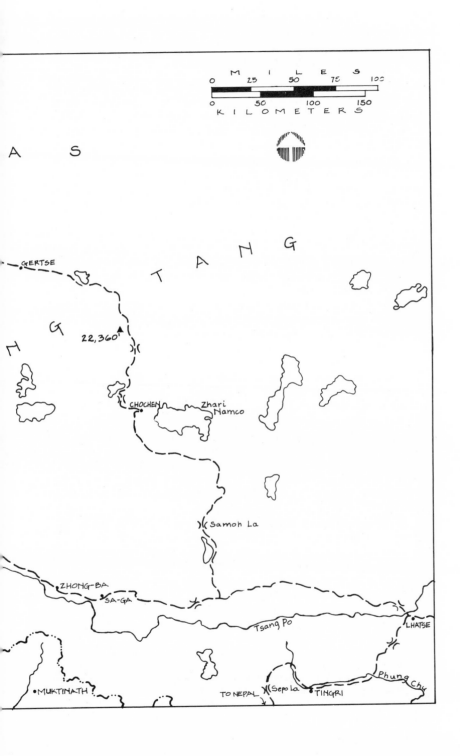

M I L E S
0   25   50   75   100

K I L O M E T E R S
0   50   100   150

A   S

C H A N G   T A N G

GERTSE

22,360'

CHOCHEN   Zhari Namco

Samoh La

ZHONG-BA
SA-GA

Tsang Po   LHATSE

Phung Chu

MUKTINATH

TO NEPAL   Sepo La   TINGRI

The Barren, Sacred Highlands

Tibet's vast Chang Tang plateau sweeps to its highest and most forbidding in the great western region called Ngari. Only scattered Drokpas, Tibet's sturdy nomads, and their herds roam beyond the horizon here. And south of Ngari's ancient goldfields lies holy Mt. Kailas, known to Tibetans as Tise or Kang Rimpoche, "Precious Jewel of Glacial Snow," perhaps the most exquisitely beautiful and sacred mountain on earth.

Until very recently, we could only dream of reaching Mt. Kailas, cobalt blue Pangong Lake, or the lost cities of Tsaparang and Toling. Following the Chinese takeover in 1951, no foreigners were permitted into Tibet for thirty years. No Westerner had visited Ngari since 1948, when Lama Anagarika Govinda* and his wife Li Gotami made their remarkable pilgrimage to Tsaparang. In 1978, however, a Mandarin-speaking Indian official told China's deputy prime minister that the world's most sacred mountain for all Hindus lay not far inside the Tibetan border with India and requested permission for pilgrimages. It took three more years for negotiations to proceed, but in September 1981 the first group of Indian pilgrims in over a generation was allowed to visit holy Mt. Kailas. Since 1984, the first Westerners in over a generation have begun to visit Ngari.

Ngari stretches 550 miles northwest to southeast from the 16,000-foot-high Aksai Chin plateau and Lingzti Tang plains to the pass above Lhatse. This far western region of Tibet is situated directly east of the Indian region of Ladakh and just north of the Indian region of Garhwal and the Nepali regions of Humla, Dolpo, and Mustang. Its northern border is the Kun Lun Range, beyond which lies Sinkiang. Today Ngari is estimated to have an indigenous (Tibetan) population of only twenty-five thousand. Like the transborder regions of Nubra, Rupshu, and Spiti in Ladakh, however, it is highly likely that the local population is more than doubled by the military, here the People's Liberation Army (PLA). Ngari's largest town is called Shiquanhe in Chinese and Ali or Ngarigar in Tibetan. Ali is a military town located on the banks of the Indus River.

Because Ngari is so barren and sparsely populated, it has always been far removed from most vestiges of any central authority. A century ago, the powerful *dzongpon,* the governor of Purang District in the southwest, kept close to his castlelike dzong in Taklakot, near the Indo-Nepalese border. Not far from his fortress, the southern approaches from India to Mt. Kailas were crisscrossed by roving bands of *dacoits* (brigands) bent on pillaging any pilgrim hoping to slip by and reach the sacred confines of the holy mountain and its monasteries. From all accounts, including

---

*Lama Govinda was born in Europe; early in life he traveled to India, becoming an Anagarika, a "homeless one," and a lama by the age of thirty-three. He was a unique combination of West and East and through his writing did much to explain Tibetan Buddhism to the Occident. Li Gotami, an Indian-born Parsi (Zoroastrian), was a talented painter who accompanied her husband on his pilgrimages to Tibet.

those of Giuseppe Tucci (the renowned Italian Tibetologist who made eight lengthy trips to Tibet) in 1936 and Lama Govinda and Li Gotami in 1948, every pilgrim rich or poor once feared these dacoits. Both Tucci's and the lama's sirdars managed the same successful ruse when mounted robbers appeared: they elevated their employers' importance and announced that strong retribution would follow if any untoward incidents occurred. Now, a generation and a half later, the descendants of those highwaymen escort Indian and other foreign pilgrims around Mt. Kailas.

Ngari's People, the Drokpas

Who are the Drokpas, these nomads who populate much of Ngari's harsh but beautiful landscape? Drokpas aren't the sophisticated Lhasa shopkeeper types who can charm a tourist into buying a Kathmandu-made "Tibetan" rug. Not at all. Most Drokpas are dark complected with sun-burned faces of sandpaper and rawhide. They aren't at home in town or on a truck. They're only at home around their campfires or in their tents, pitched somewhere on what Giuseppe Tucci called a "temporary halt in an eternal wandering."

I first saw Drokpas in the far distance, roaming the infinitely wide countryside with their herds of sheep, goats, and yaks as I rumbled overland by truck from Sinkiang into Tibet. But I first got close to these people of the high plains in Ali's small bazaar. Three dust-covered Drokpas walked, almost glided, into town, moving lightly, animal-like. They were bent at the waist from many hours sitting about yak-dung fires. But if they shifted directions or even looked intently in a new direction, they *moved*, catlike and out of place in the shop-lined street. They each wore wide-brimmed felt hats, beneath which hung two thick black braids. Their heavy coats were sewn sheep hides turned so that the wool faced inward, like thick comforters. Homespun woolen pants and modified Tibetan *somba*s (shoes), completed their outfit. Their new-fashioned footwear consisted of the upper of the traditional somba, a carefully constructed multilayer, multi-color woolen legging (which can help identify the origin of its owner by its design), sewn onto the bottom of a modern factory-made gym shoe.

Shop by shop the three went, pricing cigarettes first of all. They expressed great surprise at the price of the brand they chose and switched to another, cheaper package. Then it became a buying spree conducted in loud, basic Tibetan with Chinese shopkeepers and low, guttural talk with the local shopkeepers. Oblivious to my following and photographing them, they purchased milk powder, porcelain cups, and finally many pairs of brightly colored tights for their wives minding the tents. Later, with the assistance of other locals translating for me, they stopped while I took a photograph of them. They didn't know what a camera was and thought I was looking at them through a telescope, so the locals had to urge them to be still for the shot. Now when I look at the picture, there is the perpetual squint, their mouths part grin, part grimace. Later I also met Drokpa women, circling Mt. Kailas with their families, and our curiosity about each other was mutual. Their glistening black hair was plaited in scores of small braids; some had colorful fanlike hats. They all wore wide skirts lined with wool that reached nearly to the ground, and bells hung from their waist straps.

Contemporary Tibet

The days of dacoits are over, but a different cloud, a political one, has darkened the sky. In the minds of most Tibetans, theirs is an occupied country, and the situation is unfortunately not likely to change. Most Tibetans had rarely been affected in a day-to-day fashion over the centuries by the political winds that blew first one way, then another about Lhasa, the capital. But after Lhasa fell to the overwhelming Chinese People's Liberation Army in 1951, the changes imposed by the alien authorities were, for a time, genocidal (forceable planting of wheat instead of barley, forced resettlement of Tibetans, and collectivization) and affected nearly everyone. There has also been a rapid (and involuntary) migration of ethnic Chinese (Han) into Tibet to the point where they now outnumber Tibetans in Lhasa. Expatriate Tibetan sources claim that the number of Han throughout Tibet now exceeds the Tibetan population.

Tibet's land and people are still adjusting to triple catastrophies: first came the military takeover (when Lhasa, Ganden, and numerous other towns and dzongs were howitzered and bombed from the air) and the takeover of government by the Chinese. Then in the mid-1960s came the Cultural Revolution, when most of the remaining thousands of shrines and monasteries and much of the nation's vast cultural heritage was systematically plundered and dynamited by the Chinese. This left skeletons of ruined buildings that are still visible throughout much of the country, central Tibet's Tsang Po Valley in particular. Finally, during this entire time there were programs of forced resettlement, government ownership of livestock, and other aspects of collectivization, including the attempt to completely destroy the monastic way of life. Even teaching the Tibetan language was prohibited for nearly a generation. Now many of these ill-advised policies have been relaxed, and mistakes have been admitted. Nonetheless Tibetans remain second-class citizens in their own country. They are not permitted to travel freely and are often forced from their ancestral lands. Tibetans are discriminated against when it comes to medical care, schooling, and jobs in the lucrative tourist industry.

Travel in Tibet

A few generations ago Lhasa, Tibet's mysterious capital, was the ultimate prize for the occasional foreign explorer. Now the attitude is quite the opposite. The current Chinese government has opened Lhasa for tourism but would just as soon foreigners didn't wander away from town

unless they are on an officially escorted group tour with a fixed itinerary.*
A permit has been required for individual travel outside Lhasa (this includes
traveling from Lhasa to Golmud or to the border of Nepal). Many people
have, nonetheless, struck out on their own with success. If you travel on
your own in Tibet (just as when you travel anywhere off the beaten track),
you may have an entirely different reception than someone who arrived a
day or an hour earlier. The experience you have depends on who you are,
who you meet (or don't meet), and how each of you is feeling at the time.

If you are traveling in Tibet as part of a group, you have paid well to
forego the rigors described in this and the following paragraphs. Buses or
Japanese landcruisers are provided for members of foreign groups who
travel outside Lhasa. If, however, you are traveling individually in Tibet,
the information in the following sections is for you.

Getting to Lhasa

As noted in Chapter 2 (see "Passport, Visas, and Immunizations"),
you will need a visa to enter China before you can proceed to Tibet.
Currently most people reach Lhasa by flying from Peking or Canton to
Chengdu, then flying on directly from Chengdu to Lhasa. It is also possible
to fly from Kathmandu, Nepal to Lhasa. The most popular overland route
to Lhasa (when the road is unobstructed and the border is open) is to
proceed from Kathmandu. This route is noted below under "From
Kathmandu to Lhatse" and "From Lhasa to Lhatse" (this latter section will
have to be followed in reverse to complete the description of the way from
Kathmandu to Lhasa). Some people reach Lhasa overland by taking a bus
from the town of Golmud to the north in Ching Hai Province. An intrepid
few have even traveled from Chengdu to Lhasa by the difficult, rutted land
route, a journey that can take several weeks if you don't have a through ride.

Transportation Within Tibet

Western Tibet is far too vast a domain to consider approaching on
foot, so we will look at it in this chapter from the perspective of motoring
from one area of interest to another.

It's difficult for us in the West to imagine a region larger than any
state in the United States outside of Alaska where private or foreign-owned
vehicles are not permitted. But such a place is the Xizang Autonomous
Region (as Tibet is now officially called). Tibet continues to suffer from
a serious lack of transport, especially outside its few large towns along the
central Tsang Po Valley. Not only are vehicles few and far between, but

*In October 1987 following internationally publicized rioting against the government,
Tibet was closed to individual travelers, then to all tourists. The Chinese authorities
recognize a difference between foreigners on a group tour (who pay high rates and
can be kept track of) and individuals (who contribute far less to government coffers
and are able to strike up friendships and often travel where they are not supposed
to). Whether Tibet will be open to all foreigners, closed to individual travelers only,
or closed entirely may change several times over in the 1990s.

the official policy of restricting individual travel by foreigners outside Lhasa has been well publicized to all local vehicle drivers. Note, however, that permits for Mt. Kailas were being given in Lhasa for the first time in 1987. That summer, two separate buses were hired by individual travelers to make the long journey to Mt. Kailas. This change in policy bodes well for the future, but the problem of finding affordable transport (even if it is legal to travel to west Tibet) remains little changed.

It is very difficult to obtain a ride by waiting along a road and trying to hitchhike. You may have to arrange a ride ahead of time by personally contacting the driver, perhaps in the truck compound where the vehicle he drives leaves from. Speaking a few words of Tibetan or Mandarin helps immeasurably. Always be polite and be ready to return several times to chat and make friends with the driver. Now is the time when a quietly proffered color photograph of the Dalai Lama can come in very handy, if the driver is Tibetan, or a few packs of Marlboro or 555 cigarettes if the driver is Han. Indicate that there are more photos or coffin nails where those came from. Or consider asking someone who is fluent in the language to assist you in finding a ride. Chinese travelers from Hong Kong, who are very westernized, can be quite helpful if they wish to assist you. Using your wits to obtain long-distance rides may remain a crucial matter, for until there are more vehicles on the roads, it may continue to be difficult for individuals to travel across western Tibet. Remember that the locals are also scrambling for rides, with fewer funds but far more savvy than you or I.

Weather and When to Go

Weather and when to go are very important considerations if you intend to visit western Tibet. With the modern miracles of disposable income and jet transport, we can very quickly put ourselves in deep yak dung if we are not careful in Tibet. Drokpas still living in the fifteenth century pitch their tents near hotels lodging those of us from the twentieth century. But when weather extremes hit, as can always happen in Tibet, the traveler, be he Drokpa or Westerner, needs to be well prepared. The Drokpas are. Will you be?

Regardless of whether you travel to Lhasa for three days or Ngari for three months, and regardless of the size of your bankroll: if you travel to Tibet, you have gone to some trouble to get there. No one leaves for Lhasa with thongs and a day pack like the proverbial ill-prepared person who flies to Kathmandu, gets a visa, and wanders out of town into the hills. Have rain protection (a tough multipurpose poncho perhaps) and enough down or miracle-fiber clothing to keep you warm in temperatures with a zero-degree windchill factor. As you rise up into Tibet on the overland route from Nepal, for example, you cross the 17,100-foot Sepo La. Picture what might happen if your vehicle broke down hereabouts and you can begin to imagine the possible consequences. This is no imaginary scenario: a heavy snowfall in October 1987 trapped several busloads of people for eight days near the Sepo La. No one died, but for food the foreigners aboard had their first taste of raw mutton, and some who were inadequately clothed got frostbite. Clouds, wind, or rain can radically change the weather in any season, particularly at Ngari's high elevations, usually between 14,000 and 16,000 feet. Snow can fall any month of the year in Ngari.

Lhasa may be visited anytime, now that frequent jet flights from Kathmandu and Chengdu are available, but visiting Ngari is a different matter. Snow on the passes into the area is the limiting factor in reaching western Tibet before April or May or after early October during most years. Tibetans themselves visit Mt. Kailas between the months of April and October, and those months should be considered the earliest and latest to travel to Ngari. July and August are traditionally considered the rainy season in Tibet. As you read "Today's Routes to Western Tibet," below, note that every single road into the area crosses at least one pass higher than 17,000 feet. Remember the Sepo La in October 1987.

How long will it take to reach, visit, and return from Mt. Kailas or anywhere else in west Tibet? If you don't have a least a month of time, you would be well advised not to attempt the arduous journey.

Acculturation

It is sad and bizarre that Tibet is being governed and resettled by people with no interest in the country's rich culture, its religion, or its language. The great majority of Chinese who live in Tibet rarely interrelate with Tibetans or even trouble themselves to learn the first words of the local language. Two different worlds live near each other with virtually no assimilation. For you, the traveler, it is helpful to know whom you are talking with. Remember the adage "Speak to people in their own language." Use whatever few words you know, in whichever language is appropriate. Your attempts at communicating, however small, will always be appreciated.

When you travel in Tibet, you may imagine yourself to be a modern-day Giuseppe Tucci, Lama Govinda, or Li Gotami, but the locals have different ideas. Just pausing to note these different perceptions can help you as you travel in western Tibet. Setting aside sophisticated Lhasa shopkeepers and the very few Tibetans whose job it is to work with Westerners, your average highland nomad or valley farmer will call a Westerner the same name that he calls a goods trader from Nepal or a pilgrim from India. To the Tibetan, we are all *rongpa*s, meaning "valley men," or "men from where the forest grows." Nowadays the locals tend to see two kinds of Westerners, if they see any at all. One kind of rongpa is the kind that goes in groups to the Potala Palace and Jhokhang Monastery in Lhasa, then zooms off in a Toyota landcruiser to the next destination in a tightly packed itinerary. The other kind of rongpa usually isn't in such a rush and may even try a few words out on the people he sees. As always, those of us in tour groups, unless we speak Tibetan, are going to be moved through places so fast that it will be hard to do much more than take a few photographs. The individual traveler is often better able to pause and use some words of Tibetan if the desire to use the language is there or if the rare local acquaintance who can translate is found. (See Milan M. Melvin's "Tibetan Glossary" at the end of this book.)

What we visitors don't always realize is that although this may be the first time for us in this strange and exciting land, the locals often have preconceived ideas about us because of the rongpas who have preceded us. The landcruiser ones usually have cameras pasted to their faces and leave quickly. The others are often lost when it comes to such basic, simple matters as having enough food supplies or getting from place to place. But a Tibetan, above all, loves a good joke, even if it is on himself. If you can greet people and toss in a few quick one-liner phrases, you will stand out from other rongpas. The fact that you may in fact appreciate a place for the night or some food will matter less. With a few words of Tibetan, you are a fellow traveler, not just a helpless rongpa. You *can* learn how to communicate like the Tibetans and "speak with hands and feet."

Explaining your presence to Tibetans in their own terms is most helpful. Tibetans, like most desert peoples, are inveterate travelers, so the concept of "just passing through" is familiar to them. After all, travelers are an integral part of the traditional society. Tibet's largest clan is the nomadic Drokpas, who may be found moving from anyplace to anywhere. Other Tibetans travel hundreds of miles to trade or to buy and sell goods. Another well-established reason for travel in Tibet is to go on pilgrimage. If you have been to Lhasa, you have undoubtedly seen clusters of country people, mouths agape, looking lost and roaming the streets between the Jhokhang, the Potala, and the camping ground. Those folks are all on pilgrimage, which they call *naykor* (literally "going around places"). Tibet has many pilgrimage sites, as far apart as La Brang Monastery (now in Ching Hai Province) and Kang Rimpoche, on opposite edges of traditional Tibet and far away from the populous central Tsang Po Valley. Currently, each of these sacred places, and many more, harbors scores of pilgrim tents for much of the year. When I've been in Tibet, I've said that I'm on naykor and that has always sufficed, even with no explanation, since I've always just been going to or coming from Kang Rimpoche. I'm a rongpa on naykor to an extremely holy place, so I have a good reason to be in Tibet. Likewise, you can work out your own explanation for traveling through P'ö.

If you want additional general information about Tibet, consult one or more of the following books listed in the bibliography: *The Tibet Guide*, by Stephen Batchelor, and *Tibet: A Travel Survival Kit*, by Michael Buckley and Robert Strauss. My aim in this chapter is to inform you about Ngari more completely than the guides that cover all of Tibet.

Today's Routes to Western Tibet

Swami Pranavananda, a unique combination of Indian holy man and ever-observant scientist, wrote two books in the 1940s on Tibet in which he described twelve separate routes to Mt. Kailas, stretching from Kashmir and Ladakh in the west to the route from Lhasa in the east. Today we can approach western Tibet from Kathmandu and Lhasa to the east and from Sinkiang far to the northwest (this route has been officially open only to groups). In the future it may become legally possible to enter Ngari directly from northwestern Nepal by walking about four days up-valley from the Humla region. And, finally, Indian pilgrims in strictly controlled groups again trek and ride along the ancient pilgrim route from India that crosses Lepu Lekh Pass. I will describe each of these four routes in turn, but note that only the first two are legal now, while the third may possibly open. Distances are given and points of interest along the way are mentioned. If you want to travel directly between Lhasa or Kathmandu and Kashgar in Sinkiang, then continue along the route described in "From Lhatse to the Junction of the Northern and Southern Routes," "The Northern Route from the Junction to Ali," and "From Sinkiang to Ali," all below.

A note on place names: One part of the all-pervasive attempt at Sinofication in Tibet is the renaming of every feature on the map. With this in mind, the first time a place name is given, I will always mention as many names as I know for it. On subsequent uses, the traditional or best-known name will be used. Let's take two quick examples. The Tibetan name for the great western region of Tibet is Ngari, but the "ng" sound is difficult to pronounce in Mandarin. So, the Chinese name for the area is Ali. This can be confusing, because the Chinese name for their new district head-quarters on the banks of the Indus is Shiquanhe, whereas both Tibetans and the Uighurs who come to town in the summer usually call the town Ali. Shiquan He (*he* means "river") is the traditional Chinese name for the Indus River, but now that name has been given to the town also. And so it goes. This is like the time when government surveyors in Nepal gave new names to places in political Nepal that were ethnically Tibetan. In this way, Dzong Sarba became today's Jomosom. Welcome to the wonderful world of nomenclature in Tibet. Finally, remember that the Tibetan name for their own land is not Tibet, but P'ö!

From Kathmandu or Lhasa
to Western Tibet

If you want to reach Ngari from either Kathmandu in Nepal, or Lhasa in Tibet, the route you must take passes on a ferry across the Tsang Po (Brahmaputra) River just west of the town of Lhatse. Here, I'll give a description of the route from Kathmandu to Lhatse, then quickly mention a few places of interest along the way from Lhasa to Lhatse. A brief section on the road from Lhatse to the junction of the northern and southern roads to west Tibet follows. Lastly I'll describe both the less-traveled southern route to Mt. Kailas and the more popular, northern route to Ali from this road junction.

From Kathmandu to Lhatse

The ancient walking route from Kathmandu to Mt. Kailas once led through Muktinath, a sacred and very beautiful location in Nepal now visited yearly by thousands of foreign trekkers and local pilgrims. Presently the only legal route from Nepal to Tibet for foreigners lies along the paved 70-mile road, called the Arniko Rajpath, from Kathmandu to Kodari, Nepal's border town. Just north of Kodari, the road crosses the new Friendship Bridge into Tibet or Xizang, "The Western Storehouse," as it translates from Chinese. About 4½ miles from the bridge by road (or considerably less if you hike the steep Nepali-style trail directly up the hill) lies the bustling town of Khasa (Nepali), called Zhangmu by the Chinese. In Khasa (circa 7,500 feet), you can find occasional buses leaving for Lhatse, Shigatse, or possibly even Lhasa. You may also be able to get onto an empty truck. If you ride on the back of a truck, be sure to read the next paragraph and be prepared with warm clothes. To find a ride, discuss your transportation needs with locals. If price is no concern, talk with the management at the government-run hotel in Khasa. They will probably be able to provide a landcruiser or bus. (*Note:* Due to severe landslide problems in both countries, the road in the Khasa region may be rerouted.)

Khasa is a rapidly expanding town filled with Nepalis, located in the forest-choked, monsoon-drenched Bhote Kosi Valley. At Khasa, it's just like being in Nepal's middle hills, but the valley changes rapidly as you ascend it. Once you begin traveling up-valley on the road hacked out of the steep gorge, your muscles tense from eyeing the unguarded 1,000-foot drop-offs below. Twenty miles along, you'll arrive at the town of Nyalam, populated only by Hans and Tibetans. Climbers attempting Mt. Shishapangma (26,390 feet) approach the mountain's eastern side from the valley angling northwest above Nyalam. Beyond Nyalam the valley opens out and vegetation rapidly diminishes. The ever-rising road now gains its altitude in grand, sweeping bends rather than the gear-wrenching hairpin turns that you've been frightened witless of since you left Kathmandu.

Welcome to the beginning of the real Tibet. You will pass a few tiny villages, but basically you are out there crossing the barren, soaring plains for 100 unpopulated miles until you reach Tingri. The road climbs steeply again, now through hilly desert. To the south, the northern slopes of the Eastern Himalaya come into view. Menlungtse (24,000 feet) is the closest high peak, and behind it lies Gauri Shankar (23,560 feet). To the west you begin to have a great perspective of Shishapangma. Finally, you reach the 17,100-foot Sepo La. The prayer flags and stone marker signaling the pass sit on an almost-level dune, and it's hard to imagine yourself on a pass. Now you are wearing clothes that would have stifled you at the border. Khasa, nearly 2 vertical miles below, is already a distant memory.

The wide valley you descend into north of the Sepo La is part of the vast upper basin of the Phung Chu, the river that becomes the mighty Arun in Nepal. Hundreds of years ago this valley must have been fertile, for ruins of ancient buildings dot the flat valley floor. Tingri village, slightly off the main road, is the traditional trading partner of Namche Bazaar south of the Great Himalaya Range in Nepal, across the Nangpa La. Standing in

Tingri on a clear day, you can see a sweeping panorama, including a low point where the 19,000-foot Nangpa La hides behind intervening hills. To the east of the pass is Cho Oyu (26,750 feet) and to the east again lies Chomolungma, the mountain we know as Mt. Everest (29,030 feet). Veteran Nepal hand Brot Coburn stood in Tingri in 1984 and estimated he could walk to the Nangpa La in a day and a half. But the Tibetan atmosphere is crystal clear and plays tricks on the eyes. Brot walked hard for four days before skirting the checkpost on the east side of the pass approaches, reaching the pass, and descending southward into Khumbu in Nepal.

The route continues to the east along flat, barren country. Then, as it begins to turn northeasterly, a side road angles off toward hills to the southeast. This secondary route crosses the Pang La and continues on to Rongbuk Monastery and the northern approaches to Mt. Everest. A branch of this side road leads lower down the Phung Chu Valley to the town of Kharta and the way to the Kangshung, or East Face, of Mt. Everest. Not far north of the Rongbuk turnoff is the larger road to the west leading to the village of Shegar, just visible some 5 miles away. Shegar's ancient fortress, ruined in the Cultural Revolution, still climbs the heights above town. For some time there has been a checkpost just south of the Shegar junction. This post monitors and sometimes turns back domestic traffic as well as foreign. But the Dalai Lama performed the Kalachakra ceremony (also called the "Wheel of Time," an important tantric initiation ceremony for lay people as well as monks) in Bodh Gaya, India, in December 1985. Tibetans came in such droves that the checkpost was inundated and some twenty thousand people poured through; their documents, or lack of them, went unchecked.

North of the Shegar turnoff, the road rises out of the Phung Chu Valley, reaching the 17,200-foot Lakpa La. Gradually, then directly, the route descends into a steep, rock-walled canyon and plunges down into the Tsang Po River Valley. This road leading to Nepal joins Tibet's principal east-west route in a 4-mile stretch of road midway between Lhatse and the Tsang Po River crossing. The total distance from Kathmandu to Lhatse has been 310 miles.

From Lhasa to Lhatse

To reach Lhatse (or Nepal) from Lhasa, you must travel along the main road through Gyantse and Shigatse. If you are touring with a group, you may not be able to stay very long at Gyantse, because the official, bland, overpriced hotel is in Shigatse. But if you are traveling individually, Gyantse is definitely the place to stop. The town has been left relatively undisturbed in recent years, and its population remains primarily Tibetan. On a rocky hill above town is the fortress that the British commander Francis Younghusband and his punitive force of troops stormed in 1904. But far more striking is Gyantse's intricate Kumbum Chorten. This tall, luminous white shrine, also known as the Temple of the Hundred Thousand Buddhas, may well be the world's most complex and awe-inspiring chorten.

The statuary and frescoes in its many interior rooms were made by crafts-men of the Newari clan from Kathmandu. Lama Govinda passed months there studying the stupa and said of it, "The amount of iconographic material contained in it could not have been exhausted in a lifetime!" Next to the Kumbum is the massive, block-shaped Palkhor Chode, which also contains wall upon wall of Newari-painted frescoes.

Early one morning I barreled into the compound housing the chorten, ready to do a few koras (circumambulations) around it. The whispy-bearded *chowki*, the compound's guardian, walked over to me, as if to head off the interloping foreigner. But I smiled and repeated, "Kora yakpo yakpo. Kora yakpo yakpo. La, dro." "Let's go, let's do kora." He laughed and joined me for a good walk around the nine-tiered shrine. People can be welcoming in Gyantse, and there are many places of interest both in town and in the nearby hills.

One last note about the Gyantse area. The road to Shigatse divides just south of town. The lesser-used branch route leading eastward heads over a pass and across the plains north of Bhutan's beautifully symmet-rical Mt. Chomolhari. The lucky foreign interloper on that road passes Phari Dzong (Pali in Chinese) just after Chomolhari, then drops into the narrow wedge of Tibet that lies between the Indian state of Sikkim and Bhutan. This is the Chumbi Valley, with a river that flows south through the Great Himalaya Range and drains into Bhutan. Yatung (Yadong in Chinese), at the junction of two rivers, is the large down-valley town in a valley green with cultivation. It lies tantalizingly close to both Bhutan and Sikkim, and locals from both places flood Yatung's bazaar to trade, buy, and sell.

The main road west from Gyantse heads down-valley a fertile 60 miles to Shigatse (Xigaze in Chinese). Shigatse lies south of the Tsang Po River and is home to the Panchen Lama. This man was traditionally the secondmost powerful regent in Tibet (second in power to the Dalai Lama). Unlike the Dalai Lama, the present incumbent did not leave the country and was jailed for many years. The Panchen Lama has been forced to make his residence in Peking but is periodically permitted to visit Tibet, where he is still venerated. Like Lhasa, Shigatse is being torn apart to make way for new, boxlike buildings, and it is also receiving many Han immigrants. But the large, active compound housing the Tashilhunpo Monastery is pure Tibet. The old town lies to the northeast of the Tashilhunpo. People have arranged rides from Shigatse to Ngari by asking at truck compounds in town and through word of mouth. Getting a ride west from Lhatse can be more of a last resort, so do inquire hereabouts if you haven't lined up sure transport before reaching Shigatse. The road from Shigatse to Lhatse is a short half day's drive and traverses the Po La, a pass I first crossed in the back of an open truck just after a chill dawn. West of the Po La, up-valley from Lhatse and 16 miles south of the main road, is Sakya. Its large monastery contains what is probably Tibet's largest repository of images, frescoes, and texts.

From Lhatse to the Junction
of the Northern and Southern Routes

Lhatse is the door to Ngari from central Tibet.* When you leave Lhatse, you will not see another fully grown poplar or tall willow tree until you reach Taklakot, tucked away north of the Great Himalaya Range 400 air miles to the west. In all of Ngari you will not see such trees aside from Taklakot at 11,000 feet on the Humla Karnali River and Toling in the Sutlej Valley at roughly the same elevation. If you are traveling on your own, Lhatse is the last sure place to find food supplies until you reach either Ali or Taklakot. You may possibly find food cooked along the way, but don't count on it. If you are riding on a truck, do count on possible delays due to mechanical problems, unexpected pilgrimages off-route, or halts to sell merchandise. When I arrived at Lhatse's hotel, I had been riding for five dawn-to-dusk days coming from Ali on the back of an old, never-quit "Liberation" truck. In Lhatse I drank my first sweet tea and ate rice for the first time since leaving Ali.

So here you go west of Lhatse, loaded with rations and ready for Ngari. The road leads 4 miles from Lhatse to the Tsang Po River, passing the southward route to Nepal midway. The Tsang Po is a wide river even this far up-valley, and a steel-hulled ferry to its north bank provides the key to reaching Ngari. The ferry is powered by a winch operated by four Tibetan women and has an enormous six-person wooden sweep oar for steering. This ferry has a capacity of four trucks, plus assorted foot travelers and animals, but the ferry doesn't operate when the Tsang Po is in flood, a common occurrence during the monsoon. On the north bank of the Tsang Po are a few teashops-cum-inns. Presumably there is also some authority who observes who passes and may well try to turn you back if you don't have a permit to travel west. Rides have materialized here, but you may have to wait for some time to get one. From the river, the road climbs to a pass and continues westerly for some way along a valley that parallels the Tsang Po. You'll pass Ngam Ning, Sang Sang, and Raka, the latter an isolated inn. West of Raka lies an extremely important T road junction. The route continuing to the west (following the telephone poles) is the direct southern route to Mt. Kailas and Taklakot.† The road to the north is the more frequented route to Ali.

---

*There is also a rarely used northern road into Ngari. This route goes from the town of Amdo and proceeds north of Nam Tso, the great salt lake. It connects with the principal road into Ngari east of Gertse.

---

†There may be a road to the south from somewhere west of this junction that crosses the Tsang Po and joins the road to Kathmandu west of Tingri, not too far from the Sepo La. Ask drivers or locals about this route when in Khasa; it could be a good shortcut from Kathmandu to Ngari if it's open to traffic and if the Tsang Po can be crossed. But you would have to have food and transport arranged before taking this route.

The Southern Road to Mt. Kailas   *by Peter Overmire*

[This direct southern road to Mt. Kailas is open only in spring after the snows have melted and before the monsoon begins. The road reopens in autumn after the high water from the monsoon and snowmelt has receded and before the first snows. Peter Overmire, a veteran Asia hand from San Francisco, traveled this route in both directions in 1985. At that time, Peter was escorting the first American group to circumambulate Mt. Kailas. The following is his excellent account of this route as far as Barkha, another important T junction just north of Lake Manasarovar.]

Marco Pallis, in *The Way and the Mountain*, says that a pilgrim to Kailas "approaches from the golden plains to the south, from the noon of life. . . . He enters the red valley . . . in the light of the sinking sun, he goes through the portals of death between the dark northern and the multicolored eastern valleys . . . and descends, as a new-born being, into the green valley on the east. . . ."

The southern route to western Tibet is surely Pallis's approach from the golden plains. It follows the Tsang Po River for about 400 miles, then continues to Darchen. Seemingly, all military and most civilian traffic uses the route farther north. The southern route is a much less used, poorer road, certainly less dependable than the northern route. All supplies and fuel must be taken with you—there are few settlements and fewer places to spend money. At the time of our trip, the fords of the Tsang Po and other rivers were up to 50 feet wide and 2 to 3 feet deep before the heavy August rains, and as much as 300 feet wide and 4 feet deep (worse when the driver lost the right track) during and after the rains. In addition, many washouts and long, deep muddy stretches were encountered. It's essential to have two vehicles traveling together during the rainy season. Our group accomplished the trip in three and a half days westbound from Lhatse to Mt. Kailas. The return trip took five days because of rain; one of these days was over eighteen hours on the road.

The track wanders through beautiful rolling hills, always changing, never monotonous. To the south the ice and snow of the Himalayan crest are seldom out of sight and often close, and to the north lie the rounded hills of the Tibetan Plateau (the Chang Tang). The hills are mostly golden, but with a covering of green during the monsoon. The rain shadow of the Himalaya is something of a myth: heavy rains can be anticipated during July and August.

The road goes by Sa-Ga, an uninteresting Chinese army camp of some size. It's called Sa-Ga Dzong on Tibetan maps, but there is no sign of a ruined village or dzong. There is an ill-stocked general store here, apparently the only one on the whole route. The next significant settlement is Zhong-Ba, a dingy village with a partially destroyed gomba surrounded by acres of flattened rubble, mostly mani stones carved in thin purplish slate.

There are no other settlements of note visible from the road. A few ruins are seen, and a ragged little road maintenance post or an occasional communal resettlement compound pops up from time to time. The Chinese are attempting, with limited success, to turn the Tibetan nomads into farmers.

The rewards of the southern route are enormous: vast green pastures with Drokpa camps; countless flocks of sheep and goats being milked and sheared; long yak trains carrying wool to be traded at Taklakot; and an occasional pilgrim or two, walking to Kailas, making better time than a motor vehicle on the zigzags over a pass, then falling far behind on the straight stretches. In some of the broad valleys there are stone fences running for miles, straight as an arrow.

After crossing the Marium La (16,900 feet) on the last day, the route passes through serene greenish gold plains populated by small herds of wild animals: kiang and either gazelle or antelope. They gallop along, keeping pace with your vehicle, paralleling the road several hundred yards away, interested but wary and without doubt hunted by the Chinese. You'll find that almost all of the Chinese, military and civilian alike, carry guns, expressing concern about the dangers of "wild animals and bandits." The Chinese are unwilling to sleep anywhere but in a compound. Shortly after crossing the Marium La, you'll get your first view of Kailas, all the more exciting for the hardships of the road.

The Northern Route from the Junction to Ali

Now back to the more traveled northern route to Ngari. The northern road via Chochen and Gertse is usually the main route between Lhatse and Ali because of the seasonal nature of the southern road. This northern way is also the principal road between Lhasa, the capital, and Ali, the western provincial headquarters. But when you leave those telephone poles along the southern road behind and head north, you're truly heading for some wide open spaces. The first noteworthy location on this road is a series of hot springs by the road at the base of the first range of peaks north of Raka. When the truck I was riding in reached this place, everyone emptied out long enough to sponge off, particularly their long-ignored feet. This proved a real morale booster, after which local, then Western, songs were exchanged by those of us on the back of the truck.

The road continues northward and gains elevation, passing a small lake, then a long one, traversing high meadows and aiming for the flat Samoh La (circa 18,000 feet), the highest pass between Lhasa and Sinkiang. Just south of the Samoh La, our driver stopped in front of a nomad's tent with a painted sign in front, written in Tibetan, announcing tea and chang (beer) for sale. We Westerners quickly dubbed it the World's Highest Teashop. North of the Samoh La the route continues down a very long valley drained by a clear stream. Black and white Drokpa tents dot the meadows, and yak herds enjoy prime high-level grazing lands. Emerging from a narrow gorge, the road arrives at Chochen (Coqen in Chinese), several miles west of the vast Zhari Namco Lake. Chochen is a settlement of several compounds where Khampas sell supplies and plastic beads to Drokpas and PLA soldiers try to keep warm. In the room next to ours, nomads were resting from their ride on another truck. They heated tea, in good Ngari fashion, with a hand-held blowtorch.

The north-to-south stretch on either side of Chochen is considered the best area (outside of the Marium Pass vicinity on the southern road) to see large mammals from the road. Kiang, the wild Tibetan ass (now quite rare), have been seen, as well as antelopes, wolves, foxes, and many, many hares. It was en route to Chochen that Alun Edwards, a tough Welshman I roomed with in Kashgar, had to walk alone for three days. He passed no real shelter the whole time and, lacking a through ride, took two weeks to reach Ali from Shigatse. Please heed the remoteness of this region if you intend to travel here.

North of Chochen the road rises in steps on old shorelines of Zhari Namco Lake, for this lake is receding, like others in this region. You pass another lake to the west and ascend to a rolling pass. Northwest of this pass lies a sacred mountain, 22,360 feet on the ONC Series H-9 sheet (see Appendix A, "Map Information"). Ringing its base are several bright splashes of green meadows grazed by herds of sheep. Then as the road begins to enter flatter, wetter country, it joins with the road that goes east to the town of Amdo, which lies on the road between Golmud and Lhasa. Just north of this ill-defined junction the road turns westerly through flat, sometimes boggy country and aims for Gertse, the next semideserted cluster of compounds. At Gertse, more Khampas sell glass beads and coral to more Drokpas. Gertse boasts a larger inn than the few rooms at Chochen, and all about town the wide, level horizon extends to infinity.

East of Gertse lies the single large mud-walled compound named Oma, which means "milk" in Tibetan. Oma's fortresslike walls are distinguished by low, round parapets with rifle slits. The road continues to the west over the next 200 miles, crossing five ridges along the way. Descending from the fifth ridge, our route enters the river valley that we call the Indus, the Tibetans call the Senge Kabab, and the Chinese call the Shiquan He. Hereabouts, old maps of Tibet proclaim the intriguing words "Gold Fields," and the Indus turns southerly toward its source north of Mt. Kailas. In midsummer the river is turbid, but as summer turns to autumn, it becomes clear and pairs of ducks float lazily in its waters. One last outpost named Gegyai remains, its two halves lying a long mile apart. Here you are a mere 70 miles west of Ali, and the road follows the river's north bank the rest of the way to this thriving minimetropolis. The distance from Lhatse to Ali is approximately 780 miles.

From Sinkiang to Ali

The road from Kargalik (Ye Cheng in Chinese) in Sinkiang to Ali in western Tibet is 680 miles long and traverses some of the world's highest level terrain. Beginning in the dry wastes of the Takla Makan Desert, the route crosses four passes higher than 17,000 feet until it reaches the 17,500-

foot pass marking the border of Sinkiang and Tibet. This pass, just south of the area called Aksai Chin and 445 miles from Kargalik, is marked by a lone 2-foot-high concrete marker. The description of the road up to this point is outside the scope of this book, but you can find an account of the route in the companion volume on trekking in India and Pakistan.

Presently this road from Kargalik is legally open only to foreigners traveling in escorted groups. In this case the authorities have some real justification to prohibit individual travel. For, like the Dolpo region in Nepal, once you enter the area, there are virtually no places to resupply provisions: you're truly on your own, and many of us simply aren't prepared. Nevertheless, let's suppose that you are with a group or that you've been able to finesse a ride along this barren route.

Soon after descending from the boundary pass dividing Sinkiang from Tibet, you'll begin to see widely scattered white canvas and black yak-hair tents belonging to the few Drokpa herders who inhabit these high plains in the summer. Scanty grass grows over wide areas of the rolling valleys and hills hereabouts, and the elevation averages over 16,500 feet. The road continues in a southerly direction, proceeding along a sandy desert. Your vehicle will eventually make a sweeping left turn in a swirl of dust and arrive at Domar (15,100 feet), the first settlement in 185 miles. Domar has a modern military compound and a one-dish restaurant. You'll also see

Pangong Lake stretches eighty miles from Ladakh in India, but is widest here at its eastern end in west Tibet.

Tibetan nomads and their tents, close up. But the most pleasing sight of all are Domar's grasslands, bisected by a clear stream. South of Domar the road follows these inviting grasslands, where horses graze in muck up to their knees. Then the land once again becomes dry as you cross a gentle ridge and descend, passing a series of brackish lakes.

Now, keep looking straight ahead and soon you'll see the easternmost end of Pangong Lake (13,840 feet). This eastern segment of the nearly continuous lake is also called Nyak Tso. Over a generation ago, Lama Govinda and Li Gotami visited the western shores of this lake, nearly 100 miles away near the then-undemarcated fringes of Ladakh. Later, in *The Way of the White Clouds*, Lama Govinda wrote that the lake "was as luminous and as sharply set off from the background as the surface of a cut jewel from its gold setting, and it emanated an intensely blue light, as if it were illuminated from within." This is the lake you see from the road to Ali, but one aspect of its waters is different. Lama Govinda noted that the water he saw was undrinkable and incapable of supporting plant or animal life. This he ascribed to a high magnesium concentration in the water. But here at the lake's eastern end, ducks swim and plants grow right up to the shoreline. Remembering what Lama Govinda had written, the first thing I did upon reaching the shore was to sip the water. Here, it tastes delicious. Wong, the driver whose truck I was riding in, stopped his head-long rush south, extracted a watermelon from the cargo, and we had a picnic and waded in the lake as if we'd reached paradise.

The road follows the eastern end of the lake for the better part of an hour's drive, then turns to the south, passing wide, bumpy meadows grazed by contented horses. If you have food and shelter and aren't concerned with onward transportation, consider a walk west along the southern shore of Pangong, beginning where the road turns away from the lake. The two-part town of Rudok (Ri Tu in Chinese) lies between the meadows and a sandy plain not far south of Pangong. Rudok is 92 miles south of Domar and 73 miles north of Ali. Unlike Domar, with its few buildings, this town is home to several hundred people and a sleepy military compound. Note that you may pass a checkpost south of Rudok. The narrow valley you slowly ascend south of town is quite verdant and is grazed by numerous herds of sheep. Farther along, the valley widens, the vegetation becomes sparse, and finally you reach a pass that Wong called Ali Daban (*daban* means "pass"). Wong drove the creaking, loaded truck in a circle around the pass cairn, then barreled down-valley the remaining short hour's drive to Ali.

From Humla to Taklakot

The shortest route to western Tibet is through Nepal's remote Humla Valley in the northwestern corner of the kingdom. As of 1988, this border was not officially open to foreigners. Still, each summer in the mid-1980s, a few people with visas for Nepal have been trickling south into Humla from Tibet. The Nepalese government has officially announced that this route may be opened to trekkers in the future, and regional officials on both sides of the border would like the frontier derestricted because of the expected influx of money it would bring into their respective regions. Anticipating the possible opening of this border, here is a brief look at the way north from Humla to Taklakot.

First, how in the dickens do you get to Humla? Easy: get a trekking permit for Simikot in Kathmandu and take one of the two or three weekly flights from Kathmandu or Nepalganj to Simikot. The way from Simikot up-valley to the Tibetan border is described under "From Jumla to Humla" in Chapter 4. Note that your passport and permits will be scrutinized first in Simikot, the district headquarters, then up-valley at Munchu. Munchu, about a day and a half's walk from the border, has been Nepal's last major checkpost in the Humla Valley for many years. You will not be permitted to proceed beyond Munchu if you do not have the appropriate permit. A few words to the wise: people entering Humla from Tibet who do not have visas have been held by the authorities for over a week at Munchu. Figure about four days' walking time up-valley from Simikot to the border and a day less if you are descending the Humla Valley. As noted in Chapter 4, food is scarce in upper Humla, so be prepared to pay well for supplies there.

West of the Nara La, the trail approaching Nepal's border follows the south bank of the Humla Karnali River. A small bridge across the river takes you directly into Tibet, since the river forms the border hereabouts for 2 miles. Continue up-valley for 1 or 2 miles from the bridge and you will reach the important monastery of Khojarnath (Kejia in Chinese). Surrounded by a small village, Khojarnath's ochre-colored monastery comprises two large buildings. The structures themselves are intact, but the solid silver images within were hacked to pieces and removed in the late 1960s. Formerly this gomba of the Kagyupa lineage was under Bhutan's protection, like several of the monasteries at Mt. Kailas. These buildings are held in high regard by the locals, and unless you speak Tibetan, are traveling with locals, or are with a group, you may encounter difficulty in entering. Khojarnath is the largest active monastery in Ngari.

At Khojarnath you are 10 miles away from Taklakot. A road connects the two towns, and in the summer many traders from Humla follow this path to Taklakot, urging along their pack-ladened sheep and goats. Some Humlis actually carry firewood up-valley to sell at Taklakot, while others transport wood on yaks. If you do not encounter a vehicle, it is an easy day's walk from Khojarnath to Taklakot or vice versa. You'll pass through several villages and have to ford some streams.

From India to Taklakot
on the Old Pilgrim Route

Since 1981, strictly controlled groups of Indian pilgrims called *yatris* have been following centuries-old pilgrim trails through the Kumaon region of Uttar Pradesh State and across the 17,000-foot Lepu Lekh Pass into Tibet. Their route, however, crosses the "Inner Line" at the Gorig

River, beyond which foreigners are not permitted. Thus you and I cannot travel the trails they do. Still, approximately two hundred Indian yatris a year in so-called batches of twenty-five have been making the pilgrimage across the border, so this path should be noted, if only in passing. The pilgrims ride as far as the roadhead at Tawaghat. Then, accompanied in India by physicians who monitor their health, they proceed in stages up to Kalopani, the last camp in India. From here they climb the Lepu Lekh Pass, located less than 2 miles west of the Nepalese border, and descend into Tibet to be met by their Chinese escorts. They continue on foot, then by bus to the government guesthouse in Taklakot. From there they proceed in a bus to Lake Manasarovar. At the sacred lake their escorted group divides in half: part of the group circumambulates Lake Manasarovar, and the other part drives to Darchen at Mr. Kailas for their walk. The two groups then change locations.

Now a final note on routes to west Tibet: Presently there are no commercial airports in western Tibet, and only occasional military helicopters fly into Ngari. But a survey has been made for an airport at Ali, and the Nepalese government has requested that an airport be constructed near Taklakot, as this would facilitate tourism. Who knows? You may be able to *fly* to Ngari in the future!

Ali and the Way to Mt. Kailas

I heard that if they caught you in Ali, they would send you back where you came from. So I walked for ten miles across the sand dunes north of town to avoid the place.

Bob Dutton, 1985

Ali is Ngari's administrative headquarters and the largest town between Shigatse and Kargalik, yet it isn't even depicted on most maps. Ali is located on the banks of the Indus River at the T junction of the north-south road leading from Sinkiang to Taklakot and the (east-west) northern route to Lhatse and central Tibet. Even the town's name is up to question. The Chinese call it Shiquanhe, also their name for the Indus, but the locals call it Ali (or Ngarigar). Chinese authorities are fond of saying that Ali didn't even exist ten years ago, but the presence of several old mud-walled compounds belies this. Ali is primarily a military town, quartering troops involved in guarding the disputed border not far to the west. But for the Uighur merchants from Sinkiang and the Khampas from the east who come in the summer, Ali is a place to do business. There is a bazaar near the river where Uighurs and Chinese have shops. The Khampas merely come to town and set up their tents behind the bazaar's long concrete platforms; then they sell merchandise directly from their movable homes.

For foreign travelers, Ali is a town to stock up on food supplies and get a ride onward to the north, east, or south. A new government store where you can purchase various canned goods and even dried fruits has been constructed at the town's main intersection. Ali boasts several restaurants, Chinese and Uighur, where you can fill up after the long ride from Sinkiang or central Tibet. There is even a new hotel at the eastern edge of town where foreigners are expected to stay, although older inns used by locals may still be available. Ali has been theoretically restricted to individual foreign travelers, whom the Chinese dub "unorganized tourists." But once people arrive, they have rarely been ushered out of town. Some people, including myself, have even been able to get visas extended at the local Public Security Office. And then there was Mark, the Englishman who made it to Ali from Kashgar by virtue of successfully masquerading as a Uighur. He was even given a ride by the police in their motorcycle sidecar to the rickety truck that was taking thirty locals and us Westerners east. If you find yourself at odds with the local authorities, maintain a polite demeanor. It's better to plead forgiveness than ask permission. The trick is to tell the officials that you came from the place where, in fact, you wish to proceed. When foreigners are apprehended in restricted areas, if they aren't held, they will be invariably sent back where they came from—after a self-criticism has been written.

You didn't come to Ali to see the town or the sand dunes to the north, however. Moving on is your only reason for coming here in the first place. Remember that there is no commercial transportation into or out of Ali. If you are with a group, your transportation will be provided. If you want to go to Sinkiang, ask a Uighur in the bazaar the location of the *maachine serai*, the truck yard. Every few days there will be trucks leaving for Kargalik. Getting a lift east to central Tibet on the road through Gertse and Chochen can be a good deal more difficult, and you may have to be patient. If you get out of town in less than a week on the road to the east, you've done well. If there are any English-speaking Hong Kong Chinese travelers in town, they may be able to help you. Talk with Tibetans in the bazaar. And remember that you should only take a ride east that is going at least as far as Lhatse or you may become stuck in an even more remote location.

Going south from Ali toward Mt. Kailas should be easier than reaching Ali. Trucks leave every few days from Ali carrying both merchandise for Taklakot's bazaar and Tibetan pilgrims going to Mt. Kailas. Carry food with you and try to sit toward the front of the truck: it is not dusty there, and you will be jostled far less as the truck bounces along.

The road from Ali to Darchen at the base of Mt. Kailas is 205 miles long, and many of those miles are sandy, bumpy, or both. A landcruiser can make the trip in a day, but if you are on a truck, it may take as long as two days to reach Darchen. After an hour's ride across the sandy desert south of Ali, you'll cross the Gar River and begin the long drive up this nearly level tributary valley of the Indus. Maps of the region depict the town of Gar (or Gartok) roughly midway between Ali and Mt. Kailas, but the most you'll see now are a few humble mud homes. They are all that remains of what was once the largest trading center in Ngari north of Taklakot. About 80 miles south of Ali is an easily missed turnoff to the west. This side road leading up the dry ridge is the lesser-used route to the Sutlej Valley and the ancient temples of Toling and Tsaparang (see "The Lost Cities of Toling and Tsaparang," below). This little-used road crosses a 17,050-foot pass, then a 17,385-foot pass to reach Toling, some 90 miles from the Ali-to-Taklakot road.

The road up the Gar Valley continues to Baher, a godforsaken walled-in road maintenance post. Here the larger road to the Sutlej Valley diverges from the main road. This recently constructed route crosses a single pass and reaches Toling in 112 miles. The main road south begins to climb and after crossing several false passes, gains the last rolling, grassy ridgeline, a pass that Swami Pranavananda called the Chargot La. You now descend into the drainage of the Sutlej River, and the road traverses rolling meadows where scattered Drokpas graze sheep. The wide valley closes in, and after crossing a bridge, you arrive at Mensar, or Missar (Menshi in Chinese), the first real town since Ali. Here you are only about 35 miles from Mt. Kailas, and you can find a cooked meal and a room to sleep in.

Mensar is important because it is the junction for the side road leading 7 miles to the ancient pilgrimage site of Tirtapuri. In the old days, no pilgrimage to Mt. Kailas by Hindu or Tibetan was complete without going to Tirtapuri. In a cave there Padmasambhava (the mythical saint, also known as Guru Rimpoche, who is credited with bringing Buddhism to Tibet) once meditated and achieved *samadhi* (satori). Nearby are some warm springs and outcroppings of a white substance containing calcium that is collected by pilgrims as a sacred powder.

South of Mensar the road crosses rolling plains cut in several places by large streams. These waters have their sources in the Kailas Range, now rising high above you to the east. If you are traveling in a truck carrying pilgrims, the mood becomes exhalted as your companions sight these snowy outliers of Mt. Kailas, often mistaking them for the holy mountain itself. You'll also begin to see the majestic Central Himalaya, an unbroken line of peaks far to the south forming the border with India and Nepal. The road curves to the east as you descend onto the vast, flat Barkha Plain. Then, floating above all other peaks like an island of light, the sacred mountain comes into view. When you first glimpse symmetrical Mt. Kailas, its beauty is so great that you won't doubt for an instant that you've finally seen it. Now there are only a few more streams to cross. One of these creeks is quite large and seems to delight in trapping vehicles during the afternoon, when its waters are highest. The small settlement of Darchen at the base of the mountain is now visible a mere 3 miles away up the gently sloping plain.

You may, however, approach Mt. Kailas from Taklakot, like the Indian yatris. The trails from India and Nepal that join at and pass through Taklakot have been the traditional path for many pilgrims going to the mountain.

Taklakot: A Tale of Three Towns

Taklakot is situated above the Humla Karnali River at an elevation of about 11,000 feet. Taklakot and its neighboring villages downriver are the lowest towns in all of Ngari. Yet south of town and visible from it are the gleaming white peaks of the Central Himalaya. And tucked away in those high mountains less than a day's walk away are two high passes: the Tinkar Lepu La, crossed daily in the summer by goods caravans of mules, leads into Nepal's remote Tinkar Valley. And the Lepu Lekh Pass is the high point on the ancient pilgrim path into India.

In the winter Taklakot slumbers beneath many feet of snow, but in the summer the town is a well of activity. Tibetans from several nearby villages come and go. Khampas set up their tents and sell goods brought from the east. Tibetans call the bazaar Purang, the same name that used to be given to the entire region. Chinese administrators and customs agents (these latter dressed in shiny green uniforms quite out of place in this dusty town) regulate commerce and collect taxes. Taklakot has several private restaurants, a Chinese-run hospital, a sleepy government resthouse, and a busy government store jammed with Tibetans and Nepalis. The Chinese name for the village is Burang or Pulan, depending on which of their maps you consult. But to the outside world, the town has traditionally been known by its Nepali name, Taklakot, the name used in nearly every old account of the region.

The Chinese have their compounds on the north side of the Humla Karnali, east of the area's only clear stream (which is the best local place to wash) and somewhat removed from the main bazaar. The Khampas set up their tents right in the main bazaar on the north bank of the river. But, for me, the most interesting part of town lies south of the river where the Nepalis stay for a four-month period in the summer. There are actually two Nepali bazaars. Each bazaar is composed of small, stone-walled rows of shops that also serve as sleeping quarters. These rudimentary cubicles have canvas roofs that are taken down during the winter. Just across from the main part of town is Humla Bazaar, run by men from Nepal's Humla District down-valley to the east. Out of sight, over a barren ridge a fifteen-minute walk away, lies the larger Darchula Bazaar. The people from Darchula District in Nepal live a four-to-five-day walk south of Taklakot beyond the Himalayan crest. These merchants have good access to Kathmandu via roads through India, so some of the lucrative wool business out of Ngari passes through their hands. From morning til dusk, the long alleys of Darchula Bazaar resound with the cries of men loading and unloading caravans of mules, sheep, and goats. Other people take raw wool that has been brought south by Drokpas and twist it into long ropelike strands. These thick woolen ropes are further twisted into small round bales to be carried south. From old photographs we can see that these methods of baling wool have not changed in fifty years. A year after it leaves town, this raw wool will have been cleaned, carded, spun, and woven into the Tibetan rugs that are sold in Kathmandu and around the world.

Wool is by no means the only commodity bought and sold in Taklakot's Humla and Darchula bazaars. Drokpas bring rock salt and borax to trade with the Nepalis, and the Khampas make good business with bricks of tea and manufactured items. Nepalis need no permits from the Chinese to come as far as Taklakot. They take full advantage of the fact that Indian merchants are banned from Tibet and bring bolts of Indian cloth to sell or trade. The Nepali businessmen also sell Indian *gur* and *meeschery*, two types of unrefined sugar that Tibetans favor. Over a cup of tea I asked one shopkeeper if he sold anything at all from his own country. Looking over

This Drokpa standing next to his canvas tent in western Tibet looks as if he is ready for whatever the elements send his way.

his piles of cloth and gur, he said, "All I have from Nepal are these Yak cigarettes."

Atop a stony ridge 500 feet above Darchula Bazaar, the ruins of Simbiling Gomba pierce Tibet's clear sky: another stark reminder of the cultural devastation wrought in the late 1960s. Lama Govinda and Swami Pranavananda each described Simbiling as an active monastery housing 150 monks. Their photographs of the gomba from the 1940s depict tall whitewashed buildings topped with gold-plated ornaments. Below, maroon-robed monks smile, looking quizzically at the camera. Climb the hill to Simbiling. Taklakot's main bazaar is out of sight below, and the giant massif of 25,390-foot Gurla Mandhata (climbed for the first time in 1985) rises into view to the north. In the opposite direction the Central Himalaya of the Nepalese and Indian borderland gleams brilliantly. As I slowly walked up, slipping on round pebbles, I imagined water carriers in ages past struggling upward with their loads. The extensive ruins stretch for 100 yards along the crest of the narrow ridgeline. I explored from room to room in the bright sun, inevitably reminded of the Buddhist doctrine of impermanence. Nothing of any value remained. Not a single mani stone or fresco. The dynamite had done its work with appalling thoroughness. Finally, in one room with three empty niches, a single stick adorned with tattered prayer flags was propped up by rocks.

Looking below to the base of the next ridge to the west, I noticed scores of caves cut from the conglomerate rock. Scrambling and sliding down the scree-covered slopes, I approached these long-deserted grottoes, fantasizing I was a latter-day Aurel Stein (a Hungarian-born archeologist and explorer who made many collections and discoveries in Central Asia during the first half of this century). Other similar aeries are cut into the sheer cliffs above Humla Bazaar. Later, taking a circuitous route, I found and chatted with a lone kindly Nepali ascetic in one of those caves high above the bazaar. On impulse I gave him a few small notes of currency. He went into his little alcove and returned, giving me a sacred white chunk of soft stone from Tirtapuri. But here, well above town, I was utterly alone as I investigated cave after cave. Each grotto was about 6½ feet high. Some of the rooms interconnected, and many had shelves hacked out of the conglomerate. The ceiling and upper walls in each room were coated in black, hardened soot from countless cookfires set by their former occupants. Later on I asked a Nepali merchant in the bazaar about the caves above town. He replied, "I used to come to Taklakot with my father when I was a boy. In those days, the loudest sounds in the morning came from the many *damaru*s (small hand-held drums) in the caves."

From Taklakot to Lake Manasarovar and Mt. Kailas

In the past, when Taklakot was the capital of the autonomous region of Purang, the governor's authority did not extend far beyond town. Once away from the villages near Taklakot, pilgrims and locals alike had to fend for themselves against roving dacoits (brigands). Swami Pranavananda, writing in 1948, recommended that pilgrims in this region fire off a gun each night before retiring to warn nearby outlaws. But of course those days are now history.

It is 75 miles from Taklakot to Darchen. Your landcruiser or truck will climb the hill out of Taklakot, and soon you will leave the last willow trees behind. The road gains altitude rapidly at first, then levels off somewhat, crossing barren wastes below the base of Gurla Mandhata. Then, as you continue northward, you'll cross streams from this giant mountain that rises alone and north of the Great Himalaya Range. Shrubs and grasses now appear, and you may see a herd of grazing livestock. Hills embrace the road, which steepens as it climbs to the Thalladong Pass (circa 16,000 feet), topped by a cairn of stones and prayer flags. At this viewpoint you can first see oblong Rakas Tal. Beyond, radiant in the distance, sacred Mt. Kailas rises above its nearby cluster of peaks. Of the Gurla Pass, not far away on the old foot trail, Lama Govinda said, "It certainly is one of the most inspiring views of this earth, a view, indeed, which makes the beholder wonder whether it is of this world or a dreamlike vision of the next."

The road descends and soon you are skirting the stony southwestern shores of Rakas Tal (Langak Tso in Tibetan) at about 14,900 feet in elevation. Rakas receives the waters from its larger neighbor Lake Manasarovar via an intermittent stream named the Ganga Chu. Rakas Tal is situated south of Mt. Kailas, and indeed the waters from the sacred mountain flow directly into it. Yet Manasarovar is considered to be the sacred lake, whereas Rakas Tal was traditionally considered by Tibetans to be the Lake of the Demons. In the past, Manasarovar was encircled by eight gombas on or near its shores, while Rakas was home to only a single monastery.

Turning toward the east, the route ascends the narrow, hilly finger of land that separates the lakes. Here, near their southern shores, the lakes are less than 2 miles apart. Lake Manasarovar (not more than 50 feet higher than Rakas Tal) again comes into view to the east. Now you are as close as the main road gets to Manasarovar. A spur road angles directly off toward the lake's rocky shoreline. Next to the waters a high, triangular pillar is covered with Tibetan prayer flags that flutter in the breeze. Nearby stands a stark, recently built structure that is good for shelter from the incessant afternoon wind. Not far north of this place the steep bluffs to the west of the lake come down near the shore, and there are several caves where Tibetan pilgrims circling the lake often sleep. Lake Manasarovar is also extremely important for Hindus. To them, the lake symbolizes the receptive, female aspect of creation, the yoni, while Mt. Kailas symbolizes the active, male aspect, the lingum. In 1948 some of Mahatma Gandhi's ashes were ceremonially scattered at Lake Manasarovar. Some Nepalis who visit the holy lake do not even go to Mt. Kailas. Imagine the awe of a Nepali villager from the hills (who at most has visited Gosain Kund Lake in his own country) as he first sees sparkling Lake Manasarovar.

Lake Manasarovar is 54 miles in circumference. Swami Pranavananda has made the *parikrama* (circumambulation) of the holy lake thirty-three times (and he has made an equal number of trips around Mt. Kailas). As a guide to the length of time it takes to walk around the lake, keep in mind that it has taken Pranavananda as few as two days and as many as four days to do his parikrama. Summer is the most likely time for foreigners like you and me to be at Manasarovar, but it can be a difficult time to walk around the lake because of the high runoff from streams that flow into the lake from the north and east. There are also marshy areas on the lake's northern shore. Going with a local and a horse is recommended: you may be able to hire both of these at Houre (pronounced "Hor"), a village located 17 miles east of Barkha, near the lake's northeastern shore. (The Indian yatris begin their parikrama of the lake at Houre and do part of the circuit by bus because of the marshes—and the lack of time in their tightly packed itinerary!)

To reach Barkha, continue north along the Taklakot-to-Ali road between the lakes. You will cross the area where gold has been mined, then reach the Ganga Chu. In the last few years the streambed has been dry prior to the monsoon, but after the rains and runoff begin, the Ganga Chu becomes so full it is not fordable by foot. Just north of here and visible from the road is Chugu Gomba (also called Chiu Gomba), where a friendly lama has recently been in residence. If he is still there, he may be able to help you find a local with horse. The road continues northward, crossing a final rolling, scrub-dotted ridge, and descends to an important road junction at Barkha. Here, with a magnificent view of Mt. Kailas across the flat Barkha Plain, you meet the less-traveled southern road across Ngari coming from Lhatse. Barkha consists of a few compounds, and its residents have usually not been helpful to outsiders. Go to Barkha well supplied with food from Ali, Taklakot, or elsewhere if you intend to circle the lake.

Now, with Kang Rimpoche shimmering across the plain, the main road north continues the remaining 15 miles from Barkha to Darchen at the southern base of Mt. Kailas. Now it's time to explore some of the important places around the holy mountain and meet some of the pilgrims who have traveled so far to visit Mt. Kailas.

Mt. Kailas, Jewel of the Snows

The mountain known to Hindus as Kailas ("Crystal Shining") and Tibetans as Tise or Kang Rimpoche ("Precious Jewel of Glacial Snow") is about 21,850 feet high. But height alone is not important. To take one example: most people who visit Khumbu, at the southern base of Mt. Everest, leave with more words of admiration for 22,494-foot Ama Dablam than for Everest itself. Kang Rimpoche is located near the headwaters of the Indus, Sutlej, Karnali, and Tsang Po (Brahmaputra) rivers, which radiate away from the region in the four cardinal directions. The mountain has a remarkably symmetrical shape when viewed from the south or north. Its vivid mythological history goes back to the time when it was considered the embodiment of Mt. Meru, the invisible center of the earth. Kailas is the most sacred mountain on earth to the world's 800 million Hindus as well as Jains, Tibetan Buddhists, and Bon Pos. Hindus consider Kailas to

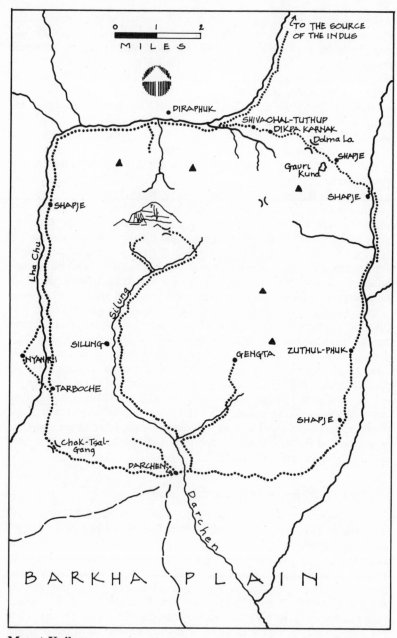

Mount Kailas

be the abode of Shiva, the god of destruction and rebirth. Tibetan Buddhists believe the peak is the home of Demchog, a major guardian deity, and his consort Dorje Phangmo. It is beyond the scope of this book to delve into the many religious associations connected with Kailas, but two recent books have done an excellent job. If you are interested, do look at *The Sacred Mountain*, by John Snelling, and *Sacred Mountains of the World*, by Edwin Bernbaum. Lama Govinda's *The Way of the White Clouds* and Swami Pranavananda's *Kailas Manasarovar* are also excellent, combining Kailas's spiritual and explorative aspects. All of these books are noted in the bibliography.

Due to the mountain's remote location in western Tibet, few people of any faith have visited Kang Rimpoche. The first non-Asian person to circle the sacred mountain was the indomitable Swedish explorer Sven Hedin in 1907. Between then and 1984, when the Ngari region slowly began to open to foreign tourists for the first time, only sixteen Westerners had ever walked around Kailas. When I began to hear that it might be possible to visit Mt. Kailas, I headed for Ngari in 1985 and was able to reach Kang Rimpoche. Like many pilgrims before me, I discovered that the rigors of the journey to Kailas exceeded the difficulties of the actual walk about the mountain. Prior to 1988 the mountain had never been climbed. Local opinion has always been that since the mountain is sacred, why should anyone wish to surmount it? More important is that a person be consumed and reborn by the experience of circling Kailas. To climb the mountain would only be a sacrilegious act of ego.

Enough background, however. Now to get our feet on the ground and begin looking around.

Darchen and Vicinity

Darchen (also written as Tarchen on some maps and called Daerjing in Chinese) is a small settlement at about 15,000 feet, just 100 yards from the southern base of the foothills of Mt. Kailas. There are no permanent dwellers at Darchen, for the area is abandoned in winter to the bitter winds and drifting snow. A photograph taken by Hugh Ruttledge (then British deputy commissioner in Almora, India) in 1926 pictures Darchen much the way it appears today with its gomba, a few small huts, the Darchen Chu (stream), and the black yak-hair and white canvas tents of visiting Drokpa pilgrims. Recently a small resthouse has been constructed to accommodate the Indian yatris. The small gomba is nominally owned by the Buddhist Drukpa Kagyupa sect from Bhutan. Its foreign ownership may possibly be the reason that the small monastery was spared ruination during the Cultural Revolution. This gomba is one of six in the immediate area surrounding the sacred mountain.

By late summer of 1986, a mud-walled eight-room "hotel" had been constructed at Darchen, with a government-owned store located in one room of the building. Don't count on being able to purchase food supplies there, for the selection of items can be hit or miss: when I visited, there were plenty of bottles full of rot-gut alcohol, some very nice Kang Rimpoche souvenir pins, but precious few food items. Nearby, two young, enterprising Han lads had erected a tent and were serving noodle soup and rice dishes. Their "greasy spoon" saved me from having to exist on the many cans of Spam-like pork I had purchased in Ali. More facilities are inevitable if Mt. Kailas remains open to visitors. The scores of visiting Tibetan pilgrims all carry their own food to the area.

Before or between your own pilgrimages around Mt. Kailas, here are four suggestions for hikes from Darchen:

South across the Barkha Plain. The best time for this hike is in early morning or late afternoon when the sky is apt to be clear on the mountain. At Darchen you can just see the very top of Kang Rimpoche. But as you walk away from the settlement, the hills recede and a wonderful perspective of Mt. Kailas opens up.

Up the ridge to the north. This hike offers the best overall views of the area and is likewise best taken in late afternoon as the sun's intensity diminishes and the day's clouds evaporate. Walk due north past the pilgrim tents on the west side of the stream that runs through Darchen. Climb up the rocky outcropping and continue uphill following the rolling grass- and shrub-covered slope along the ridgeline that angles to the northwest. Soon Darchen disappears below. You will begin to see the Silung Valley leading north to the base of the mountain, and the views to the south become ever more spectacular as you proceed. The thin air and grand views may tempt you to stop. But I strongly recommend keeping a slow pace and going to the highest point on the hill. It will take you somewhat over an hour to reach this place, but you will be greatly rewarded for your efforts.

Gaze to the south: the green Barkha Plain sweeps away to Rakas Tal, here seen at its full 18-mile length. Lake Manasarovar, invisible at Darchen, gleams azure blue in the distance. Gurla Mandhata rises like an island in front of the Central Himalaya. And away to the southwest in India, Nanda Devi's rounded peak juts 5,000 feet above its encircling summits. To the north, Mt. Kailas floats neatly framed between outliers on either side. The horizontal strata forming the summit cone appear most nearly symmetrical from this perspective. Here you can see the entire snow-filled couloir that perfectly bisects the pyramidal south face. Hindus call this striking feature the Stairway to Heaven.

North to Gengta Gomba. Formerly the largest of the area's six gombas was Gengta, a cube-shaped building poised neatly on a ridge that rises among meadows south of the mountain. Inexplicably spared the depredations of the late 1960s, the monastery again houses a few monks. Take lunch or be prepared for a lengthy half day's walk to reach the building and return. First, cross the Darchen Chu to the east bank. Walk uphill, steeply at first, then more gradually as you disappear into the hills. Follow the trail, keeping to the eastern fork of the stream as it divides. The valley opens out into a large green basin, and the gomba is situated above and slightly to the east of the long, Ladakhi-style prayer wall in the meadow.

North to the base of Kang Rimpoche. You can walk right up to the southern base of Kang Rimpoche, but first, here are two caveats: Don't attempt to walk from Darchen to the mountain's base and back in one day unless you are a very strong and well-acclimatized hiker. Secondly, tradition states that you are not supposed to walk to or near the base unless you have done thirteen koras (circumambulations) of the mountain. Now you've been warned. Your *karma* (action and its consequence) is your own.

Begin this walk as you would the hike to Gengta Gomba. But at the point a half hour up from Darchen where the streams divide, cross the eastern stream (which is smaller) and follow the east bank of the western valley. Now you begin ascending the curving Silung Valley, which you saw from the viewpoint described in the ridgeline walk, above. Across the valley you'll see the ruins of Silung Gomba, about an hour's walk above Darchen. It is probably easiest to follow the bottom of the valley on the way up, for there is no path. On the way back, you can take a high route if you wish. About three hours' walk from Darchen, you'll have an excellent view of Kang Rimpoche's south face and you'll reach another stream junction. At this point I forged up to the east, looking for two small lakes described by Swami Pranavananda. The ponds may be up the eastern valley somewhere, but if so, they are well hidden indeed and far above the valley floor. You would probably prefer to follow the western tributary at this point. The way is steep initially, then levels off into a rolling, rocky basin. Now you are right at the southern base of the sacred mountain. Given good weather, a night passed within this lovely amphitheater would be an ethereal experience.

The Walk Around Mt. Kailas

Tibetans, Buddhist and Bon Po alike, always walk around their sacred places, regardless of whether they are monasteries or mountains. They call their circumambulations koras, as I've already noted. The only difference is that Buddhists walk clockwise, while Bon Pos, who are many fewer in number, proceed counterclockwise. Thus, when you see a Tibetan approaching on a pilgrim path, you can usually surmise that he or she is Bon Po (we will meet one notable exception to this rule below). Whenever I met people walking around Kailas, I always greeted them by singing out the Bon Po's sacred (and untranslatable) mantra "Om matri muye sa le du." Of course this was always highly appreciated. The Hindus who visit from India always circle the mountain clockwise. Their parikrama is an ancient Indian gesture of devout respect.

The pilgrim trail encircling the sacred mountain is 32 miles long, and for the most part, quite level. Most Tibetans who camp at Darchen do repeated koras: three, five, or the highly auspicious thirteen. Some locals arise in the middle of the night, cook a meal, and accomplish their koras in one long day. This saves having to carry much food or shelter. But such rigorous exercise is best left to the sturdy Tibetans. Foreigners, including the Indians, usually do the walk in two and a half days. Now to begin, but don't forget to keep well hydrated at this high elevation. Drink plenty of water as you proceed, and you'll be much less tired as you go. The path begins at Darchen Chorten and immediately passes a low prayer wall. Then for several miles you follow the rolling foothills with the vast Barkha Plain and Gurla Mandhata on your left. Wild hares bounce away uphill, and marmots shriek warnings to their kin as you progress. The trail rises to cross a ridge topped by a pile of stones, and the summit of Kang Rimpoche becomes visible. Now you begin walking northward, descending gently into the flat, green Lha Chu Valley. The next few miles provide some of the loveliest scenery of the entire walk. On either side of the valley, layer upon layer of subtly shaded horizontal strata rise toward the heavens. Ancient prayer walls trimmed with dark green nettles (the food that sustained poet-ascetic Milarepa) follow one after another.

Soon you reach the place called Tarboche, where there is a tall pole covered with prayer flags. Each year during the spring full moon that signifies Buddha's birth, enlightenment, and death, a fair was held at this place. This venerable tradition has begun anew in recent years with the relaxation of prohibitions on religious practices. Be careful as you proceed, for the trail is vague at Tarboche. Keep away from the seductive hill to the east that leads directly toward Kang Rimpoche's peak, or like me, you'll have to scramble down a steep incline to rejoin the path.

Along this grassy plain you may meet the most pious of all Tibetan pilgrims. Wearing long leather aprons and leather gloves, they glisten with sweat and proceed by prostration after prostration as if in a trance. They are not Bon Po, for they have already circled the mountain and are retracing their route. Like a man saying his beads and returning back to the beginning of the string, they are coming back to Darchen. They fall forward so that their foreheads touch the ground. Then they mark the spot reached by their dust-covered foreheads, stand up, and repeat the process. This repeated act of full prostration is called *gyang chatsel* in Tibetan (meaning "to salute stretched out"). Performing this type of prostration helps to gain more merit toward the possibility of a higher incarnation in the next life. When they are finished for the day, they will mark the point they have reached. Then they return to their tents somewhere behind, slowly moving their camp forward, day by day. One kora done in this fashion takes from two to three weeks.

The south face of Kang Rimpoche slowly disappears behind the intervening hills as you walk along. Across the valley, several hundred feet up on the western slope lies Nyanri, also called Chuku Gomba. Now the path slowly rises onto a series of low alluvial fans. Mt. Kailas has four distinct faces, each facing one of the four cardinal directions. Soon you begin to see, high above, a foreshortened view of its dark west face. The flat strata are layered with snow like a many-layered chocolate cake with white frosting. Now look carefully as you go and you'll see the first of many *shapjes* along this pilgrim route. A shapje is an indentation on rock supposedly made by the footprint of a sacred, mythical person or animal. This shapje is one of at least two near Kang Rimpoche supposedly made by Buddha himself as he touched the earth. Coins and paper notes are stuck onto the rock with butter. You can clearly see Buddha's footprint, an impressive 18 inches in length. The valley begins to bend, and soon you are heading to the east. Hereabouts most Westerners make their camp for the night. Ahead, above the river's north bank, lies Diraphuk Gomba, 12 miles beyond and barely 1,000 feet above Darchen. Branching up from the river's south side across from Diraphuk is a narrow valley, initially quite steep, that leads toward the sacred peak. After you have rested, if the weather is good, be certain to walk up the west bank of this side valley. I had to force myself to clamber up this rocky hill because I was tired, but was I ever rewarded! About 700 vertical feet up is a viewpoint where you can see the entire north face of Kang Rimpoche. The face is practically perpendicular, some 4,000 feet or more from top to bottom. Of this view (as seen from the top of Diraphuk Gomba), Swami Pranavananda wrote, "One can spend days and nights like minutes without being tired, watching the splendour of the Sacred Kailas Peak. . . . The grandeur and sublimity of the view and the spiritual atmosphere pervading there is simply indescribable."

The main valley turns away toward the north, where a pass eastward leads to the headwaters area of the Indus River (see "To the Headwaters of the Indus," below). The main trail crosses the Dolma La Chu on a new bridge, and the path begins the first of several upward steps that alternate with flat terrain. Now the valley widens, and you'll see nomad tents below in these highest grazing meadows. Soon you reach a patch of ground littered with clothing. This place is called Shivachal-Tuthup, and the clothing is part of an ancient practice. To the devout, whether Hindu or Buddhist, the kora of Kang Rimpoche involves an experience of death and rebirth. As a symbol of dying, you must leave behind an article of clothing, a piece of your old life. As you approach the next hill, hundreds of stone cairns dot the horizon. Here among these many cairns, you enter the highest basin, a rocky arena with a small lakelet at its bottom. Look at the magnificent view behind in the direction you've come: now you'll have one of your last views of Kailas's north face and the valley you've been ascending. The path makes a sweeping bend to the right and climbs to the pass over stony terrain. Water is available up to the base of this last hill to the pass.

The Dolma La (circa 18,300 feet) is crowned by a large boulder. This rock is festooned with strands of Tibetan prayer flags that radiate outward, and it is coated with dabs of butter and money (both local and Nepali currency), like other important places along the way. If you arrive at the pass along with any Tibetan pilgrims, you will see them prostrating in the direction of the boulder and perhaps adding to the many strings of prayer flags. Often people add a few flags, then take one or two old ones to place on their altars at home. And they always make the required three koras of the large rock. But the wind can be fierce here, and you may not stay for long if the weather is bad. Below the pass lies the gray-green Gauri Kund, a lake known by its Hindu name. Gauri Kund is the place for baptism into your new life. Only the most pious bathe there, however, for it is quite frigid and lies well below the trail. The path descends steeply for more than a mile over rocky terrain, then reaches the valley bottom. Just down-valley from the hill you'll see a large, lone boulder that is also a shapje of Buddha, although the indentation of his foot is not easily seen here. Look beneath this rock and you'll see how Tibetan pilgrims have torn off threads of clothing and left them hanging attached by the ubiquitous dabs of butter. Near the shapje, the main trail crosses the stream to its left bank. Here the waters temporarily disappear beneath rocks from an ancient avalanche. Again the valley levels out. Although the trail crosses some marshy places, they are not nearly as wet as some sections of the lesser-used route along the right bank. Look up across the valley to the right as you go, for if the weather is clear, you can see just the topmost portion of Kang Rimpoche's east face. Now, keep a close eye on the trail: a couple of miles from the shapje, the path recrosses the river to the right bank on a series of grassy hummocks and rocks that dot the streambed.

As I came down this valley, I had two pleasant encounters. First, I caught up with an old woman who was walking alone quite slowly twirling a hand-held prayer wheel and walking with a staff. I said my usual "Kora, yakpo, yakpo." She replied, "Ah, kora yakpo." Then she began a long monologue that appeared to be about the difficulties she had encountered in reaching the holy mountain. She stopped. We agreed. Then she said merely, "La so" and resumed her slow pace.

A little farther on a tall man caught up with me. He said he was from Kham, but did not have long hair like most Khampas. As we walked, he began asking me for a photograph of the Dalai Lama in typical Tibetan fashion: raising his hands waist high, he made two fists and pumped his thumbs up and down, all the while repeating, "Kuchee, kuchee, kuchee, kuchee . . ." ("Please, please, please, please . . ."). As usual, I pretended not to have any photos. After walking together for about a mile, while he continually asked, "Kuchee, kuchee, kuchee" (Tibetans can be very persistent), I stopped to rest. He stopped with me, and we shared some tsampa he carried and some dried cakes of mine. I began to relent, indicating that I'd swap a few shots of him from my camera for a photo of the Dalai Lama (thus perpetuating the myth that Westerners all carry such photographs). He briefly touched the picture to his forehead in the Tibetan gesture of veneration and headed for Darchen, a happy man.

Tibetans on kora circle the sacred places along the way and often say their prayers or mantras aloud, spinning prayer wheels or doing their beads as they walk. Walking at these high elevations doesn't trouble them, and their gusto, jocularity, and piety is both delightful and contagious. The Indian yatris doing their parikrama are usually urban dwellers from the lowlands, and most are noticeably out of their element. The leader of one group of Indian yatris said to me, "Only four of them even brought a cup and a plate. They are not used to camping." Some yatris ride yaks requested from their Tibetan escorts. These local guides can be most attentive, even refilling exhausted yatris' water bottles. I was surprised to hear a Khampa escort intone the Sanskrit mantra, "Om namo Shivaya" along with his charges. But he said, "Chelo" ("Let's go" in Hindi), with much more fervor. The pilgrims from India appreciate their good fortune in being picked to visit Lake Manasarovar and Mt. Kailas. Once I was asked to sit in with a group during their morning prayer sesson. And I can never forget the mantra they often repeated while walking: "Jai Kailas puttee-ki, Om namo Shivaya" ("All victory to Lord Kailas, Hail the name of Shiva").

Zuthul-Phuk (or Miracle Cave) is the remaining monastery near Mt. Kailas. It is located about 5½ miles down-valley from Buddha's shapje and lies above an area of lovely green meadows. Most pilgrims visit this gomba, for it is directly on the main path. Zuthul-Phuk, like Diraphuk and Nyanri, has been rebuilt, having been demolished in the late 1960s. The name Miracle Cave refers to a small underground alcove that is said to have been made by the poet-saint Milarepa during his visit to this place. Foreign tour groups and the Indian yatris camp near this monastery on their second night out of Darchen.

The remainder of the circuit around Mr. Kailas involves a gentle two-and-a-half-hour walk from Zuthul-Phuk. The path continues down the grassy valley you have been following, and you'll pass prayer walls topped with yak horns carved with the sacred words "Om mani padme hum" in Tibetan. Milarepa's nettles grow from the base of these walls, as if the rocks themselves provided nourishment. At one place, you ascend a slight rise where the river flows through a narrow gorge. Here the view back up-valley is particularly delightful, and you can also see the Barkha Plain ahead. Then the trail angles downward and to the west. You proceed along the edge of Kang Rimpoche's foothills with the plain sweeping south all the way to Rakas Tal. Rounding a slight rise, look ahead and see the pilgrim's tents and the gomba at Darchen. Jai Shri Kailas!

Now I must explain something. I have walked around Mt. Kailas not once but three times. And, mostly traveling alone, I visited the sacred mountain not once, but twice. After circling Kang Rimpoche initially in 1985, I returned home and thought during the winter about the long and rewarding overland journey I had undertaken from Kashgar to Ngari (and on to Lhasa and Kathmandu). Finally, I decided to repeat the part of the trip as far as the circumambulation of Mt. Kailas. I began my second kora of Kang Rimpoche a year to the day after my first and my third kora a few days after that.

All the while there had been a remarkable man at Darchen named Choying Dorje. Dorje was born at Darchen and attended a missionary-run school in Kalimpong, near Darjeeling in India. Later he continued his education elsewhere in India and speaks several languages, including Hindi and English. Dorje has many duties at the sacred mountain. He assists the Tibetans who come on pilgrimage and also sees that both the Indian yatris and other groups (usually European or Japanese) who come to Mt. Kailas are provided with local guides and yaks to carry their gear. Dorje needed a break from his work, so he and I set off to circle Kang Rimpoche: he for the seventy-sixth time and I for the third. We must have presented an unusual sight to the discerning observer. Dorje wore his maroon Tibetan chuba but also carried a camera with a bright yellow Nikon strap and sported a Western-style brimmed hat. As always when trekking, I wore baggy brown Pakistani shalwar and used a black umbrella against the intense sun. Come along with Dorje and me as we go on a special kora around the sacred mountain.

It is early afternoon as we begin by circling the Darchen Chorten. Then we start to walk, each carrying only a light day pack. We reach the first low ridge, and Dorje tells me it is called Chak–Tsal–Gang, "Prostration Pass." Then he rapidly intones a series of prayers involving several prostrations. Instead of heading for Tarboche, we strike out away from the path across the gently undulating terrain. From this perspective Kang Rimpoche's symmetrical, rounded peak stands out against the deep blue sky as if it were crafted in heaven. Now we head for the Lha Chu and wade across. Dorje waits patiently on the far side, for my tender feet take a long time to make the crossing. We climb up to Nyanri (Chuku) Gomba. Dorje explains that Nyanri is the name of the mountain above. Chuku refers to the white marble image inside, which is considered to be the brother of the marble image of Avalokitesvara (the Buddha of Compassion) at Triloknath in Lahoul, Himachal Pradesh, India. We have tea and tsampa with the monks and look at the recently rebuilt main prayer room. In it, the monks have constructed a unique periscope. By kneeling down and looking into a mirror, you can see the summit of Kang Rimpoche. As you do this, your eyes also rest on the plate for donations, just inches away from your nose.

We continue up the La Chu Valley across the river from the main pilgrim trail and pass some Drokpas who speak to Dorje with obvious concern. Dorje tells me that they are grazing their animals here improperly; they have asked him not to fine them, for they are poor people doing kora. He told them that it was none of his business. It is up to the locals who belong here to charge them. Dorje points out Rainbow Waterfall on the west side of the valley and, across from it, Sweet Milk Waterfall. Soon we reach a black yak-hair tent. Inside sits Dorje's "uncle," a soft-spoken, rock-hard man with a bright red shirt and long braided hair who herds the yaks belonging to three families. We drink more tea with tsampa and carry on up-valley, fording two streams as we go.

Evening is full upon us as we reach Diraphuk Gomba, where we will stay for the night. A year before, Diraphuk lay in ruins, but it has been rebuilt for the most part. The lama inside is an old friend of Dorje's. This man has done sixty-five koras of Kang Rimpoche and twenty-five koras of Lake Manasarovar, two of which were done with full prostrations. Besides ourselves there are a bearded lama and an old monk from Halji in Limi (located in Nepal's Humla region). For dinner we have butter tea and a delicious soup made from tsampa, yak cheese, and meat. Dorje and his friend are still talking in the smoky room as I fall asleep. In the morning we look at the gomba's new *du-khang* (prayer room). At the rear of the room is a small cave where a saint named Ghalwa Gotsangpa is said to have meditated for nine years, nine months, and nine days. This saint is highly venerated hereabouts and is considered the first person to have circumambulated Mt. Kailas. We walk out of the gomba to find that snow had fallen not far above (and this was August!). I expect a cold river crossing, but instead we walk up-valley to a place where we can leap across the main stream from rock to rock.

Dorje stops to pray at Shivachal-Tuthup and I catch my breath. Farther along we reach Dikpa Karnak, "The Sinner's Testing Stone." This white rock with black flecks has a red swordlike mark (representing the sinner's blood). Beneath the stone is a narrow gap that we each, in turn, squirm through to determine whether our sins will prohibit us from reaching the other side. As we ascend the pass, Dorje says prayers aloud while he walks; the best I can do is try to keep up with him. We circle the boulder at Dolma La three times and pause to eat some dried fruits and wheatcakes. I mention to Dorje that there had been more currency stuck onto the boulder with butter the last time I was here. He replies, "Yes. Some people leave it and other people take it away." A good example of impermanence, just as the Buddha preached long ago.

Halfway down the steep hill beyond the pass, Dorje shows me two more shapjes and says there are about fifteen along the entire route. Dorje always begins his comments about any shapje by saying, "This rock is very important." Then he shows me the proper way of rubbing the shapje with the fingertips of his right hand, then placing his fingertips on his forehead, throat, and heart.

Shadows lengthen across the Barkha Plain and the sunlight casts a brilliant golden hue on the nomads' tents as we arrive back at Darchen. Two days later as I leave, Dorje gives me a kata, a prayer scarf, and my eyes glisten with emotion.

To the Headwaters of the Indus   *by John V. Bellezza*

["Jungly Jaan" Bellezza has done a great deal of solo trekking in India, Pakistan, and Tibet. Here he describes the strenuous walk from the north-ernmost part of the pilgrim track around Mt. Kailas to the headwaters of the Indus River. John is probably the first Westerner in many generations to reach these fabled headwaters. He just put an impossibly heavy pack on his back and set off. Another person who applied for official permission was told by the authorities in Taklakot that it would cost $20,000 to make the trip. Hail the Funky Trekker!]

An interesting but difficult trek can be made to the source of the Indus River (Senge Kabab in Tibetan) located 150 miles southeast of Ali. The easiest way to reach Senge Kabab ("Lion Fountain River") is from the Mt. Kailas circuit. It is approximately a 49-mile hike from Diraphuk Gomba on the Mt. Kailas trail to Senge Kabab, and one major pass needs to be crossed. The upper Indus region, with its numerous streams and marshes, abounds with water. Like most headwaters in Tibet, the area is green and very lush, particularly during the summer monsoon. Kiang (the wild Tibetan ass) and their major predator, the wolf, can be sighted. Wolves present little danger to people, but mastiffs belonging to the occasional Drokpa family are a very real threat. There is no assurance that people will be in the region, so plan accordingly. You will have no one to rely on but yourself. Senge Kabab is higher than Darchen, so even during the summer you will need winter clothing and equipment. One last word of caution: do not make this trek alone. It is far too risky.

Just east of Diraphuk Gomba on the north side of the Mt. Kailas circuit, the path to Dolma La veers away from the Lha Chu Valley. To reach the source of the Indus, you must follow the Lha Chu Valley to the north. Both sides of the valley are walkable, but the east bank is a little easier. The trail is indistinct, but the terrain is not difficult. The biggest problem will be swampy ground: try jumping from tussock to tussock, and you might be able to keep your feet dry. Elevation gain is gradual during this first section of the trek. The Lha Chu Valley trends northerly for about 8½ miles, then turns to the east. Be on the lookout for the first side valley to the north, about 1½ miles beyond the eastward bend in the valley. From the confluence of the Lha Chu Valley with this side valley, it is about 4 miles to the Testi Lachen La. The side valley is boulder strewn and quite narrow initially, but in 1½ miles it opens up into a large amphitheater. As long as you head in a northerly direction, you won't have any orientation difficulties. Continue north along an ancient moraine and don't head east toward a likely looking gap in the range. The route to the Testi Lachen La is distinguishable but faint.

The approximately 18,000-foot-high Testi Lachen La lies on the crest of the Kailas Range and separates the Sutlej River drainage on the south from the Indus watershed. The pass is marked by a row of cairns and several prayer flags. The panorama of Mt. Kailas and the range named for the sacred mountain is a breathtaking sight. From the pass you gradually descend in an easterly direction. In about 6 miles the stream leading down from the pass drains into a larger watercourse flowing north. This valley is very wide and contains no less than four vivid blue tarns. The next river you reach is the Indus, 15 miles downstream. Turn right, easterly, and walk 5 miles upstream to a fork in the river. From here the eastern fork leads in 9 miles to the actual source of the Indus. I pursued the southern fork here and had to hike for about 12 miles before I came to the spring that creates this alternate source. This route also has several lovely tarns. There are many streams in the area that form the headwaters, and all are worth exploring. You will probably encounter Drokpa encampments in this region. If you wish to visit the shepherds, proceed cautiously and announce your presence so the herders can restrain their ferocious mastiffs.

To return to the Mt. Kailas circuit, go back the way you came unless you have a guide (which is highly recommended). There are alternate trails, but they are very remote and little used. It would be challenging but foolhardy to take a different way back without a local to indicate the way.

The Lost Cities of Toling and Tsaparang

Mile upon mile we had jogged along in utter silence. Dark clouds had massed in the west and a sudden chill had set in. Then, all of a sudden, just around a bend we sighted Tsaparang far ahead of us, our eyes following an undulating path that led to it. There it stood, high on a hill riddled with holes, which were at one time inhabited caves. A rainbow now arched above it, and as we came nearer the clouds parted and a flood of light shone forth, bathing the entire scene in sparkling gold. To us it looked very beautiful and unreal.

Li Gotami, 1951

Our landcruiser jolted from bump to bump as we descended the dry gulch. Somewhere ahead lay the Sutlej River and, across it, whatever was left of the 900-year-old fortress temples of Toling and Tsaparang. Finally we reached the main valley and turned east, heading upriver. Photographs taken by Lama Govinda and Li Gotami that appear in *The Way of the White Clouds* and *Tibet in Pictures, Volume 2*, had prepared me for the fantastically eroded sandstone formations in this valley. But the reality was much, ever so much more grand than Li Gotami's black-and-white photographs. Up and down the valley a myriad of wind- and water-shaped buttresses and gulches lay beneath high buttes and higher mesas. The fading rays of the sun lit the pastel colors of yellow, ochre, and gray in the hills and turned them into radiant golden sculptures carved by nature that seemed to glow from within.

The origins of the two branches of this road leading into the Sutlej Valley have been noted in "Ali and the Way to Mt. Kailas," above. Remember that the better-used route into the area begins near the road maintenance post named Baher. But the road from Baher is nonetheless rarely frequented by traffic. The few truck drivers that do travel along this road are not always willing to pick up hitchhiking foreigners, and you will not likely find any sources of food in the Sutlej Valley. So, if you travel on your own in this area, carry plenty of supplies to tide you over. A Hong Kong Chinese friend had to wait for three days to get a lift from Baher to Toling. Of course if you are traveling with a group, transportation and food will be provided. If traveling alone, you can rent a Jeep (with driver) from the government resthouse at either Ali or Taklakot, for which you will be charged by the kilometer to drive to the Sutlej Valley.

As you approach Toling along the Sutlej Valley, you can glimpse parts of the temple ruins across the river above the south bank of the Sutlej. The road crosses the river on a modern steel bridge that is situated right next to an ancient log bridge supported beneath by wooden cantilevers and above by long, rusting iron chain links. Below, the brown Sutlej flows westerly, contained between high sandstone banks. Toling lies several miles to the west of the bridge. What is left of its temples is hidden by rows of poplar trees as you approach from this side of the river. There are now a hotel, restaurant, and government shop at Toling, and restoration work on the temple complex is proceeding. Before we take a quick look at Toling and then the more interesting ruins at Tsaparang, let's briefly note the history of these ancient fortress temples.

Toling and its neighbor Tsaparang some 14 miles to the west are deserted castles, temples, and monasteries that were once protected by fortifications. Both complexes were built in the beginning of the eleventh century A.D., a vast undertaking that must have required many hundreds of laborers. The finest artists from Kashmir were commissioned to paint the intricate frescoes and construct the graceful images located in the large prayer halls of both complexes. These were the same families of craftsmen who painted the exceptional frescoes at Alchi in Ladakh and Tabo in Spiti (both located in northern India). Toling was founded by the Tibetan artist, translator, and scholar Lotsava Rinchen Zangpo. He also assisted in the building of Tsaparang. In doing so, he provided the inspiration to create two centers of Buddhist learning that were as important, in his day, as any across Tibet. At that time both monastic complexes were part of the independent dynasty called Guge (pronounced "Goo-gay"), of which Tsaparang was the capital. The region was fertile and well watered by glacial melt from above. Antonio De Andrade, a Portuguese Jesuit Father, actually reached Tsaparang and set up a Christian mission there that lasted from 1625 until 1635. Five hundred families then lived at Tsaparang.

By the end of the seventeenth century, however, several calamities caused these vibrant cities to become the deserted, empty shells that twentieth-century scholars have rediscovered. The region suffered from an epidemic of smallpox in the seventeenth century, and by the end of that century, Guge had come under the control of Lhasa in central Tibet. In the mid-nineteenth century the forces in the area were attacked and defeated by a powerful army led by Zorawar Singh from Kashmir. But what seems to have ultimately led to the area's total decline was increasing desertification that has affected Tibet as a whole over the centuries. Rainfall has diminished in western Tibet, and glacial waters no longer flow into Toling or Tsaparang. Giuseppe Tucci, who visited the area in 1936, noted that he saw ancient irrigation works in places that were then practically deserted. When Lama Govinda and Li Gotami arrived in 1948, they found a single impoverished caretaker at Tsaparang. When I arrived (adopted temporarily by an Austrian group) at the end of August, thirty-seven years later, we found only two people in charge of the ruins and temples at Tsaparang.

Toling is called Zada or Zanda in Chinese. The main group of buildings that comprise Toling lies on a dry, flat plain not far from the south bank of the Sutlej River at roughly 11,000 feet in elevation. Long rows of head-high chortens lie to the north of the complex. The largest structure is the former Golden Temple of Toling. In the eleventh century it was the greatest seat of learning in western Tibet. Its maroon paint has faded with the ages, and now it is merely a collection of high, mazelike walls. Only four large chortens at its corners still remain. This temple was still in use when Lama Govinda and Li Gotami visited in 1948. Only two buildings have survived both the elements and the destruction wrought by the madness of the late 1960s. During the time that I visited, only one of these buildings could be entered. This was a large prayer hall, a du-khang, with a 15-foot-high ceiling. No statuary remained, but the intricate frescoes, which covered all the walls from floor to ceiling, were untouched. The only sign of restoration inside the building was the tall wooden roof supports stretching from floor to ceiling, which had been painted a bright Chinese red.

We were told that all the remaining statuary from both Tsaparang and Toling was stored inside the other building (a statement greeted with skepticism by everyone, including the guide from Peking). The wooden door at the front entrance was marked by Chinese letters written in black paint and held closed by a cheap padlock. Just to the right of this door a weathered chorten had broken open, and its contents lay exposed to the elements. Chunks of dry clay lay in a pile interspersed with pages from prayer books, many of which were hand written in gold lettering. An aged prayer wheel was burst apart in the debris. Its pages were made of thin layers of birchbark printed with the sacred mantra "Om mani padme hum." There are no birch trees in this part of the valley, and the bark must come from far down-valley. Standing alone, across a dry gully to the west, is the massive 20-foot-high chorten that Lama Govinda called "the Great Chorten of Toling." Its golden top (shaped like lotus petals) is gone, and the chorten has been eroded by the elements. But it still stands, pointing to the benign gods above.

A good road leads west from Toling toward Tsaparang (Gugo in Chinese), some 14 miles away. By the time you reach the area, there will probably be a good road the last 2 miles to Tsaparang, but there was no such road when we roared up in landcruisers. We first turned sharply south about 12 miles from Toling and followed the telephone poles up the dry valley to the high, rolling plateau 1,000 feet above the valley. Only then did we realize that we were headed for the frontier posts along China's undemarcated and disputed border with India. Not far south of us lay the Mana Pass, the route that Father Andrade had taken to reach Tsaparang 360 years before. What you must do when the main road turns abruptly south is to follow a minor road downward. First you'll cross dry wastes, then pass a few small homesteads. Now as you slowly drive or walk along, look ahead to the southwest. Keep looking as you go. No, not on the highest ridges, but in the midst of the eroded sandstone layers. If it is early morning, the rock appears to be the color of burnt sienna, but by midday, it turns a pale yellow, even gray.

Now you begin to see Tsaparang: a tangle of ruined buildings tumbling up and down a 500-foot-high butte that juts into the valley. As you come closer, individual structures emerge. A solid red building shaped like a giant brick draws your attention first. Ironically, this is called the White Temple, and in it are many well-preserved frescoes. On the very top of the high, narrow butte are the walls of the former chapels and palaces of the kings. At the base of the vertical city are several well- preserved chortens of different styles. As you come closer up the dry, pebble-covered valley floor, Tsaparang towers over you. From the photographs taken by Li Gotami in 1948, it appears that the structures themselves have escaped further ruination since then. But the same cannot be said for the scores of exquisite images within the large temples. To see some of those statues, you will have to consult Li Gotami's *Tibet in Pictures, Volume 2*.

The feeling of walking into an untouched lost city was inescapable as we began to file upward into the ruins, led by a caretaker carrying a few small keys. A Japanese photographic crew had preceded us by a year, and we understood that a small Italian group had visited Tsaparang earlier the same year. Some Chinese graffiti with the dates 1981 and 1983 marked the only foreign intrusions to the place. The memories of Lama Govinda and Li Gotami echoed silently among the ruins. They had planned their trip to Tsaparang for ten years. To be certain they could enter the temples, they traveled overland in 1947 from India to Gyantse in central Tibet. It took them eight months to acquire the necessary passes (*lamyiks*) from the Dalai Lama's government to travel in western Tibet and enter the temples at Tsaparang. They returned to India and outfitted another expedition, this time to western Tibet. Once they arrived at Tsaparang, they were able to stay for three months before being forced to leave by an "ill-tempered, autocratic Dzongpon, or governor." During their time at Tsaparang, they had to contend with bitter cold inside the buildings, lack of food, and

The "Great Chorten of Toling" rises above a temple complex that has been decimated by both man and the elements.

thievery. But they made excellent use of their precious time at the temples and were able to take hundreds of interior photographs and return with stacks of watercolors and tracings of frescoes.

We were not so fortunate, for the caretaker had "bakshee," tips, on his mind, and initially we were not permitted to take pictures inside or out. First we headed for the massive White Temple, the largest enclosed structure at either of the two sites. The keeper of the keys unlocked the tiny padlock and pushed open the aged wooden door. As my eyes became accustomed to the dim light, I could see that nearly the entire wall space was covered with wall paintings. Most of these frescoes depicted row upon row of larger and smaller figures, their hands arrayed in various positions called mudras. Scenes from the life of the Buddha were depicted in one small portion of the large room (Buddha meditating rib-thin in the deer park was particularly beautiful). The wooden ceiling must have been nearly 20 feet above the floor, and it too was covered with paintings, mostly designs and mandalas. But virtually every statue of the various divinities and protectors of the faith that Li Gotami had so expertly photographed was gone. The few images that remained were damaged, and gaping holes attested to the force used to pull out these missing statues. Water damage had ruined some of the wall paintings. This was not surprising since the building had not been repaired for hundreds of years. A few Tibetans had found their way to the temple, however, for they had left behind prayer scarves and had burned incense sticks at the otherwise-empty altar.

Outside again, I began climbing onto the ruins. Not far along, the few tracks in the dust completely disappeared. Several times it was necessary to double back to find the correct path. The way was narrow, and in places a false step would have sent me skidding down in a puff of dust. From one lookout, I could see large rectangular cavities below with thick stone walls, suggesting giant grain storage containers. Twice I bent low and climbed tunnels angling upward cut directly into the sandstone. Finally, emerging through a wooden door frame, I reached the top of Tsaparang. Here the ruined fortress was highly eroded by centuries of weathering. A lone inner chamber stood intact: one room dedicated to Demchog and his consort Dorje Phangmo, the same deities said by Tibetans to inhabit Mt. Kailas. The exquisite frescoes of these deities and of intricate mandalas in this small room are still in excellent condition. Outside, puffy white clouds drifted across the wide horizon. Far below, a single patch of green meadow next to some barley fields provided the only contrast to the surrounding desert and bleached sandstone hills.

Later that day back at Toling, I played a hunch. A high, eroded ridge similar to the kind that supports Tsaparang lies to the south of the buildings at Toling. Some old ruins lie partway up the ridge, and at the very top, separated by 300 feet of near- vertical sandstone, a few ancient foundations are just visible from Toling. Still exhilarated from exploring Tsaparang, I headed for the high ridge and began climbing up its lower talus slope in spattering rain. The ruins revealed little of interest aside from a good view of Toling. Then I continued along around a bend and up the highest scree at the base of the sheer sandstone walls. Rain played fitfully and small stones fell about, each adding its own small weight to the slope along which my feet were angling. Ignoring the rain and encroaching darkness, I slowly made my way toward a black hole ahead. Just as I hoped, this opening turned out to be a tunnel. Clawing my way up into the darkness from the loose talus, I gingerly continued as, inches from my head, screeching birds flew out of their sanctuary. The low, steep tunnel led to a miniature, fantastically eroded valley above. Faint tracks, slippery in the rain, led upward. Following them, digging my boots in the oozing mud, I reached the top of the ridge, a thousand feet above Toling. The Sutlej Valley disappeared west in the dark toward India. And my ecstatic song could probably be heard all the way to Mt. Kailas.

10
Bhutan: Land of the Thunder Dragon

No one has been this way in six years.
Three bridges are missing.
And there are bears.

Trekking escort in eastern Bhutan, 1981

One new virgin peak will be opened every two years for
mountaineering expeditions. . . . Each peak is likely to defy
a few attempts before yielding.

Bhutan Tourism Corporation brochure, 1985

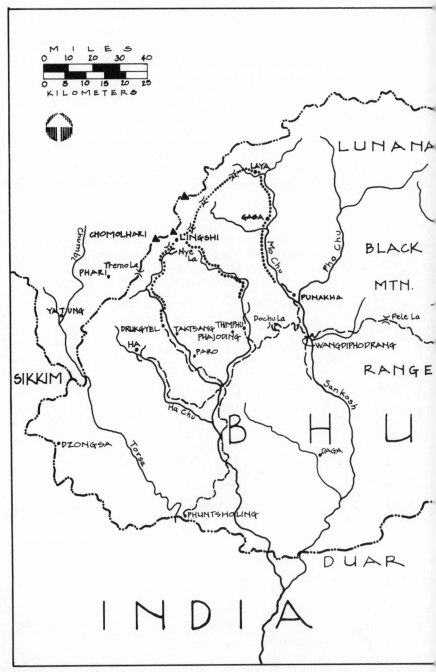

Bhutan

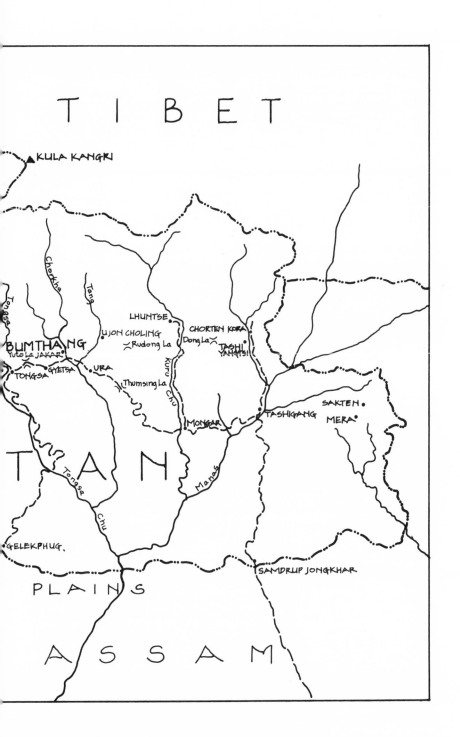

TIBET

▲ KULA KANGRI

Chorkha

Tang

Tongsa

BUMTHANG

Yuto La JAKAR

TONGSA GYETSA URA

LHUNTSE

LJON CHOLING

Rudong La

Thumsing La

CHORTEN KORA

Dong La

TASHI
YANGTSI

Kuru Chu

MONGAR

TASHIGANG

SAKTEN

MERA

TAN

Tongsa

Chu

Manas

GELEKPHUG.

SAMDRUP JONGKHAR

PLAINS

ASSAM

A Small Kingdom Allows a Few Visitors

Druk Yul, "Land of the Thunder Dragon," is known as Bhutan to those of us who live beyond its borders. The name Druk Yul is intriguing enough, but consider Bhutan's great seal: a double *dorje* surrounded by two thunder dragons. A dorje is a diamond scepter, a symbol of the eternal, unchanging self. The double dorje represents diamond-clear wisdom or indestructable selfhood. A double dorje surrounded by two thunder dragons, symbolizing twofold strength and invincibility, is a powerful representation of clear purpose—for Bhutan a very apt symbol.

Bhutan is a small, oval country, not much larger than Switzerland. It is 200 miles from east to west and just over 100 miles from north to south. Like Nepal, Bhutan is situated between the world's two most populous nations: India and China. It is located just east of Sikkim and north of the Indian states of Assam and West Bengal. The country's northern border follows the lofty summits of the Great Himalaya Range. Beyond these forbidding peaks, most of which have never been climbed, lies Tibet.

Situated north of the monsoon-generating Bay of Bengal, most of Bhutan is inundated with more rain than any other region of the Himalaya. Over half the country is forested, and more than 2 million of these acres have been set aside as national parks, forest reserves, or wildlife sanctuaries. Given Bhutan's small population (about one million), deforestation is not presently of concern as it is in most other Himalayan areas. Virtually all of the country is hilly or mountainous, and entire watersheds in the sparsely populated northern regions have barely felt human impact.

There are eight major rivers in Bhutan (give or take one or two, depending how you count them), and they flow generally north to south. Only in recent years has a west-to-east national road been constructed across the grain of the land, but due to the strong summer monsoon, heavy snow in winter, and landslides that can occur in either season, the road is often blocked. If people need to travel across the country, they may have to go south into Assam's Duar Plains, cross them, and then go north again into Bhutan. Only locals can use this route, however, as Assam is closed to foreigners without special permit. Bhutan's snow-clad peaks, its forested hills, and its deep gorges all so inhibiting to travel and commerce are idyllic places to outsiders who visit but do not have to make a living from the soil.

From the extremely scanty evidence available, the area that is now Bhutan was sparsely populated by scattered independent principalities from about the tenth century onward. As an integrated political entity, however, Druk Yul's history only began in the early seventeenth century with the ascension to power of Ngawang Namgyal, the first Shabdung or Dharma Raja (a spiritual and temporal sovereign).

Until the middle of this century, Bhutan's rulers actively discouraged foreign penetration of its mountainous terrain, just like the authorities in all Himalayan regions as far away as Hunza and Kashmir and as near as Nepal and neighboring Sikkim. After all, outsiders might hurt themselves on the precarious paths leading up from the plains, they might bring disease, and they often spread unwelcome information about the outside world. Between 1626, when two Portuguese missionaries were welcomed as "pandits from the far western world," and 1921, only thirteen expeditions from the West entered Bhutan.

Until 1907 Bhutan was essentially divided into two regions, the west, with Paro Dzong as its center, and the east, ruled from the great Tongsa Dzong. These regions and the districts within them were governed from large fortresses, or dzongs, which were unique in that they contained both offices for civil officials and quarters for monastic authorities. Many of Bhutan's important dzongs were built in the seventeenth century at the order of Ngawang Namgyal. Today some of these dzongs are still the headquarters for Bhutan's nineteen districts, housing the offices of *dzongdas* (equivalent to governors in the United States) as well as shelter for monks. Dzongs were sometimes built at river confluences—for example, Punakha and Wangdiphodrang. More often, they were constructed high on strategic points for defense purposes—for example, Lingshi, Tongsa, and Tashigang dzongs. The attempt was always made to build each dzong in harmony with the land it protects, and often dzongs seem to grow directly out of the ridges they are built upon.

In 1907 Sir Urgyen Wangchuck, who ruled from Tongsa Dzong (the country's largest fortress) and had been knighted by the British for his assistance to Francis Younghusband's 1903–1904 expedition to Lhasa, was acclaimed by leading secular and religious officials across the land as the country's first Druk Gyalpo, or king of Druk Yul. This ended the Shabdung system, established a hereditary monarchy, and effectively united the eastern and western regions of the country. Sir Urgyen's grandson Jigme Dorji Wangchuck ruled from 1952 until 1972 and began the momentous task of transforming an extremely isolated society into a country willing to grow and interact with the modern world while continuing to maintain its rich cultural heritage. (Readers who are interested in learning about Bhutan's engrossing recent political history should consult Leo Rose's excellent book *The Politics of Bhutan*, noted in the bibliography.) Bhutan joined the United Nations in 1971, sponsored by India, and set up its own permanent mission the next year. Since that time Bhutan has joined a number of international aid consortiums, but its authorities have always been extremely careful to proceed at a pace appropriate to the country's direction and capacity for change. The double dorje surrounded by thunder dragons continues to guide Druk Yul's destiny with clarity and strength.

Presently, Jigme Dorji Wangchuck's son Jigme Singye Wangchuck is the Druk Gyalpo. Few monarchs or heads of state command the respect and affection of their people as does the king of Druk Yul. Nowhere else adjacent to the main Himalaya ranges (excepting the Hunzakuts from what was once Hunza State in Pakistan) do a region's inhabitants have such quiet, assured pride in their land. And in no other country anywhere do its sons and daughters who go abroad to study so willingly return to live in their own country and improve their homeland.

Bhutan's original inhabitants are said to have come from the east and are called Sharchops. The other principal Bhutanese ethnic group is the Ngalops, who are descended from Tibetans that migrated centuries ago to the land now called Druk Yul. Finally, there are many Nepalis who have moved into the southern hills within the past century. The majority of Bhutanese work the land and raise livestock, as for the most part theirs is a subsistence economy. The national language is Dzongkha ("language of the dzong"), which comes from the west and is a dialect of Tibetan. English is the medium of instruction in the schools, and, effectively, the language used by administrators. Across the country, particularly in the east, fifteen different dialects are spoken, and as you walk, you may find the local language changing from day to day. Most Bhutanese belong to the Drukpa branch of the Kagyupa sect of Mahayana Buddhism, the kingdom's state religion. Most Bhutanese are very devout, and every home has an altar where devotional practices usually take place.

The favorite dish of most Bhutanese is *eema dashi*—red rice, chilies, and cheese—a very spicy meal, indeed. Red rice is a hearty, tasty variant of the white rice favored throughout much of Asia, and the hard white cheese, usually obtained from the milk of yaks or cattle, is excellent when rehydrated and cooked. The chilies, however, whether green or red, are searing to most Western palates. They do look lovely as they dry on rooftops across the land. The red rice (similar to that grown in Nepal's Jumla region) cannot grow much above 8,500 feet, so in the northern regions, people eat graincakes of wheat or buckwheat. Uplanders also eat tsampa, the roasted, ground barley kernel so popular throughout the Himalayan highlands. Soup, called *thupa*, made preferably from meat and whatever else is available, also provides sustenance in the north. Salted yak-butter tea is the preferred drink in Bhutan, and chang (beer) and *arrah* (distilled chang) are also popular. The Bhutanese have a great lunchbox, called a *banchung*, woven from thin bamboo strips in two interlocking basketlike parts, each with a thick lip. Inside go rice, meat, chilies, and cheese. But no liquids, for they would seep out!

Bhutanese men wear a long robe called a *kho*, which is supported by a woven sash at the waist. The pocket formed above this sash provides a handy place to store one's banchung, drinking cup, and the ubiquitous betel leaf, lime powder, and areca nut (together called *doma* and known as *pan* in India). The waist strap also holds the *ghechu*, a straight knife used for everything from cutting toothpicks to slicing meat to hacking limbs from trees. At night the waist strap is removed, and the kho falls down to its full length below the feet to provide a perfect sleeping robe. Women wear a long length of homespun cloth called the *kira*, which is held up by two brooches, one at each shoulder blade. If you knew enough about the various styles of cloth and the ways of wearing the kira, you could tell which part of the country or even which village a woman comes from. Both men and women wear their hair in similar pixie-style haircuts unique to Bhutan.

If you are Bhutanese, you are not supposed to enter a dzong unless you are attired in both a kho or kira and a ceremonial scarf. For men the scarf is called a *kamni*, and for women it is a *rapchu*. More than a scarf, actually, the kamni is a long length of cloth wound back upon itself, while the rapchu is somewhat smaller. The rapchu is a woven design, different for each area, but the kamni is distinguished only by its color. Most men, including lower officials, wear a white kamni. Village headmen, called *gups*, wear red-and-white scarves, while important civil and religious officials and high court judges wear red kamni. If you are a representative of the people in the National Assembly, you may wear a blue scarf; if you are a minister, orange is your appointed color. Only the Druk Gyalpo and the Je Khempo (the country's highest religious figure) may wear a saffron kamni. The rule about the necessity of wearing a kho into a dzong is not always strictly enforced in the more remote areas. When I was trekking in central Bhutan, my escort wore Western-style clothes but was permitted to enter the local dzong on the technicality that the dzongda was absent.

Like card playing in Nepal and watching television in the West, the Bhutanese have their own form of mass entertainment: archery. Sundays are reserved for archery contests in towns and hamlets across the country. This is the time for Bhutanese to wave at the fates and laugh at the sky. And they do this and more with great gusto. Archery contests often begin at eight in the morning and continue until five in the afternoon. The targets are a series of concentric rings painted on white wooden paddles some 15 inches wide and a yard in length, with a pointed end tapped into the ground. These small targets are placed 420 feet from the archers, so far that we foreigners can barely see the bull's-eye at the far end. An archer gets to shoot two arrows per turn, his team urging him on from the opposite end of the range, where they stand clustered near the target, casually dodging the incoming arrows.

At Paro Dzong is a proper archery range in a long grove of willows. There I saw a man with a Western compound bow, which didn't ensure his accuracy but did establish his prestige. Now many people have these modern, foreign-made bows. At Paro, two groups of women chant refrains in support or mockery of the respective teams, for women themselves never shoot. In Thimphu, the capital, archery contests take place every Sunday on the large, flat sports field. Here, many contestants are shod in the shiny, black, thick-heeled shoes favored by cosmopolitan men of rank and importance, but rarely do the women gather to sing, for they are busy at the nearby weekly market. Compared to other places, archery in Thimphu is more sedate, but here you will find the biggest tournaments with the best archers. In the fall, an archery contest is held at Thimphu in which only traditional bows and bamboo arrows are used.

My favorite memories of archery come from the first such contest I saw. The game took place below Lhuntse Dzong in the northeast, where the villagers had challenged the administrative workers from the dzong. Targets were set up in small cleared areas on opposite sides of a stream. Each archer would chant his own particular lucky word or phrase as he drew back his long bowstring in a steady motion. When it seemed he had the arrow sighted, he would give a quick, jerky pull and let loose the arrow, running after it for several steps to urge it along. The chang and arrah flowed. When an arrow landed on or even near the target, the team standing nearby would begin a circle dance. The men danced and sang—arms flung out, a bow in one hand, legs akimbo—first in one direction, then another, twisting in midair and kicking in midflight. Then another swig of arrah and it was back to the match. The contest didn't stop until the sun was long gone beyond a far ridge.

Tourism and Trekking in Bhutan

The government of Bhutan has wisely decided not to open the floodgates to uncontrolled tourism. Wide-open tourism just wouldn't work in this underpopulated and traditionally oriented country. The authorities have pursued the proper course, given the natural hospitality of the Bhutanese and the inability of the kingdom to absorb hundreds of low-budget travelers. Bhutan has very few towns as such and even fewer hotels outside of Thimphu and Phuntsholing (on the southern border). Stores are practically unknown away from a few bazaars like Thimphu, Phuntsholing, and Tashigang. In Bhutan's traditional society, each family raises enough food for itself or trades with other families for what is needed, and in most parts of the country, a cash economy is still little known. Unregulated tourism would be a mistake.

In the 1970s, realizing the need for hard currency and the need to become better known by other countries, Bhutan established the Bhutan Tourism Corporation (BTC) as part of the Ministry of Communication and Tourism. It is the job of this corporation to promote tourism and to provide the facilities and infrastructure to handle the people who come. Strict limits are placed on the yearly number of tourists who can enter the country, based on the facilities and staff available to handle visitors. At first, the ceiling was five hundred people a year. Subsequently it has been raised in steps to approximately three thousand people per year and may ultimately reach a maximum of about five thousand people a year. Hotels with restaurants have been built at Phuntsholing, Paro, and Thimphu. Lodges have been constructed at Tongsa and Jakar in the central part of the country, and a campground is in operation near Punakha. Other facilities will be built as time goes on.

Formerly, all visitors to Bhutan had to enter the country by the overland route, arriving at Phuntsholing on the southern border and then driving to either Paro or Thimphu. This necessitated getting a transit permit from the Indian government, for the area immediately south of Bhutan was and still is restricted to foreign travelers. In 1983, the new national airline Druk Air began flying sixteen-passenger Dornier propjets into the previously constructed airfield at Paro. Currently, flights leave from Kathmandu in Nepal, Dhaka in Bangladesh, and New Delhi and Calcutta in India. Service will expand in the future, particularly to the rest of the capitals of countries that are part of the newly formed South Asian Association for Regional

Cooperation (SAARC), which includes Pakistan, India, Nepal, Sri Lanka, Bangladesh, and Burma. Passengers on Druk Air who are members of groups arranged through tour operators have their air tickets into Paro included as part of their entire tour package.

The Bhutan Tourism Corporation has slowly increased the number and types of tours it offers. Initially, few places other than Paro, Thimphu, and the old capital of Punakha could be visited. Only one trek was offered, a hike to the base of 22,997-foot Chomolhari, north of Paro. Subsequently, the high village of Laya and Gasa Dzong were opened to group trekking, and in 1982, central Bhutan was opened for both tours and treks. This meant that you could visit Tongsa Dzong and the Bumthang region. Specially arranged groups have also traveled to Tashigang and Lhuntse in the east. If you wish to trek in Bhutan, you have to join a group organized by a tour operator (such as Mountain Travel or Innerasia in the United States or Hauser Excursions or DAV in Germany) that makes its arrangements through the BTC. In the United States, the most experienced tour operator is Bhutan Travel, Inc. at 120 E. 56th Street, Suite 1430, New York, NY 10022. Group treks in Bhutan are usually more strenuous than hikes in Nepal or India. Some people have gone so far as to call them "forced marches," but I prefer to think of them as vigorous and energizing. Group baggage in Bhutan is carried by either horses or yaks, both of which can cover more distance than porters. The first group I went with in Bhutan walked from 9,000 feet to 14,000 feet the second day of the trip. There were some rather tuckered-out trekkers by evening.

Aside from joining a group on one of the several prearranged routes, your only other option so far as trekking goes in Bhutan is to make up your own group of six people or more. Then you can try to arrange your trek directly with the BTC or, better yet, with one of the tour operators used to working with the BTC. If there are at least six of you, you can try to arrange a special itinerary in any part of the country, perhaps to an area you will have read about here. If you want to trek in a region where treks don't normally go, you will need a lot of lead time for your planned itinerary to be approved and arrangements to be made. Six months to a year ahead is not too soon to initiate your request. All special arrangements have to be confirmed (not requested, but finalized) at least two months in advance. So plan ahead if you want to arrange your own group. Note that there are two rate structures in Bhutan: sightseeing and trekking, and that the highest rates are in April and October. Trekking rates are lower and will only apply if the number of nights you are on trek exceed the number of nights you spend in hotels. Remember that everything is covered in the cost of any specially arranged tour in Bhutan: your in-country transportation, meals, group escort, tents, the works. The daily cost to trek in Druk Yul is no higher than a night's room in any first-class hotel in the United States. You will be trekking in one of the most traditional areas of the Himalaya, and you'll be helping to keep it unspoiled by traveling in an escorted group.

The address of the Bhutan Tourism Corporation is:

Bhutan Tourism Corporation
P.O. Box 159
Thimphu, Bhutan
Telex: 0890-217-BTC#TPU#BT *or* 31-62377 SARC IN
Cable: Bhutrism

On January 1, 1988, Bhutan officially closed its monasteries, temples, and the monastic assembly halls and temples in its dzongs to foreign tourist groups. This law came into effect because of the government's desire to protect the aura of sanctity pervading the kingdom's places of worship. Trekking has been unaffected by this change in regulations. Hikers should be aware that if they approach the occasional temple in the hills with respect and propriety, they may still be permitted to enter.

The following sections explore Bhutan from west to east, irrespective of which areas are or are not "open" for trekking. If you organize your own group, are patient with your request, and start the process far enough in advance, you may well be able to walk in areas that have never seen Westerners before. It's still quite possible to do this in Druk Yul.

Western Bhutan

Bhutan's far west, like western Nepal and western Tibet, is something of a terra incognita to foreigners. However, unlike the western reaches of Nepal and Tibet, which are open to foreigners but difficult to reach because of lack of transport, far western Bhutan is prohibited to foreigners, and practically no outsiders have been there. Ever. The westernmost dzong in Bhutan is Dzongsa Dzong, about 3,000 feet in elevation. Situated on a hill above the confluence of three rivers and overlooking land that at one time belonged to Sikkim, Dzongsa was probably built to protect the kingdom's western flank from unauthorized entry. Over a ridge to the east of Dzongsa is the Torsa River Valley. This is the forested lower gorge of the Chumbi Valley in Tibet, which forms a wedge between Sikkim and Bhutan. The town of Yatung not far across the border into Tibet has buildings similar to upland Sikkimese and Bhutanese architecture.

The pine-forested Ha Valley is the next valley to the east. It is known for its excellent livestock and is said to have the best yaks in the kingdom. Many years ago the Ha Chu was stocked with brown trout carried by runners from Darjeeling, and for all we know brown trout are still happily swimming in the river. Ha Dzong (about 9,100 feet), a rectangular three-story building on the western bank of the river, once housed some of the powerful Dorji clan, the former rulers of western Bhutan. High above the dzong is a trio of forested hills called the Three Brothers. If you drive into Bhutan from Phuntsholing, you can see the lowest reaches of the Ha Valley to the west as the road you are following climbs toward the junction of the Paro and Thimphu valleys.

Paro and the Trek to Chomolhari

Paro Dzong (circa 8,100 feet) is located in a flat valley awash with rice fields that lie above a narrow gorge, much like Ha Dzong to the west and Punakha and Jakar dzongs to the east. This fertile valley was the seat of power in western Bhutan during the nineteenth century, and Paro's large dzong testifies to the area's former importance. The tall rectangular fortress with a large central tower sits just above and east of the Paro Chu, next to a covered bridge, and dominates this part of the valley. As you enter the dzong's courtyard, you'll see several colorful frescoes, including one of the Mystic Spiral, that are symbolic renderings of the cosmos and earth's infinitesimal place within it. Inside the dzong is a large room, known as the Hall of a Thousand Buddhas, where the National Assembly once met before its venue was changed to Tashichho Dzong in Thimphu. Paro Dzong is the location of a large *tsechu*, or festival, each spring. At dawn on the last day of the tsechu, a gigantic 60-by-60-foot tangkha (painted wall hanging) portraying Guru Padmasambhava is unfurled to cover the entire outer wall of a nearby temple. Padmasambhava, also known as Guru Rimpoche ("Precious Teacher"), is a legendary figure said to have introduced Buddhism to Bhutan after having done the same in Tibet, where he overcame the then reigning Bon Po deities. Padmasambhava's appearances throughout much of Tibet and the eastern and central Himalaya, like Milarepa's, are numerous and on the order of "George Washington slept here" in the eastern United States.

Above Paro Dzong on the hill to the east stands its former watchtower, the unusually round Ta Dzong. This building's original function has become outmoded, and for over twenty years Ta Dzong has been the home of Bhutan's National Museum. Here a growing collection of medieval artifacts, tangkhas, and artistic treasures is displayed in the narrow circular hallways of the stone-walled fortress. You can look out of Ta Dzong's small windows and relieve your incipient claustrophobia by snatching views of the large dzong and lovely wide valley with its rice terraces below.

Paro Valley is the place where many of us first alight on Bhutanese soil, since the country's only airport is located here. Visas are issued on arrival, and then people either drive to Thimphu or go to the Olathang Hotel on the western side of the valley. Each room in the original part of the hotel is a separate cottage, and every one of these outsize dollhouses is built in miniature local style, utilizing many painted wooden beams in its construction. Not far north of Paro is the Kyichu Lhakhang, one of the oldest temples in the country, set up by propagators of the Buddhist faith who entered the valley from Tibet in the early part of the seventh century.

Taktsang, also called the Tiger's Nest or Tiger's Den (9,840 feet), is a small temple perched high on a rock face above the eastern side of the valley about 10 miles upriver from Paro. People walk up the steep forested trail to an overlook near the temple, stopping en route to take an obligatory photograph of Taktsang framed in clusters of hanging moss. Inside the main building are a large image of Padmasambhava and numerous tangkhas depicting him. The temple's nickname derives from the legend that Padma-sambhava was transported to this dizzying place from Tibet on the back of a flying tiger.

For many years the road up the Paro Valley has ended at Drukgyel Dzong (8,300 feet), the Victorious Fortress. This dzong was built in the seventeenth century to protect western Bhutan from Tibetan invaders who crossed the Tremo La from Phari Dzong in the Chumbi Valley. Drukgyel served its purpose, for the forces garrisoned within twice fought off the Tibetans as well as an invading force of Mongols. But a generation ago Drukgyel was swept by a fire started by a votive butter lamp, and the dzong now stands vacant, a relic of history. People walking to the base of the sacred mountain of Chomolhari begin or end their trek at Drukgyel, which is appropriate, since the top of the peak can be seen from here on a clear day. The hike to Chomolhari is probably the most popular trek in Bhutan, a route that takes eight days from Drukgyel to the Thimphu Valley or vice versa.

The route from Drukygyel to Chomolhari begins by circling fields of grain in which large boulders protrude. Walking up the gently rising Paro River Valley, you will cross to the river's east bank within the first hour. As you continue, the valley narrows to a gorge, and a mixed forest replaces the fields. By the third day's walk, the valley, which has been angling slightly west of north, divides and you take the trail up the western fork, which lies below the Tremo La, the pass to Phari Dzong in Tibet. The path along the upper valley runs parallel to and far below an unbroken string of high white peaks, including Chomolhari, that form Bhutan's northwestern border with Tibet. The forests have gradually diminished to windblown scrub trees, then shrubs, and finally yak pastures. Hereabouts and in several formerly glaciated U-shaped upper valleys that extend as far east as Laya village are some of Bhutan's best yak-grazing areas.

You will be able to enter a yak herder's black yak-hair tent with your Bhutanese escort once you are sure that the snarling, chain-pulling mastiff that guards the site is well tied down. Inside the tent is a scene that has changed very little over the centuries. Sit down quickly on the blanket where you are directed, for the acrid smoke is less intense toward the ground. Across from you a tiny, unkempt child may shrivel up next to its mother for protection as the woman smiles indulgently at him and pours you and your Bhutanese friend a cup of butter tea. Some say that Tibetan-style butter tea is an acquired taste, so think of bouillon or a Tibetan herbal broth, not tea, and the salty, buttery mixture will taste delicious. About you are stacked blankets, firewood, yak dung, pack saddles, wooden con-tainers, and more blankets. A large metal cauldron of milk is being pas-teurized outside the tent, but here on the inside, the small yak dung fire simmers tea or heats thupa for the next meal. Look up at the woven yak hair that forms the tent and you'll be able to see the sky very clearly between the loosely knit strands. Somehow these fibers admit only a fine mist from the heavy storms that often sweep across the region, while slowly permitting the smoke from within to waft away. As you are sipping tea, your Bhutanese companion will very likely be purchasing some of the white yak cheese, called *choogo*, produced by the herdsmen. Inch-long rectangular chunks of cheese are strung together by a thin yak-hair cord and are cheaper and fresher than those sold in Thimphu. In some areas where coins are still rarely seen, these white nuggets are used to make change.

Chomolhari (circa 24,000 feet), lying just north of the trail up the valley you are ascending, is a steep, rather symmetrical peak that tilts slightly in a westward direction. It is one of the few mountains in the Himalaya that looks much the same from the north as it does from the south. If you were to see the mountain from Bhutan, then traveled to Tibet and drove south of Gyantse, you would immediately recognize its leaning form from the flat plains north of Phari Dzong. Chomolhari's summit is considered to be the abode of the god Jomo Lhari. It is easy to imagine how the mountain came to have a religious association, for its nearly perpendicular fluted sides gleam in the sunlight, suggesting an unassailable stronghold of the gods. Chomolhari was first attempted (from the Tibetan side) by the British explorer F. Spencer Chapman in the 1930s, but the sacred peak was first climbed in 1970 by a joint Indo-Bhutanese expedition, which left a sanctified image of Buddha on the peak. The second group from the same expedition to attempt the summit completely disappeared in a sudden storm that enveloped the mountain.

Late one afternoon I went alone directly toward the southern base of Chomolhari, walking above a tributary stream past the remnant of a stone fort that had once guarded the upper valley. The path was faint and the light was dim as I hurried up several low hills, walking through thick grasses and onto an old moraine. It seemed this valley was a place where the locals had turned their largest yaks loose to graze, for never anywhere had I seen such black behemoths. Not wanting to irritate the beasts, I scurried past, finally reaching the mouth of the small valley glacier. Directly above, Chomolhari's flutings of snow and ice turned from white to violet to gray. Darkness had crept in with an ominous chill, and it was well past time to head back in the deepening gloom.

Your last camp in the upper Paro Valley will be in a yak pasture slightly above 13,000 feet. Then you'll climb a path up the rocky Nye La (about 15,500 feet) and descend on a trail along a long moraine toward Lingshi Dzong. This small fortress stands completely alone on top of a grassy hill in the midst of a wide valley and was once an important lookout, for the Lingshi La leading from Tibet is not far out of sight. The pass is hidden beyond the high, sloping meadow that rises over 1,000 feet to the north of the dzong. When our group camped near Lingshi, a herd of nearly a hundred bharal grazed high above on this meadow. And that herd was not the first large band of bharal we had seen: it was the third or fourth. We had already begun to lose count. Bharal are surely the least timid wild mammal found in the Himalaya, which accounts for the reason they have been so decimated in most regions. In Bhutan most bharal will let a person get within 100 yards before moving away, and then they move only, it seems, with some reluctance. Buddhist strictures against taking life have been closely followed in Druk Yul up to now, so these northern areas of Bhutan are probably the best you can trek in throughout the Himalaya if you want to see bharal and possibly other mammals (let alone gargantuan yaks).

If you are on a trek to Chomolhari, your group will turn south from Lingshi and ascend a trail to the 16,200-foot Yali La, the highest pass of the trek. At the pass you'll have your last views of Chomolhari (given clear weather, which is not always a given in these parts), and from here on you continue down, slowly at times, for the rest of the trek. There are enchanting forests of rhododendron, bamboo, and pine en route as you trek to the south, then east for a day. Finally you join the Wang Chu, the valley that leads to Thimphu, but you will drive the last part of the way to the capital.

You may, however, be with a group that is going east of Lingshi Dzong to the high village of Laya and to Gasa Dzong. If so, you will follow paths east of Lingshi and on successive days cross the 14,000-foot Gobu La, the 15,000-foot Jare La, and the 16,000-foot Singe La. All the while you'll be passing herds of yaks as you proceed. To the north rises the narrow range of high snow peaks that form the border. You can ask your Bhutanese escort the names of these peaks, and he will ask the local yak drivers, whose animals are carrying your gear. You will get an answer, but don't give it too much credence, for there are so many peaks and often the same mountain has several names. Some days there may be delays as the yak drivers hunt their errant charges, who often have an infuriating tendency to head home instead of grazing nearby during the night. While you are in this area, you may possibly glimpse a rare animal, the takin (*Budorcas taxicolor*). This creature tends to travel in a small herd and somewhat resembles a small American bison, for it stands about 5 feet high, with a large head and front quarters. The Bhutanese call it *rougimsee*. Good luck in sighting the shy takin. Your best chance to see the animal is in a fenced-in compound a five-minute walk west of the Motithang Hotel in Thimphu.

The large village of Laya at 12,750 feet is a center of yak herds and is also the northernmost village in Bhutan. Laya is unique in another respect: its women are the only ladies in the kingdom who do not have the short pixie haircut. Both women and girls wear their hair long, and they do not braid it like Tibetan women but let it fall loosely over their shoulders. They wear pointed hats of woven bamboo with a wood-and-bamboo decoration at the peak that resembles a child's toy top. This kind of hat is found only in Laya, and it isn't the same shape as the flatter bamboo hats worn in central Bhutan. South of Laya you cross a high forest-cloaked spur called the Pale La (12,300 feet) and continue southward high above the Mo Chu ("Mother River Valley") to reach Gasa Dzong (9,600 feet), built in the seventeenth century. Gasa is in a heavily forested area, and south of and below the small rounded dzong are some hot springs called Gasa Tsachu.

In less than two days of hiking down the deep gorge, you will reach the roadhead at Tashitang (5,300 feet), north of Punakha Dzong. All the way down this valley your Bhutanese escort will shout and sing to warn away any bears that might be nearby. East of Laya and Gasa Dzong, across three high passes, lies the remote area called Lunana. As with Nepal's remote Dolpo region, one is reminded of the old Maine saying "You can't get theyah from heyah." Of course, locals do get in and out of their hidden reboubt, but they don't follow rigid "day 1, day 2" itineraries as foreign trekkers must. A few trekking groups have reached Lunana and briefly tramped up and down the upper valley, passing through its several villages. But no one in recent years has lingered to savor the area, get to know the locals, or otherwise learn much about the region. In 1986, unseasonably stormy weather marooned one group between two passes as it tried to leave Lunana, and food had to be dropped in by helicopter.

Thimphu

Bhutan's small capital of Thimphu (about 7,900 feet), with a population of about twenty thousand, is not an entirely new town, but most of its buildings have been constructed since 1960. Initially the attempt was made to build every structure according to traditional Bhutanese architectural practices, utilizing dovetailed joints and no nails. Thus you'll see a gas station at the south end of town that on first glance resembles a small temple. But practicality has outstripped aesthetics, and many new buildings, particularly residences, have been built along utilitarian lines. Video rental shops have replaced the now-forbidden tungba (millet beer) stalls, and vehicles are not the rarities they once were in town. The local Tipsy Beer may not get you tipsy, but the distilled Bhutan Mist certainly will. When you reach Thimphu you will probably stay at the Motithang Hotel, a former royal guesthouse several miles west of town. Less regal but right in Thimphu is the Bhutan Hotel. Everyone who visits Thimphu is usually taken to the Handicrafts Emporium, but if you fancy the local handwoven textiles, be sure to search about in some of the smaller shops. (In Bhutan you can either spend the beautifully designed local currency, the *ngultrim*, or Indian rupees, for the ngultrim is tied to and worth the same as an Indian rupee.) Most people also visit Tashichho Dzong in Thimphu, the second-largest dzong in the country. King Jigme Dorji Wangchuck chose Thimphu as Bhutan's permanent capital in 1960, and extensive additions (carried out without nails or written plans) were made to the dzong during the 1960s to prepare it for its new role. This giant complex of buildings is something like Parliament, Westminster Abbey, and Eton rolled into one, for it houses the National Assembly Hall, the quarters of the royal kingdom's Lord Abbot (the Je Khempo), and a school for young monks. In addition, the Thimphu Tsechu takes place at Tashichho Dzong every autumn. About 6 miles east of Thimphu and just off the road lies Simtokha Dzong. Simtokha is the oldest dzong in the country, built in the 1600s by Ngawang Namgyal and used to guard the Thimphu Valley from the south. Presently a school is located at Simtokha for training teachers to instruct Dzongkha, the national language.

High above Thimphu to the west is Phajoding Monastery (circa 11,000 feet), recognizable by the many tall white prayer flags that flutter in a ring about the temple complex. If you have a free day in Thimphu and want to walk in the country rather than about town, take something for lunch and walk uphill from the Motithang Hotel. If you keep going, you'll get to Phajoding within a few hours. You can see Thimphu very well from Phajoding, but for the best view of all, take the trail that angles upward and north from the monastery. Another 800 feet up brings you to the Dongtsho La with its large stone chorten and a row of vertical prayer flags. From this vantage point the whole Thimphu Valley is spread beneath you. To the east is the Black Mountain Range, which separates western Bhutan from the central part of the country, and to the north lie the white border peaks of the eastern Himalaya. If you continue along the trail west of here, you'll enter an area with yak pastures and nomadic yak herders. The steep, rounded peak northwest of Dongtsho La is called Trup Chula. When an important religious figure dies, he is taken to this mountain and cremated.

South of Thimphu on the northern edge of the Duar Plains is Phuntsholing (800 feet), Bhutan's bustling border town with India. Until the airport at Paro was put to use, everyone entered and left Bhutan beneath the stylized wooden entrance gate at the edge of Phuntsholing. If you enter Bhutan here, you will stop briefly just beyond the gate to get your visa stamped. Then you'll proceed several miles beyond town to the isolated Kharbandi Hotel, where you'll stay the night. The next day you'll proceed the 112 winding miles up to Thimphu or go to Paro to continue your tour in Bhutan.

Punakha and Wangdiphodrang

Punakha Dzong (about 5,200 feet) is situated in Thimphu District across the 10,200-foot Dochu La east of Thimphu. Like most dzongs in Druk Yul, it is not surrounded by or even near a town of any size, reminding us again that Bhutan is predominantly a rural country. The dzong lies just north of the junction of the Mo Chu and the Pho Chu, the "Mother" and "Father" rivers, which now together form the Sankosh River. More than once a wall of water has rushed down the Pho Chu after a glacial lake high in Lunana has burst its banks. Bridges have been torn out, villages have been isolated, and people have been killed by the torrent, but miraculously Punakha's dzong has never been harmed. The large fortress is especially busy in winter, when hundreds of monks from Thimphu and Tongsa move to Punakha to escape the inclement weather at their own dzongs. The Je Khempo, the kingdom's spiritual leader and head of the monk body in Bhutan, also comes to Punakha in the winter. Most visitors to Bhutan make a day trip across the Dochu La from Thimphu to see Punakha and Wangdiphodrang down-valley. To reach the dzong at Punakha, you walk across a suspended bridge over the Mo Chu. Within the dzong are many elaborate frescoes, including one of the Mystic Spiral, like that seen at

Paro. Punakha's importance lies largely in the past, when it was Druk Yul's capital, but the elaborate religious art within and the dzong's sheer size give a hint of Punakha's former days of glory.

Wangdiphodrang Dzong (about 4,500 feet) is located on a narrow, windswept bluff above the junction of the Sankosh and Tang Chu rivers down-valley from Punakha. The only approach to Wangdi from the west used to be across a cantilevered footbridge that could be locked against intruders at night. At the dzong the bright national flag—gold and orange separated by the thunder dragon—ripples high on a staff, just as at any dzong that is a district headquarters. Wangdi is the headquarters of one of Bhutan's largest districts, an administrative region that stretches from Tibet to within 15 miles of the southern border. The dzong has a pleasant grassy courtyard that is patrolled by a large rooster. In 1981 the pavement on the west-to-east national road ended at that point. Referring to the beginning of the tarmac, a sign by the roadside once read: Metalled Road Starts: Thank God The Agony Is Over.

East of Wangdiphodrang Dzong the road winds up the long Tang Chu Valley. At one place along the way, if you look carefully to the south, you can see more than a dozen honeycombs not far above the river's thrashing waters. These oblong dark brown combs are oozing with rich honey, but they hang firmly attached to an overhanging rock, where they are quite safe from any intruder, human or animal. Gradually the road leaves the terraced fields and scattered homes of the warm lower valley and snakes back and forth upward through a thick forest. The tall conifers you pass through lie on the western slopes of the north-to-south series of high, sparsely populated hills called the Black Mountain Range. These hills separate western Bhutan from Tongsa Dzong and the area called Bumthang, which comprise the central region of the kingdom.

Central Bhutan

The Pele La (circa 11,000 feet), 38 miles east of Wangdi, is in a wide, unique bamboo grassland in the midst of the 12,500-to-14,000-foot Black Mountain Range. East of the pass the road continues downward, passing the clustered village of Rukubji. It then meanders alongside an isolated white chorten, named Chendebji, with four sets of baleful eyes facing the four cardinal directions. This chorten is similar in shape to the round, white chortens at Bodnath and Swayambhu in Nepal's Kathmandu Valley. The twisting, narrow route keeps its elevation as the river valley falls away far below. Ahead a large north-south gorge opens out into the Tongsa (or Mangde) Valley. A road wends its way up this thickly forested valley to Tongsa Dzong from Gaylegphug on Bhutan's southern border. Soon you can begin to see massive Tongsa Dzong (about 7,100 feet) far across the steep gorge to the northeast. The view of the surrounding forest-clad hills is spectacular hereabouts. When I walked along this way, a small sign jutting out from the side of the road caught my attention. The inscription read simply: Proposed Viewpoint.

The road continues contouring nearly level for miles, high above the bottom of the gorge, until it reaches Tongsa Dzong, 80 miles beyond Wangdiphodrang. There is a guesthouse at Tongsa, and a small bazaar of little shops has been built along the road. When I passed this way, I was walking with Arlene Blum, a friend from California, and several Bhutanese. We trekked the entire way from Tashi Yangtsi Dzong in eastern Bhutan through Tongsa to Wangdi, a walk that took thirteen days.

Formerly only one major trail led across Druk Yul from east to west. (With some alterations, that path has become the east-to-west national road.) At Tongsa Dzong the path led out of a large door at the base of the dzong. Like the passage across the bridge at Wangdi, this door could be closed at night or whenever the authorities wished, thereby effectively stopping any east-west traffic. Since I was exiting from within the dzong, I pulled back a thick wooden bar on this door and let myself out. Then I scampered downhill on the old, rarely used path to the bottom of the gorge. A covered bridge with small stone portals at either side reached over the river, leading to the equally steep trail up the far bank. You can't see the old bridge from above, but it will probably remain standing for a good many years, a mute reminder of the days when this narrow span was part of the only trail across the country.

Tongsa Dzong, built in stages from 1543 until the middle of the seventeenth century, is a vast, echoing white fortress that appears to grow directly up from the narrow green ridge on which it is constructed. The dzong is a series of connected buildings that house over twenty prayer halls (*lhakhangs*), chapels, and rooms housing the district administrators. Formerly the seat of government for all of central and eastern Bhutan, Tongsa is where Sir Urgyen Wangchuck came to power and went on to unify Druk Yul in 1907. Even now, the crown prince of Bhutan must first ceremonially become the Tongsa Penlop (an old title meaning regional governor) before he can become the Druk Gyalpo. As you walk from courtyard to courtyard and enter a few of Tongsa's many large lhakhangs, you will undoubtedly breathe a few ineffable wisps of the mystery and authority that once emanated from this giant dzong.

The road from Tongsa curls around a steep hillside beneath the Tiger Fortress, three round watchtowers connected by enclosed stone passageways that once stood guard over the dzong below. Then the route rises through forest to cross the Yuto (or Wanspe) La (circa 11,300 feet), leading to the Bumthang region and Gyetsa (9,800 feet), the next small settlement. Gyetsa sits among fields of buckwheat, which are in turn surrounded by pine forests whispering with thick hanging strands of moss. Well back from the road on the gently sloping valley floor is a large square temple resembling Samye Monastery in central Tibet. At one time the Karmapa, former head of the Kagyupa sect, used to live in this impressive gomba. Other temples are located in the opposite direction, high on a steep rocky cliff several miles north of town.

When we passed through Gyetsa, our Bhutanese escort Yeshe Wangchuck hired a retired soldier to guide us over the traditional trail to

Tongsa. This wonderful roly-poly man was delighted to show us the old path, a route that had become rather overgrown since the road had been built. Our new friend pointed out the grassy meadow where the former king always ate lunch on his way from Gyetsa to Tongsa and showed us an ancient tree that gave its name to a resting place, as well as another tree with large burls used to make drinking cups. His enthusiasm and knowledge of local lore truly sparked our walk that day. As we descended toward Tongsa, I told him (with Yeshe translating) that I highly respected him and that he had known and been involved with an era of history that was now all but gone. With a twinkle in his eye, he replied that he knew this. Yet what could he do but return home and finish building a storage shed for his potatoes.

The region called Bumthang is a series of several interconnected valleys, clustered in some areas with temples and monasteries. Bumthang's vales lie 8,000 to 10,000 feet high, and the rounded pine-clad slopes above them are reminiscent of Nepal's Jumla Valley or high valleys in western Colorado. But those places have not known the numerous mythical events that centuries ago occurred in Bumthang, epic mysteries commemorated by the many large and small temples built locally as memorials. In Bumthang you can find the Lotus Grove Monastery, the Iron Castle, the Gomba of the Happy Message, and the Broken Bell Lhakhang. Padmasambhava converted the inhabitants of this region to Buddhism in the eighth century, and there are several temples dedicated to his honor. The most important of these is Kuje Lhakhang, where Guru Padmasambhava left an impression of his body in solid rock. Jakar Dzong (9,200 feet), the Castle of the White Bird, is Bumthang's principal dzong and headquarters of the district administration. The long, narrow dzong rises up upon a soft, green prow of a hill near the main road in the wide Chorkha Valley, Bumthang's largest vale. Jakar was constructed upon the spot where a group of monks saw a large white bird land, a bird that was surely King of the Geese.

Wild cannabis grows in Bumthang and other parts of Bhutan, but unlike virtually everywhere else in the Himalaya, the plant is not rubbed by hand to make hashish or dried as is to be smoked. Instead, the Bhutanese feed it to their pigs. With respect to cultivated crops, the locals construct elaborate scarecrows adorned with old clothing and also make wooden faces to help protect the buckwheat fields. When the buckwheat begins to get ripe, people must sleep in tiny frame huts on stilts that are scattered along the upper edges of the fields near the forest. Then when a bear comes to eat the crop, they must frighten it away. "How do you scare it?" I asked. "Oh, we must make a very loud noise by yelling and hitting pots and lids together."

Northeast of the Chorkha Valley is the Tang Chu. As our small group was descending into this valley from the east along an old, rarely used path over the Rudong La, I saw a large building to the north and began walking toward it. Even though the tall wooden structure was well off the route we were supposed to be following (and farther away than I imagined), the building was so stunning I just had to see it close up. A monk, who must have been surprised to see two Westerners, told us this was a monastery named Ujon Choling and showed us about the nearly deserted structure, which contained many old frescoes, including a circular one, surrounded by clouds, depicting the mythical kingdom of Shambhala.

South of the Tang Chu and along the main road is the hamlet of Ura, surrounded by buckwheat fields, its small dzong tucked away within rolling hills of evergreens. The road then climbs to 12,400 feet, where it crosses the fog-shrouded Thumsing La, the highest point traversed by a road in Bhutan. As you descend from this pass, you leave Bumthang and enter eastern Bhutan.

Eastern Bhutan

From 12,400-foot Thumsing La, the road twists and turns its way down for over 10,000 feet, from high, wet rain forests into the lowlands of eastern Bhutan. Southeastern Bhutan does not get the heavy rainfall that the rest of the country receives, and the valleys here are drier than anywhere else in Druk Yul. Because the land is not as fertile as in other regions, shifting cultivation is common. Corn grows well in this part of the kingdom and is often cooked until parched, then eaten for breakfast and snacks. Eastern Bhutan is the land of the Sharchops, who speak Sharchopkha. *Shar* means "east," just as it does with regard to the Sherpas who live in the Khumbu region of Nepal. So Sharchop (like Sherpa) means "person from the east." At the bottom of the ridge beyond the Thumsing La flows the Kuru Chu. And near the road just east of the river is another white chorten, similar in style to Chendebji (west of Gyetsa). But here by the Kuru Chu, instead of moss growing among the surrounding evergreens, banana trees grow between the pines.

A road ascends the Kuru Chu Valley northward for some 30 miles as far as Lhuntse Dzong (about 4,500 feet), another district headquarters. Lhuntse, situated 500 feet above the river on the valley's western slopes, is a solid, almost-square fortress with a round entrance portal. When we arrived at the dzong from the east, the dzongda most hospitably served us with orange squash, sweet tea, salted tea, then arrah as he plied us with questions about our dome tent and asked for the address where he could order one. But this didn't happen until the day's archery contest was finished. First things first, of course. Kuenga, one of our group, came from a village north of Lhuntse. He had left home ten years before to attend school in Darjeeling and had not been back since. So he walked two stages in a day, visited his parents, and hiked back after a single day at home. When we left Lhuntse, we hiked up toward the west, and nowhere in the wide upper valley beyond Lhuntse was there a single sign of human habitation.

East of the Kuru Chu the road rises directly up to a ridge where the district headquarters of Mongar Dzong (over 3,000 feet) is located, near a small bazaar. Then the route continues east and into the large Manas River Valley. The largest town in eastern Bhutan is Tashigang (perhaps 3,500 feet), situated high above the river. A road from the southern border town of Samdrup Jongkhar joins the east-west road at Tashigang, and a prestigious college (equivalent to a U.S. junior college) is located near town. Tashigang's large three-hundred-year-old dzong, head of the district's administrative apparatus, rests precariously at the end of a narrow spur overlooking the wide valley. At a butcher's shop in town, a sign in English noted, among other items: Yak meat only: 9 ngultrim. Meat with bone: 7 ngultrim.

Whether you are in Ha or Tashigang, Bhutan's solid, rectangular houses have many similarities. Most homes are at least two stories high with an open space beneath the roof for food storage. Usually the thick walls are made of pounded earth or mud blocks, but in some areas, such as Bumthang, the walls are constructed from stone. The majority of homes are whitewashed on the outside with crushed lime, like the dzongs, but some houses remain brown. The ground floor is always used as a stable and storage for tools. Then you climb a ladder inside or reach the living area on the second floor by means of a porch. The flooring is made of thick, well-worn planks of wood; vertical planks divide the sleeping quarters and altar from the main kitchen and living room. Many homes are roofed with wooden shingles held down by large rocks. These distinctive wooden roofs cover homes, temples, and shrines and were formerly used to protect the large dzongs (now maroon-painted corrugated metal is used for dzongs).

A Brokpa in far eastern Bhutan wears a "spiderman" hat with rain gutters. (Photograph by Daniel Miller.)

Dovetailed woodwork decorates the windows and porches of all buildings. Well-to-do homeowners hire painters to add bright touches to their houses; shrines and temples also have a great deal of decorative painting on the woodwork.

North of Tashigang, the road passes Tashi Yangtsi Dzong (about 5,400 feet), a small dzong surrounded by mixed forest. It was here at Tashi Yangtsi that Arlene and I began our walk to Wangdiphodrang. Before we began, we observed a routine that is a holdover from the old days, whereby orders come down from the central authorities to provide services for official guests. To transport our food and gear, locals and their horses were needed. The people who would go were to be paid by our escorts from Thimphu, and the locals would change each time we crossed a district boundary. The headman at Tashi Yangtsi, the *gup*, had received a message from the dzongda in Tashigang requesting him to provide men and horses to carry our supplies. The gup, in turn, was required to call together the local farmers, and while we watched, he asked, cajoled, threatened, and finally ordered six men to go. Initially unwilling to undertake the difficult walk to Lhuntse, the men were excellent companions and hard workers once we got under way.

The road beyond Tashi Yangtsi continues as far north as Chorten Kora (circa 5,450 feet), another white chorten, similar to Chendebji. Chorten Kora, however, is partially encircled by a small community of homes, reminiscent of a miniature Bodnath, the large stupa northwest of Kathmandu. Chorten Kora has a comfortable, used aspect since people live nearby, unlike the other two chortens in central Bhutan, which are quite isolated.

A road has now been constructed from Tashigang partway to the far eastern village of Sakten. In this easternmost part of Bhutan live the Brokpas. These people raise crops and are also pastoralists. Sometimes the Brokpas are nicknamed Spidermen because of the thick, black hats of wiry yak hair they wear. These round, brimless hats have five tails that act as rain gutters.

So there you have an overview of Druk Yul from Dzongsa Dzong in the far west, across the kingdom's many hilly, forested valleys to Sakten near the eastern border. Most trekkers won't be able to see this much of Bhutan, but now you can understand why the Bhutanese are not ready to receive foreigners wandering randomly in every area of their kingdom. Bhutan is wisely being opened to outsiders by its government at a pace that is proper to the country's situation.

11

Himalayan
Natural History

by Rodney Jackson

Introduction

Since the Himalaya's origin less than 25 million years ago, it has molded the region's fauna and flora by limiting Indian species from moving northward and Tibetan species from moving southward. Because of its youthfulness in geological terms the Himalaya has not yet evolved plant and animal life uniquely adapted to its terrain; flora and fauna are instead an amalgam of forms native to India, Southeast Asia, the Mediterranean, and Europe. Himalayan rivers were in place before the mountains were; consequently, the courses of the rivers have remained unchanged while they have cut ever-deeper gorges. These valleys have provided the main avenues of contact between Indian and Eurasian wildlife. Animals adapted to cold climes, such as wolves, brown bears, and rose finches, moved south from Eurasia, while tropical species moved north into the foothills, eventually meeting in the high mountains.

The main Himalaya, stretching for 1,900 miles and varying in width from 50 to nearly 200 miles, really consists of three parallel ranges. The low hills of the Outer Himalaya, or Siwaliks, adjoin the Indian plain and in few places exceed 3,000 feet in height and 30 miles in width. For much of their length the Siwaliks are separated from the main Himalaya by elongated *dun*s, or flat valleys, such as the Vale of Kashmir. The Middle Himalaya forms the southern edge of the Inner or Great Himalaya Range, which extends from Kashmir to Bhutan and China. The Middle Himalaya's peaks vary in height from roughly 6,000 to 14,000 feet. This zone supported extensive and magnificent forests of conifers, oaks, maples, laurels, and magnolias until intensive woodcutting in recent years decimated them. The Inner Himalaya is distinguished, of course, by its high peaks, which abut the so-called Trans-Himalaya Range, in reality not a range but a series of ridges, ranges, and plateaus forming the southern edge of Tibet. Examples of individual ranges considered part of the Himalaya include the Zanskar Range, the various Ladakh ranges, the Hindu Kush, and the Karakoram.

The Himalaya is a biological wonderland. To the north lies Tibet, the Roof of the World, a vast area of plains, mountains, and gorges that is only now being explored by naturalists. Neither altitudinal nor latitudinal factors hold much sway, given the region's high base elevation and rigorous climatic regime. Harsh winters, a short growing season, and paucity of moisture have far-reaching effects on the vegetation and wildlife. The area referred to in this guide consists of dry shrub steppe of sagebrush and several species of low, much branched, often-spiny shrubs that seem to barely survive on the stony or sandy ground. Scattered mats of the shrub *Carigana versicolor* occur in parts of the Tsang Po Valley; otherwise ground cover is virtually nonexistent. There are no trees on the windswept plains. In wetter places, especially those drainages not too heavily grazed by livestock, there is a sparse mat of grass and sedge. Very few places have the alpine flower displays that characterize the Himalaya grasslands.

Tropical heat and arctic cold are telescoped into a span only 40 miles wide in the Himalaya of Sikkim and Bhutan, and the region as a whole boasts a richness and variety of plants and wildlife that is perhaps unequaled in the world. On a circuit of the Annapurna massif you will pass from tropical forest to the barren mountain desert of the Tibetan Plateau: two major biogeographical zones. Botanists have estimated that at least 6,500 species of flowering plants grow in Nepal alone. Although the British botanist Joseph Hooker cataloged many Himalayan plants in the mid-nineteenth century, the region's fauna is not well known. A new order of amphibians was discovered in Nepal in the early 1970s, and only recently have the first field studies been conducted on large ungulates (hoofed animals), such as the bharal, or blue sheep.

This trekking guide obviously cannot provide more than a brief glimpse of the area's natural history. The number of plants and animals that can be described here is quite limited, and the descriptions that are included suffer from incompleteness. But if this account stimulates the reader to explore further, it will have served its purpose. In the bibliography you will find references to the most useful natural history books, field guides, and magazine articles. For flowering plants, I recommend Polunin and Stainton's *Flowers of the Himalaya*, with its excellent plates and descriptions. For birds, the latest edition of the *Birds of Nepal* will enable you to identify most species. Prater's *The Book of Indian Mammals* remains the only mammal guide for the area; since it was written in 1965—before any field studies were made of the mountain species—it has some misleading information. However, the plates will help you identify any large mammal you are likely to see. Another source of information are the numerous articles on Himalayan wildlife and natural history appearing in popular magazines published by the world's many conservation groups and zoological societies. One day the Himalayan trekker will be able to take along a completely portable library, making identification of plants and animals routine. Until then, interest, ingenuity, and perseverance will be the primary tools for exploring life in the Himalaya.

Life Zones

Biologists recognize a number of vertical (or altitudinal) and horizontal (or regional) zones that support distinctive fauna and flora (see accompanying diagram). The eastern Himalaya is considerably wetter than the western (Kashmir and Kumaon) or northwestern (Hindu Kush and Karakoram) Himalaya because as the yearly monsoon moves northwestward from the Bay of Bengal, the moisture it carries is rapidly dissipated. And the northern slopes of the Himalaya and the Tibetan Plateau, sequestered in a rain shadow beyond the monsoon's reach, are dry and practically rainless. As one would expect, then, forests, flowering plants, and wildlife are most diverse and prolific in the east. The eastern Himalaya supports lush tropical montane forests, while at the same elevations in the west is found sub-

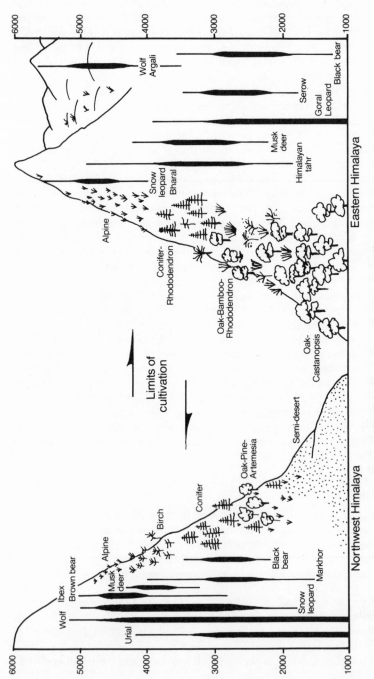

Vertical zonation of vegetation and altitudinal distribution of large mammals in the northwestern and eastern Himalaya. Altitude in meters. (Reproduced courtesy of University of Chicago Press, 1977).

tropical thorn or sage scrub. In the north, coniferous or deciduous forests grow on some of the more moist slopes, yet other slopes are entirely unforested. In arid Ladakh, for example, the only trees are those planted near villages and along irrigation ditches. The change from east to west is not abrupt, however. Most biologists recognize the Kali Gandaki River as the eastern boundary and the Sutlej River as the western boundary of a gradient along which plant life changes significantly, with Southeast Asian species to the east and Mediterranean-Eurasian ones to the west.

Vertical zonation results from changes in temperature and moisture with increasing elevation. Temperature decreases while moisture increases to a point and then, at higher levels, decreases. In general, the temperature drops about 3.5 degrees Fahrenheit for every 1,000-foot rise, and the timberline seems to coincide with elevation levels having mean temperature of about 50° F for the warmest day of the year. Timberline varies from about 12,000 to 13,500 feet; it is higher on southern than on northern slopes, and higher in the west than the east.

Equally dramatic is the effect of aspect. Steep north-facing slopes receive substantially less sunshine than those that face southward. It is not unusual to cross from hot, oak-covered or bare slopes over a ridge into the snowbound cool of a north-facing fir or birch forest. Even in the dead of winter, you may see grasshoppers and agamid lizards feeding or basking in the sun on one slope, while a few yards away the ground is covered by deep snow and all animals are hibernating.

The permanent snow line is another limit that determines plant and animal populations. Its height varies according to summer temperatures, amount of snowfall, and exposure, fluctuating greatly even within the same range. In the central and western Himalaya the permanent snow line may be 2,000 feet lower on a north slope than on a south slope and in the eastern Himalaya, perhaps as much as 3,000 feet lower on a north slope. Precipitation actually may be less on the higher peaks, and conditions are generally more severe than in temperate America or northern Europe because the steep slopes and strong winds of the Himalaya usually prevent deep accumulation of snow, with its moderating effect.

Five major vertical zones have been recognized. From highest to lowest, they may be briefly described as follows:

aeolian (snow line and higher)
alpine (timberline to snow line)
subalpine (a narrow transition zone)
temperate (a broad belt)
subtropical and tropical (warmer, low-lying belts)

The accompanying table shows how the location of each zone varies in elevation from region to region and notes the dominant plant life of each zone. (In the table, the temperate and subtropical/tropical zones are further subdivided.) The elevations given in the table should serve only as a general guide to the zones and their characteristic plant communities, for they vary considerably as a result of exposure, soil depth and moisture, the underlying rock type, and such human influences as logging, burning, and grazing. Although the transition from one zone to the next is gradual rather than abrupt, the change may be dramatic if steep slopes and strong shifts in aspect prevail or if man has removed the original plant cover.

Simplified Vertical Zonations of Himalayan Vegetation

Zone	Northwest [a]	West [b]	East–Central [c]
Aeolian	lower limit unknown bacteria, fungi, lichens	15,000 ft. plus bacteria, fungi, lichens	15,000 ft. plus bacteria, fungi, lichens
Alpine	alpine meadows 9,600–? ft. pioneer plants	alpine meadows 11,700–15,000 ft. pioneer plants	alpine meadows 11,400–15,000 ft. pioneer plants
Subalpine	subalpine scrub 9,000–11,400 ft. birch, juniper, sagebrush	subalpine scrub 10,200–12,000 ft. birch, juniper, fir, rhododendron, willow	subalpine scrub 10,200–12,000 ft. birch, juniper, rhododendron
Temperate	temperate coniferous forest 6,000–10,200 ft. pine, Himalayan edible pine, west Himalayan fir	temperate coniferous forest 7,500–10,500 ft. deodar (Himalayan) cedar, west Himalayan fir, Himalayan hemlock, blue pine, cypress	conifer-rhododendron forest 7,500–10,500 ft. blue hemlock, east Himalayan fir, spruce
	forest and sage steppe 6,000–8,400 ft. chir (long-needled) pine, sagebrush	temperate mixed forest 6,000–9,000 ft. oak, deodar (Himalayan) cedar, spruce	temperate evergreen forest 4,500–7,500 ft. oak, rhododendron, magnolia, maple
Subtropical and Tropical	subtropical, semi-desert scrub 1,800–6,000 ft. *Capparis, Pistacia,* wild olive	pine forest 2,700–6,000 ft. chir (long-needled) pine	subtropical montane forest 2,400–4,500 ft. chilaune, chestnut, oak, alder
	subtropical thorn 1,800 ft. acacia, *Zizyphus*	subtropical thorn 2,400 ft. acacia, bauhinia, *Albizzia*	tropical evergreen rain forest 150–2,400 ft. sal, bauhinia, *Terminalia*

[a] Northwest = Pakistan, Jammu, and Kashmir

[b] West = Himachal Pradesh, Uttar Pradesh, and western Nepal

[c] East-Central = Nepal east of Kali Gandaki Valley to Bhutan

Aeolian Zone

The permanent snow line is considered the lower limit to this zone. Flowering plants are absent here, and life is limited to bacteria, fungi, insects, and crustaceans that subsist upon airborne food particles blown up from below. Much ground is exposed because snow seldom accumulates evenly. Lichens encrust rocks, and spiders, springtails, and glacier fleas are able to survive in protected microclimates among the rocks and in the soil. Jumping spiders have been found at the 22,000-foot level on Mt. Everest, presumably preying upon other insects that live beneath the snow or that are blown there by the wind. Microorganisms have even been found in soil sampled from the very top of Mt. Everest. At the 19,000-foot level, temporary glacial pools in the eastern Himalaya are known to support large populations of fairy shrimp. And birds and mammals are occasional though transient visitors; the snow leopard, for example, may use high passes to move from one valley to another, and such flocking birds as snow pigeons and cloughs frolic in the thermals. Some birds may rest on high cols as they migrate across the Himalaya, although their flights are usually nonstop.

Alpine Zone

The alpine zone extends from timberline to snow line. It is a zone characterized by harsh winters, short summers, shallow stony soils, strong winds, and a lack of moisture. At the upper limits of vegetation, a few pioneering rock plants grow in sheltered places—beneath rocky ledges and beside protective boulders—where they form small cushions. Typical plants include the stonecrops and rock jasmines, which have basal rosettes of succulent leaves, and the drabas or stoneworts with their densely matted, cushionlike stems. *Stellaria decumbens* has been found at 20,129 feet and is listed in the *Guiness Book of World Records* as the highest plant in the world; however, the rock-encrusting *Arenaria bryophylla* has been recorded at 20,277 feet. Delicate purple or red primroses are often seen flowering immediately adjacent to melting snow. The plants are typically widely scattered and, unless they are in bloom, easily overlooked. The alpine zone also supports such plants as the edelweiss or sow's ear, having fuzzy, hairy leaves and a tufted, or clustered, growth pattern (adaptations to the scarcity of water in a form available to plants).

In sedge and grass meadows, wildflowers often form spectacular displays. These profusions of color are greatest where snowmelt collects and where deeper soils have developed over the ages. Some species bloom into late summer, especially at higher elevations and on more exposed sites. Anyone familiar with the mountain flora of North America or Europe will recognize many genera: there are buttercups, anemones, larkspurs, everlasting flowers, asters, dandelions, thistles, saxifrages, cinquefoils, louseworts, geraniums, lilies, and gentians. The diversity is staggering; in Nepal alone more than sixty-seven species of primrose occur, many of them in the alpine zone. Worth looking for are the sky blue *Meconopsis* poppy—the so-called queen of Himalayan flowers—and the delicate purple gentians and poisonous monkshood. Carpets of wildflowers are all the more remarkable in the northwestern Himalaya, where soils are absent or thin and water very precious. Small and vulnerable hanging alpine meadows relieve the otherwise-barren landscape of this region. Alpine scrub is found along streams and in U-shaped valleys. Typical species include the *Cotoneaster*, a rigid and much-branched shrub that produces an abundance of red berries in the fall; *Caragana*, a member of the pea family that bears thorns and is widespread in central Asia; *Ephedra* or Mormon tea; rose; and several species of procumbent (a flattened growth form) rhododendrons, junipers, and cinquefoil. This community is characteristic of the dry valleys behind the main range, such as Dolpo, Ladakh, and large parts of Tibet. In Bhutan, relatively lush stands of rhododendron, grasses, and sedges prevail.

The high Deosai Plains of Baltistan are vegetated by sagebrush and willow, with moist grassy meadows along the watercourses. In contrast, the alpine zone in Ladakh has very little plant life and virtually no trees, except those people have planted and the odd, stunted juniper that grows in protected places. All plants in this region are adapted to conditions of extreme dryness. Much of the Karakoram consists either of barren scree or arid steppe in which sagebrush is the chief ingredient.

The animals found in the alpine zone tend to be of Eurasian origin, with preexisting adaptations to the severe conditions of northern latitudes. Typical mammals include bharal, pikas, marmots, red foxes, weasels, voles, and mice. Snow leopard, lynx, wolves, and brown bears are found near the Tibetan border, and in this zone in the western Himalaya the ibex is a characteristic ungulate. A few large birds, such the snow cock and snow partridge, are permanent residents. In summer there is a dramatic influx of songbirds, which breed in the grassy meadows. Snakes and lizards are typically scarce.

Subalpine Zone

The subalpine zone is most accurately considered a transition between the temperate coniferous forest and the alpine belt, in effect delineating the timberline. Stunted, windblown birch, juniper, and rhododendron characterize this zone, except in the northwest, which has, instead of rhododendron, sagebrush, poplar, and willow. Fir, pine, or spruce trees are interspersed with these shrubs, and some north-facing slopes support pure birch forests. Birch is easily identified by its pale, peeling bark, which in times past provided the main source of paper.

The birch forest and scrub of the subalpine zone are vital habitat for the arboreal birch mouse and the dwindling population of musk deer.

Temperate Zone

Below an elevation of 12,000 feet is a more or less continuous forest belt. Conifers such as fir, hemlock, pine, cypress, and cedar occupy the higher levels. Undergrowth is sparse in most places, consisting of rhododendron, a variety of shrubs, and in the east, bamboo. In Bhutan, Sikkim, and as far west as central Nepal, a lush, temperate evergreen forest grows between elevations of 3,000 to 5,000 feet. Almost pure stands of evergreen oaks are interspersed with laurels, chestnuts, maples, magnolias, and other trees that rarely exceed 60 feet in height. In spring the forest is ablaze with white magnolia and white, pink, or red rhododendron blossoms. Mosses and lichens clothe every oak, and numerous orchids and other epiphytes add to the "cloud forest" setting. These forests are frequently shrouded in mist, and they may be remarkably cool even in summer. Some of the steeper slopes support almost pure stands of alder, a tree with deciduous branches that break off easily and lack the moss festoons so characteristic of the oaks in the area. Alders seem to invade areas prone to landsliding and probably play a vital role in stabilizing areas that have slid. Numerous wildflowers, ferns, and orchids occur, especially in moist ravines and near streams. Look for yellow balsams, purple violets, touch-me-nots, begonias, and Solomon's seals. The flora and fauna of this temperate-zone belt are truly Himalayan in composition, but they have been little explored, cataloged, or described.

In west Nepal, Kumaon, and parts of Kashmir, the temperate forests consist mainly of oak, blue pine, and west Himalayan fir with some deodar cedar. Magnolias are absent, rhododendrons sparse, and maples occur primarily near streams or along cool northerly slopes. Farther west yet, the coniferous forests at the same elevation are patchy and steppelike with such species as oak and sage in the understory.

The northwestern Himalaya is semiarid to arid at this altitudinal zone. Forests, if present, are small and scattered. There are few conifers, and the barren landscape is dominated by shrubs.

The Himalaya is famous for its variety of "rose-trees"—rhododendrons. The greatest number of species is found in Bhutan and Sikkim. About twenty-nine species are found in Nepal, and most of these are east of Kathmandu. One, *Rhododendron arboreum*, is the national flower of Nepal. Rhododendrons range from trees 45 feet tall to low, creeping shrubs and even epiphytic climbers. Flower color is not a reliable means of identification, for a single species can exhibit shades from white and pale pinks to scarlet. The displays are best seen between late March and early May.

Conifers become increasingly abundant as one climbs higher. In the west, the forests are dominated by the five-needled Himalayan blue pine (*Pinus wallichiana*) and the west Himalayan silver fir (*Abies pindrow*), a species with a smooth, silvery bark. Other trees include the famous deodar, a magnificent Himalayan cedar that grows as high as 150 feet, with a girth of 35 feet. Also look for the hemlock (*Tsuga dumosa*), a delicate conifer, and the west Himalayan spruce (*Picea smithiana*), with its flattened leaves (in contrast to the needlelike leaves of firs) and pendulant cones. Spruce branches droop conspicuously. The Himalayan silver fir (*Abies spectabilis*) is found from Kashmir to Bhutan but is most abundant in central Nepal and westward. It is differentiated from its western cousin by its rough, fissured bark and lower leaf surfaces that have two dark bands rather than one. Another pine, the Himalayan edible pine (*Pinus gerardiana*), provides food for people in the Hindu Kush and parts of the Karakoram; the seeds, which are protected by thick scales, contain much oil. The leaves occur in clusters of three. Yet another pine that is found in almost-pure stands in the central and western Himalaya—the long-needled or chir pine (*Pinus roxburghii*)—is best distinguished by its long, light green needles (in bundles of three) and deeply fissured bark. This relatively fire-tolerant fir is common in west Nepal at elevations of 2,700 to 6,000 feet. On limestone outcrops you may well find dense stands of Himalayan cypress (*Cupressus torulosa*).

Spruce and hemlock are more likely to be found on cool, moist, north-facing slopes, especially in the drier parts of the Himalaya (for example, north of the Annapurna and Dhaulagiri massifs). Larches (*Larix* spp.) are found only from central Nepal eastward, while the Himalayan cypress occurs only west of the Kanjiroba Himal of Nepal. Junipers (*Juniperus* spp.) are characteristic of the more arid higher elevations throughout the Himalaya, although they are more common in the alpine or subalpine belts.

The fauna of the temperate zone is diverse and in many respects rather unique. Large mammals include the serow; goral; the takin of Bhutan, Burma, and China; and the Himalayan tahr. At lower elevations macaque monkeys forage on the ground; the langur monkey, which spends much of its time in trees, is found up to around the 12,000-foot level. Less frequently seen wildlife includes Himalayan black bears, forest leopards, yellow-throated martens, red pandas, and a number of small cats. There are numerous small rodents, from wood mice to flying squirrels. Frogs, toads, and snakes, few of which are cataloged, also occur. But the greatest variety is in the avifauna. Most trekkers will attest to mysterious and wonderful calls from birds heard but not seen. The presence of trees, shrubs, and ground vegetation provides many foraging niches for birds that would otherwise compete with one another. Laughing thrushes, babblers, and minias flit about the ground and tangled brush, while nuthatches and tree creepers comb conifer branches for food. Tits and warblers forage among the foliage, and woodpeckers work on dead or dying trees. If you sit quietly on a trailside log, you'll be well rewarded for your patience. Many species will come close enough for you to see without field glasses.

Subtropical and Tropical Zones

Subtropical montane forests occupy the foothills of the Himalaya. Common trees include the chestnut (*Castanopsis* spp.) with yellow flowers and spiny acornlike fruits; *Schima* spp.—locally called *chilaune*—with fragrant white flowers and a nutlike fruit; and in west Nepal, the horse chestnut and walnut. Oaks are also abundant, and alders grow along drainages and on recent landslide scars.

West of Nepal's Karnali River are almost monotypic stands of long-needled pine, which at higher elevations merges with oak forests. The pines are sometimes 100 feet tall, and without an understory of shrubs or vines, the forest has a parklike appearance. Most trees bear witness to past wildfires, to which this pine is specially adapted.

The subtropical fauna is decidedly Indian in composition. For example, this zone, like much of India, has chital deer, tigers, water buffaloes, and hog deer, and in times past there were elephants. However, unless you make a special trip to a tropical reserve such as the Chitwan, you are unlikely to see these animals. And because most of these animals are not truly Himalayan, they will not be discussed further.

Below the subtropical is the tropical zone, which extends up to 4,500 feet in the east. Until the terai region of Nepal was developed, the tropical forests extended in a continuous belt along the country's southern border. They are now very fragmented. The canopy is composed of many deciduous and evergreen hardwoods, including bauhinia and teak, although sal (*Shorea robusta*) is the major species. Its large, rounded leaves, 6 to 10 inches long and a shiny yellowish green, make it an easy species to identify. Although never quite leafless, sal sheds much of its foliage during the dry season. Its flowers are yellow, and it is an important timber and fodder species. Until recently, sal trees formed an almost-continuous forest belt along the base of the Himalaya, but in many areas branches have been repeatedly lopped off and the leaves collected for firewood and livestock feed, with the result that the sal's form is typically straight and gaunt. The shrubs, bamboos, palms, and ferns that cover the forest floor decrease in density as you move west so that the sal forest becomes increasingly parklike, until it is replaced by thorn scrub in India and Pakistan. Among the arid scrubs, acacia, *Zizyphus*, and other thorny species dominate.

Himalayan and West Tibetan Fauna

Mammals

Langur monkeys, Himalayan orange-bellied squirrels, pikas, and marmots are the mammals most commonly seen on a trek in the Himalaya. Many hikers remark on the paucity of large animals, and certainly the water buffaloes or yaks you see will be domestic rather than wild ones. To see such wildlife as the Himalayan tahr, musk deer, or urial, you must go either to a national park or one of the few remaining sparsely populated valleys of the Himalaya. Reports from Tibet indicate its wildlife is under considerable pressure, and you are likely to see little. Bhutan is an exception: here wild game is still widespread, thanks to the strong Buddhist tradition and sparse human population. Because almost all species are on the decline, do not participate in their demise by purchasing wild-animal skins or horns—it may in fact be illegal to do so (and impossible to import without a special permit). Also, you'll simply encourage the local people to hunt all the more.

A few of the larger or more conspicuous mammals you may find on a trek are listed below with brief descriptions. Except where stated otherwise, the species occur throughout the Himalayan chain.

Primates. Langurs (*Presbytis entellis*) are long-limbed, long-tailed gray monkeys with distinctive black faces. They live in troops of as many as fifty and are the most commonly seen species in the Himalaya. Like the rhesus macaque, this species is sacred to many Himalayan peoples, and even the monkeys that raid agricultural fields are not killed. The rhesus macaque (*Macaca mulatta*) occurs at lower elevations and is brownish red, has a squat form with short limbs, and spends much of its time on the ground. Often seen in towns and villages.

Yeti (Abominable Snowman to some). Protected by the government of Nepal, the yeti has yet to be classified by scientists. Since its possible presence was first reported by British resident Brian Hodgson in 1832, accounts of this ape have been numerous in eastern Nepal and occasionally as far west as the Karakoram (though its existence there is even more open to question). In 1951 mountaineer Eric Shipton took pictures of "yeti tracks" on the Menlung Glacier, near Everest; these pictures are now considered the "type photos" of the yeti's apelike footprints. Eyewitness accounts generally describe the yeti as a stocky ape 5 feet or taller, with coarse reddish or grayish brown fur, a large head with a pointed crown, hairless face, and robust jaw. Its arms reach to the knees, and it moves bipedally with a shuffling gait. If the yeti exists—some evidence is tantalizing—some experts speculate it probably does so in the dense montane forests of the middle elevations. Since "yeti tracks" have usually been found on or near strategic passes, it is assumed that yetis use passes to move from one valley to another. During their mating season, snow leopards communicate with piercing, eerie "yowls": villagers sequestered in a high mountain hut during a winter snow storm would naturally think of the yeti! But more tangible evidence, in the form of scats, hair, or a conclusive photograph, is needed to decide whether this creature is real or a fancy of the human imagination. Many expeditions have endeavored to do so, and all have failed.

Pika (*Ochotona* spp.). This delightful relative of the hare is easily found amongst rocks and along mani walls above the tree line. Also known as the mouse-hare, the pika has a short muzzle, rounded ears, and no visible tail. It lives in loose colonies, spending summer days collecting grass and forbs, which it stores under rocks for the winter. Will allow you to approach closely.

Hares. Look for the woolly hare (*Lepus oiostolus*) while driving across the Tibetan plains; in many places in the south, it is the only form of wildlife you will see because everything else has been hunted out. The black-napped hare (*L. nigricollis*) takes its place in the Himalayan region.

Marmot. Marmots live in large colonies, excavating deep burrows in which they hibernate during winter. They feed outside burrows during summer and give loud whistles when sighting an intruder. Most commonly encountered above timberline. The Himalayan marmot (*Marmota bobak*) is about 2 feet long with a 5-inch tail and occurs along the Tibetan Plateau throughout the Himalaya. The long-tailed marmot (*M. caudata*), whose tail exceeds one-third of its total body length, has a rich golden orange pelage. Found in the wetter areas of Pakistan and Kashmir; common on the Deosai Plains, and in various areas of Zanskar.

Red fox (*Vulpes vulpes*). Its sign is often seen, because the red fox tends to use the same trails people do. Fairly shy, but not infrequently observed by trekkers. Preys on small rodents, such as pikas and voles. In appearance the same as the European or North American red fox.

Dhole, jackal, and wolf (*Canis alpinus, Canis aureus,* and *Canis lupus*). Jackals and dholes are larger than foxes, with black-tipped tails. The dhole, or Indian wild dog, is the larger of the two and is best identified by its bushy tail and black cheek patch. Both are widely distributed in the Himalaya but are nonetheless rare. The familiar wolf may be seen in small packs in Zanskar, Hunza, Dolpo, and other border areas in the Himalaya and is widespread in the rolling mountains of Tibet. Because wolves often kill many domestic animals, they are usually shot or trapped by villagers.

Bears. The brown bear (*Ursus arctos*) inhabits wetter alpine or subalpine meadows and scrub in Tibet and the far western Himalaya but is very rare along the central or eastern parts of the range. Its pelage (fur) is sandy or reddish brown, and it has a conspicuous hump of longish hair over the shoulder. Uses forefeet for digging out bulbs, grass, and the occasional marmot. The Himalayan black bear (*Selenarctos thibetanus*) is a widespread denizen of temperate forests at elevations of 4,000 to 12,000 feet. Black in color with a conspicuous cream-colored V on the chest. If you visit the lowlands, you may see the sloth bear (*Melursus ursinus*). Give all bears plenty of room—every year locals are severely mauled by bears disturbed intentionally or accidentally.

Red panda (*Ailurus fulgens*). The red or lesser panda of the eastern Himalaya is easily recognized by its white face, dark eye patches, rich chestnut back, dark limbs, and faintly ringed tail. It's rarely seen but worth keeping an eye out for reclining on a branch, for these pandas are not as uncommon as previously thought.

Large Indian civet (*Viverra zibetha*). May be seen in forests and scrub at low elevations. About 30 inches in length, with black-and-white-striped tail and two white throat patches. Short legs, silvery gray fur.

Martens and weasels. Species are too numerous for all to be described. The stone marten (*Martes foina*) inhabits the higher mountain steppe, avoiding forests; forests are the primary domain of the Himalayan yellow-throated marten (*M. flavigula*), which, as its name denotes, is yellow throated. Its pelt is greatly prized for making hats. The weasel (*Mustela* spp.) is a small, slender animal with a sinuous body. Frequently bold and inquisitive, a weasel may approach a quietly sitting person. Feeds on voles and other small rodents and occurs throughout the Himalaya, usually in or near meadows and brush fields.

Spotted cats. If you are exceptionally lucky, you may see a forest leopard (*Panthera pardus*) while hiking through a forest, or even the legendary snow leopard (*P. uncia*) while traversing a high meadow. Either is rarely seen, of course, but to find their sign along the trail is possible—look for the tracks in the snow or mud, and areas scraped bare with droppings nearby. The large cat tracks winding through a village at about 7,000 feet probably belong to a forest leopard (looking for dogs to eat!). Those seen at the 12,000-foot level and away from forests probably belong to the snow leopard or the lynx. The forest leopard may weigh as much as 150 pounds and usually inhabits forests lower than 10,000 feet.

Until Gary Ahlborn, myself, and our Nepali associates radio collared and tracked five snow leopards in the Langu Valley, almost nothing was known about the habits of this magnificent cat. The elusive snow leopard can melt away unseen and invariably spots the human intruder first. Over four years of study, we saw it only eighteen times. Its pelt is smoky gray with a tinge of yellow, its spots forming open rosettes. Best identified by its 3-foot-long tail and its size—about that of a large dog. Snow leopards rarely descend into the coniferous forest belt and are most frequently glimpsed north of the main Himalaya along the Tibetan border. Ibex and bharal are primary food items in large parts of their range, but with the depletion of native ungulates, snow leopards have turned to livestock for sustenance. This almost guarantees them a short life. Strongly solitary, they nevertheless communicate to each other through such signs as scrapes, scats, and scent-sprayed rocks. Look for their distinctive scrapes—shallow depressions scuffed in the ground, usually with a pile of dirt at one end—along the edge of sharp ridgelines, atop rocky promontories, and along river bluffs near stream confluences. Snow leopards rarely number more than a half dozen in a particular valley complex. Places like the Langu Valley of Nepal's Shey-Phoksumdo National Park in Nepal support as many as twelve or more cats per 80 square miles. Zanskar in Ladakh is another stronghold for the species.

The lynx (*Lynx lynx*) inhabits the barren uplands of Ladakh, the Karakoram, and Tibet, avoiding forests and deep valleys. Several other species of small cat also dwell in the Himalaya, but you are not likely to encounter them. One of these, the clouded leopard (*Neofelis nebulosa*) is restricted to the lush tropical and semitropical forests from Nepal eastward. It has a marbled appearance and a magnificent coat.

Muntjac, or barking deer (*Muntiacus muntjak*). Found at lower elevations in montane forest. Recognized by its reddish brown body with short, dainty legs. The distinctive doglike bark may be repeated at regular intervals. Partial to rocky, wooded ravines.

Musk deer, or kasturi (*Moschus chrysogaster*). The musk deer is a primitive deer about as large as a medium-size dog. It has large, rounded ears, no visible tail, and an arched back, with long hind limbs. The male sports long upper canines or tusks and has a highly prized musk gland, the contents of which are literally worth their weight in gold. Musk deer are solitary and shy most of the time, and you are more likely to see piles of their droppings than catch a glimpse of an animal. They prefer birch forests and scrub in the upper temperate and alpine zones. Local people hunt them with dogs, snares, and poisoned spears, and for some villagers they provide a major source of income. Where protected, they can become extremely tolerant of human presence—a breeding pair essentially lives within the village of Phortse in Sagarmatha National Park, and sightings are guaranteed for those willing to spend a few hours looking.

Tibetan wild ass, or kiang (*Equus kiang*). The wild ass of the Tibetan plains. Unmistakable. Regarded as the world's most handsome and horse-like wild ass, the kiang is almost 4 feet at the shoulder, with a pale chestnut or almost reddish summer coat. Typically occurring in herds of five to ten (occasionally more than a hundred), kiang feed upon the sparse desert grasses and shrubs. Said to rut in later summer, but like other Tibetan ungulates, their social life is only now being studied in the wild by George Schaller. Although able to exist under extremely harsh conditions, they have disappeared from many places at the hand of man.

Tibetan antelope, or chiru (*Pantholops hodgsoni*). A handsome antelope. Adult males stand about 36 inches at the shoulder and sport dark, saberlike horns (20–28 inches), a black face, pale tawny pelage with reddish tinges to the flanks, a white rump patch, and short tail. Females are hornless. Curious nasal sacs when inflated give muzzle a swollen appearance. Used to occur in Serengeti-like herds, but now greatly depleted.

Goral (*Nemorhaedus goral*). A widespread inhabitant of the south-facing slopes of the Himalaya to as high as the 14,000-foot level in Nepal. Stands 2 feet at the shoulder. Horns short, pointed, and present in both sexes. Color variable, but usually grayish. Solitary, but may be seen in groups of up to five. Usually the goral waits until you are nearly upon it before bounding uphill in a zigzag route and disappearing quickly.

Serow (*Capricornis serow*). Goatlike, standing about 3½ feet at the shoulder, with a stocky body, thick neck, large head and ears, and short limbs. Horns stout and conical, pointed backwards, and present in both sexes. Color generally black or reddish chestnut, with white on limbs. Inhabits forests and wooded gorges, using cliffs for escape. Usually solitary. Found at 6,000 to 10,000 feet.

Takin (*Budorcas taxicolor*). Very distinctive dark brown or golden, massive ungulate that stands 50 inches high, has short wildebeast-like horns, humped shoulders, and large mooselike face. Said to be common in Bhutan, inhabiting dense thickets and forests at higher elevations.

Bharal (*Pseudois nayaur*). Sheeplike in appearance, the bharal exhibits the behavior of a goat. Males stand about 3 feet at the shoulder and are best identified by their slaty blue body color, black flank stripes, and dark chests. Cylindrical horns curve outward; in older animals, tips are directed backward. Females lack stripes and have thin horns. Bharal are an essentially Tibetan species found north of the main range from Zanskar to Bhutan. Easily seen in India's Nanda Devi Sanctuary, in parts of Zanskar, near Shey Gomba in Nepal, the Dhorpatan area, and north of Annapurna east of the Thorong Pass. They occur in herds of more than eighty individuals, though groups of a dozen or so are more typical. Found from elevations of 9,000 to around 20,000 feet on the north slopes of Mt. Everest. Bharal are an important item in the diet of snow leopards.

Argali, or nayan (*Ovis ammon*). The wild sheep of the rolling hills and mountains of Tibet, ecological equivalent of the Rocky Mountain bighorn. Stands about 3½ feet high, is sandy colored, with massive horns and a white rump patch. Occurs in small herds; very vulnerable to human disturbance. A few can be seen in the Hemis High Altitude Park, Ladakh.

Urial, or shapu (*Ovis orientalis*). A sheep found in the large river valleys of the Karakoram and the Indus drainage, preferring gently rolling to steeply rolling terrain, up to the 14,000-foot level (though usually found much lower). A large animal, grayish in color with a long black chest ruff and white bib. Horns massive and strongly corrugated, forming an open half circle that turns inward at the end. Often seen at the lower end of such valleys as the Braldu, Shigar, and Shyok. Now much depleted.

Markhor (*Capra falconeri*). Another wild goat, with a straight or flaring set of corkscrew horns, a flowing, whitish gray ruff, and a dark flank stripe. Very localized occurrence in Chitral, Gilgit, Astor, and Indus areas. They live in herds like urial and ibex. Essentially an inhabitant of the low-lying cliffs that receive little moisture and support a dry, shrubby vegetation.

Ibex (*Capra ibex sibirica*). Easily identified by the large scimitar horns and beard so characteristic of the goat genus. Females lack the beard and have smaller horns; males stand about 40 inches at the shoulder. Like all ibex, the Asiatic ibex have a strong predilection for the steepest cliffs. They are excellent climbers, though easily killed by hunters in the winter when deep snows hinder their movements. They spend summers at 16,000 feet or higher if grassy hanging meadows are available, and their escape is always to cliffs. The most widespread ungulate of the mountains of Pakistan, occurring as far east as the Sutlej River of India.

Tibetan gazelle (*Procapra piticaudata*). An inhabitant of plateau grasslands and barren steppes, the Tibetan gazelle is probably the most widespread of Tibet's wild ungulates. Stands about 2 feet at the shoulder and is best distinguished by S-shaped horns 11 to 15 inches in length and a pale, slaty gray coat with distinctive white rump and buttocks. Both sexes have horns. Usually seen singly, in pairs, or small groups.

Himalayan tahr (*Hemitragus jemlahicus*). A large, handsome goat that is very partial to the steepest cliffs. Males stand around 3 feet at the shoulder and sport large, shaggy shoulder ruffs that are straw colored, contrasting with the black or coppery brown body color. Horns are about 12 inches long, close set, and curving backward. Females lack the ruff and are much smaller. Tahr are found within a narrow, but highly discontinuous band of land along the southern slopes of the Himalaya from west Kashmir to Sikkim. Readily seen on the cliffs above Langtang village in the Langtang National Park of Nepal, and around the village of Phortse in Sagarmatha (Everest) National Park.

Birds

The Himalaya is an ornithological paradise: Nepal has more than 800 species, and Sikkim and Bhutan many more. Depending upon whose tally one takes, this compares favorably with the 1,200 to 1,800 species found in the entire Indian subcontinent. The abundance of birdlife reflects the diversity of life zones and habitats, as well as the central position of the Himalaya between two major biogeographical zones: the Kali Gandaki

River of Nepal is usually considered the dividing line between the eastern and western avifauna. Himalayan birdlife was virtually terra incognita until recently. When Nepal opened to outsiders in the early 1950s, several species new to science were discovered, and the habitat of the spiny babbler, a common bird, was finally determined.

Visitors from Europe and America may recognize a few species from home: the golden eagle and house wren, for example. However, the vast majority of species will be new, sporting such names as crested serpent eagle, large-necklaced laughing thrush, three-toed golden-backed woodpecker, satyr tragopan, hoary barwing, Tibetan twite, white-capped river chat, Hodgson's frogmouth, Mrs. Gould's sunbird, and Guldenstadt's redstart. Birds can be seen even at the highest elevations, and many migrate over the Himalaya. Mountaineers have encountered choughs at 27,000 feet, heard snipes flying over the highest peaks at night, marvelled at geese returning from their Tibetan breeding grounds, and found dead birds on windy cols.

With one of the recently published field guides and a pair of lightweight binoculars, novice and expert alike can look forward to many hours of exquisite birdwatching. If you are interested in numbers, you can expect to enumerate lists at least as long as those back home, even restricting yourself to narrow altitudinal ranges. For the serious ornithologist, spring and summer are the best times to visit the Himalaya because birds are in their breeding plumages and generally much more approachable. You can spend hours watching rose finches, accentors, pipits, and many others amid carpets of alpine wildflowers. However, a word of caution: because of late storms or the monsoon's arrival, it may be wet and, at high elevations, cold.

For those trekkers without benefit of binoculars or field guide, opportunities for observing and appreciating are still ample. Most will surely sight a lammergeier—the bearded vulture—as it glides low over Bhotia villages and across knife-edged ridges, or will flush an impeyan pheasant on its downhill race. A few of the birds you may see are very briefly described below according to their preferred habitat. This introduction obviously cannot mention more than a few, nor can the descriptions provided allow identification of any species with certainty. The emphasis here is on alerting you to birds that are widespread and of prominent size, color, or behavioral features.

Alpine Meadows and Slopes

Rose finches (*Carpodacus* spp.). Gregarious small birds with thick bills and notched tails that are among the most common breeders in alpine meadows. Many species; most brownish with crimson or reddish breasts in males.

Impeyan pheasant, or danphe (*Lophophorus impejanus*). Nepal's national bird of nine iridescent colors. Invariably glides noisily downhill when disturbed. A heavy bird, the male is easily recognized by its white rump and tan tail. The female is a nondescript brown bird with a white rump. Found on steep grassy or rocky slopes or in winter fir forests. In late fall, many of the resplendent males gather in the fields of Khumjung near Everest to dig up potatoes and grubs.

Grandala (*Grandala coelicolor*). Unmistakable glistening blue robin of steep rocky slopes well above tree line.

Redstarts (*Phoenicurus* spp.). Robinlike birds with dark heads and chests and chestnut brown abdomens and tails.

Pipits (*Anthus* spp.) **and wagtails** (*Motacilla* spp.). Long-legged birds partial to grassy meadows. Pipits are heavily streaked, while wagtails have whitish or yellow breasts and constantly pump their tails.

Snow cocks. Giant partridges that escape by running uphill. Feed in groups and found as high as 18,000 feet. The Tibetan snow cock (*Tetraogallus tibetmanus*) is brownish with white underparts, while the Himalayan snow cock (*T. himalayensis*) is gray with rufous neck streaks and a chestnut chest band. Cannot be mistaken for the snow partridge (*Lerwa lerwa*), which is much smaller and barred gray and white.

Accentors (*Prunella* spp.). Sparrowlike ground-feeding birds with long square tails. They hop about. Many species; most gray or brownish, with dark face mask.

Streamside Habitats (above 8,000 feet)
White-capped river chat (*Chaimarrornis leucocephalus*). Black-and-maroon bird with white cap, seen skimming from rock to rock. Also pumps tail.

Plumbeous redstart (*Rhyacornis fuliginosus*). Tame, slaty blue bird that constantly moves its tail up and down. Female with conspicuous rump, male with rufous (reddish) tail.

Dippers (*Cinculus* spp.). Plump birds that feed by walking underwater. The white-breasted dipper (*C. cinculus*) has a white throat and breast. The brown dipper (*C. pallasii*) is all chocolate brown. Both bob up and down while standing on rocks.

Forktails (*Enicurus* spp.). Black-and-white birds with forked tails. The spotted forktail (*E. maculatus*) has a spotted back and a long tail that it lifts up and down slowly. The little forktail (*E. scouleri*) is a small bird seen moving amongst rocks in rushing streams.

Ibisbill (*Ibidorhyncha struthersii*). Large gray bird with prominent, decurved bill. Breeds in glaciated valleys. Bobs head and tail.

Oak and Conifer Forests
Blood pheasant (*Ithaginis cruentus*). Pheasant with coral red legs found east of Dhaulagiri. Quite tame near Tengboche Monastery, where flocks of several hundred are known to congregate in winter.

Tragopan pheasants (*Tragopan* spp.). Brilliant and very rare crimson pheasants with blue-and-black faces. Found in dense forests.

Great Himalayan barbet (*Megalaima virens*). Green, brown, and dark blue with large yellow bill and red beneath tail. Several may gather at a fruiting tree.

Himalayan jay (*Garrulus glandarius*). Medium-size gregarious bird that has a white rump obvious in flight. Lacks the dark crest of the blue-throated jay, which occurs in oak forests.

Yellow-billed blue magpie (*Cissa flavirostris*). Yellow bill and long blue tail distinguish this bird from its lowland cousin with a red bill.

Himalayan tree pie (*Dendrocitta formosae*). Noisy bird that feeds in scattered parties. Recognized by its dark gray body and white wing patch. The closely related nutcracker (*Nucifraga caryocatactes*) of pine and fir forests is a large dark bird that continuously flicks its tail, showing white patches.

Minivets (*Pericrocotus* spp.). Brightly colored (red, orange, or yellow) long-tailed birds seen feeding amid dense foliage.

Bulbuls. Robin-size birds that perch conspicuously on trees and shrubs. The red-vented bulbul (*Pycnonotus cafer*) is found at lower elevations, often in gardens. Note the red patch under its tail. The black bulbul (*Hypsipetes madagasciensis*) has a bright coral red bill and feeds in excited parties that keep up a constant chatter.

Laughing thrushes (*Garrulax* spp.). Noisy, myna-size birds; prefer areas of dense vegetation; form large feeding parties. Many species. The white-throated laughing thrush (*G. albogularis*) is olive brown with a large throat patch. The white-crested (*G. leucolophus*) has a "turban" and a brown eye streak. The white-spotted (*G. ocellatus*) is profusely spotted with white. The striated (*G. striatus*) is rich cinnamon with narrow white streaks and is usually found in shady ravines.

Black-capped sibia (*Heterophasia capistrata*). Common, light rufous bird with dark head and crest that is raised upon alarm. Jerks tail up and down and has a beautiful clear whistle.

Blue-headed rock thrush (*Monticola cinclorhynchus*). Usually found in pine forests and open shady places. The male is an outstanding cobalt blue and orange with a white wing patch evident in flight.

Mountain thrushes (*Loothera* spp.). Common inhabitant of fir forests and small forest glades. Brown or olive brown with heavily spotted breast and abdomen. Spends much time on the ground.

Whistling thrush (Myiophoneus caeruleus). Blue-black bird with bright yellow bill, often seen near rushing streams and deep cover. Song (consisting of sustained silvery notes at dawn) penetrates above sound of waterfall.

Coal tits (*Parus* spp.). Minute black birds with white cheek patches and dark crests.

Scarlet finch (*Haematospizma sipahi*). Male a brilliant scarlet with brown wings and tail; seen in heavy forest at low elevations.

Not mentioned are the cuckoos, flycatchers, warblers, leaf warblers, bush robins, nuthatches, woodpeckers, and creepers. Some are extremely numerous and so often sighted; many are difficult to identify without field guide and glasses; and others are simply inconspicuous.

West Tibetan Steppe

Lack of food and cover, in the way of ground plants, limits the diversity of birds able to exploit the windswept plains. Ground-nesting songbirds, many migratory and nondescript with brown or tawny plumages, dominate the avifauna.

Look for the Tibetan partridge (*Perdix hodgsoniae*) among *Caragana* shrubs (when disturbed it calls loudly, preferring to run uphill) or the Tibetan sandgrouse (*Syrrhaptes tibetanus*), which congregates in small flocks and inhabits very stony country. If you are exceptionally lucky, you will see the black-necked crane (*Grus nigricollis*) during its migration to lake breeding grounds; it is now very scarce in western Tibet and Ladakh. The Tibetan owlet (*Athene noctua*) is also rare; it is recognized by its relatively long legs and boldly barred (streaked) and spotted body.

The dominant birds, however, are such songbirds as the short-toed lark (*Calandrella cinerea*), Hume's lark (*C. acuttirostris*), and the horned lark (*Eromophila alpestris*), a species familiar to North Americans. Larks have melodious songs, usually sung during impressive courtship flights, and they walk or run on the ground rather than hop. The skylarks (*Alauda* spp.) are masters of song in flight. There are many accentors (see above) and several species of snow finch (*Montifringilla*), a flocking songbird related to sparrows and difficult even for the experts to separate. The Tibetan twite (*Acanthis flavirostris*) is a finchlike pale brown bird that is both tame and able to survive in the bleakest of areas.

The hoopoe (*Upupa epops*), a widespread species of Africa, Asia, and Europe, is important to Tibetans, for its arrival signifies the onset of summer. It is unmistakable with its distinctive cinnamon coloration and fan-shaped black-tipped crest.

In addition, you may see ducks, plovers, sandpipers, and snipe along the edge of Tibet's large inland lakes that are fresh enough to support aquatic life.

Other Common Species

These birds are likely to be found in a variety of habitats. Soaring birds you may see are the lammergeier, or bearded vulture (*Gypaetus barbatus*), with its 9-foot wingspan and long, wedge-shaped tail; the Himalayan griffin vulture (*Gyps himalayensis*); the golden eagle (*Aquila chrysaetos*), recognizable by its white wing patches and white at the base of the tail, which distinguishes it from the steppe eagle; and a variety of buteos or buzzards that have rounded wings and fan-shaped tails. In winter, gray or brown harriers (*Circus* spp.) can be seen hovering over open areas.

Fast-flying kestrels and other falcons literally streak by, while snow pigeons (*Columba leuconota*) wheel about in large flocks and feed in open fields like the common rock dove, from which they are unmistakably distinguished by their pale necks and abdomens. Near villages you will see ravens or crows, the common myna (*Acridotheres tristis*), house sparrows (*Passer domesticus*), and swifts. The raven (*Corvus corax*) is a large black crow with a distinctive, wedge-shaped tail and an unmistakable call: *gorak . . . gorak*. Crows (*Corvus* spp.) are small and lack the shaggy throat feathers of the raven. Choughs fly about in very large flocks; there are two species, the yellow-billed (*Pyrrhocorax graculus*) and the red-billed (*P. pyrrhocorax*).

Look as well for ducks, geese, and cranes flying over in spring and fall. High mountain lakes provide resting sites for waterfowl, though few species breed there.

Reptiles and Amphibians

Although some seventy species of reptiles and amphibians inhabit Nepal, only thirty of these are typically found in the mountains. Of these, less than a dozen are found above 8,000 or 9,000 feet. Amphibians, like frogs and toads, occur primarily in the tropical zone and the warmer, lower, temperate forest belts, although some live in hot springs at amazingly high altitudes. The number of species also declines as you move westward to the Karakoram. Salamanders are rare but were recently discovered in the forests of east Nepal. If you are observant, you may find the Himalayan rock lizard, the *Agama* (males have orange heads with bright blue throats), the long-legged *Japalura* lizard of brushy slopes, or the skink species *Leiolopisma ladacense*, which holds the record for being the highest lizard in the world, found at 18,000 feet.

Unless you visit the hot and humid lowlands or know where to look, you are unlikely to find any snakes in the Himalayan regions. Typical snakes include the rat snakes and racers, which are fast moving with large eyes, slender necks, and broad heads; water snakes, which are, indeed, partial to the aquatic environment; and the mountain pit vipers, which are uniformly dark with triangular heads. Most of the snakes are nonpoisonous. The cobra is occasionally encountered at low elevations. The only other venomous species are pit vipers; fortunately, they too are relatively rare and not often seen.

Although reptiles and amphibians have not been studied in Sikkim and Bhutan, it is likely that numerous species thrive in the favorable conditions found there.

A World in Transition: The Future of Himalayan Wildlife

Alas, as remote as Mt. Kailas in western Tibet may seem, you will be lucky to see any wildlife—unless you travel to the most remote valleys lacking roads. The vast herds of antelope, kiang, and wild yak that early explorers like C. Rawlings and Sven Hedin witnessed are history, a casualty of the Chinese takeover of the Roof of the World.

Almost all officials carry rifles and show little hesitation in shooting species on the protected list, especially when they are seen to pose threats to the expanding livestock industry. These attitudes are being passed to present generations of Tibetans, whose Buddhist precepts on the taking of life have been perceptibly altered since the Dalai Lama fled and the monasteries were sacked in the 1950s.

Wildlife is threatened not only in Tibet: throughout the Himalayan region the numbers of all large mammals have been greatly decimated and their populations fragmented as former habitat is converted to agriculture, forests felled, pastures grazed beyond their ability to sustain grass, and predators ruthlessly hunted because they had no choice but to take someone's sheep to survive. There are few national parks in the Himalaya where the local residents do not view the imposition of regulations negatively. As tourism to the stupendous mountains of Nepal, Bhutan, India, and Tibet soars, it is a tragedy that few will see a musk deer, a Himalayan tahr, or a kiang. This need not be the case. Thanks to recent efforts by biologists, including a new cadre from Asia itself, we have the basic information to reverse the downward spiral. Now politicians and the government need the commitment to follow through with innovative approaches to ensuring that man and wildlife can coexist to mutual benefit. It is imperative that the villagers participate in planning and management and that they benefit directly and significantly from the tourists who have come halfway around the world to see their sacred snow-clad peaks.

Despite their limited resources, countries like India or the Kingdom of Nepal have embarked on ambitious conservation programs. Those who visit Sagarmatha (Everest) National Park in Nepal and see a musk deer casually feeding on forest floor lichens—or easily stalk to within 50 yards to photograph a massive tahr standing calmly on a small cliff ledge, its coppery brown ruff catching the sinking sun—cannot fail to go home with memories to match the world's highest peaks. Where would their feelings soar if they glimpsed a snow leopard? I'm firmly convinced these images need not be idle phantasy. Thanks to the efforts of many, wildlife is returning in the face of protective measures. And where there is prey, the mythical snow leopard may not be far behind. Your support of such organizations as the World Wildlife Fund, Wildlife Conservation International, International Snow Leopard Trust, King Mahendra Trust for Nature Conservation, and governmental agencies can make this possible. Let them know how you would like your donation spent. Let the people of the Himalaya know your interest in wildlife does not exclude providing for their basic needs.

12

A Himalayan
Medical Primer

by Peter H. Hackett, M.D.

Preparation

Discussions of Asian travel invariably turn to matters of health. The returning traveler is asked by the inexperienced, "Did you get sick?" and by more experienced friends, "How sick did *you* get?" Infectious diseases are the most feared, and are much more common in developing countries that do not yet have adequate sewer systems, immunizations, and a high standard of living. As a result, travelers frequently have minor illnesses, many of which are no longer found in developed countries. Other problems are related to the unique environment trekkers seek: high altitude, precipitous trails, glaciers, jungle, and desert. The chances of a traveler becoming seriously ill, however, are not great. Recent statistics gathered from 1984 to 1987 by David Shlim, medical director of the Himalayan Rescue Association, may be of some interest to those planning a trip. He calculated that the risk of dying while trekking was 14 per 100,000. Most deaths were from trauma (falling off trails). For comparison, the risk of dying in a car accident in North America each year is 24 per 100,000, and of being murdered in Miami, Los Angeles, or New York, 20 per 100,000.

Adventure travel in this fascinating area of the world should result in increased vitality and enrichment of life. Even persons with diabetes, high blood pressure, heart disease, and other problems have done quite well on treks in the Himalaya. Others who were perfectly well have suffered dire consequences because of pushing themselves when they shouldn't have and, in general, not anticipating what they were getting into. Proper preparation, simple precautions, knowledge of basic medical treatment, and a proper medical kit can effectively treat minor illnesses before they become serious.

More detailed sources on the subject of travel medicine and trip preparation include your physician; the U.S. Public Health Service Centers for Disease Control, Atlanta, Georgia; your local public health clinic; special travelers' medicine clinics, which are now appearing in most large cities in North America; and university medical centers. In such clinics you can obtain expert advice, any necessary immunizations, and updated information for each country. While it is impossible in this chapter to discuss all potential medical problems that may occur on a Himalayan trip, there are a number of useful medical books that are small enough to be taken along. Especially recommended are Wilkerson's *Medicine for Mountaineering*, Darvill's *Mountain Medicine*, Auerbach's *Medicine for the Outdoors*, and Hackett's *Mountain Sickness: Prevention, Recognition and Treatment*.

A routine physical exam before trekking is of minimal value for the healthy person. However, even minor, nagging kinds of problems—such as tendinitis, headache, recurrent sinusitis, cough, or unexplained aches and pains—should be evaluated because they could easily flare up in a remote environment where adequate diagnosis and treatment may not be available. If you are under a physician's care for a special medical problem, you should of course discuss your travel plans with your doctor. Most physicians are, understandably, not familiar with special Third World or altitude problems and may refer you to an immunization clinic or a colleague with special expertise. Or you may wish to offer your doctor excerpts from this chapter or other materials to assist in your preparation. Medications should be discussed with your physician and adequate supplies prescribed for the trip. It is also a good idea to carry a small card with your passport listing medications and dosages, allergies, and past medical problems and even containing a miniature version of an electrocardiogram (EKG) for those who have had previous cardiac problems. Such cards can be invaluable.

Some trekking companies recommend stress electrocardiograms for men over age forty and women over age fifty. Unfortunately, the stress EKG is notorious for false positive results in healthy people, which can lead to unnecessary, expensive, and sometimes risky further testing. The best indicator that your heart is able to take on the stress of a trek is that it can handle similar stress before you go. In other words, the best stress test is a hiking or backpacking trip over rugged terrain and into high-altitude areas. If you experience no difficulty with that back home, you are unlikely to have any difficulty with trekking in the Himalaya, even though the mountains are considerably higher. Exercise stresses the heart much more than altitude per se. A special caution to the sedentary individual who decides to take up trekking in mid- or late life: get in shape first.

A dental checkup is advisable. Dental problems may develop because of high altitude (air trapped in cavities expands), tooth trauma, or cracked fillings, and dental care is difficult to obtain and unreliable throughout most of these regions. I have had to send more than one trekker back to civilization because of tooth problems (they didn't want me to just yank out a tooth!).

Physical conditioning may or may not be important, depending on the type of trip envisioned. Plenty of sedentary folks are able to tolerate short, easy treks without any particular problem. It's important to choose a trek suited for your level of comfort and your level of conditioning. Most Himalayan treks, however, follow a course across steep ridges and valleys, and demand a high level of fitness. Proper physical conditioning makes trekking easier and much more enjoyable. Fit persons will be bothered less by minor illnesses, for example, whereas a trekker struggling into camp each day will have little reserve left to deal with illness. A conditioning program should be started months ahead of time and should consist primarily of walking. Walking up and down steep hills, not necessarily with loads, is best. Building-bound workers in the city can get in shape by running or walking up and down flights of stairs during lunch hour. Running is excellent for cardiovascular conditioning, as are cross country skiing, swimming, and other aerobic activities. Being able to run a mile in under ten minutes is probably evidence of adequate cardiovascular conditioning for a trek. However, the principle of specificity applies to trekking as it does to any other sport: there are specific muscles and joints used for trekking, and the more these can be conditioned prior to the trip, the more effective the training. There is no specific training for altitude. Persons living at high altitude have the advantage of partial acclimatization. Aerobic fitness is important but will not lessen the time necessary for acclimatization and does not protect against altitude illness.

Every trekker should carry a small medical kit. You should discuss your particular needs with your physician. A list of recommended items for the kit is included at the end of this chapter. Contents will vary depending upon your medical sophistication, whether there's a trip physician, the number in the party, length of the trip, and availability of local services.

If possible, identify health facilities in your region of travel beforehand, as well as telegraph offices, radios for sending emergency messages, and airstrips. If you are not trekking with a local tour outfitter or agent, it is wise to register with your country's local consulate. Most Westerners working in remote regions of Nepal and India, for example, will leave emergency contacts with the American consulate, and many will leave a deposit in case a helicopter or some sort of evacuation is needed.

All trekkers, particularly those who go with groups, should consider insurance coverage. Some of the newer policies include trip cancellation insurance, default protection, supplemental collision damage waivers, and emergency medical expenses. Default protection reimburses you should a tour operator default. Trip cancellation insurance reimburses you for cancellation penalties or extra cost incurred if you must change your plans before or during a trip because of circumstances beyond your control, including illness. Any sickness qualifies that prevents you from traveling and that your doctor is willing to certify. Some emergency medical policies are reimbursement plans, which means that you still have to pay up front, while some companies provide direct payments to foreign hospitals and doctors. Excellent coverage can be obtained for $3 to $5 a day per person, or sometimes even less. Baggage insurance, helicopter evacuation, trip cancellation insurance, and medical insurance are sometimes all provided by one policy for a slightly greater cost. Always inquire whether a policy will cover emergency transportation, such as a helicopter. Determine whether your current health insurance covers foreign travel and emergency evacuations. (For more on the vagaries of helicopter evacuation, see "Rescue," below.)

Immunizations

Immunizations offer an easy and effective way to avoid some of the major illnesses associated with international travel. You need to discuss with your doctor or a travelers' clinic the particular immunizations you will need. The following is a guide to the most important ones:

Cholera. The risk of cholera is very low. The vaccines are not very effective, and vaccination is not recommended for tourists. Some countries, however, do require a booster within six months of entry for travelers arriving from infected areas. These countries are listed by the U.S. Public Health Service.

Diptheria-tetanus. Your immunization should be current (a booster shot within the last ten years).

Gamma globulin. Immune serum globulin (ISG, gamma globulin) is unquestionably effective and necessary for travel in this part of the world. The dose is 2 milliliters (ml) intramuscularly for a trip of three months or less and 5 ml every four months for longer trips. ISG prevents hepatitis A, which is endemic throughout all of central Asia, and also has some effects against tetanus, rabies, and measles. Persons with a previous history of hepatitis A are immune for life and do not require this immunization. Gamma globulin is not a vaccine. It provides passive immunity because it provides antibodies from another person's blood. A recent conference of the World Health Organization established that there has not been a case of AIDS in over 20 million doses of gamma globulin and that no chance of contracting the AIDS virus exists with this immunization. Hepatitis B vaccine is not ordinarily recommended for travelers, except for medical personnel whose work requires handling body fluids or those who expect to have sexual contacts in areas where hepatitis B is highly endemic, such as Southeast Asia.

Influenza and pneumococcal pneumonia. Two vaccines commonly overlooked by public health authorities and travelers' clinics are influenza vaccine and pneumococcal vaccine. Both are very effective with minimal side effects and should be considered by every traveler. Influenza and pneumococcal pneumonia are found throughout the world. All persons with chronic lung disease, diabetes, splenectomy, or over sixty-five years of age should receive a once-a-lifetime Pneumovax for prevention of pneumococcal pneumonia and a yearly influenza shot at the start of the flu season, usually in October. Travelers should probably have these vaccinations as well.

Measles. Anyone born after 1956 who did not receive measles vaccine after age one and does not have a documented history of infection should receive a single dose of vaccine before traveling.

Meningococcus. Because of a meningococcal epidemic in Nepal in 1984, the U.S. Public Health Service has been recommending the vaccine. The epidemic seems to be over in 1988. However, you should seek the current advice of the Public Health Service.

Polio. All travelers who have previously completed a primary series should receive a booster dose of oral polio vaccine or inactivated polio vaccine.

Rabies. The rabies vaccine is recommended only for those anticipating contact with animals that may have rabies or prolonged residence where rabies is a constant threat, such as in Nepal or India. The current vaccine is presently much easier, more comfortable, and more efficient than previous vaccines but not necessary for the general trekker.

Typhoid. Typhoid vaccine is recommended for all travelers to this part of the world, although it is not fully protective. The vaccine often causes one or two days of pain at the injection site, sometimes accompanied by fever, headache, and general malaise.

Yellow fever. Vaccination is not necessary for this part of the world.

Many of these immunizations can be given together. A measles shot has to be given two weeks before a gamma globulin shot, which is given one to two weeks before departure. Pregnant women should not receive any type of live virus (measles, trivalent polio). Cholera and typhoid vaccines are also best avoided during pregnancy, especially in the first trimester. Vaccines that pose no problems during pregnancy or breast feeding include gamma globulin, hepatitis B, rabies, diptheria, tetanus, and oral chloroquine (see "Prevention of Malaria," below).

Most experts recommend a stool examination upon return from, or just before leaving, Asia (it's much cheaper in Asia). Even if you have no symptoms, you may have acquired worms or parasites. Also recommended is a tuberculosis skin test prior to departure and a repeat after return if the initial test result was negative.

Although international health certificates are no longer required throughout most of the world, they do provide documentation for those few places where they may be mandatory and also provide a useful place for recording your immunizations.

Prevention of Malaria

Malaria is a particular problem in the lower-altitude areas of South and Southeast Asia. Since recommendations change with changing resistance in strains of malaria, you should obtain updated information just prior to travel. There is little danger of contracting malaria in Himalayan treks, since the anopheles mosquito penetrates Himalayan river valleys only to an altitude of about 3,000 feet. However, the traveler may be entering the Himalaya through malarial areas, such as the terai of Nepal, or India, Thailand, or Burma. Travel through any malaria-infested area generally requires preventive medication—for adults, usually 500 milligrams (mg) of chloroquine phosphate (one tablet) beginning one week before entering and continuing six weeks after leaving the risk area. If you are traveling in rural Thailand or Burma, you may be advised by your physician to take chloroquine plus fansidar or, alternatively, 100 mg of doxycycline once a day during exposure, since strains totally resistant to chloroquine and 80 percent resistant to fansidar have now emerged in these countries. Probably more important than medication for prevention of malaria is applying mosquito repellent when in malarious areas, using mosquito netting during sleep, and wearing long pants and sleeves when out at dusk, the time of day when the anopheles mosquito feeds.

On Trek

Diarrhea

Although usually not more than nuisance, diarrhea does affect a large number of travelers and can be especially serious in children; the smaller the child, the more quickly dehydration develops. Dehydration due to diarrhea is still the major cause of death in Asian children.

The reason infectious diarrhea is so common in Asian countries is the lack of sewer systems. The same diarrheas were prevalent in the United States and Europe a hundred years ago. Developed countries now efficiently dispose of feces, separate wastes (sewage) from the drinking supply, and disinfect tap water. These precautions have not yet become the rule throughout much of Asia and, as a result, intestinal illness transmitted by the fecal-oral route is quite common. Fecal contamination is found in the soil, raw food, on flies, on the hands of some food servers, and in the water, to mention a few places.

Diarrhea is generally not a serious illness, and "diarrhea neurosis" can ruin a trip because of excessive worry. A few sensible precautions in disinfecting water, avoiding contaminated food and beverages, and maintaining personal hygiene, will help prevent diarrhea, or at least "cut the losses."

Water Disinfection

All water in the "turd" world is suspect and requires disinfection. Even tap water in places like Kathmandu should not be trusted, although tap water is apparently good in Thailand. Simple disinfection techniques include the following:

Heat. The often-repeated recommendation of boiling water for five to ten minutes at sea level is only for complete sterilization and is unnecessary for disinfection. Giardia and amoeba cysts (parasites) both are killed in two to three minutes at 140°F; intestinal viruses are killed within seconds at 176° to 212°F; and intestinal bacteria are killed within seconds at 212°F (the boiling point of water at sea level). The higher the temperature, the less time required for disinfection. Bringing water to a boil is adequate for disinfection of all intestinal-disease-causing organisms. Although boiling point decreases with increasing altitude—the boiling point of water at 14,000 feet is 187°F; at 19,000 feet it's 178°F—these temperatures are still adequate for disinfection. The problem with using heat is fuel consumption and time: a pressure cooker saves both at any elevation.

Filtration and clarification. Water-filtering devices are limited in their efficacy by the size of their pores, which must be small enough to catch all infectious particles. Parasitic eggs and larvae and giardia and amoeba cysts are large enough to be caught in a filter, but it is very difficult for bacteria and nearly impossible for viruses, which are only 0.1 microns in size, to be caught. Filtering does remove particulate debris, however, thereby allowing a lower dose of disinfecting agents, and does improve the appearance and taste of "dirty" water, but filters clog quickly if water is dirty or has a lot of suspended particles. The appearance of water can also be improved by sedimentation—that is, by allowing large particles to settle out over a period of several hours.

Charcoal resins are commonly incorporated into multiple-layered filters to improve the color, taste, and smell of water after chemical disinfection. However, charcoal does not remove microorganisms and is therefore not itself a disinfectant.

Recommended water disinfection devices (effective for all except viruses) are Katadyne Pocket Filter, First-Need Purifier, and Water Tech Water Purifier.

Chemical disinfecting agents. Chlorine and iodine are the most commonly used disinfecting agents. Both effectively kill bacteria and viruses and giardia and amoeba cysts. The rate and percent of organism death depends on the concentration of the disinfecting agent and the exposure time.

$$organism\ death = contact\ time \times concentration\ of\ agent$$

Since "death" is a constant, doubling the contact time will allow half the amount of disinfecting agent to be used. For example, if sixteen drops of iodine solution are needed to disinfect a quart of water in thirty minutes, eight drops will disinfect in one hour, and only four drops are needed to disinfect the water in two hours. (Four drops are probably about the lowest amount of iodine that can be used to disinfect a quart of water.) In very cold water or if there is organic matter in the water, the dose needs to increase (chlorine and iodine are absorbed and therefore become less active in cloudy or polluted water). Taste can be improved by adding drink flavoring *after* adequate contact time or by pouring the water through a charcoal resin after disinfection. *Note:* The potency of some tablet and crystal forms of iodine and chlorine is affected by heat and moisture. Tablets deteriorate within a few months after the bottle is opened.

Water Disinfection by Chemical Agents

Agent	Form		Concentration/time per quart water
Chlorine	tablet	p-dichlorosulfamoyl benzoic acid (Halazone)	5 tabs/10 min. (1 tab/glass of water) or 2.5 tabs/30 min.
	solution	sodium hypochloride (bleach) 1% 4%–6%	10 drops/30 min. 2 drops/30 min.
Iodine	tablet	tetraglycine hydroperiodide (EDWGT, Potable Aqua, Globaline)	1 tab/10 min.
	solution	10% povidone-iodine (Betadine)	8 drops/15 min. or 4 drops/30 min.

Information courtesy of Howard Backer, M.D.

Note: If water is cold (less than 60° F) or cloudy, double the dose or the contact time. If both cold and cloudy, double both the dose and the contact time.

Chlorine is used in all municipal water systems and is very effective, even for giardia. For water disinfection, chlorine can be used in the form of Halazone tablets or liquid bleach.

Iodine has some advantages over chlorine since iodine is less affected by debris in the water. It is effective in low concentrations if there is adequate contact time, and the taste is better at these low levels than is the taste of chlorine. Iodine is quite safe but should not be used by people with unstable thyroid disease or iodine allergy, or during pregnancy.

Iodine in tablet form is easiest to use while trekking, but tablets come in only one strength (8 mg). Iodine in solution form—for example, the povidone-iodine preparation Betadine—is very handy since it can double as a disinfectant for wounds. Iodine crystals are also commonly used to produce a saturated solution. My own experience is that iodine solutions invariably leak in luggage—pack them with great care! I personally prefer Betadine since it's an essential ingredient of the first aid kit as well.

The accompanying table gives dosages and contact times for the various forms of chlorine and iodine. Become familiar with one system and use it regularly.

Food and Beverage Contamination

Contamination of food products is common. The motto for Third World travelers is "Cook it, peel it, boil it, or forget it." Foods freshly cooked that are still warm and have not had time to be contaminated by flies, etc., are perfectly safe. Fruits that can be peeled are safe, as is anything that can be boiled. Yogurt, one of the tastiest foods in Asia, is a pure culture of lactobacillus and is therefore generally safe unless it has been exposed to flies; in that case the top layer can be scraped off. Bottled soda drinks and beer are considered safe because of the carbonation. (Carbonation makes the pH too acid for infectious organisms, plus carbon dioxide itself kills some organisms.) Milk is safest if pasteurized or scalded. It is not necessary to actually boil it. A particular problem is home-brewed liquor. Rakshi, as it is called in Nepali (arak in Sherpa or Tibetan), is a distilled product and generally safe. Chang (Tibetan beer) is a problem since it is prepared by pouring untreated water through fermented rice, barley, or corn mash. Although chang may be unsafe, it is often unavoidable because of its role in local custom, and you might be considered rude to refuse it. Many times I have gulped down chang with a little mantra chanted to ward off illness.

Another source of contamination can be recreational drugs. I met one trekker who had bought some local hashish on a trek and decided to eat it rather than smoke it, to save the wear and tear on his lungs. It didn't take long after his eating the hashish to make a presumptive diagnosis of severe bacterial diarrhea. When I looked at the hash, it was obvious that it must have been 50 percent cow dung!

Hygiene on organized treks with reputable trekking companies is quite good. The staff usually provide boiled water so that chemical disinfection is unnecessary, and precautions in preparing food are adequate. Washing your own hands after bowel movements is important in limiting disease as well. All toilet paper should be burned or buried, both for hygiene and to avoid the visual pollution. It is a good sign to see all the kitchen help in camp washing their hands frequently. All in all, one has to use a moderate ration of common sense. Persons concerned to the point of wanting to wear disposable rubber gloves, disinfect all eating utensils before eating, and being afraid to shake hands with friendly residents, touch children, etc., are probably better off staying at home in their more secure environment. Be sensible, relax, and enjoy your trek.

Treatment of Diarrhea

Despite adequate preventive measures, diarrhea may still occur. Diarrhea is defined as a change in frequency and liquidity of stools. Dysentery is diarrhea that is associated with abdominal pain, straining at stool, and blood and mucous in the stool. Fever may be present with either. In cities, stool tests may be easily available and cheap, and establishing the exact diagnosis and subsequent exact treatment is worthwhile. In the field setting, however, determining the cause of diarrhea is difficult. In any case, it is generally safe to wait one to two days after the onset of any diarrheal illness to see if it resolves quickly and spontaneously.

While waiting twenty-four to forty-eight hours to see if the diarrhea stops, you can take a number of measures to help limit the unpleasant effects. First of all, since diarrhea generally means increased fluid loss, it is important to increase fluid intake: with voluminous stools, liters of fluid may be necessary to avoid dehydration. Water is mostly what is needed, but if the diarrhea is severe, electrolyte solutions (containing sodium, potassium, chloride, and bicarbonate) and sugar also become important. Throughout Asia, rehydration packets provided by the World Health Organization are available. In Nepal the product is called Jeevan Jal, which is an electrolyte solution made by mixing one packet in a liter of treated water. Rehydration is particularly important for children, who can very quickly get dehydrated.

Agents that slow the intestines—such as tincture of opium, deodorized tincture of opium (paregoric), diphenyxolate (Lomotil), or loperamide (Immodium)—help reduce fluid loss as well as reduce the frequency of stools and cramps. The correct dosage of Lomotil is two tablets after each loose bowel movement, and no more than ten tablets in twenty-four hours. Also effective is Pepto-Bismol, a nonprescription product in liquid or tablet form that works by an unknown mechanism. Two tablets can be taken four times a day. Pepto-Bismol contains an aspirinlike product and therefore should be used with caution by people already on aspirin or who have problems with aspirin. Kaopectate and other kaolin or pectin products are useless in treating diarrhea.

If the diarrhea is not resolving or if it is particularly severe, especially with a high fever, it's worthwhile to attempt a more definitive treatment based on some guess as to the cause of the illness. In Nepal, diarrhea-causing agents include, in order of frequency, bacteria (shigella, salmonella, and campylobactor), parasites (including giardia and amoeba), viruses (enterovirus, reovirus, and others), and worms (unusual). Unfortunately, there is little correlation between symptoms—such as blood and mucous in the stool, foul-smelling burps and gas, the color of the stool, or other easy identifiable factors—and the pathogen. Therefore, field treatment is usually blind. A good initial treatment that will cover all bacterial diarrheas (the majority of diarrheas) is the new drug ciprofloxacin, known by the trade name Cipro in the United States. One 500 mg tablet taken twice a day for five days is very effective and acts quickly. Another useful antibiotic is trimethoprim/sulfamethoxazole (Septra DS or Bactrim DS), also taken twice a day for five days. This is a sulfa drug and must be avoided by people allergic to sulfa. So many of the bacterial diarrheas are now resistant to ampicillin, amoxicillin, or tetracycline that these drugs are now unreliable.

The use of antibiotics for prevention of diarrhea is controversial and is generally not recommended by experts. Liberal use of antibiotics in this manner produces more organisms resistant to the drugs, which is an increasing problem all over the world with these bacterial diarrheas. Since the treatment is relatively simple and effective, antibiotics probably should be reserved for actual diarrheal illness treatment, not used for prevention. Pepto-Bismol is a wiser choice for prevention, since it is not an antibiotic and does not induce resistance.

If diarrhea does not respond to the antibiotic within two to three days, the cause is more likely a parasite or a virus. There is no specific treatment for viral diarrhea; the body sheds itself of viral illnesses within a week or so, and the treatment is directed to decreasing cramps and fluid loss. The two most common parasites in central Asia are giardia and amoeba, both of which are treated with a drug called tinidazole. This drug is not available in North America yet, but it is readily available in Asia; in Nepal and India it is sold as Tiniba. The dosage for giardiasis is a single, one-time dose of 2 grams (gm); for amoebiasis the dosage is 2 gm per day for three days.

Sulfurous burps and foul-smelling gas are often ascribed to giardiasis, but these are actually relatively nonspecific symptoms. Giardiasis takes two weeks to incubate and develop, whereas bacterial infections develop much more quickly. Therefore, if you've been in Asia for only a short time—i.e., less than two weeks—your diarrhea is more likely to be bacterial or viral rather than giardia. If after treatment with an antibiotic and an antiparasitic agent there is still diarrhea, especially associated with upper abdominal pain, worms should be considered, although they are not as common a cause of diarrhea as the others. However, worms can be treated rather easily with mebendazole, in the dosage of one tablet (100 mg) twice a day for three days.

Diarrhea may also be due to food poisoning. If a toxin that has been produced in a food substance is ingested (common where there is no refrigeration), it may cause immediate vomiting and diarrhea. More than once, unfortunately, I have been at dinner with a friend who quite suddenly became pale (with a greenish tint) and immediately vomited, sometimes on the table. This kind of acute explosive illness, often occurring in the first day or two in Asia, is food poisoning caused by a toxin. Fortunately, it usually lasts only a few hours, but sometimes it can continue up to twelve hours. Usually by the time a person is strong enough to seek help, he or she is already starting to get better. The fluid losses, however, can leave people weak for a few days.

Trekkers with severe abdominal pain and tenderness when the abdomen is pressed upon, especially without diarrhea, should be evacuated to the nearest hospital for evaluation for appendicitis or other potential surgical conditions.

There are other approaches to diarrhea in this part of the world: shamans treat by appeasing evil spirits, and many village health care workers treat with herbal remedies, some of which appear to be very effective. Once on a BBC yeti hunt, of which I was a deputy leader, we ran into a crisis when the cameraman was unable to go on because of severe diarrhea. I had treated him with antibiotics and antiparasitic agents, yet he continued to become weaker and weaker and finally was not able to move. As a result, we had to halt the entire expedition (at great cost) and wait for his recovery. A village health worker came over to our camp and asked to see the doctor. He asked me if I had any of the new American ulcer medicines, since he had a stomach ulcer and was always interested in new ulcer treatments. I was glad to share some of my medication, and then I asked him for a consult on the cameraman. He examined our prostrate comrade and asked for a stool sample, which was not hard to obtain. A quick look at the stool in a tin can, and he made an immediate diagnosis. He then administered a series of herbal medications and also prescribed alternating hot and cold compresses to the abdomen (which, of course, I thought were useless). He told us that within twenty-four hours all diarrhea would stop and that within forty-eight hours the victim would be strong enough to go on. Sure enough, the diarrhea stopped within twenty-four hours, and in forty-eight hours the cameraman had a remarkable recoup of his strength. Ever since then, I have had more respect for herbal remedies and have used them more often myself.

Another time, in the upper Arun Valley, for the purposes of a movie, a shaman went into a trance directed toward my diarrheal illness. After his trancelike state, he diagnosed my diarrhea as being from fear I had experienced earlier that day when crossing a particularly bad bridge made of willow strands. He said that it would be gone the next day. Well, my diarrhea was gone the next day, and I still have no idea if that was the real cause or not.

Respiratory Infections

The common cold is called common for a reason. It's likely that trekkers will pick up local viruses. The combination of jet lag, new environment, thermal extremes, dust and other particulate matter, and suppressed immunity because of high altitude and ultraviolet light can result in frequent upper respiratory infections. These are best treated, if necessary, with decongestants, such as pseudoephedrine (Sudafed), and aspirin or acetaminophen for pain and fever. With fever and facial pain indicating sinusitis, an antibiotic should be administered. Bronchitis that produces green or yellow sputum associated with fever should also be treated with an antibiotic, especially at high altitudes, since it may predispose to high-altitude illness. Sore throats are best treated with hard candies and throat lozenges to keep the throat moist and aspirin, acetaminophen, or ibuprofen for pain. At high altitude, always be aware of the possibility of pulmonary edema in yourself or others with any kind of cough or chest complaint (see "High Altitude Pulmonary Edema," below).

Headaches are common at high altitude but if associated with fever or a stiff neck, they must be taken very seriously because of possible meningitis. Rather uncomfortable muscle aches and pains associated with a bad headache and a high fever that goes on for days and days may very well be typhoid fever, which has been on the increase in Nepal. It tends to have a course of more than one week and can cause progressive, prostrating illness; it may or may not be associated with diarrhea. Anyone with muscle aches and pains, fever, headache, and shaking, bone-rattling chills away from medical care should be treated for typhoid fever. The drugs currently used are chloramphenicol or ampicillin in a dose of 500 mg four times a day.

Snow Blindness

Snow blindness is a burn of the cornea caused by excessive exposure to ultraviolet (UV) light. It is entirely preventable by wearing adequate glasses or goggles that filter 90 percent of UV-B radiation and reduce exposure from the sides also. UV light penetration increases by 5 percent for every 1000-foot gain of altitude, so there is 75 percent more ultraviolet penetration at 15,000 feet then there is at sea level. Reflection of this much UV light off snow or water can produce a burn in only two hours. Even on cloudy days, exposure is adequate for damage. Snow blindness is extremely painful and can last forty-eight hours or longer. Porters, who usually don't have adequate goggles, are the most likely victims. Makeshift goggles can be improvised by taping a piece of cardboard over the eyes, with small horizontal slits through which the porter can see but which will also block most of the UV reflection. If preventive measures are inadequate and snow blindness occurs, the eyes need to be patched to prevent the extreme irritation caused by the eyelids moving across the injured cornea. Cold compresses should also be applied and pain pills given. Earlier generations of climbers used drops of mineral oil under the eyelids to provide some increased lubrication across the cornea. Antibiotic eyedrops or antibiotic ophthalmic ointment can be applied for the same purpose and also prevents infection.

Women's Health Concerns

Gynecologic problems need to be anticipated. Some women are particularly prone to yeast infections, especially during antibiotic use, and should carry appropriate medications, since antibiotics may have to be taken for diarrhea or some other cause.

Irregular menstrual periods are common when changing multiple time zones, exercising strenuously, and going to high altitude. This should not be a concern unless there is any chance of pregnancy. The first period after missing a few may be abnormally heavy. Note that tampons and pads are not available in the hill areas.

Some authors have irresponsibly written that birth control pills should be discontinued at high altitude. Studies that I conducted in Nepal found no increased incidence of altitude problems or any other problems in women trekkers on birth control pills. It may be wise for women expeditioners who will be at 18,000 feet or above for months at a time to discontinue the pill because of the slight increased risk of vascular problems. For everyone else it is best to stay on the pill.

Little information is available about the effects of short-term high-altitude exposure during pregnancy. Conservative advice is to limit exposures to less than 15,000 feet, for periods of only a few weeks, and to take extra time to acclimatize. Pregnant trekkers need to realize the consequences of having a complication far from medical care and transportation.

Trauma

It is impossible in the space of this chapter to cover diagnosis and management of trauma in the back country. Suffice it to say that falling off the trail is the most common cause of death, injury, and helicopter evacuation in Nepal. Concentrate on walking when walking, and scenic viewing when resting or stopping. Every trekker should have sterile bandages, adhesive tape, wraparound gauze, safety pins, and elastic bandages for treatment of common injuries (see "Medical Kit for Himalayan Trekking," below).

Wounds

Most wounds can be treated adequately on trek. Extensive facial injuries that might cause a cosmetic problem, open fractures, or penetrating wounds of the abdomen, chest, or head call for evacuation to a hospital. The most important principle in the treatment of wounds is adequate cleansing and disinfection anytime the skin is broken. Small wounds can be cleaned by scrubbing with iodine solutions. After the wound has been thoroughly cleansed, it should be covered with an antibiotic ointment and bandaged; the bandage should be left in place for a long time to maintain the initial cleanliness. Larger wounds that cause gaping of the skin need to be thoroughly cleansed by irrigation with disinfected water; at least a liter should be irrigated into the wound to wash out any debris and to kill bacteria. Gaping wounds can then be taped shut and carefully bandaged. Wounds that are very extensive, going down to the bone or across tendons, or wounds that are difficult to clean properly need antibiotics as well. Penicillin, erythromycin, or cephalosporins can be administered in dosages of 250 mg four times a day for five days. Likewise, wounds not initially needing antibiotics but which later become infected should also be treated with antibiotics four times a day for five days.

Animal bites are a particular problem in central Asia because of the danger of rabies. Rabies is not carried by rodents, such as rabbits, squirrels, mice, rats, and picas. Dogs, bats, wolves, monkeys, and foxes are the common rabies carriers. All animal bite wounds first need to be treated like any wound with thorough cleansing and bandaging. The following measures must then be taken if rabies is a consideration. First, if at all possible, the animal must be captured and watched for ten days (good luck!). If there is no sign of illness in the animal in ten days, there is no danger of rabies. If it is not possible to catch the animal and observe it, the conservative measure is to proceed to the nearest urban center where rabies vaccine is available. The postexposure treatment involves five injections of HDCV (human diploid cell vaccine) over a period of one month, plus a one-time injection of rabies antibodies (rabies immunoglobulin, RIG). This injection is given as soon as possible to provide some protection while the body is making antibodies in response to the vaccine. This postexposure treatment in Kathmandu costs more than $500. If you have had a preexposure immunization series of three injections for prophylaxis, you still must have the postexposure treatment, but only an additional two shots. These treatments can be very difficult to obtain in Asia.

The rabies problem is a particularly troublesome one. Prevention is obviously the best solution. When faced with a growling dog, pick up a rock or just pretend to pick up a rock, and the dog will usually run away with its tail between its legs. Walking sticks and umbrellas are also handy.

Altitude Problems

There are a few medical conditions that preclude traveling to high altitude: these are pulmonary hypertension, moderate to severe chronic lung disease, unstable angina, unstable cardiac arrhythmias, cerebrovascular malformations, sickle cell anemia, congestive heart failure, and high-risk pregnancies. Persons with well-controlled blood pressure and heart problems and normal pregnancies seem to do just fine at high altitude but must exercise some caution. For all trekkers, not just those with medical problems, I seriously recommend a trial of high-altitude exposure before traveling to high areas on expensive and time-consuming trips. For example, you can sleep at 10,000 to 12,000 feet in the Rocky Mountains and the Sierra Nevada in North America or the volcanoes in Mexico and South America, or camp out near the tops of some European peaks. A person's response to high altitude (given the same rate of ascent) is generally predictable from one time to the next. So if you do well sleeping at 12,000 feet in North America, you will probably do well at that altitude in Asia. Doing well at 12,000 feet will make it easier to acclimatize to higher altitudes, and you should have little trouble.

As the Himalayan Rescue Association likes to point out, "The Himalaya starts where other mountains leave off." Too few trekkers seem to realize that it is the sleeping altitude that makes the critical difference in terms of the hypoxic (lack of oxygen) stress. In Tibet the *lowest* sleeping altitudes are generally 13,000 to 14,000 feet—the same as many summits in North America and Europe. For this reason the Himalaya deserves much more respect and much more knowledge of prevention and treatment of altitude illness. Recent studies have shown that approximately 30 to 40 percent of all trekkers in the Mt. Everest area develop some degree of altitude illness, with about one-third of this group becoming sick enough to change plans and not reach their destination. About 10 percent of this sick group develop life-threatening illnesses that require evacuation and/or medical attention. Only prior experience at these altitudes may help predict how your body is going to react. The three factors that determine whether you acclimatize well or become ill are (1) the altitude, (2) the rate of ascent to that altitude, and (3) your individual susceptibility to altitude illness. Men and women are equally susceptible to acute mountain sickness, and children may be somewhat more susceptible. Older folks seem to do just fine. What is hard for young, fit persons to understand is that superior physical conditioning grants absolutely no protection from altitude illness.

Prevention of Altitude Illness

The surest way of preventing altitude illness is by allowing the body adequate time to acclimatize. Avoid flying directly to altitudes over 9000 feet unless you can allow three or four days to adjust to the altitude before proceeding higher. For any mode of ascent, it is best to spend three or four days between 10,000 and 12,000 feet, acclimatizing until you feel stronger and less breathless; you should do the same between 14,000 and 15,000 feet, and again between 17,000 and 18,000 feet. Above these altitudes, it is best to get up and down as quickly as possible since the body's ability to acclimatize within the short period of time that most trekkers are exposed is limited.

Responsible trek leaders and guides will gear the rate of ascent to the people who acclimatize slowly. Everyone's physiology is different, and there is nothing to be ashamed of it you acclimatize more slowly than others. Some of the greatest mountain climbers in the world are poor acclimatizers but are able to make it up the peaks because they spend the necessary time acclimatizing before going for the summit. Other leaders and guides have no idea of the acclimatization process and consider performance at altitude a matter of strength or weakness rather than acclimatization. Unfortunately, this attitude is still too common. Acclimatization makes all the difference in the world. This is one reason I like to call altitude the great equalizer. Persons who are out of shape and not very athletic at sea level may acclimatize well and surpass marathon runners who are too incapacitated to move on the trail. Once the initial period of acclimatization is over, of course, the marathon runner will be superior in performance. But during the time of rapid adjustments in the body, when altitude sickness is likely to be debilitating, fitness is no protection, and the ones who go fast are the ones most likely to suffer.

Sometimes rapid ascent cannot be avoided. For example, the only way to enter Tibet is either by flying directly to Lhasa at 12,000 feet or by driving over the Sepo La pass from Kathmandu, which is an even worse stress. The road goes from 4000 feet in Nepal to over 17,000 feet and then down to 14,000 feet at Xegar in a matter of a day and a half or so. No wonder so many people get altitude sickness in Tibet! When faced with this kind of forced rapid ascent, especially if you know you are susceptible to altitude illness, preventive medication is prudent.

The drug of choice for preventing altitude sickness is acetazolamide (Diamox), which is a sulfa drug. Acetazolamide causes the blood to be slightly more acid, which stimulates breathing. It is also a mild diuretic. It hastens the natural processes of acclimatization, which are to increase breathing, reduce alkalinity, and diurese fluids. Therefore, acetazolamide does not mask the illness or cause any false sense of wellness. It produces changes in a few hours that normally take a few days. Acetazolamide should not be taken by people who are allergic to sulfa or during pregnancy. It can be used by both children and adults. The usual regimen is 125 to 250 mg twice a day starting twenty-four hours before ascent and continuing through the first twenty-four hours at altitude. Although this may be only four or five doses, it is very effective in speeding acclimatization and is all that is necessary. The drug can be restarted at any time if symptoms of altitude sickness develop (see below).

Adequate hydration is also helpful in preventing altitude illness. The body loses tremendous amounts of fluid from the lungs and the skin in the high, dry environment. You should drink enough to maintain a clear and copious urine output. Other measures include eating a diet high (greater than 70 percent) in carbohydrates, and going higher during the day and coming back down to sleep. Avoid sleeping near the top of passes. It's also best for acclimatization to have some mild or moderate activity rather than just to lie around. Exercise stimulates the circulation and respiration and helps the body adapt.

Your body usually offers plenty of warning signs that it doesn't like being at altitude and that you need to slow down and give it a little more time to acclimatize. However, no matter how slowly they go, some rare individuals do not acclimatize well and if not aided by acetazolamide will just have to go down. The secret is to listen to your body and heed the warning signals discussed below.

Acute Mountain Sickness

Acute mountain sickness (AMS) is the most common form of high altitude illness. Its typical symptoms are headache, lack of appetite, nausea, sometimes vomiting, and a feeling of tiredness. The initial symptoms are almost exactly like an alcohol hangover. One reason alcohol should be avoided in the first days at high altitude is that it can blur the distinction between acute mountain sickness and hangover. Another reason is that alcohol aggravates the effects of altitude and can actually impair acclimatization and make people more ill. (Contrary to popular opinion, alcohol does not exert any more effect on the brain at altitude than it does at sea level.) This stage of mild mountain sickness can be treated with aspirin or acetaminophen for headache, and perhaps other medication, such as promethazine hydrochloride (Phenergan) or prochlorperazine (Compazine), for the nausea and vomiting. However, even a headache alone must be taken as a warning sign that the body needs more time to acclimatize.

In treating acute mountain sickness, keep in mind three cardinal rules: (1) stop ascending if symptoms develop; (2) go down if they become worse instead of better with treatment; and (3) go down immediately if there is trouble with coordination, change in consciousness, or evidence of fluid in the lungs.

Rule 1: Stop ascending in the presence of symptoms. If ascent is stopped, mountain sickness will usually resolve within twenty-four to forty-eight hours but sometimes takes up to three or four days, depending on the rate of ascent, the altitude, and other factors. Acetazolamide should be administered in the same doses as for prevention to speed acclimatization. If, despite these measures, there is no improvement or symptoms become worse, you must descend.

Rule 2: Descend in the presence of worsening symptoms despite treatment. If started early enough, descent does not have to be very far; a 1,000- to 3,000-foot drop in altitude may be enough to reverse the process and induce rapid resolution. The bottom line is to descend as far as necessary for results. In Tibet in particular it may be very difficult to drop in altitude since there is no quick way off the plateau and a descent may involve going up even higher over a pass. In such circumstances it is best to treat medically and try to find oxygen. Oxygen is available in Xegar, Shigatse, and Lhasa and may be available in other places as well. If you are responsible for a group, it behooves you to inquire about the availability of oxygen in areas of travel or to carry oxygen with you. One cylinder, good for four to eight hours depending on flow rate, may save a life and a lot of problems.

Rule 3: Descend immediately if severe mountain sickness or pulmonary edema develops. The single most reliable sign of onset of severe acute mountain sickness is loss of coordination. Coordination can be tested by having the sick person walk a straight line heel to toe. A well person should be able to accomplish this feat without the maneuvers of a tightrope walker or falling off the line (and an unquestionably well person can always be used for comparison). Anyone who stumbles off the line and is obviously having difficulty with coordination needs immediate medical attention with administration of oxygen, dexamethasone (Decadron), and descent. Other symptoms associated with severe mountain sickness are recurrent vomiting, severe headache, loss of interest in all activities and surroundings, halluci-nations, bizarre behavior and thinking processes, paralysis, seizures, and unconsciousness. This type of severe mountain sickness is also called high altitude cerebral edema (HACE). Dexamethasone, which reduces brain swelling, should be given to people this ill in a dosage of 4 to 8 mg initially and then 4 mg every six hours, either by mouth or injection, depending on whether there is vomiting. Descent is mandatory.

High Altitude Pulmonary Edema

High altitude pulmonary edema (HAPE) is the form of altitude illness that most often results in death. HAPE is caused by fluid accumulating in the lungs so that the air sacs become filled with fluid instead of air, resulting in suffocation from lack of oxygen. The key to avoiding death and serious illness is anticipation and early recognition. The early symptoms of pulmo-nary edema are dry cough, decrease in exercise ability, longer recovery time from exercise, and excessive breathlessness and rapid heartbeat during exercise. As the illness progresses, shortness of breath develops even with small amounts of effort, the cough becomes worse, and fingernail beds become a dusky gray or blue color. In the late stages of the illness, the victim is breathless even at rest, usually with a resting respiratory rate greater than 24 breaths per minute and a resting heart rate greater than 100 beats per minute. The fingernails are always bluish or gray, a gurgling sound can often be heard in the chest, and the cough becomes wet and finally productive of pink, frothy sputum. At this stage, death may only be a few hours away.

If high altitude pulmonary edema is recognized early, prompt treatment can result in very rapid recovery. Treatment includes oxygen and/or descent. If oxygen is available, it should be given immediately, especially in serious cases. If the illness is discovered early, descent without oxygen is adequate and sometimes even rest alone without further ascent will make the pulmo-nary edema resolve, but this usually takes days. With descent, recovery is remarkably fast. For example, I have had patients who were unconscious at 14,000 feet wake up during the one-hour helicopter evacuation to 4,000 feet. By the time we landed they felt so well that they refused to pay the helicopter bill, claiming the illness was not severe enough to have warranted the helicopter! In reality, they would have been dead in another twelve hours or so at high altitude. This fast response to descent is one of the more puzzling, but satisfying, elements of the disease.

Other measures for treating pulmonary edema include keeping the victim warm, since cold will increase the pulmonary artery pressure and cause more fluid in the lungs; keeping the victim in a sitting position rather than lying so that breathing is easier; and avoiding overexertion. It is always easiest to have the person walk down on his or her own power—but without carrying a load and perhaps being carried on the uphill sections to avoid overexertion. Medications are not very useful for treating high altitude pulmonary edema. Oxygen and descent are the mainstays of treatment, and early recognition is the key to saving lives.

Most people who die or need to be evacuated from altitude illness have early warning signs but choose to ignore them and continue on. Often this foolhardiness is the result of group pressure: trekkers in large groups are therefore more likely to get in trouble than are individual trekkers, who are more free to change the itinerary as necessary. It is very important not to deny symptoms of altitude sickness. Although mountain sickness may be difficult to differentiate from conditions that may have the same sort of symptoms—such as alcohol hangover, flulike illnesses, bronchitis, pneumonia, exhaustion, dehydration, and hypothermia—the trekker needs to make the best judgment possible and if unsure of the cause of illness, to assume that it is due to high altitude. You must keep in mind that altitude illness, if ignored, can lead to death. Unfortunately, there is no way to tell at the first onset of symptoms whether the illness will be short and trivial or likely to progress. The best way to guarantee a progression of illness, however, is to continue on despite feeling ill.

Rescue

Evacuation from remote areas of the Himalaya is very difficult at best. The trekker must assume primary responsibility for himself or herself: the trouble you get into is the trouble you have to get out of. However, if there is an injury or a significant illness, help is usually available in the form of other trekkers or mountaineers not too far away, local villagers, porters, or guides.

The first priority is to establish the extent of injury and incapacity. You have to evaluate the situation much more carefully than if you were in the backcountry in the States because of the greater difficulty and expense of evacuation. Probably the most important determination is if the injured or sick person is well enough to move on his or her own power. If someone has fallen down a cliff, for example, and complains of pain in the lower back, you don't immobilize the victim on some sort of board and call for a helicopter and wait for help; you try to get the person to stand up and walk. Many people have been able to walk out of the mountains to the nearest airstrip with compression fractures of the vertebrae and other injuries that they might not normally have walked out with in North America. Head, neck, and spine injuries are particularly troublesome since at home we have a paranoia about possibly doing further damage by moving somebody with this type of injury. The truth is that having a person move under his or her own power is not going to cause anywhere near the stress of the initial fall or injury. Sore necks can be splinted with cut-up sleeping pads; scalp lacerations can be closed by cleaning the wound and tying the hair together across it; and people can walk out with injured backs as long as there is no paralysis or nerve damage. It is too often a fatal mistake to keep a victim of pulmonary edema at high altitude while waiting for a helicopter instead of starting right away, which is the definitive treatment and immediately effective.

Sometimes because of the severity of injury or illness there is no option but to call for help. If the person can be moved to the nearest airstrip, a seat on the next flight can usually be negotiated with the pilot or local official. If the person can't be moved at all, a runner has to be sent to the nearest radio station or police post, where a wire can be sent to Kathmandu. For the wire to bring results, however, there has to be someone reliable on the receiving end to take the message, such as an embassy, trekking agent, or other effective contact. In Nepal, for example, no helicopter will be sent after an injured person unless payment is guaranteed in Kathmandu. This is where the individual trekker is at a distinct disadvantage, since trekking companies all have agents in Kathmandu and can put money down for a flight. There are only a few aircraft available for emergency flights in Nepal, and all such mountain flights are dangerous (most of the pilots I flew with in the 1970s have since died in crashes). It is therefore critical to include the best estimate of the actual injuries or illness of the person to be rescued; the exact time and place of pickup; the victim's name, nationality, and passport number; and all other pertinent details. Some embassies will immediately guarantee payment for their nationals, whereas others will not. Sometimes family members have to be contacted in the States and payment guaranteed by telephone. Preregistration with the embassy can expedite this process quite a bit. Since these arrangements may take some time, a rescue should never be expected on the same day it is called for, although occasionally that happens. More often it is the next day or two days later that a helicopter can get in. These are just facts of life when trekking in Nepal. In Tibet the situation is far worse, for there are essentially no emergency aircraft available and there can be long, uncomfortable rides in Chinese trucks to get to the nearest hospital or to a lower altitude.

Should a fatality occur, local authorities (police) must be notified. An investigation of sorts is usually required before disposal of the body. No aircraft in Nepal will transport corpses. Cremation, if wood is available, crevasse burial, or other burial is best done on location. All details of the death should be recorded, and belongings and passport should be brought back to the consular section of the person's embassy.

The Trekker's Medical Kit

Following is a list of suggested medical supplies for Himalayan trekking. Specific items and amounts needed will vary according to medical sophistication, the number in your group, and length of trip. This list includes prescription items: in all cases their advisability, proper use, and side effects need to be discussed with your physician. How to use these drugs and proper precautions are also covered in the medical books recommended at the beginning of this chapter.

Water disinfectant: iodine or chlorine tablets, iodine tincture, povidone-iodine (Betadine), bleach, or filter

Sunscreen: sun protection factor (SPF) 10 to 15

Mosquito repellent: very important in malarial areas

Wound disinfectant: povidone-iodine (Betadine), 1-oz. plastic spout or dropper bottle (more if doubling for water disinfection)

Blister treatment: moleskin, Second Skin, or cloth adhesive tape

Adhesive strips:
  Band-Aids, #10
  ¼" or butterfly tapes, 1 package

Gauze pads: 3", #4

Gauze roll: 3" roll

Cloth adhesive tape: 2" roll

Elastic bandage: 3" roll

Thermometer

Scissors: Swiss-army type adequate

Safety pins

Matches: windproof, waterproof

Space blanket

Analgesics:
  aspirin or acetaminophen (Tylenol), #20
  acetaminophen with codeine (Tylenol with codeine), 30 mg, #10

Anti-inflammatories: ibuprofen (Advil, Rufen, or Motrin), 200 mg or 400 mg, #20

Antibiotics:
  trimethoprim/sulfamethoxazole (Bactrim DS or Septra DS) double strength (160 mg/s 800 mg), #14
  enteric-coated erythromycin, 250 mg, #28
  ciproflaxacin (Cipro), 500 mg, #10
  gentamicin (eyedrops or ophthalmic ointment)
  skin antibiotic/antifungal ointment

Antidiarrheals:
  diphenoxylate HCl with atropine sulfate (Lomotil), #30
  Pepto-Bismol tablets, #50 (more if using for prevention of diarrhea)

Antinausea drugs:
  promethazine HCl (Phenergan), 50 mg tablets, #4, *or*
  prochlorperazine (Compazine), 10 mg tablets, #5

Antihelminthic (for worms): mebendazole, 100 mg, #6

Malaria prophylaxis: individualized for traveler and trip

= quantity

Antihistamine:
  diphenhydramine HCl (Benadryl), 50 or 25 mg, #4 or #8, *or*
  chlorpheniramine
Decongestant: pseudoephedrine HCl (Sudafed), 60 mg
High-altitude trips:
  acetazolamide (Diamox), 250 mg or 500 mg long-acting, #20
  dexamethasone (Decadron), 4 mg, #10

Appendix A

Map Information

*My experience of mountains is that
the longest way round is the shortest way there.*
                    Laurens Van Der Post, 1952

The maps in this book are meant primarily for general orientation and as aids for interpreting the description of treks. For many people, these maps will be sufficient. However, in nearly all cases, this book's maps, while always drawn to scale, lack sufficient detail to be relied on for route finding off the main trails. The best thing to do when you are trekking off main trails is to walk with a local who knows the way. This appendix is designed to point out, by country, the principal maps covering, in greater detail, the regions described in this book. Sources for the maps listed here are given under "Map Ordering" at the end of this appendix.

The best single overall map of the Himalaya is the 1:4,000,000 sheet *Indian Subcontinent,* published by John Bartholomew & Son, Ltd., of Edinburgh, Scotland. This map, in Bartholomew's World Travel Series, is widely distributed and available at most large map stores. Most of the areas discussed in this book (except the routes to west Tibet and Mt. Kailas) are depicted on this excellent topographic map.

Nepal

One of the best series of maps covering a limited portion of the Himalaya are the sheets edited by the Research Scheme Nepal Himalaya and printed in Vienna, Austria. These sheets of eastern Nepal are often called the Schneider maps after Erwin Schneider, who supervised the fieldwork and mapmaking. The sheets available are, from west to east:

- *Kathmandu Valley* (1:50,000)
- *Kathmandu City* (1:10,000)
- *Patan* (1:7,500)
- *Helambu-Langtang* (1:100,000) — Helambu region and Langtang Valley
- *Lapche Kang* (1:50,000) — From the road to the Tibetan border to the western end of the Rowaling Valley
- *Tamba Kosi–Likhu Khola* (1:50,000) — Middle portion of the trek to Khumbu

- *Rolwaling Himal* (1:50,000)   Rolwaling Valley
- *Khumbu Himal* (1:50,000)   Entire Khumbu region
- *Shorong/Hinku* (1:50,000)   Area south of the *Khumbu Himal* map: upper Hinku Valley and most of upper Hongu Valley

- *Dudh Kosi* (1:50,000)   Area south of *Shorong/ Hinku* sheet

The *Kumbakarna Himal* sheet (1:50,000), which may be released in the near future, covers the area east of Khumbu (and the *Shorong/Hinku* sheet) as far as the Arun River. These maps are available in Kathmandu at the larger bookstores, or they may be ordered from the map houses listed at the end of the appendix.

A state-of-the-art map of Mt. Everest at 1:50,000 scale has been published by the *National Geographic* magazine in the November 1988 issue. This map goes as far south as Pangboche in Khumbu and covers the upper Khumbu and Imja valleys.

The best overall series of maps covering the Himalaya outside Tibet is the U.S. Army Map Service (AMS) U502 Series. These maps have a scale of almost 4 miles to the inch (1:250,000) and a contour interval of 250 or 500 feet, depending on the sheet. The U502 Series was completed prior to 1960, so it does not have current road information. However, numerous villages are shown in the hill areas, and these maps can be helpful especially if you are trekking off the main routes. The maps covering Nepal and western Bhutan are fairly accurate in most areas excepting the high mountain regions of northernmost Nepal. Black-and-white and color copies of most U502 sheets can also be ordered from Michael Chessler Books and foreign map houses, including Zumsteins, Geo Center, and Libreria Alpina. Reproduction copies of these maps should be highlighted for easier readability: try to emphasize the ridgelines and principal rivers with different-color felt-tip pens.

The principal available U502 sheets covering the hill areas of Nepal are, from west to east:

- NH 44-10 *Almora*   Westernmost Nepal as far east as Silgarhi
- NH 44-11 *Jumla*   Khaptad, Bhajang, Simikot, Rara, Jumla
- NH 44-15 *Nepalganj*   Dailekh, Jajarkot, lower Bheri River
- NH 44-16 *Pokhara*   Dhorpatan, Kali Gandaki and Pokhara valleys
- NH 45-13 *Jongkha Dzong*   Marsyangdi and Buri Gandaki valleys
- NG 45-1 *Kathmandu*   Trisuli to Kathmandu—of little use
- NG 45-2 *Mount Everest*   Middle Hills, Rolwaling, Namche, Salpa Pass
- NG 45-3 *Kanchenjunga*   Arun Valley and northeastern Nepal

The maps most often used by trekkers in Nepal are a series of bluish ammonia dye sheets made by Mandala Graphic Art in Kathmandu. These maps are of varying scales from 1:125,000 to 1:250,000, and their accuracy often leaves much to be desired. But they are readily available at bookshops in Kathmandu for less than $1 each, and they help orient you, even without a high degree of accuracy. They may be all you'll be able to get at such a scale once in Nepal. If you can't find the sheet you want, keep looking in different stores. Himalayan Booksellers usually has, or can get, any of these maps. Some of the sheets usually available (names do change) are, from west to east:

- *Jumla to Api and Saipal Himal*
- *Jomosom to Jumla, Surkhet*
- *Pokhara to Jomosom, Manang*
- *Kathmandu to Manaslu, Ganesh Himal*
- *Kathmandu, Helambu, Langtang, Gosain Kund*
- *Khumbu Himal*
- *Dhankuta to Kanchenjunga, Mt. Everest, Makalu and Arun Valley*

More a photograph than a map are the two sheets of Nepal prepared for the World Bank. These handsome false-color maps (*Western Sheet,* to Pokhara, and *Eastern Sheet*) at a scale of 1:500,000 are based on Landsat satellite imagery and are available from International Mapping Unlimited.

Two atlas-size books published in Japan by Gakushukenkusha, Ltd. (Gakken) contain many large-scale maps of areas covered in this book. The two books are part of a series called Mountaineering Maps of the World. Edited by Ichiro Yoshizawa, the individual volumes are titled *Himalaya* (1977) and *Karakorum* [sic], *Hindu-Kush, Pamir and Tien Shan* (1978). Text is in Japanese, with color photographs. These volumes have, respectively, twenty-three and twenty-five two-page shaded relief maps that cover many Himalayan regions. The books can be difficult to locate, but their maps can be copied for field use and are particularly helpful for areas with the highest concentrations of peaks.

An extremely accurate series of maps covering Nepal (and India) with a contour interval of 100 feet at a scale of 1 inch to the mile (1:63,360) has been printed by the Survey of India. These excellent maps are highly restricted, and though they are coveted by many, they are unlikely ever to become generally available.

Western Tibet

No maps yet exist of just western Tibet. Probably the best available sheets are the ONC Series, noted below. Otherwise, you will have to use maps that depict all of China.

The Operational Navigational Charts (ONC) at a scale of 1:1,000,000 are a series of maps made for pilots. These maps cover the entire world, and the information shown on them is obtained from satellites. Surficial information (mountains, lakes, rivers) is excellent, but it's best to be skeptical regarding what these sheets say about either roads or towns. The ONC H-9 sheet covers most of the areas described in the chapter on west Tibet, almost as far north as Ali (and it covers all of Nepal). The ONC G-7 sheet north of H-9 covers Ali and everything north to Kashgar. ONC Series maps are inexpensive and are carried by many agents in the United States. They can also be ordered from the National Ocean Survey.

Two maps covering all of China at a 1:6,000,000 scale are the *Map of the People's Republic of China,* published by the Cartographic Publishing House, Beijing, China, and *China and Mongolia,* published by John Bartholomew & Son, Ltd., in the World Travel Series. This scale is rather small to be of much help for west Tibet. The National Geographic Society has also published a similar-size map of China.

A map called *Kathmandu to Tibet* at the scale of 1:1,000,000 has been published by Mandala Maps in Kathmandu. This map includes the road routes between Kathmandu and Lhasa, and the ones to western Tibet almost as far as Gertse. It is available from Himalayan Booksellers.

The best maps of the Mt. Kailas area are still Swami Pranavananda's. If you can't locate his book *Kailas Manasarovar,* two of his maps have been reproduced in the endpapers of John Snelling's *The Sacred Mountain,* noted in the Bibliography.

Bhutan

The best overall map of Bhutan is made by International Mapping Unlimited. This 1:250,000 map is actually a false-color composite of Landsat satellite imagery with the names of principal towns overlain from an earlier map made by the Survey of India.

Two U502 Series sheets of Bhutan are helpful but not of good reliability: NG 45-4, *Phari Dzong* (western Bhutan), and NG 46-1, *Tongsa Dzong* (central Bhutan—poor reliability). These maps can be ordered as indicated above for the Nepal U502 sheets.

Map Ordering

In addition to the maps listed above, other good maps of specific areas have been published as well. The following sources will send lists or catalogs of the maps they sell. Ordering maps takes time, so you may have to begin the process well in advance to allow time for correspondence, particularly with the Library of Congress or overseas map sellers.

Michael Chessler Books
P.O. Box 2436
Evergreen, CO 80439
(800) 654-8502; (303) 670-0093
    At last: a company in the United States that sells a wide variety of maps, including the Schneider Series, color reproduction copies of many U502 maps (mostly sheets in India and Pakistan, however), and more.

Geo Buch Verlag
Rosental 6
D-8000 München 2
West Germany
    A large map house and bookseller.

Geo Center GmbH
Honigwiesenstrasse 25
Postfach 80 08 30
D-7000 Stuttgart 80
West Germany
    One of the biggest map houses; it also sells books.

Himalayan Book Center
Nepal Red Cross Building
P.O. Box 1339
Baghbazar
Kathmandu, Nepal

Himalayan Booksellers
Ghantaghar–Clock Tower
GPO Box 528
Kathmandu
Nepal
    These folks made a good, two-sided Kathmandu city and valley
map and a map of Nepal as well. They always carry the latest locally
produced maps and others like the Schneider maps.

International Mapping Unlimited
4343 Thirty-ninth Street NW
Washington, D.C. 20016
    Available are the Landsat-based maps of Bhutan and Nepal noted
above.

Library of Congress
101 Independence Avenue
Washington, D.C. 20540
    U502 Series maps cost a minimum of $8.50 per sheet, plus post-
age. If you know which map sheets you want, you can write direct to
the Photoduplication Division. But if you have any questions about
which map to order, you'll have to first contact the senior reference
librarian at the same address. This latter process takes two steps and
requires up to eight weeks, so plan ahead. U502 sheets from Chessler
Books are better quality.

Libreria Alpina
Via C. Coroned-Berti, 4
40137 Bologna, Zona 3705
Italy
    Excellently stocked map and book seller with a fine catalog.

National Geographic Society
Seventeenth and M Streets, NW
Washington, D.C. 20036
  National Geographic has produced a map of Mt. Everest and a
map of China (which includes west Tibet).

NOAA Distribution Branch (N/CG33)
National Ocean Service
Riverdale, MD 20737
  Sells the ONC Series of maps, if you can't find copies in your area.

Stanford International Map Centre
12-14 Long Acre
London WC2E 9LP
England
  Sells some U502 sheets and the Schneider maps of eastern Nepal.

Zumsteins Landkartenhaus
Liebkerrstrasse 5
8 München 22
West Germany
  A well-stocked map seller.

Appendix B

Trekking Outfitters in Nepal

In Nepal, if you wish to embark on a completely arranged trek for a group of friends, or by yourself, or if you only want to hire a good porter or two to cook and carry, you can contact a reputable trekking outfitter ahead of time. Kathmandu has over a hundred trekking companies (only half are licensed!), but only some of these are large enough or experienced enough to assist you, should you wish to firm up plans before arrival. You can arrange a two-day trek (including tents and hot meals) to a nearby viewpoint on the edge of the Kathmandu or Pokhara Valley, or a two-month hike to a remote sanctuary behind the far himals. Some outfitters are more interested or more experienced in arranging permits to interesting regions outside the purview of most trekkers.

Here is a short list of some trekking companies that should be reliable. These trekking outfitters can make all arrangements for you. Otherwise, for greater ease in obtaining the same services, you can contact a tour operator at home (who will in turn relay your request, probably through one of the outfitters listed below).

Above the Clouds Trekking
P.O. Box 2230
Kathmandu
Telephone 412-921

Above the Clouds Trekking
P.O. Box 398
Worcester, MA 01602
Telephone 617-799-4499
    Will try to arrange off-the-beaten-path destinations.

Ama Dablam Trekking (P) Ltd.
P.O. Box 3035
Lazimpat
Kathmandu
Telephone 410-219; telex NP 2460 AMDB TRK
    The largest trekking company in Nepal.

Himalayan Journeys (P) Ltd.
P.O. Box 989
Kantipath
Kathmandu
Telephone 211-138, 214-626; telex 2344 HJTREK
    One of Kathmandu's large trekking companies.

International Trekkers
P.O. Box 1273
Kathmandu
Telephone 224-157, 220-594; telex 2353 INTREK NP

Lama Excursions
P.O. Box 2485
Durbar Marg
Kathmandu
Telephone 220-186, 220-940; telex 2534 EPNTT NP

Mountain Travel, Pvt. Ltd.
P.O. Box 170
Durbar Marg
Kathmandu
Telephone 414-508, 411-562; telex 2216 TIGTOP NP
    The first company of all still organizes logistics for expeditions
or treks.

Nepal Himal
P.O. Box 4528
Thamel
Kathmandu
Telephone 411-949; telex 2244 ATTOUR NP
    Three well-known people started their own company: Bobbie
Chettri, Pasang Kami Sherpa, and Pertemba Sherpa.

Rover Treks and Expeditions (P) Ltd.
P.O. Box 1081
Naxal Nag Pokhari
Kathmandu
Telephone 414-373, 412-667; telex 2417 PRESSI NP
    Experienced in arranging permits to interesting areas and to Tibet.

Sagarmatha Trekking
P.O. Box 2236
Thamel
Kathmandu
Telephone 413-239

Sherpa Trekking Service
P.O. Box 500
Kamaladi
Kathmandu
Telephone 222-489, 220-243; telex 2419 STS NP
    Mostly works with European groups.

Trans Himalayan Trekking
P.O. Box 283
Durbar Marg
Kathmandu
Telephone 224-854, 223-871; telex NP 2233
    Most of its groups are Japanese.

Bibliography

The books in this bibliography are only a small fraction of those available about Nepal, western Tibet, and Bhutan. Most of the books listed should not be difficult to locate, given access to a well-stocked library. You can find more information about nearly every area mentioned in this book from one or more of the titles below. If your interest continues to grow, you can vastly expand your list of sources from the bibliographies in the books you read.

General

Barrett, Robert LeMoyne, and Katherine Barrett. *The Himalayan Letters of Gypsy Davy and Lady Ba*. Cambridge: W. Heffer & Sons, 1927.
A poetic tale of a year's travels in Ladakh and Baltistan. Hard to find, but very informative about the way things were.

Bernbaum, Edwin. *Sacred Mountains of the World*. San Francisco: Sierra Club Books, 1990.
A fascinating compilation in words and photographs of sacred mountains in the Himalaya and elsewhere.

————. *The Way to Shambhala*. Los Angeles: J. P. Tarcher, 1989.
The inner and outer quest for "hidden valleys" as symbolized in the Buddhist concept of Shambhala.

Cleare, John. *The World Guide to Mountains and Mountaineering*. London: Mayflower, 1979.
Facts about peaks, passes, access, maps, and references, intelligibly presented. Cleare picks up at snowline, where this book leaves off. Fifty pages of the book describe the Himalaya.

Heim, Arnold, and August Gansser. *The Throne of the Gods*. Translated by Eden and Cedar Paul. New York: Macmillan, 1939.
Heim and Gansser traveled light and deeply experienced the country. Excellent photographs. Contains accounts of a visit to Mt. Kailas in Tibet and the Tinkar Valley in Nepal.

Mason, Kenneth. *Abode of Snow*. Seattle: Mountaineers, 1987.
The basic history of Himalayan exploration and mountaineering.

Newby, Eric. *A Short Walk in the Hindu Kush*. New York: Penguin, 1981.
A humorous account of trekking in Nuristan, Afghanistan. Find this one: it's a must.

Rowell, Galen. *Many People Come, Looking, Looking*. Seattle: Mountaineers, 1980.
A well-written book with superb photography; one section discusses the Kali Gandaki Valley in Nepal.

Shipton, Eric. *That Untravelled World*. London: Hodder & Stoughton, 1969.
Superb writing by a master of the small expedition; about Baltistan, Garhwal, the Khumbu region, and elsewhere.

Singh, Madanjeet. *Himalayan Art*. New York: Macmillan, 1968.

An overview of wall painting and sculpture from Ladakh to Bhutan. Contains many photographs; the text is often quite technical.

Thesiger, Wilfred. *The Last Nomad*. New York: Dutton, 1980.
Although this books is only in part about the Himalaya, Thesiger has a fine approach to travel in Asia. He roamed at length and visited many remote peoples and places. Excellent photographs.

Tichy, Herbert. *Himalaya*. Translated by Richard Rickett and David Streatfeild. Vienna: Anton Schroll, 1970.
Brief but captivating accounts of voyages by Tichy and others from Chitral to Assam. Tichy has a wonderful "insider's" feel for the land and people.

Nepal

Anderson, John Gottberg. *Nepal*. Singapore: Insight Guides, 1983.
An excellent, colorful guide; the best there is for the Kathmandu Valley.

Armington, Stan. *Trekking in the Nepal Himalaya*. 4th ed. South Yarra, Australia: Lonely Planet, 1985.
This book gives good descriptions of the popular trekking routes from the Kali Gandaki to Arun valleys.

Bezruchka, Stephen. *A Guide to Trekking in Nepal*. 5th ed. Seattle: Mountaineers, 1985.
The most detailed trekking guide to Nepal's most popular trekking routes. Packed with accurate information.

Bista, Dor Bahadur. *People of Nepal*. 2d ed. Kathmandu: Ratna Pustak Bhandar, 1972.
The best book about the many clans inhabiting Nepal, by Nepal's foremost anthropologist.

Chorlton, Windsor. *Cloud-Dwellers of the Himalayas*. Amsterdam: Time-Life, 1982.
Excellently written and well-photographed account of the difficult daily lives of people in the restricted Nar-Phu Valley.

Coburn, Broughton. *Nepali Aama*. Santa Barbara: Ross-Erikson, 1982.
A delightful rendering of traditional middle-hill Nepal and its people, told largely in the words of Aama herself.

Downs, Hugh R. *Rhythms of a Himalayan Village*. New York: Harper & Row, 1980.
A sensitive account in photographs and words of life in a Sherpa village by a person who lived for two years in the area depicted.

Gurung, Harka. *Vignettes of Nepal*. Kathmandu: Sajha, 1980.
Detailed descriptions of many remote areas in Nepal by an extremely knowledgeable native son.

Hagen, Toni. *Nepal*. 3d ed. Berne: Kummerley & Frey, 1971.
A classic book on Nepal. Superb photographs by the author, who has still probably seen more of the country than anyone else.

————. Gunter-Oskar Dyhrenfurth, Christoph von Fürer-Haimendorf, and Erwin Schneider. *Mount Everest: Formation, Population and Exploration of the Everest Region*. Translated by E. Noel Bowman. London: Oxford University Press, 1963.
All the background you want about Khumbu by four eminent scholars. Information on the Sherpas is dated.

Hornbein, Thomas F. *Everest: The West Ridge*. Seattle: Mountaineers, 1980.
A sensitively written account of the 1963 American ascent of Mt. Everest.

Jest, Corneille. *Tarap, une vallée dans l'himalaya*. Paris: Seuil, 1974.
Superb documentary photographs of the Tarap Valley in Dolpo. The text is in French.

Kazami, Takehide. *The Himalayas: A Journey to Nepal*. Tokyo: Kodansha, 1968.
Still one of the best inexpensive collections of color photographs on Nepal.

Kelly, Thomas L., and V. Carroll Dunham. *The Hidden Himalayas*. New York: Abbeville, 1987.
Here's the book about remote Humla.

Kleinert, Christian. *Nepal Trekking*. Munich: Bergverlag Rudolf Rother, 1976.
Informative summaries of various treks in Nepal. Excellent fold-out panoramic photographs.

Matthiessen, Peter. *The Snow Leopard*. New York: Bantam, 1979.
Along with Schaller's *Stones of Silence* (see "Natural History" listings, below), one of the few recent published accounts about a visit to Dolpo.

Meerendonk, M. *Basic Gurkhali Dictionary*. Singapore: M. Meerendonk, 1960.
A small pocket dictionary that will help you add vocabulary to your working knowledge of Nepali. Available in Kathmandu.

Nakano, Toru. *Trekking in Nepal*. New Delhi: Allied, 1985.
Excellent maps and photographs make this an important new book. If you can't find the U502 maps, the maps in this book can give you good ideas for out-of-the-way treks.

Pilkington, John. *Into Thin Air*. London: George Allen & Unwin, 1985.
A delightful, well-written tale of a person who walked across western Nepal from Pokhara all the way to India.

Raj, Prakash A. *Kathmandu and the Kingdom of Nepal*. 5th ed. South Yarra, Australia: Lonely Planet, 1985.
A brief guide to the Kathmandu Valley.

Rieffel, Robert. *Nepal Namaste*. 2d ed. Kathmandu: Sahayogi, 1986.
A good overall guide to Nepal, but hard to locate out-of-country.

Snellgrove, David L. *Himalayan Pilgrimage*. Boulder: Prajna, 1981.
Snellgrove's insights make this "scholar's travelbook" of a trip in Dolpo and northern Nepal a very special book. Many trail facts are included.

Tilman, H. W. *The Seven Mountain Travel Books*. Seattle: Mountaineers, 1983.
Contains *Nepal Himalaya,* with its amusing, very British account of early trips into the Nyeshang (Manang) and Langtang regions of Nepal.

Tucci, Giuseppe. *Journey to Mustang*. Kathmandu: Ratna Pustak Bhandar, 1977.
The trail from Pokhara to the Kali Gandaki Valley all the way to Mustang in 1952.

———. *Nepal: The Discovery of the Malla*. New York: Dutton, 1962.
Account of a trip from Pokhara to Jumla through the Barbung Valley.

Valli, Eric, and Diane Summers. *Dolpo: Hidden Land of the Himalayas*. New York: Aperture, 1987.
An excellent gallery of photographs from Dolpo, with emphasis on a trading caravan moving south. Gets you right next to the Dolpopas.

Von Fürer-Haimendorf, Christoph. *Himalayan Traders*. New York: St. Martin's, 1975.
Dry, but very informative about people in Nepal's northern border regions.

Western Tibet

Allen, Charles. *A Mountain in Tibet*. London: Futura, 1983.
Gives some information about western explorers in the Mt. Kailas region.

Batchelor, Stephen. *The Tibet Guide*. London: Wisdom, 1987.
An excellent guide that contains some information about western Tibet.

Buckley, Michael, and Robert Strauss. *Tibet: A Travel Survival Kit*. South Yarra, Australia: Lonely Planet, 1986.
A good overall guide to Tibet, particularly the central Tsang Po Valley. Doesn't pull any punches.

Govinda, Lama Anagarika. *The Way of the White Clouds*. Boston: Prajna, 1985.
A wonderful, well-written book that describes several pilgrimages to Ladakh and western Tibet. Some information on Mt. Kailas and more on Tsaparang.

Govinda, Li Gotami. *Tibet in Pictures*, vols. 1 and 2. Berkeley: Dharma, 1979.
The best (and only) photographs you'll ever see of the now-destroyed images inside of Tsaparang and Toling. Other excellent photographs of what Tibet was like before it was invaded and irrevocably changed.

————. "The Tsaparang Expedition." *Illustrated Weekly of India*, 8, 15, 22, 29 April and 6, 13, 20, 27 May 1951.
Difficult to locate, but the best source of information for the Govinda's remarkable expedition to western Tibet, which was sponsored by the *Illustrated Weekly of India*.

Pranavananda, Swami. *Exploration in Tibet*. Calcutta: University of Calcutta, 1950.
This rare but extremely interesting book gives you lots of ideas for out-of-the-way places to explore in Tibet. Swami P. is a scientist in saffron.

————. *Kailas Manasarovar*. 1949. Reprint. New Delhi: Swami Pranavananda, 1983.
The most complete guide for the Mt. Kailas area yet written. Information about routes in western Tibet and how to reach the sources of the four major rivers that have their origins in the general vicinity of Mt. Kailas.

Snellgrove, David, and Hugh Richardson. *A Cultural History of Tibet*. Boston: Shambhala, 1986.
One of the classic overviews of Tibetan culture.

Snelling, John. *The Sacred Mountain*. London: East West, 1983.
An excellent book about the symbolism of and western explorers to Mt. Kailas. Also contains facts about the circumambulation route gleaned from many accounts.

Stein, R.A. *Tibetan Civilization*. Translated by J.E. Driver. Stanford: Stanford University Press, 1972.
Another classic book on Tibet's people, history, art, and religion.

Bhutan

Olschak, Blanche C., and Ursula and August Gansser. *Bhutan: Land of Hidden Treasures*. New York: Stein & Day, 1971.

Bhutan as experienced in the late 1960s by three insightful travelers. Fine photographs.

Pommaret-Imaeda, Françoise, and Yoshiro Imaeda. *Bhutan: A Kingdom of the Eastern Himalayas*. Translated by Ian Noble. Geneva: Éditions Olizane, 1984. Excellent overall introduction to Bhutan with lush photography by Guy van Strydonck.

Rose, Leo E. *The Politics of Bhutan*. Ithaca: Cornell University Press, 1977. Political history made interesting.

Rustomji, Nari. *Enchanted Frontiers*. Calcutta: Oxford University Press, 1971. A former advisor to the Kingdom of Bhutan (who also held similar positions in Sikkim and India's former northeast frontier), Rustomji writes from the inside about times now a part of history.

Ward, Michael. *In This Short Span*. London: Victor Gollancz, 1972. Information on Lunana with a map of the region on the back endpaper.

Natural History

Ali, Salim. *Field Guide to the Birds of the Eastern Himalayas*. New Delhi: Oxford University Press, 1978. Covers Sikkim and Bhutan, describing 535 species and illustrating 366. Detailed natural history information.

Cronin, Edward W., Jr. *The Arun: A Natural History of the World's Deepest Valley*. Boston: Houghton Mifflin, 1979. Informative account of natural history in the Arun Valley.

Dobremez, J.F. *Le Nepal: écologie et biogéographie*. Paris: Centre National de la Recherche Scientifique, 1976. A detailed account of the soils, climate, and plant communities of Nepal. In French.

Fleming, Robert L., Sr., Robert L. Fleming, Jr., and Lain S. Bangdel. *Birds of Nepal*. Bombay: Vakil & Sons, 1979. Compact field guide describing about 800 species, including some from Kashmir and Sikkim. Definitely the best available but has some misleading illustrations.

Hooker, J.D. *Himalayan Journals*. London, 1854. Available in Indian reprint editions. Account by the first botanist to visit the Himalaya and study it in depth.

Inskipp, Carol, and Tim Inskipp. *A Guide to Birds of Nepal*. Dover: Tanager, 1985. Based on reported sightings and museum collections, this book provides basic information on the distribution, habitat, behavior, and breeding of 835 species. Although illustrated with 676 distribution maps, it is not a field guide.

Israel, Samuel, and Toby Sinclair, ed. *Indian Wildlife*. Singapore: APA, 1987. An overview of wildlife in India, Nepal, and Sri Lanka, this collectively written and photographed book also contains sections on selected national parks.

Jackson, Rodney. "Snow Cats of Langu Gorge." *Animal Kingdom,* July/August 1987, 45–53. Account of author's study of the snow leopard.

Jackson, Rodney, and Darla Hillard. "Tracking the Elusive Snow Leopard." *National Geographic,* June 1986, 793–809.

Majupuria, Trilok C., *Wild Is Beautiful*. Kathmandu: S. Devi, 1981.

Introduction to the fauna of Nepal, written by Nepalese experts. Some chapters suffer from inaccurate information. Available in Kathmandu bookstores.

Mierow, Dorothy, and Tirtha Bahadur Strestha. *Himalayan Flowers and Trees.* Kathmandu: Sahayogi, 1978.
Portable guide with many color photographs of trees, shrubs, and wildflowers of Nepal for those wanting something lightweight to carry. Illustrates some of the commonly encountered species.

Polunin, Oleg, and Adam Stainton. *Flowers of the Himalaya.* New Delhi: Oxford University Press, 1984.
The guide to the flowering plants of the Himalaya, from Kashmir to Nepal. Illustrated by 690 color plates, describes 1500 plants found above elevations of 4000 feet. Though somewhat heavy and expensive, it will enable you to identify most plants encountered.

Prater, S. H. *The Book of Indian Mammals.* Bombay: Bombay Natural History Society, 1965.
Describes all large mammals of the Indian subcontinent. Recent research has changed much of our knowledge on the natural history of many primates, cats, wild sheep, and goats. Plate illustrations. Not a field guide.

Schaller, George B. *Mountain Monarchs: Wild Sheep and Goats of the Himalaya.* Chicago: University of Chicago Press, 1977.
Detailed facts about Himalayan sheep and goats. Technical but readable.

————. *Stones of Silence: Journeys in the Himalaya.* New York: Viking, 1980.
Well-written, factual information on the author's fieldwork in Chitral, Hunza, Dolpo, and the Bhote Kosi Valley.

Stainton, J. D. A. *Forests of Nepal.* London: John Murray, 1972.
Out-of-print account of the forest types of Nepal, applicable to much of the Himalaya.

Vaurie, Charles. *Tibet and Its Birds.* London: H. F. & G. Witherby, 1972.
Lists birds known to occur in Tibet, based on museum records. Includes informative accounts of the region's geography, climate, and zoogeography, with an account of early scientific explorations.

Medical Information

Auerbach, Paul. *Medicine for the Outdoors.* Boston: Little, Brown, 1986.

Bezruchka, Stephen. *The Pocket Doctor.* Seattle: Mountaineers, 1988.
Written with disease prevention in mind, this compact book includes information on medication and dosages.

Darvill, Fred T. *Mountaineering Medicine: A Wilderness Medical Guide.* 11th ed. Berkeley: Wilderness, 1985.
Small in size, this condensed guide to first aid has diagrams and describes everything from bandaging scratches to reducing a dislocated shoulder and setting broken bones in the hills.

Hackett, Peter. *Mountain Sickness: Prevention, Recognition and Treatment.* New York: American Alpine Club, 1980.
The last and most authoritative word on altitude sickness.

Wilkerson, James A., ed. *Medicine for Mountaineering.* 3d ed. Seattle: Mountaineers, 1985.
The most complete how-to medical book; covers nearly everything. Heavy to carry, however.

Glossary of
Foreign Words
Used in the Text

Speak to people in their own language.
Mushkeel Baba, 1976

This glossary is a list of foreign words found in the text. Languages are abbreviated as follows:

D = Dzongkha (Bhutan). *H* = Hindustani (Hindi or Urdu; many of the Hindustani words used herein are derived from Sanskrit). *N* = Nepali. *S* = Sherpa. *T* = Tibetan. Gurung, Limbu, and Rai are the names of local Nepali clans.

aama (N)	mother
alu (H,N)	potato
anchal (N)	zone (corresponds to a state in the United States)
Angrezi (H)	foreigner (strictly speaking, an Englishman)
arak (S,T)	distilled spirits (the same as **rakshi**)
arrah (D)	distilled chang
baatmas (N)	roasted soybeans
baba (H)	"old man," used as term of respect for older people
bakshish (H,N)	either a tip for services or a gift to the underprivileged
banchung (D)	Bhutanese lunchbox made of interlocking woven baskets
barasahib (H,N)	boss, important person (antiquated)
beautay (N)	high-quality musk
beyul (T)	hidden valley
bhaat (N)	cooked rice; also means a meal
bhanjang (N)	pass
bhatti (N)	inn; a home where you can sleep and be fed
bhit (N)	impossible or miraculous act
bibaha (N)	wedding
bistaari (N)	slowly
budgen (H)	religious song
chai (H)	tea
chaiin (N)	buttermilk
chang (D,S,T)	beer (drink only at your own risk, for it's made with untreated water)
chaulki (N)	police post
chautaara (N)	a stone-walled resting place, usually with a pipal and banyan tree planted on the top
chhatri (N)	umbrella

chiurra (N)	pounded rice; usually eaten with tea for breakfast or as a snack
chiyaa (N)	tea
choogo (D)	chunks of yak cheese made in Bhutan
chorten (T)	a reliquary shrine, also known as a **stupa** (its Sanskrit name)
chowki (T)	guardian of a monastery
chu (T)	stream or river
chuba (T)	man's or woman's robe
chumik (T)	spring of water
churpee (T)	dried cheese that comes in small pieces
daban (Uighur?)	pass
dablam (S)	charm box worn by a woman around her neck
dacoit (H)	robber, thief
dahi (H,N)	yogurt
dakshin (N)	south
dal (H,N)	cooked or uncooked lentils
dal-bhaat (N)	cooked lentils and rice; also means a meal
damaru (H)	small drum used for prayers that is held in one hand and rapidly rotated back and forth
danda (N)	ridgetop or low pass
danphe (N)	impeyan pheasant, Nepal's national bird
darra (T)	buttermilk
deurali (N)	ridgetop or low pass
dhajo (N)	red and white strips of cloth hung for a religious purpose
dhami (N)	shaman or oracle in western Nepal
dhan nach (Limbu)	rice dance, a courtship dance
dhara (N)	waterspout, usually of spring water
dharma (Sanskrit)	cosmological, religious law; loosely, religion (used in both Hinduism and Buddhism)
dharmsala (H,N)	a resthouse for pilgrims
doko (N)	woven basket carried by means of a tumpline; used in Nepal to carry nearly anything
dokpa (N)	wooden image representing a local protector diety; found in western Nepal
doma (D)	betel leaf, areca nut, and powdered lime (called **pan** in India)
dorje (T)	symbol of the eternal, indestructible self
Drokpa (T)	Tibetan nomad
druk (D)	thunder dragon
Druk Yul (D)	"land of the thunder dragon," Bhutan
dudh (H,N)	milk
du khang (T)	monks' assembly hall in a Tibetan Buddhist temple
dun (H)	flat valley in the southern Siwalik Range
durbar (H,N)	palace or any place that a potentate holds court
dzong (D,T)	fortress
dzongda (D)	district administrator, governor

dzongpon (T)	formerly a governor in Tibet
eema dashi (D)	red rice, chilies, and cheese (Bhutan's national dish)
ek dum (N)	quite, exactly
gaine (N)	clan of minstrel singers who travel from village to village
ghat (H,N)	platform by the river; some used for washing clothes, others for cremations
ghechu (D)	straight knife used in Bhutan
ghee (H,N)	clarified butter
gomba (T)	Tibetan Buddhist temple or monastery
gundruk (N)	pickled greens
gup (D)	elected village headman in Bhutan
gur (H)	unrefined sugar cane
gyang chatsel (T)	"to salute stretched out"; repeated prostrations that pious Tibetans make while circumambulating sacred places
haat (N)	hand
haat bazaar (N)	weekly market (goods pass from hand to hand)
himal (H,N)	high, perpetually snow-covered peak (more properly, *himaal*)
jhola (H,N)	small shoulder bag
jilla (N)	district (corresponds to a county in the United States)
jutho (N)	ritually impure
kamni (D)	man's ceremonial scarf in Bhutan
kang (T)	mountain
kanpat (H,N)	split-ear; name given to an order of yogis in India and Nepal
karma (Sanskrit)	action and its consequences
kasturi (H,N)	musk or musk deer
kata (T)	prayer scarf given ritually to a friend embarking on a journey or when meeting an important monk or lama
khakh shing (S)	sacred forest in Khumbu
kho (D)	robe worn by men in Bhutan
khola (N)	river or river valley
khukari (N)	sturdy, curved-blade Gurkha-style knife
khursaani (N)	green or red hot peppers
kira (D)	woman's dress in Bhutan
kora (T)	circumambulation; what Tibetans do when they reach a sacred place, be it lake, monastery, or mountain
kosi (N)	river
kot (N)	small fortress
kund (H,N)	lake
la (T)	pass, usually a high one
lagna (N)	pass
lama (T)	Tibetan Buddhist priest
lamyik (T)	permission to be in or go to a certain place
lassi (H,N)	drink made with yogurt and water that can be either "sweet," with sugar, or "sour," left plain
lato (N)	male half-wit
lekh (N)	large, high ridge that is not perpetually snow covered

lhakhang (T)	"house of the gods," chapel in a Tibetan Buddhist temple
lota (N)	metal water container with a pouring spout
lu (S)	spirit
maati baato (N)	upper trail
mala (H,N)	garland of flowers or rosary of beads
mala (T)	Tibetan rosary of 108 beads
mandir (H,N)	Hindu temple
mani stone or **wall**	stone (or collection of stones in a wall) carved with the sacred mantra "Om Mani Padme Hum," "All hail the jewel in the lotus"
masur dal (H,N)	red dal
meeschery (H)	a sugarlike lump, more refined than **gur**
membaar (N)	member of a trekking group
mudra (Sanskrit)	in India, Nepal, and Tibet, term for symbolic hand positions
naamlo (N)	tumpline
nah (T)	bharal or blue sheep
namaste (Sanskrit)	"I honor the Atman (God) within you"; loosely translated, means hello or goodbye
naykor (T)	"going around places," pilgrimage
ngultrim (D)	unit of Bhutanese currency, equivalent to Indian rupee
oma (T)	milk
pan (H,N)	areca nut and lime wrapped in betel leaf (as used in Bhutan; in India there are many types of pan, but usually built on these basic ingredients)
pangshing (T)	pine forest
pani (N)	water
parikrama (H)	circumambulation (Hindu equivalent of **kora**)
phedi (N)	"place at the base of the hill"
phul (N)	egg
pokhari (N)	pond or small lake
puja (H,N)	general term for a religious service; there are many types of pujas
quak (N)	in the Kutang region of the Buri Gandaki Valley, a local term for a volume of measure
rakshi (N)	distilled spirits (the same as **arak**), "local wine"
rapchu (D)	woman's ceremonial scarf in Bhutan
rassi (H,N)	rope
ri (T)	high mountain
rimpoche (T)	"precious one"; in the sense of worthy, used as a title for lamas, sacred mountains, etc.
rongpa (T)	valley men, or man from where the forest grows (the Tibetan name for a lowlander)
rougimsee (D)	a local Bhutanese word for the takin
sadhu (H,N)	literally, "excellent"; a Hindu ascetic: some are legitimate; others are ersatz
sahib (H,N)	loosely means "sir"
saligram (T)	ammonite

samadhi (Sanskrit)	a particular mental or spiritual realization (equivalent to satori)
sannyasi (H)	Hindu renunciate; usually a wanderer
sattu (T)	roasted barley flour; the Tibetan's basic diet (same as **tsampa**)
shakpa (S)	sherpa stew
shalwar kameez (H)	loose, flappy pants (*shalwar*) and long, loose shirt (*kameez*) worn by Muslim men and women
shapje (T)	imprint in stone attributed to a sacred person or animal
shar (T)	east
shingki naua (S)	"guardian of the wood"
sho (T)	yogurt
shri (H,N)	honorific prefix
siddhi (Sanskrit)	mental, physical, or spiritual power
sirdar (N)	here used to denote the man in charge of the porters and staff that accompany a trekking group
somba (T)	old style Tibetan shoe made from leather and woolen yarn
stupa (Sanskrit)	Buddhist reliquary shrine (same as **chorten**)
sulpa (N)	clay smoking pipe
sunpati (N)	"goldleaf"; an upper-elevation plant used as incense
suntala (N)	tangerine
suruwal (N)	Nepali-style pants: tight at the bottom and loose around the midsection
tal (N)	lake
tamak (N)	tobacco
tan (N)	wooden shrine dedicated to a local deity in western Nepal
tangkha (T)	Tibetan Buddhist painted scroll
thanna (N)	large police station
thanti (Gurung)	place
thar (Rai)	clan
thupa (T)	soup of any kind
topi (N)	man's national hat in Nepal
trisul (H,N)	trident
tsampa (T)	roasted barley flour (same as **sattu**)
tsaurie (N)	milk-giving cow-yak crossbreed
tsechu (D)	annual festival in Bhutan
tso (T)	lake
tungba (N)	type of beer made from millet (also the wooden or bamboo container of the beer)
wala (H,N)	agent, inhabitant, keeper, possessor, maker, or doer of anything ("rickshaw wala," "Kathmandu wala," "trekking wala")
yatri (H,N)	pilgrim
yersa (S)	settlement used only in summer (some of these now contain modest inns used during the trekking season)
zopkio (S)	docile but strong cow-yak crossbreed used especially for carrying loads

An Introduction
to Spoken Nepali

by Charles Gay

As recently as fifteen years ago, a village Nepali assumed that any Westerner encountered alone on the trail spoke the Nepali language. Today, on the more heavily traveled "tourist routes," this assumption is no longer made, and the Nepali expects from the trekker no more than the greeting **"Namaste"** and the Hindi word for tea, **chai.** Indeed, the villagers and innkeepers who have had contact with trekkers now know enough "trekking English" to overcome the traveler's lack of Nepali, but they would still rather speak Nepali, so even on well-traveled routes the Westerner who makes the effort to learn any amount of the language is richly rewarded. And in the farther reaches, where you still can spend days on the trail without hearing a word of English, speaking a few words of Nepali is all the more beneficial in easing your way.

Since the Devanagiri script appears imposing, it is fortunate that signs are unknown in rural Nepal and therefore a knowledge of the script is entirely unnecessary for the trekker. In fact, the spoken language is both fun and easy to learn.

The intent here is to provide information sufficient for anyone except the serious student to acquire as much facility as he or she desires, from speaking a few words for food and shelter to forming simple sentences and understanding considerably more. Traveling with a porter or guide is an excellent way to practice Nepali, although if he speaks any English, he will probably want to use that with you instead. But your Nepali may shortly exceed his English in depth and scope anyway since, after all, you are studying the language.

Children are also excellent companions for practice as they are everywhere and your passage is a major event. However, their opening exchange is likely to be **"miThai"** ("sweet"), "bon-bon" (from the French), "balloon," "chocolate," or "one rupee" as often as **"Namaste."** Your response should be a pleasant, but firm **"chhaina"** ("don't have"), or perhaps **"maagnu hundaaina"** ("you shouldn't beg"). These children are not going to grow up to be professional beggars; they simply don't know how else to strike up a conversation. Practicing your Nepali should solve the problem.

Pronunciation

Nepali is an Indo-European language. Its being written in the Devanagiri or Sanskritic script means it is based on an alphabet and is not a tonal language. As in Hindu-Urdu, Nepali has consonants that are difficult for the English speaker to master; a good ear is as important as in-depth study here, and in fact, you will likely not be able to discern the difference between some aspirated and nonaspirated consonants and between some dental and retroflex consonants—not to mention actually using them in speech. Nonetheless, in the fairly standard roman transliteration of this glossary, some differentiation of these sounds is made. For the trekker, more important than to be academically rigorous is to plunge right in and win friends, and then to imitate their speech. Realize, however, that most Nepali you will hear on the trail will be spoken by villagers (Tamrang, Rai, Gurung, Sherpa, Magar, Newar) for whom it is a second language, and they won't expect your Nepali to be proper. The native speakers (Brahmin, Chhetri) will naturally understand you anyway.

Vowels

Pronunciation of the romanized vowels is as follows:

a   as in "about"
aa as in "father"
i   as in "pit" (the long *i* has a similar sound)
u   close to "input" (the long sound as in "too")
e   as in "pay"
ai a dipthong; *a* as in "about," *i* as in "be"
o   as in "toe"
au a dipthong; *a* as in "about," *u* as in "put"
˜   denotes nasalization of a vowel sound

Consonants

The Nepali alphabet groups the consonants into five categories according to where in the mouth they are produced. We need only be concerned with two of these distinctions, the dental and the retroflex consonants. Like several of the other consonants, these are either aspirated or unaspirated; in our transliteration, they will be followed by an *h* when aspirated. Aspiration is both hard to master and difficult to detect in native speech; make an effort to differentiate it, but not to the point of distraction. Hold your hand in front of your mouth: when you pronounce an aspirated consonant, you should feel a puff of air. The vowel sound that follows is the same whether aspirated or not.

Dental and Retroflex Consonants

The pronunciation of the romanized dental and retroflex consonants is as follows:

t   dental, unvoiced, as in "tight"

th   dental, unvoiced, aspirated but still hard, not like *th* in "the"
     (Nepali has no English-style *th* sound)
T   retroflex (tongue arched back and in contact with the roof of the
     mouth), as in **baaTo** ("trail")
Th   retroflex, unvoiced, aspirated, as in **kaaThmaanDu**
d   dental, voiced, as in "dot"
dh   dental, voiced, aspirated, as in **dharma**
D   retroflex (with tongue as in *T,* above), voiced, as in **kaaThmaanDu**
Dh   retroflex, voiced, aspirated, as in **Dhokaa** ("door")

Listen closely to native speakers as they say the Nepali words used
above. You should be able to distinguish between dental and retroflex,
aspirated and nonaspirated sounds.
     Other consonants that appear unaspirated and aspirated are:

k   unvoiced, as in "kite"
kh   unvoiced, aspirated, as in **khaanu** ("to eat")
g   voiced, as in **gaai** ("cow")
gh   voiced, aspirated, as in **ghar** ("house")
ch   similar to *ch* in "church," not aspirated; this is the only exception
     to the *h* denoting aspiration.
chh aspirated, as in **chha** ("is"); no equivalent in English
j   voiced, not quite like the English *j* as in "judge"; contains an
     element of *z,* as in **bajaar** ("bazaar")
jh   voiced, aspirated, as in **jholaa** ("handbag")
p   unvoiced, as in **paani** ("water")
ph   aspirated, somewhere between *p* as in "pop" and *ph* as in "photo."
     (Nepali has no *f.*) Used in **phohor** ("dirty"), for example
b   voiced, as in **baaTo** ("trail")
bh   voiced, aspirated, as in **bhitra** ("inside")

Other Consonants

These consonants are never aspirated:

m, l, s, h as in English
y   almost a vowel sound, as in "yes"
r   not an *r* sound as in English—more like the rolled Spanish
     r. Used for example in **raamro** ("good") and **saari** ("dress")

Emphasis

Emphasis is normally on the first syllable of a word unless the first
syllable has a short sound and the second a long vowel. For example:
raam'ro ("good"); but **tarkaa'ri** ("vegetables").

Grammar

Not only is Nepali fun to learn because everybody will want to help you and the language often has a humorous ring, Nepali is fairly simple to learn—largely because of its spareness. No plural is necessary, typically there is no gender, and very little future tense is in common usage. Also, if you are disinclined to study the conjugations, **one verb ending will get you by.**

Sentence Structure

The basic sentence is arranged as follows:

Subject	Object	Verb
Haami	**bhaat**	**khaanchaũ.**
We	rice	eat.

In questions, the sentence structure generally remains the same. Raise your voice at the end of the sentence, or emphasize the appropriate word:

Which trail is going to Jumla?

Jumla	**jaane**	**baaTo**	**kun**	**ho?**	(the stress is on *kun*)
Jumla	going	trail	which	is?	

To answer questions, repeat the question's verb in the response:

What is this?   **Yo** **ke** **ho?**
                  This what is?

This is a butterfly.   **Yo** **putali** **ho.**
                         This butterfly is.

Is the trail good?   **BaaTo** **raamro** **chha?**
                       Trail good is?

Yes.   **Chha.**
         Is.

No.   **Chhaina.**
        Isn't.

Simple Negative

Add **na** to any verb or adjective to negate the concept:

na raamro   not good
na jaane   not going

Verb Conjugation

The neutral, present-tense ending **-ne** is widely heard and used and is really the only verb ending needed for simple communication in Nepal. It can be used with any personal pronoun. A typical exchange might be as follows. Villager: **"Tapaaĩ kahãã jaanuhunchha?"** (proper verb ending), meaning, "You where are going?" Trekker: **"(Ma) pokharaa/maa jaane"** (neutral ending), meaning, "(I) Pokhara/to am going." Therefore, you should at least be familiar with the proper verb endings that will be frequently heard.

Conjugation of simple present of **jaanu**—to go:

Pronoun		Affirmative	Negative
I	**ma**	**jaanchhu**	**jaanna**
you (familiar)	**timi**	**jaanchhau**	**jaandainau**
he, she	**u**	**jaanchha**	**jaandaina**
he, she (polite)	**wahãã**	**jaanuhunchha**	**jaanuhunna**
we	**haami**	**jaanchhaũ**	**jaandainaũ**
you (polite)	**tapaaī**	**jaanuhunchha**	**jaanuhunna**
they	**uniharu**	**jaanchhan**	**jaandainan**

Nepalis denote a person's rank, station, or closeness by the second- and third-person pronouns and their verb endings. **Timi** ("you," familiar) is for a close friend, relative, or person of lower stature, such as a porter. **Tapaaī** ("you," polite) connotes respect, greater age, or high caste. The same applies to **u** (third person singular, familiar) and **wahãã** (third-person singular, polite). Trekkers tend to call everyone **tapaaī**, of course.

Please and Thank You

There is no "please," as such, in Nepali. The polite imperative form of the verb is used, formed by dropping the *u* from the infinitive form and adding *os:* **"aaunos"** ("come"), **"basnos"** ("sit down"), or **"chiyaa dinos"** ("give tea"—"me" is implied). The suffix **-na** on the imperative is very polite and is close to "please," as in **aaunosna"** ("please come").

Nepali also does not have an equivalent to our "thank you," and although **"Dhanyabaad"** is common enough in its misuse for this purpose by Westerners, it is not natural for Nepalis. A nod of the head will suffice as thanks, and be correct. In areas of Tibetan Buddhist influence, such as the Sherpa homeland of Khumbu, the Tibetan word **"thuDichhe"** is commonly used as "Thank you."

The Verb "To Be"

The verb "to be" (**hunu**) has two forms, **ho** and **chha**. They are not interchangeable.

Ho (negative, **hoina**) is used for defining something or somebody:

This trail is going to Ilam.

Yo	**ilaam**	**jaane**	**baaTo**	**ho.**
This	Ilam	going to	trail	is.

My name is Charles.

	Mero	**naam**	**Charles**	**ho.**
	My	name	Charles	is.

Chha (negative **chhaina**) is used to locate things and people, or to state their quality:

Do you have any tea?	**Chiyaa**	**chha?**	
	Tea	do you have?	

The trail is not good.	**BaaTo**	**naraamro**	**chha.**
	Trail	not good	is.

or

	BaaTo	**raamro**	**chhaina.**
	Trail	good	is not.

Impersonal Verb Constructions

Some important concepts are expressed in Nepali with impersonal verb constructions. The verb is third person singular, and the subject always takes the postposition **-laai** (see "Prepositions," below).

Need: use **chhainchha** or the negative, **chhaindaina.**

I need help.	**Ma/laai**	**maddat**	**chhainchha.**
	Me/to	help	is needed.

What do you need?	**Tapaai/laai**	**ke**	**chhainchha?**
	You/to	what	is needed?

We don't need eggs.	**Haami/laai**	**phul**	**chhaindaina.**
	Us/to	eggs	is not needed.

Necessity: **parchha** or (negative) **pardaina** is affixed to the infinitive form of a verb to express "should" or "have to."

We have to go.	**Haami/laai**	**jaanuparchha.**
	We	have to go.

You don't have to carry this.	**Timi/laai**	**yo**	**boknupardaina.**
	You	this	don't have to carry.

Like and dislike: use **man parchha** or (negative) **man pardaina.**

I like Tibetan beer very much.

Ma/laai	**chang**	**dherai**	**man parchha.**
I	Tibetan beer	very much	like.

We don't like local wine.

Haami/laai	**raksi**	**man pardaina.**
We	local wine	don't like.

Do you like our country?

Tapaai/laai	**haamro**	**desh**	**man parchha?**
You	our	country	like?

I like it very much.	**Dherai**	**man parchha.**	
	Very much	(I) like	(it.)

Desire or want: **man laagchha** or (negative) **man laagdaina** are affixed to the **-na** form of a verb to express desire.

We don't want to stay here.

Haami/laai	**yahãã**	**basna man laagdaina.**
We	here	do not want to stay.

Do you want to go to the monastery?

Tapaaĩ/laai	**gompa/maa**	**jaana man laagchha?**
You	chapel/into	want to go?

I want to drink tea.

Ma/laai	**chiyaa**	**khaana man laagchaa.**
I	tea	want to eat (drink).

Feelings: use **laagyo** to make a phrase.

Ma/laai	I am	**bhok laagyo**	hungry
Tapaaĩ/laai	You are	**thakaai laagyo**	fatigued
Haami/laai	We are	**tirkhaa laagyo**	thirsty
		nidraa laagyo	sleepy
		raksi laagyo	drunk
		jaaDo laagyo	cold
		garmi laagyo	hot
		Dar laagyo	scared
		haawaa laagyo	wind-blown

Simple Past

Transitive verbs: Add **-le** to the subject noun or pronoun and **-eko** to the verb root (remove the suffix **-unu** or **-nu**).

What did you do?	**Tapaaĩ/le**	**ke**	**gareko?**
	You	what	did do?

Intransitive verbs: **-le** is not used; **-eko** is affixed to the root.

I stayed in Junbesi.	**Ma**	**junbesi/maa**	**baseko.**
	I	Junbesi/in	stayed.

Irregular verbs: some common verbs are irregular in the simple past as well as in other forms.

I went to Jumla	**Ma**	**Jumla/maa**	**gaeko.**	[from **jaanu**]
	I	Jumla/to	went.	

Possessives

The possessive is formed by adding the suffix **-ko** to a noun or pronoun, demarcated by a slash (/):

Yo	**gaaũ/ko**	**naam**	**ke**	**ho?**
This	village's	name	what	is?

Tapaaĩ/ko	**naam**	**ke**	**ho?**
Your	name	what	is?

A few important exceptions are:

mero (my)

haamro (our)
timro (your, familiar)
usko (his, hers)

Prepositions

Prepositions are actually postpositions in Nepali, and also are demarcated as romanized here with a slash (/) after the noun:

maa (in, on, or to):

Bholi	**ma**	**ghar/maa**	**baschhu**	(basne).
Tomorrow	I	house/in	will stay.	

The suffix **-laai** must be attached to the subject when the verb is impersonal (see "Impersonal Verbs," above) and also to indicate the preoposition "to" for an indirect object.

Ma/laai	**bhaat**	**dinos.**
Me/to	rice	give.

Conversational Situations on the Trail

Life on the trail settles into a routine that encourages the repetition and mastery of several basic exchanges. With the above fundamentals in mind, and when you have heard how the language sounds, the following phrases and vocabulary for a typical day on the trail should enable you to travel from the lowest valley to the highest settlement on your own. The acceptable simpler **-ne** verb form is in parentheses.

Making Friends and Chatting

The phrase for chatting is **"gaph garne."**

Hello, goodbye.   **Namaste.**

How are you?   **Tapaaĩ/laai   kasto chha?**
                              You/to   how is?

Fine, and you?   **Sanchai,   tapaaĩ/laai?**
                              Fine,   (and) you?

Are your parents living?   **Aamaa,   baabu   chhan?**
                                          Mother,   father (your)   are?

Are you married?
Bihaa gareko chha? [or]   **Tapaaĩ/ko   bihaa   bhayo?**
Marriage   (your) has been?   Your   marriage   was?

Have you eaten rice?   **Bhaat   khaanubhayo?**
                                      Rice   have you eaten?

Why have you come to Nepal?
Kina   nepaal/maa   aaeko?
Why   Nepal/to   have you come?

I've come to sightsee.   **Ghumna jaana   aaeko.**
                                        To sightsee   (I) have come.

I've come to look at the snow peaks.
Himaal herna   '   aaeko.
Snow peaks to look at   (I) have come.

Do they eat cow meat in your country?
Tapaaĩ/ko   desh/maa   gaai/ko   maasu   khaane?
Your   country/in cow's   meat   (do they) eat?

Food and Lodging

No Nepali traveler camps when houses are nearby.

Is lodging available . . .

in your house?	**Tapaaĩ/ko** Your	**ghar/maa** house/in	
here	**Yahãã** Here		**basna** staying **paainchha?** is available?
where	**Kahãã** Where		

Is food available there? **Khaana   tyahãã   paainchha?**
                          Food   there   is available?

It's available over there. **Utaa   paainchha.**
                            Over there is available.

(Please) cook me meat. **Maasu   pakaaunos.**
                        Meat   (for me)   cook.

(Please) only give me a little bit. **Ali ali   maatra   dinos.**
                                     A little bit only   give.

(Please) don't put in chili pepper. **Kursaani   nahaalnos.**
                                     Chili pepper   do not put in.

It is customary to pay for food, wood used, and lodging just prior to departure:

(Please) make the bill. **Hisaab   garnos.**   [in a house or inn]
                         Bill   make.

(Please) give the bill. **Bil   dinos.**
                         Bill   give.

Altogether, how many rupees? **Jamaai   kati   rupiyãã?**
                              All together how many   rupees?

So let's go, eh? Farewell. **La,   jaaũ   e?   Namaste**
                            So   let's go,   eh?   Farewell.

Porterage

It is important for your porter to understand his daily salary (with or without food), destination and duration of the trek, and the likely conditions (e.g., will he encounter snow and need warm clothes and adequate shoes?)

I need (one, two, three) porters.

Ma/laai   (eutaa, duitaa, tintaa)   kulli chaainchha.
To me   (one, two, three)   porters are needed.

Where are you going, sahib?   **Kata   jaane,   saab?**
                                Where   going,   sahib?

I'm going to the Annapurna Sanctuary.

Annapurna   sanctuari/maa   jaane.
Annapurna   Sanctuary/to   going.

We must go in snow.   **Hiũ/maa   jaanuparchha   (jaane).**
                        Snow/in   must go   (going).

Do you have warm clothes?

Timro   nyaano   lugaa   chha   ki   chhaina?
Your   warm   clothes   yes   or   no?

Yes, sahib.   **Chha,   saab.**
                Yes,   sahib.

Well, show them to me.   **La,   dekaau.**
                           Well,   show.   [to me]

Don't have any, sahib, I must buy.

Chhaaina,   saab,   kinnuparchha   (kine).
No,   sahib,   must buy   (buy).

How many rupees per day?   **Din/ko   kati   rupiyãã?**
                             A day/for   how many rupees?

With or without food supplied?

Khaana   khaaera   ki   na khaaera?
Food   eating   or   not eating?

With food, forty rupees is enough.

Khaana   khaaera   chaalis   rupiyãã   pugchha.
Food   eating   forty   rupees   is enough.

I don't have a basket.   **Mero   doko   chhaaina,   saab.**
                           My   basket   isn't,   sahib.

Twenty rupees isn't enough.   **Bis   rupiyãã   pugdaaina**
                                Twenty   rupees   isn't enough.

What to do? [Heard every day!]   **Ke   garne?**
                                   What   to do?

I'll go alone.   **Ma   eklai   jaanchhu   (jaane).**
                   I   alone   will go   (go).

How much do you need for the return?

Pharkana/ko laagi   din/ko   kati   rupiyãã   chhaainchha?
For returning   a day/for how many rupees   (do you) need?

Route Finding and Resting

Remember there are no signs but many trails in Nepal. For directions, hail the nearest farmer:

e **daaju** (man older than you, older brother)
  daai
e **bhai** (man younger than you, younger brother, boy)
e **didi** (woman older than you, older sister)
e **bahini** (girl younger than you, younger sister)
e **baabu** (old man, father)
e **aamaa** (old woman, mother)

Which is the trail to Manang?

Manang	**jaane**	**baaTo**	**kun**	**ho?**
Manang	going to	trail	which	is?

Go this way.

Yetaa	**baaTa**	**jaane.**
Here	from	go.

Go that way.

Utaa	**baaTa**	**jaane.**
There	from	go.

How far is Namche?

Namche	**kati**	**taaDa**	**chha?**
Namche	how	far	is?

Two hours

Dui	**ghanTaa.**
Two	hours.

How many hours does it take?
[Nepalis will tell you how long it
would take them to cover the
distance. It will take you longer.]

Kati	**ghantaa**	**laagchha?**
How many	hours	(does it) take?

Is the trail very steep uphill?

BaaTo	**dherai**	**ukaalo**	**chha?**
Trail	very	uphill	is?

Is it uphill and downhill?

Ukaalo	**oraalo**	**chha?**
Uphill	downhill	it is?

No, it's level [for a Nepali].

Hoina,	**samaai**	**chha.**
No,	level	it is.

Where are you going?

Kata?	
Where	(are you going)?

Where are you coming from?

Kata	**baaTa?**
Kahãã	
Where	from (are you coming)?

Where have you been?

Kata	**pugera**	**aaunubhayo?**
Where	(did you)	arrive and come (from)?

Can one go as far as Beding on this trail?

BaaTo/maa	**Beding**	**samma**	**jaanasakchha?**
Trail/on	Beding	as far as	(one is) able to go?

Not able to.

Sakdaaina.
Not able.

When is the weekly market?

Haat bajaar	**kahile**	**hunchha?**
Weekly market	when	is?

Take it easy.	**Bistaari**	**jaaũ.**	
	Slowly	go.	[Said upon departure.]

Let's go fast.	**Chitto**	**jaaũ.**
	Fast	let's go.

Let's sit in the shade.	**Sital/maa**	**basaũ.**
	Shade, cool/in	let's sit.

I must take a rest.	**(Ma/laai)**	**araam garnuparchha (garne).**
	(I)	must rest.

Tomorrow, we must go extremely early in the morning.

				jaanuparchha
(Haami/laai)	**bholi**	**ekdam**	**bihaana/maa**	**(jaane).**
(We)	tomorrow	extremely (early)	morning/in	must go.

I have to urinate.	**(Ma/laai)**	**pisaab garnuparchha**	**(garne).**
	(I)	urinate have to.	

Red mud, slippery trail.	**Raato**	**maato,**	**chhipalo**	**baaTo.**
[A trail proverb guaranteed to get a laugh.]	Red	mud,	slippery	trail.

Nepali Time

If you have a visible watch, you will be asked the time. If you inquire about time, you will get widely disparate answers; every watch in village Nepal shows different time. You can usually generate a lively discussion by asking what day of the week it is:

What is today?	**Aaja**	**ke**	**baar**	**(ho)?**
	Today	what	day	(is)?

Today is Sunday.	**Aaja**	**aitabaar**	**(ho).**
	Today	Sunday	is.
	[or]		

	sombaar	Monday
	mangalbaar	Tuesday
	budhabaar	Wednesday
	bihibaar	Thursday
	sukrabaar	Friday
	shanibaar	Saturday

What time is it?	**Kati**	**bajyo.**
	What	time is it?
	[literally, How many struck?]	

Four o'clock.	**Chaar bajyo.**
	Four o'clock.

We should stop around five o'clock.

Pããch baje	**tiraa**	**basnuparchha (basne).**
Five o'clock	around	must or should stop (sit).

We should arise around six o'clock.
Chha baje   utnuparchha   (utne).
Six o'clock   should arise.

When are you going? **Kahile   jaane?**
                     When   are (you) going?

                     Bholi-parsi.
Tomorrow or the next day. Tomorrow or the next day.
                     [the Nepali equivalent of *mañana*]

How many days are you staying?
Kati   din   basnuhunchha (basne)?
How many   days   are you staying?

I'll stay three days. **Tin   din   baschhu (basne).**
                       Three   days   I will stay.

Medical Problems and Evacuation

It is still possible to find yourself several days' walk from a wireless and even farther from a landing strip (**hawaj-jahaaj giraund**). If you must get out, walking or being carried is the only possibility, short of helicopter rescue.

I need a porter. **Ma/laai   kulli   chaainchha.**
                  Me/to   porter   is needed.

(Please) carry me as far as Jomosom.
Jomosom   samma   ma/laai   boknos (bokne).
Jomosom   as far as   me   carry.

My friend is sick. **Mero   saathi   biraami   bhayo** (or **chha**).
                    My   friend   sick   is.

I am sick. **Ma   biraami   chhu.**
            I   sick   am.

My stomach hurts. **Mero   peT   dukhchha   (dukhne).**
                   My   stomach   hurts.

(Please) send a message to Kathmandu.
KaaThmaanDu/maa   samaachaar   pathaaunos   (pathaaune).
Kathmandu/to   message   send.

Bargaining

For a Westerner to bargain in Kathmandu is not as easy as it once was. However, the same ancient rules still apply in the village and at the **haat bajaar** (weekly market) in the mountains.

How much are tangerines? **Suntalaa   kati   parchha?**
                          Tangerines   how much   cost?

Two for a rupee. **Rupiyāā/ko   duitaa.**
                  For a rupee   two.

Give me three for a rupee.

Rupiyãã/ko   tintaa   dinos.
For a rupee   three   give (me).

OK.   **Hunchha.**
All right.

How many rupees is this?

Yasko   kati   ruipyãã?
For this   how many   rupees?

Ten rupees.   **Das   rupiyãã.**
Ten   rupees.

That's expensive, I'll give eight.

Mahango   bhayo   [or chha],   ma   aaTh   dinchhu   (dine).
Expensive   it was   [or it is],   I   eight   will give.

OK, take it.   **La,   linos.**
Very well,   take (it).

Food

apple	**syaau, nashpati**	millet	**kodo**
banana	**keraa**	oil	**tel**
beans	**simi**	onion	**pyaaj**
beer		orange, tangerine	**suntalla**
bottled	**istar biyar**	peanuts	**badaam**
Nepali	**jããr**	potato	**aalu**
Tibetan	**chang**	pumpkin	**parsi**
bread	**roti, chapaati**	relish (hot)	**achaar**
(unleavened)		rice	
butter (clarified)	**ghiu**	cooked	**bhaat**
chili	**khursaani**	in the field	**dhaan**
corn	**makai**	pounded	**chiuraa**
egg	**phul**	in the store	**chaamal**
boiled	**umaaleko phul**	salt	**nun**
fish	**maachhaa**	soybeans	**bhaTmaas**
flour	**pitho**	sugar	**chini**
roasted barley	**tsampa** (Tibetan)	sweets	**miThai**
fruits and	**phalphul ra**	water	
vegetables	**tarkaari**	boiled	**umaaleko paani**
garlic	**lasun**	drinking	**khaane paani**
greens (spinach)	**saag**	hot	**taato paani**
lemon, lime	**kaagati**	washing	**dhune paani**
lentils	**daal**	wine, local	**raksi**
mango	**ããp**	yogurt	**dhai**
meat	**maasu**		
buffalo	**raango/ko maasu**	**Verbs (infinitive form)**	
chicken	**kukhura/ko maasu**	ask	**sodhnu**
		ask for	**maagnu**
cow	**gaai/ko maasu**	bathe	**nuhaaunu**
goat	**kasi/ko maasu**	boil	**umaalnu**
milk	**dudh**	buy	**kinnu**

carry	**boknu**	bottle	**sisi**
chat, gossip	**gaph garnu**	boy	**keTaa**
close	**banda garnu**	bridge	
come	**aaunu**	large	**pul**
cook	**pakaaunu**	small	**saanghu**
do	**garnu**	cat	**biraalu**
eat, drink	**khaanu**	children	**chhoraa-chhori**
enough (to be)	**pugnu (pugyo)**	clothes	**lugaa**
forget	**birsanu**	country	**desh**
get up, awaken	**uThnu**	cow	**gaai**
give	**dinu**	daughter	**chhori**
go	**jaanu**	day	**din**
hear (listen)	**sunnu**	dog	**kukur**
kill	**maarnu**	door	**Dhokaa**
laugh	**haasnu**	evening	**beluka**
learn	**siknu**	eye	**ããkhaa**
light (a lamp)	**baalnu**	face	**mukh**
look	**hernu**	field	**khet**
look for	**khojnu**	fire	**aago**
meet	**bheTnu**	firewood	**daura**
open	**kholnu**	floor	**bhuĩ**
put (down, in)	**raakhnu**	fly (house)	**jhingaa**
read	**paDhnu**	foot	**khuTTa**
repeat, say again	**pheri bhannu**	foreigner	**bideshi**
please repeat	**pheri bhannos**	forest	**ban**
return	**pharkanu**	friend	**saathi**
see	**dekhnu**	girl	**keTi**
sell	**bechnu**	government	**shri paanch/ko**
send	**pathaaunu**	(His Majesty's)	**sarkaar**
sing	**git gaaunu**	hair	**kapaal**
sit, live	**basnu**	hand	**haat**
sleep	**sutnu**	head	**Taauko**
speak	**bolnu**	help	**maddat**
take	**linu**	hill or ridge	**lekh, DanDaa**
talk, say	**bhannu**	holy man (Hindu)	**saadhu**
teach	**sikaaunu**	ice peak	**himaal**
understand	**bujnu**	inn	**bhaTTi**
urinate	**pisaab garnu**	junk, knickknacks	**jilli-milli**
walk	**hĩDnu**	kerosene	**maTTitel**
wash	**dhunu**	king	**raaja**
work	**kaam garnu**	knife	**chakku**
		Gurkha-made	**khukari**

Nouns and Pronouns

		lake	**taal, pokhari, tso**
afternoon	**diũso**		(Tibetan)
baby	**bachha**	lamp (kerosene)	**batti**
bamboo	**bãäs**	launderer	**dhobi**
book	**kitaab**	leech	**jugaa**

luggage, stuff	**saaman**	male	**raango**
man, person	**maanchhe**	week	**haptaa**
mat (grass)	**gundri**	what	**ke**
match	**solaai**	(is this?)	**yo ke ho?**
medicine	**ausadhi**	which	**kun**
morning	**bihaana**	who	**ko**
mosquito	**laamkhuTTe**	whose	**kasko**
mountain	**pahaaD**	window	**jhyaal**
name	**naam**	woman	**aaimai**
night	**raati**	work	**kaam**
outhouse	**chharpi**		
pass, saddle	**bhanjyang, la** (Tibetan)	**Adjectives**	
place	**Thaaũ**	ago	**aghi**
plate	**Thaal**	all	**sabai**
porter	**kulli, baariya**	bad (or not good)	**na raamro**
queen	**raani**	big	**Thulo**
rain	**paani (parchha)**	bitter	**tito**
religion	**dharma**	cheap	**sasTho**
resting place (on the trail)	**chautaara**	clean	**saphaa**
		cold	**chiso**
river	**khola** or **khosi**	colorful (multicolored)	**rangi-changi**
road	**motor jaane baaTo**	delicious	**miTho**
		different	**pharak**
room (in a house)	**koThaa**	difficult	**muskil**
shed	**goTh**	dirty	**phohor**
shirt	**kamij**	downhill	**oraalo**
shoes	**juthaa**	easy	**sajilo**
shopkeeper	**saahuji**	good	**raamro**
sir (in response to being addressed)	**hajur!**	hot (spicy)	**piro**
		hot (temperature)	**taato**
snow	**hiũ**	how many (or much)	**kati**
socks	**mojaa**		
son	**chhoraa**	little (small)	**saano**
spoon	**chamchha**	little (a little bit)	**ali-ali**
stone, rock	**Dhungaa**	long	**laamo**
store	**pasal**	many	**dherai**
stove (of mud and stone)	**chulho**	new	**nayãã**
		OK (it is)	**Thik (chha)**
sun	**ghaam**	old	
things	**chij-bij**	(things)	**puraano**
tiger	**baagh**	men	**buDho**
trail	**baaTo**	women	**buDhi**
tree	**rukh**	only	**maatra**
village	**gaaũ**	short	**chhoTo**
water buffalo		sick	**biraami**
female	**bhaisi**	sour	**amilo**

sweet	guliyo
tall	aglo
that	tyo
this	yo
uphill	ukaalo

Adverbs

after	pachhi
again	pheri
always	sadhaī
down	tala
far	TaaDhaa
fast	chhiTo
here	yahāā
how	kasari
inside	bhitra
near	najik
outside	baahira
secretly, on the sly	luki-luki
there	tyaahāā
today	aaja
tomorrow	bholi
up	maathi
very	dherai
where	kahāā
why	kina
yesterday	hijo

Conjunctions

also	pani
because	kina bhane
maybe	holaa

Money

coins	paisaa
rupee	rupiyāā
1½ rupees	DeDha rupiyāā

1 rupee = 100 paisaa
mohar = 50 paisaa
sukaa = 25 paisaa

Numerals

one-half	addha
one	ek
two	dui
three	tin
four	chaar
five	pāāch
six	chha
seven	saat
eight	aaTh
nine	nau
ten	das
eleven	eghaara
twelve	baarha
thirteen	terha
fourteen	chaudha
fifteen	pandhara
sixteen	sorha
seventeen	satra
eighteen	aThaara
nineteen	unnais
twenty	bis
twenty-five	pachhis
thirty	tis
thirty-five	païtis
forty	chaalis
forty-five	païtaalis
fifty	pachaas
fifty-five	pachpanna
sixty	saaThi
sixty-five	païsaThi
seventy	sattari
seventy-five	pachhattar
eighty	asi
eighty-five	pachassi
ninety	nabbe
ninety-five	panchaanabbe
one hundred	sae
two hundred	dui sae
one thousand	ek hajaar

Tibetan Glossary

by Milan M. Melvin

The following list of Tibetan words and phrases is all too brief but sufficient for you to acquire the basic necessities and, depending on your inclination, to get out of or into trouble. Tibetans are wonderful, fun-loving people and even this small snatch of their language can launch you into some unforgettable relationships.

Pronunciation

The vowel *a* must be pronounced like the *a* in "father"—soft and long, unless it appears as -*ay,* in which case it is pronounced as in "say" or "day." A slash through a letter indicates the neutral vowel sound *uh.* The words in this glossary have been divided into syllables to help with pronunciation.

Word Order

Simple Tibetan sentences are constructed as follows:

Subject	Object	Verb
I	mountains	going
Nga	**kang ree la**	**dro ge ray**

The verb is always last.

Verb Tenses

Tibetan verbs are composed of two parts: the *root,* which carries the meaning of the verb, and the *ending,* which indicates the tense (past, present, or future). The simplest and most common verb form, consisting of the root plus the ending **-ge ray,** can be used for the present and future tenses. The root is strongly accented in speech. In order to form the past tense, substitute the ending **-song.**

nyo-ge ray means, loosely, "buying, going to buy"
nyo-song means "bought"

Only the verb roots are given in this glossary; remember to add the appropriate endings.

Vocabulary

Phrases

Hello! Greetings!	**Tashi delay**	I do not	**Ha ko ma song**
Enough! Stop!	**Deek song**	understand	
Finished	**tsar song, deek song**	I understand, I know	**Ha ko gee doo, ha ko song**

Right! Really! yes	**ray, la ray**
Very important	**kay chem bo, ne ka chem bo**
What is this called?	**Dee ming la ka ray see ge ray? Dee ka ra ray?**
How much is (this)?	**(Dee la) gong ka tzø ray?**
It doesn't matter	**Kay kay chee ge ma ray, kay kay so ge ma ray**
Be careful, slowly	**Ka lee ka lee**
I am hungry	**nge tro ko to kee doo**
Are/is there any (onions)?	**(Tsong) doo-ay, (Tsong) doog-ay?**
Please bring (onions)	**(Tsong) kay sho ah**
OK, thanks	**La so**
Goodnight	**Sim jam, Sim jam nang ro**
How far is (Lhasa)?	**(Lhasa la) gyan lø yø ray?**
How are you?	**Kirang sook po day bo yeen bay? Kirang ko sook day be yeen bay?**
I am fine	**Sook po day bo yeen, Day bo doo**

Pronouns

I	**nga**
you (s.)	**kirang**
he, she, it	**korang, ko**
we	**nga-tso**
you (pl.)	**kirang-tso**
they	**korong-tso**
this	**dee la**
my, mine	**nge, ngay, narang kee**
your, yours (s.)	**kirang kee**
his, hers, its	**korang kee**
our, ours	**narang-tso yee**

your, yours (pl.)	**kirang-tso yee**
their, theirs	**korong-tso yee**

Relations

name	**ming la**
child	**poo goo**
boy	**poo**
girl	**po mo**
man, husband	**cho ga**
woman, wife	**kyee men**
brother	**poon dya**
sister	**poon kya, ah jee la**
father	**pa ba, pa la**
mother	**ah ma**

Time

minute	**ka ma**
hour	**tchø zø**
day	**nyee ma, shak ma**
week	**døn ta**
month	**da wa**
year	**lo**
day before yesterday	**ke nyee ma**
yesterday	**ke sang**
last night	**dang gong**
today	**ta ring**
tomorrow	**sang nyee, sang**
day after tomorrow	**nang nyee**
now	**tanda, ta ta**
always	**tak par**
morning	**sho kay**
afternoon	**nyeen goon**
night	**tsen la, tsem mo**

Numbers

one	**cheek**
two	**nee**
three	**soom**
four	**shee**
five	**nga**
six	**trook**
seven	**døn**
eight	**gye, kay**
nine	**koo, goo**

ten	**tchoo**	corn	**droo**
eleven	**tchoop cheek**	delicious	**shimbo**
twelve	**tchoog nee**	dinner	**kong dak ka lak**
thirteen	**tchook soom**	egg	**go nga**
fourteen	**tchoop shee**	flour	**to sheep, pak pay**
fifteen	**tchoo nga**	food	**ka lak**
sixteen	**tchoo trook**	fruit	**shing dong**
seventeen	**tchoop don**	lunch	**nyeen goong ka**
eighteen	**tchup kyay**		**lak**
nineteen	**tchur koo**	meat	**sha**
twenty	**nee shoo tamba**	milk	**o ma**
twenty-one	**nee shoo sak**	millet	**ko do**
	cheek	onion	**tsong**
twenty-two	**nee shoo sak nee**	potato	**sho ko**
twenty-three	**nee shoo sak soom**	rice	**dray**
twenty-four	**nee shoo sup shee**	soup	**thupa**
twenty-five	**nee shoo say nga**	spirits	**arak**
twenty-six	**nee shoo sar trook**	sugar	**chee ma ka ra**
twenty-seven	**nee shoo sub dón**	tea	**cha**
twenty-eight	**nee shoo sap kay**	vegetables	**ngup tsay, tsay**
twenty-nine	**nee sar koo**	wheat	**tro, dro**
thirty	**soom tchoo**		
	tamba	**Other Nouns**	
forty	**sheep joo tamba**	bag	**gye mo, gye wa**
fifty	**ngup tchoo tamba**	blanket	**nya tee, gam lo,**
sixty	**trook tchoo tamba**		**nye zen**
seventy	**dón tchoo tamba**	blue sheep	**nah**
eighty	**kyah joo tamba**	book	
ninety	**koop tchoo**	common	**teb**
	tamba	religious	**pay zya**
one hundred	**gyah tamba**	boots	**som ba, lam**
two hundred	**nee gyah**	bridge	**sam ba**
three hundred	**soom gyah**	candle	**yang la**
		cave	**trak poo, poo goo**
Food		cigarette	**ta mak**
barley	**droo, nay**	circumambulation	**kora**
roasted barley	**tsampa** or **sattu**	cup	**mok, cha gar**
flour		dog	**kee, kyee**
beef	**lang sha**	donkey	**poon goo**
beer	**chang**	fire	**may**
breakfast	**sho kay ka lak**	hill	**ree**
butter	**mar**	house	**kang ba**
buttermilk	**sho**	kerosene	**sa noom**
cheese	**choo ra**	kettle	**tib lee**
small pieces	**chur pee**	knife	**tee, tree**
chicken meat	**cha sha**	lake	**tso**
chili peppers	**mar tsa**	matches	**moo see, tsak ta**

medicine	**men**	be hungry	**tro ko tok**
pill	**ree poo**	learn	**lap**
monastery	**gom ba**	look	**meek tang**
moon	**da wa**	make, fix	**so**
mountain	**kang ree**	see	**ton**
pass (mountain)	**la**	sell	**tsong**
pilgrimage	**nay kor**	be sick	**na**
pot (cooking)	**hai yoom,**	sit, stay	**day, shook**
	rak sang	teach	**lap**
rain	**char pa**	wait	**goo**
river	**tsang po, tchoo,**	work	**le ka chee**
	chu		

Adjectives

robe	**chu ba**	
rock	**do**	lost	**lak song**
room	**kang mee**	thirsty	**ka kam**
shoe	**som ba**	good	**yak po**
snow	**kang, ka**	bad	**yak po min doo**
spoon	**tur ma, too ma**	big	**chem bo**
spring	**chu mik**	small	**choon choon**
star	**kar ma**	weak	**shook choon**
stomach	**tro ko**		**choon**
sun	**nyee ma**	strong	**shyook chem bo**
thread	**koo ba**	empty	**tong ba**
Tibet	**Pø la**	full	**kang**
Tibetan language	**Pø kay**	beautiful	**dzay bo**
Tibetan people	**Pø pa**	delicious	**shimbo**
trail	**lam ga**	expensive	**gong chem bo**
umbrella	**nyee doo**	cold	**trang mo**
water	**tchoo, chu**	hot	**tsa bo**
Westerner	**in gee, pee ling**	different	**kye per,**
wind	**loong bo chem bo**		**cheek be ma ray**
wood	**shing**	same	**nang shing**
		few	**tet see tet see**

Verbs

		much, many	**mang bo**
		light	**yang bo, yang**
arrive	**lep**	heavy	**jee po, jee ba tsa**
bring	**kay sho**		**po**
buy	**nyo**		
carry	**kay**		

Adverbs

feel cold	**cha**		
come	**yong**	up	**ya la**
cook	**ka lak so**	down	**ma la**
drink	**toong**	near	**nye bo**
eat	**shay sa**	far	**ta ring bo,**
forget	**jay, chay**		**gyang bo**
get up	**lang**	here	**deh roo**
give	**tay, nang**	there	**pa roo, pa ge**
go	**dro, do**	left	**yom ba**

right	**yay ba**	maybe	**cheek chay na**
slow	**ka lee**	sometimes	**tsam tsam**
quickly	**dyok po, dyok po**	other	**shem ba, shen da,**
really, very	**she ta, she tai**		**yem ba**
		what	**ka ray**
Miscellaneous		where from	**ka ne**
and	**tang, ta**	where to	**ka ba, ka par,**
another	**yang ya**		**ka roo**
how much, how	**ka tzø**	who	**soo**
many		why	**ka ray chay nay**

Index

Numbers in italics refer to illustrations.

Notes

Notes